T0305129

Financial Innovation

WILEY

SERIES IN FINANCIAL ECONOMICS
AND QUANTITATIVE ANALYSIS

Series Editor: Stephen Hall, *London Business School, UK*

Editorial Board: Robert F. Engle, *University of California, USA*
John Flemming, *European Bank, UK*
Lawrence R. Klein, *University of Pennsylvania, USA*
Helmut Lütkepohl, *Humboldt University, Germany*

Further titles in preparation
Proposals will be welcomed by the Series Editor

Financial Innovation

Philip Molyneux

University of Wales, Bangor

&

Nidal Shamroukh

Algorithmics Inc.

JOHN WILEY & SONS

Chichester • New York • Weinheim • Brisbane • Toronto • Singapore

Other Wiley Editorial Offices

John Wiley & Sons, Inc., 605 Third Avenue,
New York, NY 10158-0012, USA

WILEY-VCH Verlag GmbH, Pappelallee 3,
D-69469 Weinheim, Germany

Jacaranda Wiley Ltd, 33 Park Road, Milton,
Queensland 4064, Australia

John Wiley & Sons (Canada) Ltd, 22 Worcester Road,
Rexdale, Ontario M9W 1L1, Canada

John Wiley & Sons (Asia) Pte Ltd, 2 Clementi Loop #02-01,
Jin Xing Distripark, Singapore 129809

Library of Congress Cataloging-in-Publication Data

Molyneux, Philip.
    Financial innovation / Philip Molyneux and Nidal Shamroukh.
        p.   cm. – (Financial engineering)
    Includes index.
    ISBN 0-471-98618-6 (pbk. : alk. paper)
    1. Financial engineering.   2. Risk assessment.   I. Shamroukh,
Nidal.   II. Title.   III. Series: Wiley series in financial engineering.
HG176.7.M65   1999
332′.042—dc21   98–41437
                                                                   CIP

British Library Cataloguing in Publication Data

A catalogue record for this book is available from the British Library

ISBN 0-471-98618-6

Typeset in 10/12 pt Times by C.K.M. Typesetting, Salisbury, Wiltshire
Printed and bound by CPI Antony Rowe, Eastbourne
This book is printed on acid-free paper responsibly manufactured from sustainable forestry,
in which at least two trees are planted for each one used for paper production.

Contents

Acknowledgements

This text was inspired by doctoral work conducted in the University of Wales, Bangor, and is the result of on-going collaboration between a doctoral student and his former supervisor. In the course of the original research particular thanks go to John Goddard who provided excellent advice and support with some of the technical sections, as well as to Shanti Chakravrty for feedback on some of the main methodological issues covered in parts of the study. Thanks also go to other colleagues from the School of Accounting, Banking and Economics and the Institute of European Finance who were most supportive of this work. We would also like to thank participants of a Conference sponsored by the Federal Reserve Bank of Cleveland on 'Derivatives and Intermediation', November 1st–3rd 1993, for their input into various methodological issues associated with modelling the diffusion of financial innovations. The detailed comments and feedback provided by Allen N Berger were particularly helpful.

Finally, we would like to thank our families and loved ones for their encouragement while working on the text, especially Nadege, Delyth and the children (Lois, Rhiannon, Gethin and Gareth).

Publisher's Note

The publisher wishes to thank the following who have kindly given permission for the use of copyright material. The destination of the reproduced material is indicated in square brackets.

American Economic Association for:
[Table 2.2] W. Silber (1983) Financial Innovation 1972–82. *American Economic Review* May, 89–1995.

American Marketing Association for:
[Figure 5.5 and Table 5.5] L. A. Fourt and J. W. Woodlock (1960) Early prediction of market success for new grocery products. *Journal of Marketing* **28**, 31–38.

Bank for International Settlements (BIS) for:
[Table 2.7 and Table 2.8] *Recent Innovations in International Banking* (1986).

Basil Blackwell Publishers for:
[Figure 3.1] M. D. Desai and M. Low (1987) Measuring the opportunity for product innovation. In M. de Cecco (ed), *Changing Money: Financial Innovation in Developed Countries.* Figure 5.1 on p.116.

The Economic Society for:
[Table 5.3] E. Mansfield (1961) Technical change and the rate of imitation. *Econometrica* **29**, 741–766.

Elsevier Science for:
[Table 6.2] A. W. Drew (1995) Accelerating innovation in financial services. *Long Range Planning* **28**, 11–21.

Euromoney Plc for:
[Table 7.1 and Table 7.2] Euromoney (1987) Special Survey, p.12 Table Top 20 Underwriting Banks in the NIFs market and Top 20 NIFs Arrangers.

Institute for Operations Research and the Management Sciences (INFORMS) for:
[Figure 5.1] K. F. McCardle (1985) Information acquisition and the adoption of new technology. *Management Science*, Vol 31, No. 11 (November) Figure 1, p.1374.
[Figure 5.4] F. M. Bass (1969) A new-product growth model for consumer durables. *Management Science*, Vol 15, No. 5 (January), Figures 2 and 3, pp.217–218.
[Figure 5.6] G. Lilien, A. Rao, S. Kalish (1981) Bayesian estimation and control of detailing effort in a repeat purchase diffusion environment. *Management Science*, Vol 27, No. 5 (May), Figure 2, p.496.

International Thomson Publishing for:
[Figure 2.11] T. Kim (1993) *International Money and Banking*, Table 1, p.202, Routledge: London.

MIT Press Journals for:
[Figure 4.4] G. C. Loury (1979) Market structure and innovation. *The Quarterly Journal of Economics* Vol 93, No. 3 (August) pp.395–410. © 1979 by the President and Fellows of Harvard College.

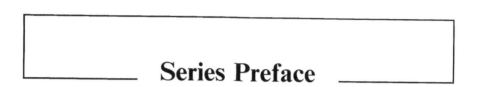

Series Preface

This series aims to publish books which give authoritative accounts of major new topics in financial economics and general quantitative analysis. The coverage of the series includes both macro and micro economics and its aim is to be of interest to practioners and policy-makers as well as the wider academic community.

The development of new techniques and ideas in econometrics has been rapid in recent years and these developments are now being applied to a wide range of areas and markets. Our hope is that this series will provide a rapid and effective means of communicating these ideas to a wide international audience and that in turn this will contribute to the growth of knowledge, the exchange of scientific information and techniques and the development of cooperation in the field of economics.

Stephen Hall
London Business School, UK and
Imperial College, UK

Preface

The increasing importance of the process of financial innovation has attracted considerable interest in recent years. Financial innovation has been one of the most influential trends prevailing in international financial markets in the 1980s and 1990s. Increased innovation, reflected in the growth of securitisation, for example, has resulted in the emergence and growth of a large number of off-balance-sheet activities (including euromarkets business, contingent banking, bank assets securitisation and derivative instruments). There are a large number of studies which document the emergence and growth of new financial products and analyse their demand/supply factors. More recently, various theoretical approaches have been advanced that attempt to explain financial innovation as a process. At the same time, a number of hypotheses that explain securitisation and the growth of OBSAs have emerged in the literature. These latter studies are mainly concerned with the question of which banks are more likely to adopt OBSAs.

These studies, however, assume a static framework which ignores the strategic and competitive interactions between firms. The presence of network and informational externalities, two important aspects of innovation competition in financial markets, can have a significant impact on an individual bank's decision to adopt an innovation and on the innovation's diffusion among banks. The industrial economics literature provides an extensive analysis of the competitive and strategic interactions between firms in the context of innovation adoption and diffusion. There has, however, been little effort made to relate the findings of this literature to the banking industry. This book aims to fill this gap.

1

Technical and Financial Innovation: An Introduction

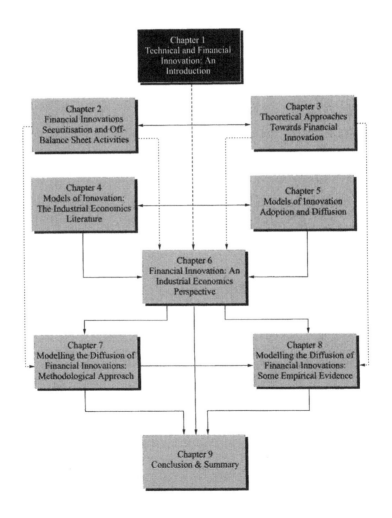

1
Technical and Financial Innovation: An Introduction

Without technical and financial innovation, the economic scene offers nothing, but uninteresting, foreseeable reproduction of goods, services and financial and material means of production. The wants of consumers, as well as the products and the methods of production, tend to be unalterable. The original factors of production, nature and labour, have the same appearance over time and do not reflect any qualitative change. The process of capital formation is an endless repetition along the lines of the savings-investment mechanism, known since the days of Robinson Crusoe. In such a world, devoid of innovation, equipment that has reached the end of its useful life will be replaced by new but otherwise identical equipment.

Arnold Heertje, 1988, p. 1

1.1 TECHNICAL INNOVATION AND THE INDUSTRIAL ECONOMICS LITERATURE

Economists have long realised the important role played by technical progress as a determinant of economic growth. Adam Smith's (1776) *Wealth of Nations* identified inventions and improvements in machinery as one major way in which the division of labour promotes productivity. Technology and technical advances were among the central forces at work on society in the early theories of Karl Marx (1900) and Alfred Marshall (1898). Economists first became aware of technical innovation's quantitative importance in the 1950s while analysing the factors contributing to economic growth. Interest in technological innovations stems in no small part from the results obtained by these empirical studies which indicated that technical change, broadly defined, provided the most significant contribution to the increase in labour productivity in the nineteenth and twentieth centuries. Abramowitz (1956), Solow (1957), and Denison (1974) estimated technology's contribution to increased productivity at 62.5%, 87.5%, and 48%, respectively. Even ignoring the different methodologies underlying such quantitative studies, the fact remains that technical change is an important factor affecting our standards of living. A recognition by economists of the importance of technical progress raised serious doubts about the adequacy with which traditional micro-economic models allow one to understand the functioning of modern market economies and to develop policy prescriptions. The lack of attention paid to new products and processes in most economic texts reflects the difficulty of incorporating the topic within the traditional analytical framework. Adopting the assumptions of perfect information and using a form of analysis that is largely *static* is inappropriate for the discussion of change (Ferguson, 1988).

Schumpeter criticised mainstream economics for failing to realise that capitalism consists of *change* and cannot be analysed in static terms; 'capitalism, then, is by nature a form or method of economic change and not only never is but never can be stationary', Schumpeter (1942, p. 82). Static analysis of welfare economics shows perfect competition as a welfare maximising system. It may however be necessary to sacrifice short-term efficiencies to gain long-term welfare maximum, a hypothesis that cannot be examined by static analysis. As Schumpeter (1942, p. 83) puts it, 'a system—any system, economic or other—that at *every* given point of time fully utilises its possibilities to the best advantage may yet in the long run be inferior to a system that does so at *no* given point of time, because the latter's failure to do so may be a condition for the level or speed of long-run performance'.

Innovation, as Schumpeter's broad definition suggests, is the 'fundamental impulse that sets and keeps the capitalist engine in motion'. Mainstream economics focused on price competition, but according to Schumpeter it is competition in the innovative activity market that matters. 'It is not that kind of competition [price competition] which counts but the competition from the new commodity, the new technology, the new source of supply, the new type of organisation—competition which commands a decisive cost or quality advantage and which strikes not at the margins of the profits and the outputs of the existing firms but at their foundations and their very lives' (Schumpeter, 1934, p. 84). Capitalism, according to Schumpeter, is a process of *creative destruction* that incessantly revolutionises the economic structure from within, incessantly destroying the old one, incessantly creating a new one. It is through this concept of *competition through innovation* that the two patterns of innovative activity, mostly associated with Schumpeter, emerged. In the first pattern, Schumpeter (1934) examined the typical European industrial structure of the late nineteenth century characterised by many small firms. The pattern of innovative activity was characterised by technological ease of entry in an industry and by a major role played by new firms in the innovative activity. New entrepreneurs entered into an industry with new ideas, new products or new processes, and launched new enterprises which challenged established firms and thus continuously disrupted the ways of production, organisation and distribution and eliminated the quasi rents associated with previous innovations (Malerba and Orsenigo, 1995, p. 47).

Schumpeter's somehow revised view of the dynamics of the innovative activity, and the one now most associated with him, is found in his *Capitalism, Socialism and Democracy* (1942) which was inspired by the American industry of the first half of the twentieth century. Emphasis according to this view was on the institutionalisation of the innovative activity, the industrial R&D laboratory for technological innovation and the key role played by large firms. According to this view, the pattern of innovative activities is characterised by the prevalence of large established firms and by relevant barriers to entry for new innovators. Large firms' advantages stem from their accumulated stock of knowledge in commercially-critical technological areas, economies of scale and economies of scope in large scale R&D projects, and from their distributional and financial superiority.

The work by Schumpeter motivated a stream of empirical and theoretical studies of the relationship between market structure and innovation. Models of the timing of innovation examine how the expected benefits, the cost of research and development programmes (R&D), and the strategic aspects of competition in an industry determine the time pattern of expenditures across firms and over time, the date of introducing the innovation, and the characteristics of the innovating firms. In these models the firm must select the optimal amount to spend on R&D where there is uncertainty regarding either the timing or value of the innovation, or both. Decision-theoretic models solve for the optimal rate of R&D spending for a single firm, and evaluate the effects of changes in the parameters of the model (as a measure of market structure) on that rate. Game-theoretic models compare the socially optimal number of concurrent research efforts with the amount of research performed by firms in a competitive versus a co-operative (i.e. socially planned) environment.

Another branch of the literature focuses on the second phase of the innovative activity; *diffusion*. Diffusion is a crucial part of any theory of innovation. The assumption of imperfect information, together with a differential response by firms, ensures that innovators will be rewarded by a period of abnormal profit before it is subsequently eroded by imitation. Where agents have perfect information, any disequilibrium will be transitory. In practice, markets are likely to be in disequilibrium for some time; equilibrium will not be restored until diffusion has eliminated all perception of potential profits (Ferguson, 1988). Empirical studies suggest that innovations *diffuse* into use over time, instead of being adopted by all potential adopters simultaneously, and that the diffusion period can vary significantly between one innovation and another. Models of innovation adoption explains this pattern of diffusion by modelling the adoption decision of individual firms. Key factors that explain diffusion are: heterogeneity in the population of adopters regarding at least one characteristic affecting their adoption decision, uncertainty regarding the benefits of adoption, exogenous factors such as declining incremental benefits to later adoptions and declining adoption costs, strategic behaviour by firms, positive informational and network externalities, and institutional and competitive bandwagon pressures caused by the sheer number of adopters. Diffusion models focus on the industry-aggregate diffusion rates and evaluate industry- and innovation-specific factors. These models distinguish between two categories of adopters, those who adopt the innovation because of their individual assessments of the innovation's profitability, and those whose adoption decision is influenced by the number of firms that have adopted the innovation.

1.2 FINANCIAL INNOVATION

As mentioned above there is an extensive and long-established literature analysing the innovative activity in the real sector. There has been, however, little effort made to relate the findings of the industrial economics literature to the financial industry. In recent years, the process of financial innovation has received a lot of interest from researchers. The interest in this process stems from the significant impact financial innovation can have on the practice and characteristics of financial institutions and markets. Although not a new phenomenon, recent growth in financial innovation has transformed financial markets. A large number of new financial products and instruments have been innovated as the traditional barriers between financial institutions have increasingly been eroded. Banks are increasingly competing with markets for what was once considered to be traditional intermediated credits. Markets are becoming more global and competition between financial institutions has intensified. This increase in financial innovation has taken place in an environment of steady deregulation coupled with significant advances in information and communication technologies. Securitisation, perhaps the most important trend prevailing in international financial markets in the 1980s and the early 1990s, continues to redefine the operations of banks and has important regulatory implications. Both bank and non-bank financial institutions are relying more on income from off-balance-sheet activities (OBSAs). A greater share of credit now flows through capital-market channels, which may be characterised by less supervision with comparison to banks (BIS, 1986). Given the significance of innovation in reshaping the financial industry, a sound theoretical understanding of the dynamics of the process of financial innovation becomes very important.

Considering the extensive study of technical innovation in the industrial economics literature, the study of financial innovation is at an early stage. The bulk of the literature consists of mainly descriptive studies which explain why innovations occur and the factors affecting demand and supply of financial innovations. Deregulation, improved technology, growing competition, and volatile exchange and interest rates are often quoted as the main stimulus for financial innovation. A specific branch of the literature has focused on the growth of OBSAs and on the characteristics of banks most likely to engage in them. Most of these studies, however, are static and ignore the strategic and dynamic aspects of diffusion processes and innovation adoption. Recently, a new approach has emerged in the literature which examines financial innovation in a general equilibrium context and analyses the risk-sharing aspects of new financial securities (e.g. Allen and Gale, 1994 and Duffie and Rahi, 1995). With comparison to earlier literature, this offers a formal framework which theoretically models the incentives of innovation. This, however, still falls short of the extensive analysis of the innovative activity in the industrial economics literature.

A main reason perhaps which explains the lack of studies that relate the industrial economics literature to the financial industry concerns the unique characteristics of the financial industry. For example, there is an absence of patent laws and many new financial products require little capital investment and can be developed within a much shorter period of time than in the real sector. There is also a lack of empirical studies of financial innovation which makes it difficult to choose among models with different underlying assumptions. These differences, however, do not imply that industrial economics is irrelevant to the study of financial innovation. Rather, it suggests that a detailed study of the industrial economics literature is needed so one can evaluate existing models and see if they can be used to describe the unique characteristics of the financial industry. Moreover, some models in the industrial economics literature are general enough to account for these characteristics. This is particularly true for adoption and diffusion models. Examples of such models that are particularly applicable to the financial industry can be found in the literature (e.g. Anderson and Harris, 1986 and Kapadia and Puri, 1995).

This book aims to investigate banks' decisions to adopt new products and to evaluate these products' diffusion patterns based on existing literature in the industrial economics literature. To accomplish this goal, we first examine the empirical and theoretical characteristics of the process of financial innovation (Chapters 2 and 3). This helps us to establish the unique characteristics of financial innovations, a prerequisite for evaluating the industrial economics literature (reviewed in Chapters 4 and 5). Based on our review of both literatures we then offer a theoretical and empirical analysis of the adoption and diffusion of two financial innovations: junk bonds and note issuance facilities (NIFs).[1] This should fill a considerable gap in the existing literature on the process of financial innovation. Theoretically, this book offers new insights into the determinants of banks' adoption of new financial products and analyses the competitive, strategic and informational aspects of the diffusion processes of financial innovations. Empirically, the book establishes features which characterise the competitive and strategic nature of adoption and diffusion of financial innovations. The bringing together of the finance and the industrial economics literature, and the empirical findings of this book, should stimulate further research in this area which can improve our understanding of the process of financial innovation, which, in spite of its increasing importance, currently is an under-researched area.

1.3 STRUCTURE OF THE BOOK

The structure of this book is organised as follows. Chapter 2 examines the emergence of a number of financial innovations in international financial markets and reviews the main structural trends prevailing in the financial industry. Most of the process of financial innovation in recent years has been reflected in the trend towards securitisation and the growth of OBSAs. The chapter discusses a demand-driven theory of innovation related to the functions financial innovations perform in the financial system. Factors affecting the supply of financial innovations are also examined. A number of studies focus on the determinants of an individual bank's decision to adopt OBSAs (e.g. standby letters of credit, loan sales, loan commitments). Important factors include banks' comparative advantage in originating and servicing loans, the size of banks, regulatory taxes, and the need to diversify. At the industry level, various hypotheses explaining the securitisation phenomenon have been proposed and tested empirically. The empirical evidence supports the market discipline hypothesis which argues that OBSAs are uninsured contingent claims whose value increases with the safety of the issuing bank. Thus safer banks have a comparative advantage in issuing these claims.

Chapter 3 reviews the literature on theoretical models of financial innovation. Most of this literature is descriptive and attempts to highlight the factors responsible for the emergence of specific financial innovations. The main factors often quoted in the literature as causes of financial innovation are regulation, competition, globalisation, technology, and volatile exchange and interest rates. An important fact that emerges from this literature is that new financial products remain and continue to grow even after the initial stimulus that led to their introduction (e.g. a certain regulation) is no longer present. One explanation for this is that financial products for which there exists a demand may not be introduced due to supply-related competitive and strategic factors. The initial stimulus makes it worthwhile for a few banks to introduce the innovation and thus starts the diffusion process. Banks' responsiveness to the initial stimulus vary according to certain bank-specific factors such as those highlighted in Chapter 2 (e.g. size, business portfolio, need to diversify). Subsequent entry to the market by more banks, and the associated growth of the market, are independent of the initial stimulus and governed by strategic and competitive factors (such as the increased liquidity in particular markets). This view of the diffusion of financial innovations forms the basis of the theoretical framework adopted in this book (Chapters 5 and 6), and motivates the empirical analysis (Chapters 7 and 8).

In Chapters 4 and 5 we turn our attention to the industrial economics literature. Chapter 4 focuses on the issue of the timing of innovation in a dynamic and competitive environment. The bulk of the literature can be characterised as models of R&D competition focusing on the timing and intensity of investing in R&D to perfect a given single innovation. In these models the firms must select the optimal amount to spend on R&D where either the timing or value of the innovation is random. The decision theoretic formulations solve for the optimal rate of R&D spending for a single firm and evaluate the effects of parameter changes on that rate. The game theoretic formulations compare the socially optimal number of research projects with the amount of research performed by firms in a noncooperative game. The conclusions drawn in both cases focus upon the effects of market structure on the timing and intensity of the innovative activity. At the industry level (i.e. game-theoretic models), and allowing for market uncertainty, the following two conclusions emerge:

1. An increase in the number of competing firms leads to an earlier expected industry introduction date of an innovation, and (with fixed development cost) to a higher level of equilibrium investment rate at the firm level.
2. Competitive entry leads to a larger number of firms than is socially optimal.

Chapter 5 reviews models of innovation adoption and diffusion. Motivated by the empirical observation that innovations often *diffuse* over time rather than being adopted by all firms simultaneously, adoption models attempt to explain this observation by analysing the individual firm's decision to adopt an innovation, and the timing of adoption. Adoption models explain diffusion by assuming a heterogeneous population of potential adopters. *Ex ante* heterogeneity stems from differences in firms' characteristics that are critical to the adoption decision (e.g. firm size). *Ex-post* heterogeneity stems from either exogenous factors including declining incremental benefits for later adoption and declining adoption costs or endogenous factors such as bandwagon effects where the sheer number of firms that adopt the product creates a pressure on non-adopting firms.

Empirical diffusion models are general mathematical functions which focus on the aggregate industry diffusion rate by depicting the successive increase in the number of adopters or adopting units of an innovation over time. The most basic of these is a mixed-influence diffusion model which distinguishes between two categories of adopters: internal and external adopters. Internal adopters are firms which are influenced in the timing of their initial adoption by the number of firms that have already adopted the innovation. External adopters, on the other hand, are influenced in the timing of their initial adoption by exogenous factors other than the number of early adopters. In relation to models of adoption, external influence can be viewed to represent the influence of exogenous factors which leads to the initial introduction of the innovation. The differences in the timing of external adopters are due to the *ex ante heterogeneity* in firms' characteristics which affect the optimal timing of adoption. Internal influence, on the other hand, captures the effects of bandwagon pressures, and changes in the return/cost characteristics of the innovation that are related to the number of firms that have already adopted the innovation. That is, it captures the *ex post heterogeneity* generated by, or related to, the number of firms that have already adopted the innovation.

A number of interesting facts emerge from our discussion of industrial economics models of innovation, innovation adoption and diffusion processes. Firstly, innovations are often developed, adopted, and diffused in a dynamic environment where strategic interactions between rivals can impact strongly on the behaviour of these firms, and on the features of the eventual equilibrium that prevails at the aggregate industry level. Static theoretical and empirical studies of OBSAs which ignore these interactions are inadequate to explain factors determining these instruments adoption by banks. Secondly, informational and network externalities are two important features of which there is no systematic analysis in the financial context, even though these factors are particularly important in financial markets. The combination of these observations with the one from Chapter 2 (i.e. that financial innovations often continue to grow even after the initial stimulus is no longer present) forms the basis of our theoretical framework of innovation adoption and diffusion in the financial industry.

Chapter 6 uses the findings of the previous chapters to formulate this theoretical framework. This framework distinguishes between two categories of adopters. External adopters are banks which adopt the innovation based on their individual assessments of the innovation's profitability, which is determined by exogenous factors that lead to the initial emergence of the innovation. These banks do not necessarily adopt the innovation simultaneously; optimal timing of adoption is defined by key firm-specific factors which are described by a distribution of values across firms and not a single value. We do not specify these factors, nor do we determine *a priori* the time-pattern of external innovation adoption.

Internal adopters are banks whose adoption decision is influenced by the number of banks that have adopted the innovation. These banks may base their decision on individual assessments of the innovation's profitability, in which case the change in their assessments is due to positive informational or network externalities related to the number of banks that have adopted the innovation. These banks may also adopt the innovation due to competitive and institutional bandwagon pressures created by the sheer number of banks that have adopted the innovation. In both cases, internal adopters are influenced in their decision to adopt an innovation and in the timing of adoption by the number of banks that have already adopted the innovation. This relationship is in the form of either updated assessments due to positive network and informational externalities, and/or in the form of competitive and institutional bandwagon pressures. The framework analysed in this chapter motivates the empirical analysis conducted in Chapter 8.

Chapter 7 explains the methodology applied in the empirical analysis. The models tested fall into two groups; single-adoption and repeat adoption models. The main goal is to test for the presence of internal and external factors in the diffusion patterns of two financial innovations, junk bonds and NIFs, and to assess which factors are responsible for internal influence. These can be either in the form of rational efficiency factors (e.g. increased liquidity, information transfer) or bandwagon pressure factors (institutional and competitive bandwagon pressures). Single adoption models (the logistic model and the non-uniform influence, NUI model) allow us to assess whether an increase in the number of banks that have introduced the innovation makes it more or less desirable for other banks to enter the market. Repeat adoption models (the NUIR, the NUIR 1, and the NUIR 2 model) assess the impact new entry by banks to the market for innovation has on the desirability of the innovation as measured by the total number of banks active in the market during each period of time.

Chapter 8 presents the results of our empirical analysis. The empirical evidence obtained from the first part of our analysis supports the hypothesis that innovation adoption by one bank makes it more likely that other banks will introduce the innovation. Mansfield (1961) explained this *imitative* nature of diffusion processes, often encountered in the real sector, on the grounds that as more firms adopt the innovation, more information accumulates regarding the innovation's profitability (reduced uncertainty through information transfer from early adopters to other members of the population of potential adopters) and increased bandwagon pressure on nonadopters. Others argue that the profitability of adopting increases (due to positive network externalities), or the adoption cost decreases (due to the elimination of the fixed-cost component of adoption cost) as the number of firms adopting the innovation increases.

Using the NUI model's results, the analysis shows that internal influence is in fact an increasing function of the cumulative number of banks that adopted the innovation. That is, the larger the number of banks that have adopted the innovation, the larger is the impact that *subsequent* adoption by more banks have on non-adopting banks. One would expect the internal influence to be a decreasing function of the number of banks that introduced the innovation if enhanced liquidity or reduced uncertainty were responsible for the internal influence. This is so because new entry to the market is likely to have a greater impact in terms of enhanced liquidity and reduced uncertainty in the early stages when there are fewer banks in the market than in the later stages of the diffusion process. An increasing internal influence thus suggests that it (i.e. the internal influence) is mainly in the form of institutional and competitive bandwagon pressure.

The analysis is extended to account for repeat adopters, i.e. how new entrants to the market impact the total number of banks engaged in the market at any point of time. The results of three repeat-adoption models suggest that, for NIFs, new entry by banks to the market has a positive impact on the total number of adopting banks which continue to operate in the market at any period of time. This suggest that the positive impact of new entry on the market's profitability, due to increased liquidity for example, more than offsets the expected decrease in incumbent firms' market shares. The results show that the emergence of the NIFs market can be characterised by an imitative diffusion pattern where the growth of the market can be ascribed mainly to institutional and competitive bandwagon pressures. For junk bonds, new entry seems to have had little impact on the number of adopting banks engaged in the market at any point of time.

The contribution of this book is not limited to the empirical findings. The theoretical framework motivating the empirical analysis is based on a review of three separate literatures (R&D competition, innovation adoption and innovation diffusion models) which have developed separately. The bringing together of this literature and establishing links provides interesting and important ideas for future research. The review of the industrial economics literature, for example, shows that innovations are developed, adopted, and diffused in a much more dynamic environment than is often assumed by banking researchers. The empirical findings also suggest that strategic, competitive, and informational factors play an important role in shaping the diffusion pattern of financial innovations. These results should also stimulate further work on modelling the process of financial innovation. Economists have benefited from a substantial empirical literature on innovation and market structure in formulating their theoretical models of technical innovation. The lack of empirical studies of financial innovation limits our ability to develop theoretical models of competition in the innovative activity and the timing of innovation in financial markets. Future research in this area can attempt to answer questions such as: under what conditions are we likely to observe bandwagon effects and what factors govern the extent of these effects? Which type of financial innovations are likely to be dominated by external adoption or internal adoption? Which banks are most likely to create bandwagon pressures and which banks are likely to be influenced by these pressures? Finally, the analysis can be extended to incorporate certain pre-defined exogenous variables (e.g. regulatory factors) into the model so as to assess their impact on the diffusion patterns of financial innovations.

ENDNOTES

1. Innovation adoption by banks in this context simply means the participation of banks in the market for the innovation (i.e. junk bonds or NIFs) as underwriters, managers, or arrangers. It excludes banks that participate in the market as issuers or investors in these instruments.

2

Financial Innovations—Securitisation and Off-Balance Sheet Activities

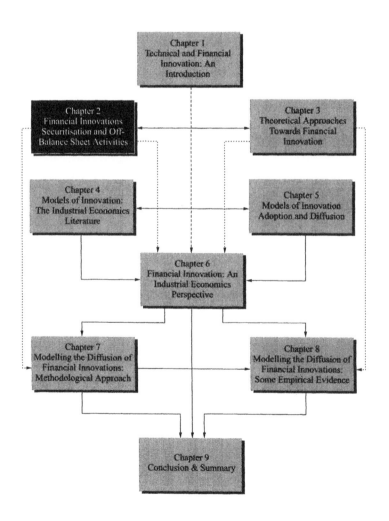

2
Financial Innovations—Securitisation and Off-Balance Sheet Activities

2.1 INTRODUCTION

Financial systems have experienced a dramatic change over the last twenty years. A sharp acceleration in the pace of innovation has transformed the international financial system significantly. These developments have been mainly due to the interaction of a number of factors. Deregulation, improved technology, growing competition, and volatile exchange and interest rates are often quoted as the main stimulus for financial innovation. Regulatory authorities have also become more concerned with the impact that financial innovation could possibly have on the stability of financial systems. Both bank and non-bank financial institutions nowadays rely much more on income from off-balance sheet activities. A greater share of credit now flows through capital market channels, which may be characterised by less supervision with comparison to banks. On the other hand, innovation can improve the efficiency of international financial markets by offering a broader and more flexible range of instruments for borrowing. It also provides hedging instruments which can help banks, borrowers, and investors to manage the risks associated with volatile exchange and interest rates.

Most of the growth of financial innovation in recent years has been illustrated by the trend towards securitisation. This trend has been reflected in the growth in the number and market size of off-balance sheet activities (OBSAs). These instruments can be broadly divided into four groups as shown in Figure 2.1; underwriting debt, derivatives, contingent banking, and bank assets securitisation. In this chapter, we aim to provide an overview of the emergence and growth of a number of new financial products, as well as the major structural trends that international financial markets have witnessed recently. In this chapter we focus on innovations that have been mainly introduced in wholesale markets rather than retail markets. The causes of financial innovation and the demand and supply forces underlying this process are examined. Particular emphasis is placed on securitisation and the growth of OBSAs.

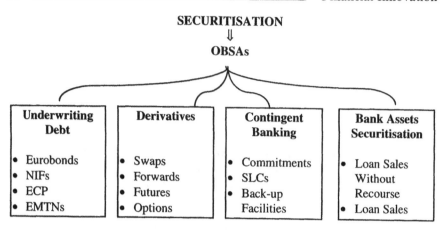

Figure 2.1 Securitisation and OBSAs

2.2 FINANCIAL INNOVATION OVER THE LAST 20 YEARS

Financial innovation is not a new phenomenon, as all financial instruments and markets that exist today were at one time invented. What is new, however, is the acceleration in the last two decades in the pace and range of financial innovation. Silber (1975) lists 25 innovations that have been introduced in the financial services industry in the period 1850 to 1974 (Table 2.1). Eight years later, Silber (1983) lists 38 new financial products or practices that emerged during the 1970–82 period (see Table 2.2 below). As stressed by Silber (1983), any single entry in this list could be expanded into additional specific innovations. Interest rate futures, for example, could be divided into numerous individual new futures contracts. Matthews (1994) identified more than 70 financial innovations introduced in the 1980–86 period, 40 of which were introduced in 1985–86. Finnerty (1993) provides an even more extensive listing with his own interpretation of the incentives for innovation for each new security. These studies clearly indicate a large increase in the growth of financial innovation over the last twenty years or so.

The structure of the financial system in the United States is relevant to any study of the process of financial innovation and its causes. In a comparative study of country shares in selected financial markets (foreign exchange, merger and acquisition advice, syndicated bank loans, Eurobonds, international equities, Eurocommercial paper, and Euro medium-term notes markets), Smith (1992) shows that most of these instruments have been innovated in the United States or by US institutions, mostly as a response to certain regulations. 'With hardly any qualification the United States obtained the largest shares of these markets at

Table 2.1   Financial Innovations—1850–1974

Innovation (Date)	Types of Innovation[a]	Cause of Innovation
1. Commercial Banks		
(a) Enter investment banking (1908)	(2)	Portfolio regulation
(b) Trust subsidiaries (1913)	(2)	Portfolio regulation
(c) Consumer loans (1928)	(3)	Weak loan demand
(d) Term loans (1933)	(3)	Weak loan demand
(e) 'Computer banking' (1950s)	(4)	Available technology
(f) Negotiable CD (1961)	(1)	Rate reg.; exp. loan dem.
(g) Subordinated debentures (1963)	(1)	Rate regulation
(h) Short-term promissory n. (1965)	(1)	Rate regulation
(i) Eurodollars (1966)	(1)	Rate regulation
(j) Evolution fed. funds mkt (1960s)	(?)	?
(k) Credit cards (1960s)	(4)	Technology
(l) Bank-related commercial paper (1969)	(1)	Rate regulation
(m) Loan RPs (1969)	(1)	Rate regulation
(n) Working capital acceptances (1969)	(1)	Rate regulation
(o) Floating prime (1971)	Reduced risk	Change in competition
(p) Floating rate notes (1974)	(3)	Rate regulation
2. Savings banks		
(a) Savings bank life ins. (1907)	(2)	Regulatory change
(b) Christmas clubs (1911)	(3)	?
3. Savings and loan associations		
(a) Serial plan (1850)	(3)	Orig. chr. too confining
(b) Permanent plan (c. 1880)	(3)	Orig. chr. too confining
(c) Brokerage of savings accts. (c. 1950)	(3)	Rising yields
(d) Mortgage participations (1957)	(?)	Rising yields
4. Life insurance companies		
(a) Tontine (1968)	(2)	Declining surplus
(b) Industrial insurance (1875)	(2)	Slowdown in growth
(c) Group insurance (1911)	(3)	Slowdown in growth

Note a: Types of innovations:

(1) Endogenizing an exogenous item in the firm's balance sheet (by modifying the instrument or accepted practices with respect to it).
(2) Introducing an existing financial instrument (from another industry or another country) in the firm's portfolio.
(3) Attempting to generate demand for credit or demand for liabilities by modifying an existing asset or liability in the portfolio.
(4) New item.

Source: Silber (1975), p. 72.

Table 2.2   Financial Innovations—1972–82

Innovations	1a	1b	1c	2	3	4	5	6
Cash management								
Money market mutual funds	•				•			
Cash management/Sweep accounts	•							
Money market certificates	•					•		
Debit card	•				•			
Now accounts	•							
ATS accounts	•				•			
Point of sale terminals					•			
Automated clearing houses					•			
Chips (same day settlement)					•			
Automated teller machines					•			
Investment Contracts								
(i) Primary market								
Floating rate notes				•				
Deep discount (Zero Coupon) bonds	•		•	•				
Stripped bonds	•		•	•				
Bonds with put options or warrants	•			•				
Floating prime rate loans				•				
Variable rate mortgages				•				
Commodity linked (Silver) bonds				•				
Eurocurrency bonds	•						•	
Interest rate futures				•				
Foreign currency futures							•	
Cash settlement (Stock Index) futures						•		
Options on futures				•		•		
Pass-through securities						•		
(ii) Consumer-type								
Universal life insurance				•				
Variable life policies		•						
IRA/Keogh accounts			•			•		
Municipal bonds funds			•			•		
All-saver certificates						•		
Equity access account		•		•				
Market structures								•
Exchange-traded options								
Direct public sales of securities								
Green Mountain Power Co.				•				
Shelf Registration				•		•		
Electronic trading								
NASDAQ					•			
GARBAN					•			
Discount brokerage						•		
Interstate depository institutions					•	•		
Institutional organisations								

(Continued)

Table 2.2 (*Continued*)

Innovations	1a	1b	1c	2	3	4	5	6
Investment bankers/Commodity dealers	•			•				
Salomon/Phibro, Goldman								
Sachs/J.Acron, DLJ/ACLI								•
Brokers/General finance								
Shearson/Amex, Bache/								
Prudential, Schwab/Bank of America								
Thrifts with commercial banks	•			•		•		
Financial centres (Sears Roebuck)								•

Column headings: (1) Inflation: (a) Level of interest rates, (b) General price level, (c) Tax effects; 2. Volatility of interest rates; 3. Technology; 4. Legislative initiative; 5. Internationalisation; 6. Other.
Source: Silber (1983), p. 91

both the beginning and end of the periods in question (1986–89), and its share has been greater than 50%' (Smith, 1992, p. 70).

Innovations also spread between domestic and international markets in both ways. As Harrington (1992, p. 52) puts it, innovations are frequently tried out first in the less controlled international markets and, if successful, are subsequently introduced into different national markets. Alternatively, when innovations occur in domestic markets, they are rapidly adopted in international banking and from there they spread quickly to other domestic markets. On this view, the large international financial markets play a crucial role in the innovation process, both as a source of innovation and/or the means of their diffusion. However, one should not underestimate the influence that British and other non-American other institutions have had on the process of financial innovation. Vittas (1985) states that European and Japanese institutions have been able to adopt, and quite often improvise, new instruments and techniques with considerable speed and flexibility. The introduction of currency options, future rate agreements, flip-flop perpetual notes, mismatch and minimax medium-term variable rate notes as well as of multiple component facilities, notes tender panels, and swap tender panels often owes as much to the inventiveness and ingenuity of British and other non-American institutions as to the large US names (Vittas, 1985, p. 50).

2.3 SECURITISATION AND OBSAs

2.3.1 Overview

The shift in international financial markets from bank loans to marketable debt securities has been highlighted by the emergence and growth of new financial markets and instruments such as Eurobonds, Floating-Rate Notes (FRNs), Euro Medium-Term Notes (EMTNs), Note Issuance Facilities (NIFs), and EuroCommercial Paper (ECP), the instruments of contingent banking (e.g. commitments and standby letters of credit), and also by the increased marketability of banks' traditional assets through loan sales with or without recourse. The growth in these markets has reflected an important recent trend in international financial markets, namely *securitisation*. Securitisation is seen by some analysts and regulators as the major banking innovation for the 1990s. It implies a shift of credit flows from bank lending to marketable debt instruments. In long-term debt markets, securitisation has been reflected in the growth of the Eurobond and FRNs market. Securitisation has been fostered by the maturing and increasing efficiency of the Eurobond markets. In short-term debt markets, securitisation has been reflected in the growth of euronote facilities (i.e. NIFs, ECP, and EMTNs), and the temporary decline (between 1982 and 1985) in the syndicated Euro-loans market.

During the 1980s, the composition of new international credit shifted from mainly syndicated bank loans to predominately securitised assets. Table 2.3 below shows the change in the composition of international credit during the 1980s. International bonds and euronote facilities grew substantially during the 1980s and early 1990s. While less than half the market of the eurocurrency syndicated credit in 1981, the market for international bonds and euronote facilities were three times as much as the syndicated credit market by 1994.

Another important aspect of securitisation in recent years is reflected in the increased marketability of banks' traditional assets. Asset securitisation and loan sales have enabled banks to unbundle the different components involved in lending (i.e. originating, funding and monitoring). By moving loans *off* their balance sheets, banks have been able to improve their capital ratios while maintaining profitability through income fees.

Table 2.3   Trends in the international credit and capital markets, 1981–94, US$ billions

Product/Year	1981	1982	1985	1988	1993	1994
International Bond issues	44	71.7	163.1	225.5	485.4	422.1
of which:						
Floating Rate Notes	7.8	12.6	55.3	23.1	68.5	92.7
Euronote facilities	1	2.3	49.49	76.4	117.4	193.3
of which:						
CP	0	0	16.31	58.25	24.2	36.4
EMTNs	0	0	0.8	19.196	92.7	157
NIFs/RUFs	1	2.3	33.14	3.7	0.5	0.5
Eurocurrency Syndicated Credit	96.5	100.5	18.92	102	221.2	248.6

Source: Compiled from various issues of Bank of England Quarterly Bulletin

Overall, securitisation and the growth of OBSA banking has had a significant impact on the functions performed by the financial sector in general and banking firms in particular. Figure 2.2 below shows how securitisation and OBSA have transformed the traditional manner in which banks carry out their operations. Banks which traditionally played the role of deposit taker/loan provider can now be viewed as a bundle of separate contracts (Lewis and Davis, 1987). Much more diverse and sophisticated types of financial intermediation are now being performed by banks compared to the more traditional deposit–loan intermediation function. Securitisation, new instruments, and hedging techniques emphasise the shift towards transactional banking and away from relationship banking (Pawley, 1991). We examine banks' asset securitisation and loan sales in more detail later in this chapter.

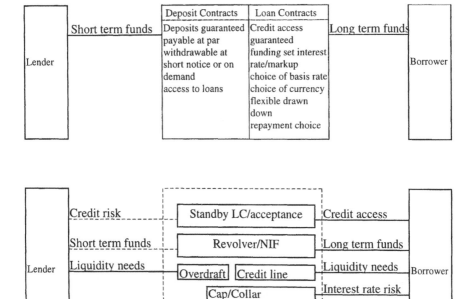

Source: Lewis and Davis (1987)

Figure 2.2 Off- and on-balance sheet banking

2.3.2 Eurodollar Market

A major development in the evolution of the present international financial system was the invention of the eurodollar market. In its origins, the market mainly consisted of dollar deposits held outside the United States, principally in Europe and especially in London. Eurodollars were mainly dollar deposits held in the immediate post-war period by former Communist bloc countries seeking to avoid their possible sequestration in the United States. Eurodollars maintained a high growth due to a continuing United States balance of payment deficits and the presence of large volumes of petrodollars attributable to the oil price increases in the mid-1970s (Smith, 1992, p. 42). With American banks eager to offset disintermediation problems created by regulation Q in the 1960s, the eurodollar market grew most rapidly during the 1970s as a substitute of domestic uninsured deposits. In 1970, overseas deposits of US banks accounted for 8% of total deposits at US banks. By 1980, deposits at overseas branches of US banks accounted for 25% of all deposits at US banks, while for the nine largest US banks they accounted for a little more than half of deposits (Baer and Pavel, 1988, p. 10). Together with certain American regulations which were introduced to strengthen the dollar, the presence of substantial financial funds in the form of Eurodollars has been a source for further innovations. Most dramatic of these innovations is the development of the Eurobond market.

2.3.3 Eurobond Market

A Eurobond is a bond issued in a different country to that of the currency in which it is denominated. In the 1960s, large international borrowers had every incentive to tap the eurodollar market. Borrowers which previously relied on issuing foreign bonds in the United States redirected their attention to the eurodollar market when in 1963 an interest equalisation tax, along with other financial regulations, was introduced in the United States to strengthen the Dollar. Besides eurodollars, eurobond issues are denominated in a number of other currencies, including Deutschmarks, French francs, Sterling, ECUs, Yen, Australian dollars and Canadian dollars.

The eurobond market has experienced substantial growth since its initial development. Figure 2.3 below shows the size of the market, in terms of volume and number of issues, for the period 1963–93. From US$148 million in 1963, the market reached US$175 760m in 1988 and more than US$400 000m by 1993. US financial institutions dominated the market, as book runners of eurobond issues, with 28.3% of the market in 1989, followed by Japanese and British institutions.

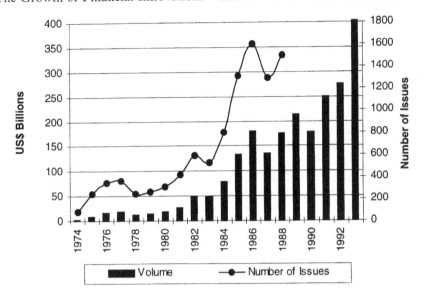

Source: 1974–1989, *Euromoney*, 20th Anniversary Supplement June 1989, and 1990–1993, *Euromoney*, Global Financing Guide April 1994

Figure 2.3   Growth of eurobonds, 1974–93

In 1990 the prospects for growth in the eurobond markets were downgraded by the Gulf war, fierce competition and lack of profitability. Interestingly, many market observers began to doubt whether the eurobond market could sustain its success once the regulations affecting domestic markets which initially gave rise to the development of eurobonds were eroded. Hamilton (1986), for example, argued that many of the laws and rules that once made the eurobond market so distinct a European phenomenon have been abolished. Smith (1992, p. 54) argues that by 1989 the regulatory barriers in the world's domestic bond markets, which led to the creation of the eurobond market, have been gradually removed: 'if this process continues the eurobond market won't have a reason for living anywhere'. Despite these developments, the eurobond market regained its substantial growth rates reaching three successive records of $249.2 billion, $275.9 bn, and $402 bn in 1991, 1992, and 1993, respectively. The experience of the eurobond market suggests that the development and subsequent growth of the markets for new financial products can be independent of factors that led to these products' initial introduction. As Davis (1995, p. 112) puts it, 'although some of these factors proved temporary [factors that led to the introduction of the eurobond], the initial stimulus was enough to provide the eurobond market with sufficient critical mass (size and diversity of issuers and investors, reputation, relationships and expertise of intermediaries) to survive their abolition'.

2.3.4 Floating-Rate Notes and Eurodollar Floating Rate Notes

Floating-rate notes (FRNs) originated in Europe and appeared in the US in the early 1970s. The market for FRNs expanded substantially with the development of the eurodollar and eurobond markets. During the 1970s and 1980s, large and unpredictable shifts in interest rates encouraged borrowers and lenders alike to minimise the accompanying risk exposure, providing an optimal arena for the development of a eurodollar FRNs market (Allen and Gale, 1989). Eurodollar FRNs are FRNs issued in the dollar section of the eurobond market. Euro-FRNs which were also dominated in a number of other currencies emerged as a close substitute to syndicated euro-bank loans. Within the category of FRNs, there has been considerable innovation, mainly in new types of interest structure (e.g. capped FRNs, interest mismatched).

The trend towards floating interest rate was especially pronounced in the dollar sector of the eurobond market. In 1985, the volume of FRN issues exceeded that of fixed-rate issues of dollars. It should be noted however that the increase in the prominence of FRNs does not necessarily imply that more international credit is at a floating rate. FRNs mainly replaced syndicated loans, which were largely placed on a variable rate basis (BIS, 1986, p. 134). In 1986 investor demand for FRNs began to weaken, as concerns about oversupply heightened and as interest rates fell (Bank of England, 1991, p. 522). This coupled with capital adequacy regulation introduced by the Japanese Ministry of Finance led to a sharp sell-off of perpetual FRNs and a drying up of liquidity. The market, however, survived and FRNs revived sharply during the period 1991 to 1994 as expectations grew that dollar short-term interest rates were reaching their trough and that European rates would fall (Bank of England, 1994). The revival of FRNs was partly due to the increased demand for structured FRNs (e.g. reverse FRNs, collared FRNs, step-up recovery FRNs) which are designed to respond to investor's views of future interest rate trends and yield curve patterns, but without exposing the issuer to interest rate risk.

Figure 2.4 below shows the growth of international bond issues and FRNs (left-hand scale) over the period 1981–94. As shown in Figure 2.4, issues of FRNs increased from $21.8 bn in 1991 to $43.2 bn in 1992, $68.5 bn in 1993 and $92.7 bn in 1994, their highest level ever. It should be noted, however, that the growth in FRNs in the last few years was also accompanied by the substantial growth in international bond issues. From $44 bn in 1981, international bond issues reached $422.1 bn in 1994. The line in Figure 2.4 measures the ratio of FRNs issues to international bond issues (the right-hand scale). Although this ratio increased consistently between 1991 (at 6.5%) and 1994 (at 22%), it was still below its highest level of almost 34% in 1985.

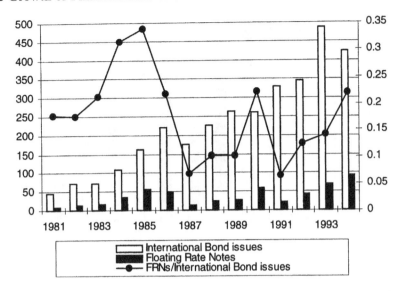

Source: Compiled from various issues of the Bank of England Quarterly Bulletin

Figure 2.4   Growth of floating-rate notes, 1978–94: new issues announced

2.3.5 Euronotes: NIFs, ECP, and EMTNs

The development of the euronote market dates back to the late 1960s. The euronote market refers to instruments or facilities designed to allow borrowers to issue a series of short term euronotes and include note issuance facilities (NIFs), revolving underwritten facilities (RUFs), eurocommercial paper (ECP), and euromedium-term notes (EMTNs), each dominating the euronote market in different periods (see Figure 2.5 below). NIFs, between 1981 and 1985; ECP between 1985 and 1990; and MTNs between 1991 and until 1994.

The euronote market was first created with the development of ECP due to various financial regulations in the US in 1968 which established certain restrictions on US business enterprises making transfers of capital abroad (Bullock, 1987, p. 1). US investment banks which had long experience in acting as dealers on domestic commercial paper programmes found a profitable opportunity in relocating the US commercial paper model abroad. Their experience and their existing market base gave them considerable competitive advantage over possible rivals. The ECP market survived for six years until its effective termination in 1974 due to modifications of the relevant regulation in the United States (Smith, 1992, p. 63). The market was to be re-established later in the 1980s.

During 1974–80, short term lending activities in the euromarkets were largely confined to direct bank lending. The large volumes of eurodollars resulted in

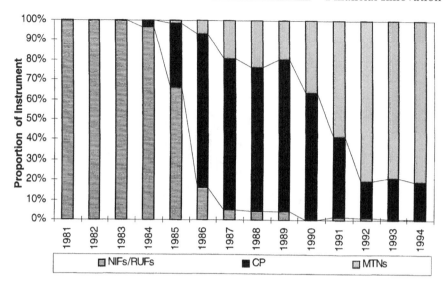

Source: Compiled from various issues of the Bank of England Quarterly Bulletin

Figure 2.5   The three phases of the euronote market, 1981–94, based on data of new issues announced

a continuing liquidity in the banking system which intensified competition among commercial banks for short-term lending, and caused lending margins to decline. Loans syndicated by a lead manager amongst a group of banks became a common financing structure, with intense competition to win the mandate from a borrower to lead manage such a facility (Bullock, 1987, p. 10). The euronote market developed as an alternative to the syndicated credit market in the early 1980s (Bank of England Quarterly Bulletin, 1988). Euronote arrangements became known as note issuance facilities (NIFs), which is an arrangement by which a bank or group of banks agree to act as managers underwriting a borrower's issue of short-term paper as and when required and to back the facility with medium-term credit should the note not find a market. Originally called 'note purchase facilities', NIFs took on a variety of names as different banks used them for the differing customer needs. They were sometimes known as: CD-issuance facilities, euronote issuance facilities, or revolving underwriting facilities. Different names were generally used to refer to different distribution methods (e.g. sole placing agency versus tender panel) that commercial banks (i.e. underwriters) used to place the notes with investors. Between 1982 and 1985, the euronote market was confined to NIFs in its various forms.

By 1985, it had been recognised by issuers and banks that existing distribution methods made it difficult to develop a stable, satisfied investor base as the supply of paper was unreliable under these methods. The combination of the underwriting and placement process necessitated the participation of a large number of banks, and required a lengthy administrative procedure. Banks recognised that the decoupling of the underwriting process from note placement, the main feature of commercial paper, ensured a distribution advantage over NIFs. In a typical ECP facility, a borrower appoints a dealer(s) to a programme without any underwriting commitment.[1] The dealer's responsibility is to place the issuer's notes with investors and to develop and maintain an investor base for the programme. Due to these advantages, the ECP market re-emerged in 1985 and continued to grow at the expense of the NIFs market. The growth in NIFs and ECP, among others, reflect two important prevailing trends in the international financial markets: securitisation and the increase in off-balance sheet activities. More recently, the ECP market seems to be threatened by a new instrument, euro medium-term notes, which have been the largest issued instrument in the euronote market since 1991.[2]

The international market for euro medium-term notes evolved only in 1986. Originally initiated by General Motors in 1972, there developed an active domestic United States market for EMTNs during the 1980s prior to its extension into the European markets (Walmsley, 1988). EMTNs showed high growth rates since their introduction into the European market in 1986 (see Figure 2.6 below). Within the spectrum of financial instruments EMTNs fit between bonds and commercial paper programmes. They differ from the former in that they are issued under a programme which ensures their availability on a continuous basis and they have a relatively short maturity. Compared with

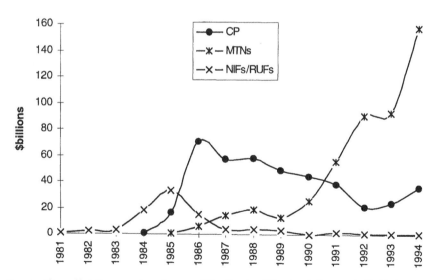

Source: Compiled from various issues of the Bank of England Quarterly Bulletin

Figure 2.6　Euronote market by instrument, 1981–94, new issues announced

commercial paper, however, their maturity is relatively long, from nine months to ten years (Smith, 1992, p. 68). A financial institution acts as an agent on the issuer's behalf making no underwriting provisions.

As can be seen from Figure 2.6 above, in 1991 EMTNs replaced ECP as the dominant instrument in the euronote market. Since then, the EMTNs have grown substantially, reaching more than $156 bn, compared to less than $37 bn new issues in the ECP market. Regulatory changes allowed EMTNs to be issued in more currencies, notably Sterling and Deutschmark (Euromoney, 1991b). Flexibility may be EMTNs' main advantage as issuers can borrow in a number of currencies with the same set of documentation. Issuers of EMTNs use this instrument and currency swaps in many different ways.[3] An EMTNs programme now consists of the documentation which allows an issuer to launch a whole series of complex private placements, reverse FRNs, puttable FRNs, commodity-linked and index-linked deals. As the size and complexity of the EMTNs market increases, its traders and salespeople have become more sophisticated. Traders in EMTNs must be familiar with the issuing regulations and execution problems of 18 currency sectors. They need to be able to give views on, say, the Sterling–Deutschmark rate and the long end of the Lira yield curve. The growth in the EMTNs market was at the expense of the ECP in particular and the NIFs market which have almost disappeared since the early 1990s. The market is expected to continue growing into the 21st century. Unlike the ECP market, the EMTNs market is nowhere near reaching its peak.

2.3.6 Euronotes and Syndicated Loans

As mentioned earlier, the emergence of the euronote market in the early 1980s was seen by some as a threat to the syndicated credit market (Bank of England, 1988) and reflected the trend towards securitisation (BIS, 1986). During the 1980s it was taken as read that the process of disintermediation combined with the development of interest rate and currency swaps would render the syndicated market obsolete (Banking World, July 1994, p. 32). Figure 2.7 below shows the trends in the syndicated credit market and compares it to the development in the international bonds and euronotes markets. As can be seen from the figure, syndicated credit entered the 1980s as the most important method of financing in international markets. Since then, however, international bond issues have increased dramatically. The syndicated credit markets contracted with the development of the euronote market between 1984 and 1987.[4] Between 1986 and 1990, the euronote market remained relatively stable and showed little growth. This was because the growth in the EMTNs market was mainly offset by a decline in the ECP market. The same period, i.e. 1986–90, witnessed a revival in the syndicated credit market. The syndicated credit market, most of which is variable-rate based, began to recover in the last

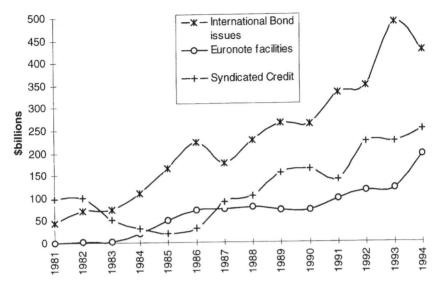

Source: Compiled from various issues of the Bank of England Quarterly Bulletin

Figure 2.7 International bonds, euronotes and syndicated credit, 1981–94: new issues
announced

quarter of 1986, and particularly during 1987 with the liquidity crisis in the
FRNs which caused a temporary decline in new issues in the international
bonds market. Since then, the syndicated credit market has remained an
important element of the Euromarkets. Nevertheless, Figure 2.7 clearly shows
the strong trend towards securitisation during the 1980s as reflected by the
growth of international bonds issues and euronotes.

2.3.7 Bank Asset Securitisation

A second dimension to the process of securitisation is reflected in the increased
marketability of banks' traditional assets. Banks have sought to increase the
negotiability of their conventional assets in two ways; through asset securitisation and through loan sales.

The pressures for generating fee income and meeting capital requirements
have led all banks, and especially large ones, to securitise their assets, mainly
loans. Securitised assets are attractive because they remove assets from a bank's
balance sheet, thereby improving capital ratios. Securitisation in this respect
refers to the separation of two main components of the traditional bank lending
function; origination and funding (and monitoring). The process of securitisation involves five basic parties (Sinkey, 1992, p. 689): (i) the loan originator

(bank or financial intermediary); (ii) the loan purchaser (an affiliated trust); (iii) the loan packager (underwriter of the securities); (iv) a guarantor (insurance company), and (v) investor (e.g. individual or other banks) who buy the securities. Figure 2.8 illustrates an example of this process. In general, banks have been motivated to securitise their assets by the implicit tax on bank capital, by competitive pressures on bank profits, and by the desire to exploit their advantage as originators of loans (Sinkey, 1992, p. 693). There are, however, barriers to asset securitisation, the most important of which is size. Arnold

---

Step 1
Party: The originating bank
Function: Originator and servicer
Cash flows/claims: Loans (downstream)
                      Loan principal + premiums if any (inflow)
                      Interest + principal (passed through over time)
Example: Marine Midland, automobile receivables

Step 2
Party: Subsidiary or separate trust
Function: Buys the loans from the bank and issues the securities
Cash flows/claims: Loans (inflow)
                      Loan principal + premiums (upstream outflow)
                      Interest + principal (passed through)
Example: Salomon Brothers affiliate and a separate trust

Step 3
Party: Investment bankers
Function: Underwrites and packages the securities and advises the trust
Cash flows/claims: Collects fees and sells securities issued by the trust
Example: Salomon Brothers

Step 4
Party: Guarantor
Function: Wholly or partially insures securities
Cash flows/claims: Insurance fees (inflow) and services (outflow)
Example: Companies specialising in financial guarantee insurance
                      (e.g. Travellers insurance company)

Step 5
Party: Investors
Function: Buys securities
Cash flows/claims: Cash outflow (principal) to buy securities
                      Hold securities (claims)
                      Interest + principal (cash inflow over time)
Example: Certificate for Automobile Receivables (CARs) purchased
                      by individuals, small banks, thrifts, and institutional investors

---

Source: Johnson and Murphy, 1987, p. 31

Figure 2.8   The process of asset securitisation

(1986) estimates that it takes a minimum pool of assets of $50m to cost justify a private placement and a pool of $100m for a public offering. This is mainly due to legal considerations and the minimum investment banking fees involved.

2.3.8 Loan Sales[5]

Banks, especially large ones, are increasingly originating loans with the idea of selling them or offering participation. Outright sales of loans by banks, not involving packaging them into securities, have also expanded rapidly in the United States. The cumulative total of loans sold reached $45 bn at the end of 1985 (BIS, 1986, p. 136). By 1990, loans sold by all insured commercial banks in the United States reached a total of $742 bn, of which $545 bn of these were sold by the nine money-center banks.[6] Small banks lack the size and reputational capital to be active in selling loans. They do, however, play a significant role as buyers of these loans. For small regional banks, loans bought offer an effective tool for diversification. Table 2.4 below shows the relation between banks' size and their role in the process of loans selling/buying. The ratio of loans purchased to loans sold declined considerably as bank size increased. Banks' profit from loan sales comes in the form of either a fee charged and/or a spread. Besides the desire to generate fee income on off-balance sheet activities, banks engage in loan sales to maintain relationships with top-quality customers.

Foreign banks play a significant role in loan sales in the United States. Loans purchased provide an access to top-quality borrowers for these banks which usually have little previous experience in lending to US corporations. In addition, loans purchased offer a higher rate of return than most money market instruments. Loan purchases as such can be viewed as a substitute for other short-term investments such as commercial paper, CD, or Euro-dollar deposits. Foreign banks' involvement in this market is an aspect of the trend towards globalisation and integration of financial markets.

Table 2.4 Bank Size, Loans Sold, and Loans Bought in the US—Dec. 31st 1990

Bank asset size class	Loans ($ bn)		
	Sold	Bought	Bght./Sold (%)
Banks < $5bn	54.6	33.8	61.9
Banks > $5bn, excluding MC banks	141.7	24.1	17.0
Nine money-center banks	545.7	6.0	1.1
All insured commercial banks	742.0	63.9	8.6

Source: Sinkey (1992, p. 688)

2.3.9 Other Off-Balance Sheet Activities (OBSAs)

So far this chapter has discussed the growth of various OBSAs in terms of a more general trend towards securitisation (e.g. NIFs, ECP). These, however, are only a few among a large number of OBSAs which emerged during the 1980s. The early 1980s experienced a tremendous increase in banks' OBSA items. Generally, we may divide OBSAs in two main groups. The first group is related to the so-called contingent banking phenomenon, and consists of financial innovations such as back-up facilities, bank guarantees, standby letters of credit, and loan commitments. These activities involve 'contingent' commitments not captured as assets or liabilities under conventional accounting procedures. A loan enters as an asset on a bank's balance sheet, whereas a promise to make a loan is a contingent liability; that is, an obligation to provide funds should the contingency be realised and does not appear on the balance sheet until after that occurrence. This group of OBSAs are also known as 'invisible banking' or 'assetless banking'.

The second group is related to the concept of *financial engineering* and includes innovations such as interest-rate and currency swaps, forward foreign exchange transactions, currency futures and options, and interest-rate options and caps. These items are generally interest rate and foreign exchange rate agreements, in most cases binding on both parties, but in some cases exercisable at one party's discretion (e.g. options). With the exception of swaps, no exchange of principal is usually involved (Lewis and Davis, 1987, p. 118). Derivative instruments can be divided into exchange-traded and over-the-counter (OTC) financial derivatives. A recent study by the central banks and monetary authorities in 26 countries estimates the notional amounts (i.e. the nominal value on which payments under derivatives contracts are based) of OTC contracts at $40.7 trillion at the end of March 1995 (BIS, 1996, p. 27). This is compared to only $8.8 trillion reported by exchanges at end-1994. The composition of the instruments varies considerably between OTC and exchange traded-markets as well. Single-currency interest rates (mainly swaps) accounted for 65% of the OTC total, followed by foreign exchange products at 32% and those on equity and commodity price risks at 1% each. On the exchange-traded market contracts on interest rates accounted for 95% of the total, stock indices for 4% and currencies for 1%.

Derivative instruments experienced high growth rates during the period from 1986 to 1994 as can be seen from Table 2.5 and Figure 2.9 below which show the total notional amounts outstanding world-wide at the end of each year from 1986 to 1994. Both exchange-traded and OTC instruments grew overall by over 40% per year with swaps, futures, and options showing the greatest growth rates. OTC interest rate swaps grew from $400 bn in 1986 to more than $3850 bn in 1992. The market for exchange-traded instruments concentrated heavily in interest rate futures with outstanding notional principal amounting to $5757.4 bn by the end of 1994.

Table 2.5 Markets for selected derivative instruments world-wide: notional principal amounts outstanding at year-end (US$ bn)

	1986	1987	1988	1989	1990	1991	1992	1993
Exchange-traded instruments								
Interest rate futures	370	488	895	1,201	1,454	2,157	2,902	4,960
Interest-rate options[a]	146	122	279	388	600	1,073	1,385	2,362
Currency futures	10	14	12	16	16	18	25	30
Currency options[a]	39	60	48	50	56	61	80	81
Stock market index futures	15	18	28	42	70	77	81	119
Options on stock market indices	38	28	44	72	96	137	168	286
Subtotal	619	730	1,306	1,768	2,292	3,523	4,641	7,839
of which:								
In the United States	518	577	950	1,152	1,262	2,130	2,684	4,329
In Europe	13	13	178	251	461	710	1,110	1,820
In Japan	63.5	108	107	261	424	441	576	1,194
Over-the-counter (OTC)[b]								
Interest rate swaps (IRS)	400	683	1,010	1,503	2,312	3,065	3,851	—
Currency and cross-currency IRS[c]	100	183	320	449	578	807	860	—
Other derivative instruments[d]	—	—	—	450	561	577	748[e]	—
Subtotal	500	866	1,326	2,423	3,451	4,449	5,459[e]	—
Grand total	1,119	1,596	2,632	4,191	5,743	7,972	10,100[e]	—

[a] Calls plus puts
[b] No statistics available on forward agreements or OTC foreign exchange options
[c] Adjusted for reporting of both currencies
[d] Caps, collars, floors, and swaptions
[e] Author's estimates based on grand total of US$2 trillion for forward rate agreements (FRAs) (which are not included in the IMF data)

Source: IMF 1993, 1994: GAO 1994

The table also gives a breakdown of the number of contracts by region for exchange-traded instruments. The United States has dominated the markets of derivative instruments throughout the 1980s with more than 65.1% of the notional principal amounts having been transacted in the United States in 1989, compared with only 14.1% in Europe and 14.7% in Japan. The 1990s however showed substantial growth rates of derivative activities outside the United States as can be seen from Figure 2.9. This was accompanied by a world-wide increase in the use of exchange-traded derivatives which reached US$8838 bn in 1994, almost double the corresponding figure in 1992 and four times that in 1990.

A more meaningful economic measure than the notional amounts is the gross replacement value (GRV) of contracts outstanding (BIS, 1996, p. 28). This, at

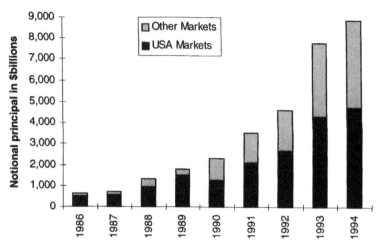

Source: IMF (1994, p. 119), BIS (1996, p. 54)

Figure 2.9   Notional amounts outstanding for exchange-traded derivative instruments
—1986–94

any point in time, represents the costs incurred had long contracts been replaced at prices prevailing at the time. The study by the central banks mentioned earlier estimates the GRV of OTC contracts at $1.7 trillion, or 4% of the total reported notional amounts. The growth of derivative instruments can also be gauged by examining Table 2.6 below which shows the total number of contracts traded each year in the exchange market. The table also gives a breakdown of the number of contracts by region. A similar picture emerges. The United States has dominated the markets for derivative instruments throughout the 1980s with more than 68% of the contracts transacted in the United States in 1989, compared with only 15.3% in Europe and 10.8% in Japan. The 1990s however witnessed substantial growth rates of derivative activities outside the United States as can be seen from Figure 2.10.

On the supply side, banks engage in derivatives to gain fee income (as a third party agent in guaranteeing and arranging swaps in the OTC market) or spread income (as one of the exchanging parties) and/or to hedge their interest rate and foreign exchange rate exposure. On the demand side, high levels of interest and foreign exchange rate volatility create an increasing demand for hedging instruments. The derivatives business is also a highly concentrated market. A Federal Reserve report, for example, showed that six US commercial banks accounted for 90% of the derivatives business in 1992 (Euromoney, 1993, p. 45).[7]

Although derivative instruments are often perceived and presented as exposing firms, and financial systems in general, to large new risks (Brown, 1996,

Table 2.6 Annual turnover in derivative financial instruments traded on organised exchanges (millions of contracts)

	1986	1987	1988	1989	1990	1991	1992	1993
Futures on short-term interest rate instruments	16.4	29.4	33.7	70.2	75.8	84.8	130.8	166.8
Futures on long-term interest rate instruments[a]	74.6	116.3	122.6	130.8	143.1	146.1	199.3	260.2
Interest rate options[a]	22.3	29.3	30.5	39.5	52.0	50.8	64.8	82.9
Currency futures	19.7	20.8	22.1	27.5	29.1	29.2	30.7	38.0
Currency options[a]	13.0	18.3	18.2	20.7	18.9	22.9	23.4	23.8
Stock market index futures	28.4	36.1	29.6	30.1	39.4	54.6	52.0	60.7
Options on stock market[a] indices	140.4	139.1	79.1	101.7	119.1	121.4	133.9	141.8
Total	314.8	389.2	335.8	420.4	447.7	509.8	634.9	774.2
of which								
in the United States	288.2	317.2	251.0	286.2	310.3	300.7	339.4	379.0
in Europe	10.3	35.9	40.7	64.4	83.9	110.5	185.0	255.9
in Japan	9.4	18.5	23.1	45.7	60.6	66.2	51.7	57.8

[a] Calls plus puts.
Source: IMF (1994, p. 120)

p. 297), the consensus view of the Basle Committee on Banking and Supervision in June 1994 does not support these perceptions: 'Derivatives tend to reduce volatility under normal circumstances, enhance market efficiency, facilitate better risk pricing, and provide low transaction costs. They also expand a range of hedging opportunities for market participants and thus lessen their

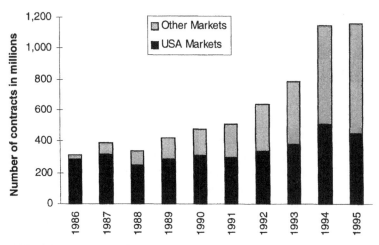

Source: IMF (1994, p. 120), BIS (1996, p. 54)

Figure 2.10 Number of exchange-traded derivative instruments contracts—1986–95

dependence on any one particular market. In these ways they dramatically improve the functioning of the financial system.' Nevertheless, it is still believed that current accounting rules and definitions on derivatives are inadequate and inconsistent, reducing rather than increasing the transparency of a firm's exposures and those of the derivative system as a whole. The need for a more reliable disclosure system becomes stronger the larger the contribution of derivatives to total trading income of major banks. In 1993, this totalled US\$2.251 bn for four US banks (Chase Manhattan, Chemical, Citicorp, and JP Morgan), up 34% on the respective figure in 1992. US banks are making more efforts to disclose notional and marked-to-market data on their derivative books, in varying degrees of detail. European banks have also started to disclose notional amounts (which they did not do in 1992), but they still lag behind the US banks, although disclosure is still greater than for Japanese banks (*Risk*, September, 1994, p. 91).[8] A study conducted by *Risk*, September 1994, reveals that, in terms of market value, five of the top 10 leading derivative players are European, including the big three Swiss banks. The top eight had portfolios with a market value of more than \$21.9bn with JP Morgan at the top with \$30.7 bn.[9]

The growth of OBSAs as briefly described in this chapter have been generally influenced by similar factors that caused the trend towards securitisation. Specifically, these are the desire of banks to earn fee income and to improve their capital ratios. Additionally, volatile exchange and interest rates helped to create demand for derivatives, the tools of financial engineering, as hedging instruments. Derivatives can also be used to exploit market imperfections and provide access to foreign markets. The ability to exploit differential rates between different national markets enhances integration of these markets.

2.4 FACTORS AFFECTING SUPPLY OF FINANCIAL INNOVATIONS: GLOBALISATION, TECHNOLOGY, AND COMPETITION

As discussed above, securitisation, which has materialised mainly through the growth of OBSAs, has been one of the dominant trends reshaping financial markets in recent years. Three other related factors have been influencing international financial markets during the 1980s. These are globalisation, increased competition, and advances in technology. These factors have, in particular, influenced the supply side of financial innovations. Sinkey (1992) proposes a model of financial innovation which captures the effect of these factors. Specifically, Sinkey formulates his model as follows:

TRICK + Rational Self-Interest = Financial Innovation.

The five components of TRICK are: technology, reregulation, interest-rate risk, customers, and capital adequacy.

The components of TRICK should not be examined in isolation as they interact with each other. Globalisation, for example, which refers to the internationalisation of financial institutions and markets is very much inter-related with the other trends. Specifically, the trend towards globalisation has a cause/effect relationship with securitisation, regulation, technology, and competition. Among these it seems that securitisation was the major driving force behind globalisation. Securitisation led to globalisation in two main ways. Firstly, banks involved in euro-markets had to broaden their geographical presence world-wide. Table 2.7 shows foreign banking presence in selected countries in terms of number of institutions (or number of banking offices) and

Table 2.7 Foreign banking presence in selected countries

Host Country	1960	1970	1980	1985 end-June
Number of institutions				
Belgium	14	26	51	57
Canada	0	0	0	57
Italy	1	4	26	36
Netherlands	n.a.	23	39	40
Switzerland	8	97	99	119
United Kingdom	51	95	214	293
Number of banking offices				
France	33	58	122	147
Germany	24	77	213	287
Japan	34	38	85	112
Luxembourg	3	23	96	106
United States	n.a.	n.a.	579	783
Foreign banks' operating in assets as a % selected of total assets countries of all banks				
Belgium	8.2	22.5	41.5	51.0
Canada	n.a.	n.a.	n.a.	6.3
Italy	n.a.	n.a.	0.9	2.4
Netherlands	n.a.	n.a.	17.4	23.6
Switzerland	n.a.	10.3	11.1	12.2
United Kingdom	6.7	37.5	55.6	62.6
France	7.2	12.3	15.0	18.2
Germany	0.5	1.4	1.9	2.4
Japan	n.a.	1.3	3.4	3.6
Luxembourg	8.0	57.8	85.4	85.4
United States	n.a.	5.8	8.7	12.0

Source: BIS, 1986, pp. 151–52.

their assets in a foreign country as a proportion of total assets of all banks operating in that country. It is clear from the table that the importance of foreign banking increased significantly between 1960 and 1985. Table 2.7 also reveals the large foreign banking presence in London as the financial centre of the euro-markets: 62.6% of all bank's assets operating in UK were held by foreign banks in 1985, compared to 12.0%, 3.6%, and 2.4% in the US, Japan, and Germany, respectively. London's place as the leading international financial centre in Europe is also confirmed by the results of a survey of foreign exchange markets carried out by the central banks in the main centres (The Banker, November, 1995). At $464 billion, the average daily turnover in London is more than the markets of New York and Tokyo put together.

Secondly, most OBSAs have also contributed directly or indirectly to the process of globalisation. Due to the increase in the volume of OBSAs, the resulting growth of securities markets during the 1980s has been accompanied by a growing integration between domestic and international markets. A key factor in this development was the increasing use of swaps to arbitrage away international rate differences (Gardener, 1991). NIFs also have contributed significantly to the global integration through the development of multiple-option funding facilities (MOF). Under these facilities, the issuer can raise funds in a variety of different currencies and variety of different instruments. This provides the issuer with the opportunity to take advantage of any discrepancy which arises between rates, and arbitrage them away. Also, NIFs are usually distributed via a tender panel consisting of a large number of banks from different countries, usually unrelated to the issuer's country. As potential issuers of NIFs were spread all over the world, banks competing to arrange a NIF facility had to increase their international presence. This is not confined to NIFs but is also true for most euro-type financial innovations including ECP, EMTNs, FRNs and syndicated euroloans. The Banker's (November, 1995) list of foreign banks in London, for example, includes more than 450 entries, almost 50% of which are branches as opposed to offices or subsidiaries.

Generally, the globalisation of financial markets is facilitated by the growth of OBSAs which are international in nature. New financial instruments adopted in international markets create a pressure on domestic authorities to allow their issuance in local currencies and by local institutions. Regulations with regard to capital inflow/outflow and market participants have been liberalised in a number of countries.[10] Technological advances, especially in telecommunications and information processing, enabled the connection of different domestic markets around the globe, and thus have created a global financial market. This encouraged investors, borrowers, and financial institutions to seek profitable opportunities world-wide. Moreover, technology has been a major factor in reducing the costs of entry for new competitors through cheap computer facilities, and allowing customer databases to be used for more effective selling of innovations to targeted customers (Pawley, 1991).

Globalisation and deregulation have increased competitive pressures. Financial institutions with international outlooks have had to face competition from institutions from different countries operating under different regulatory regimes. Given the view that certain regulations (e.g. capital adequacy regulation) impose a kind of 'profit tax' on banks (e.g. Baer and Pavel, 1988), then banks subject to one regulatory regime may be disadvantaged if other competing banks are subject to less strict rules. Against this background, the convergence of capital adequacy regulations has emerged as one of the big issues of the 1980s and 1990s (Gardener, 1991, p. 107).

Certain aspects of the process of globalisation are of special relevance to this book. Specifically, we are interested in the role of international capital markets in the diffusion process of financial innovations. Most financial innovations have tended to originate in dollar-denominated markets, and to be dominated by large US financial institutions. In 1986, a BIS report concluded that the long-run trend towards diversification out of a dollar base in the international financial markets had been limited. This is mainly due to national regulations controlling the variety of new instruments available for non-dollar borrowing, the lack of investor demand in some foreign currency sectors and the dominant role of US financial institutions in the international financial markets. Given, however, that there has been a wave of deregulation in the early 1980s, and judging by the example of the eurobond markets, one would expect that financial innovations have geographically spread more in the last few years in terms of issuers, arrangers, and investors.

2.5 WHY BANKS ISSUE OBS ASSETS

A number of recent studies in the academic finance literature have examined why banks engage in OBSAs.[11] These studies focus primarily on US banks' engagement in loan sales, commitments, and standby letters of credit (SLCs). Benveniste and Berger (1986, 1987) have argued that securitisation enables banks to optimise the allocation of risk sharing by shifting risk from risk-averse to risk-neutral investors (the *collateralisation hypothesis*). Banks can do so by securitising their safest assets off balance sheet and retaining their risky assets on balance sheet. This hypothesis predicts a positive relationship between securitisation and bank risk because the pooling problem (of mixing risky and safe assets on balance sheet) is more acute in risky banks. Moreover, Benveniste and Berger (1986) and Thomas and Woolridge (1991) suggest that securitisation motivated by fixed-rate deposit insurance encourages banks to become even riskier (the *moral hazard hypothesis*). The argument is that banks have a comparative advantage in originating loans, but a disadvantage in warehousing low-risk loans. Due to the moral hazard problem associated with fixed-rate deposit insurance, banks can increase their risk while retaining their comparative advantage in originating loans by selling relatively high-quality low-risk loans and issuing standby letters of credit. Pennacchi (1988) argued that loan sales may be motivated by differences in loan and liability opportunities among financial institutions (the *comparative advantage hypothesis*). While some institutions may enjoy comparative advantages in loan funding and warehousing (e.g. small and foreign banks), other institutions enjoy comparative advantages in loan originating. These advantages stem from differences in the regulatory taxes that banks must pay in the form of federal deposit insurance premiums, forgone interest rates from holding required reserves, and mandatory capital requirements that exceed those that would be maintained in the absence of regulation (the *regulatory tax hypothesis*, Pavel and Phillis, 1987). Carlston and Samolyk (1995) developed a market-based model of bank asset sales in which information asymmetries create the incentive for unregulated banks to originate and sell loans to other banks, rather than fund them with expensive deposit liabilities. A loan sales market in their model allows banks with private information (e.g. within their localities) to sell loans to banks with fewer capital constraints seeking profitable projects. Thus, securitisation provides a means by which relatively inexpensive funds raised by banks with good liability opportunities and poor loan opportunities can be used to fund relatively profitable loans at banks with good loan opportunities and poor liability opportunities.

In contrast to the above, Boot and Thakor (1991), Berger (1991) and Koppenhaver and Stover (1991) argued that off-balance-sheet securitisation may occur in larger quantities for safer banks or induce riskier banks to become safer. The argument here is that standbys and commitments are uninsured contingent claims whose values increase with the safety of the issuing bank. This provides an incentive for banks which issue these claims to increase their safety and it also offers relatively safer banks a comparative advantage in issuing these claims (the *market discipline hypothesis*). Berger and Udell (1993) argued that the growth in disintermediation-type securitisation (e.g. loan sales without recourse), due to changes in the technology of monitoring, is independent of bank risk and liquidity. They argued that this type of securitisation may change the size of the banking sector but not the economic role of banks as holding risky, illiquid, information-problematic loans (the *monitoring technology hypothesis*).

A number of studies have tested the empirical implications of the competing hypotheses outlined above. Pavel and Phillis (1987) attempted to explain why banks sell loans by estimating two logit models to determine the probability that a bank will sell loans and by estimating a tobit model to determine the dollar amount of loans that the bank will sell annually. They found that a bank's comparative advantage in originating and servicing loans had a larger impact on a bank's probability of selling loans than regulation did, and it had the largest impact in determining the amount of loans that a bank will sell. Other important factors included the need to diversify and the size of the bank.

Koppenhaver (1986) estimated models to determine the key factors that affects a bank's decision to engage in loan commitments, standby letters of credit, and commercial letters of credit. He found that the most important factors are bank quality, regulatory taxes, and customer demand. Benveniste and Berger (1987) used a reduced form logit regression to test the empirical predictions of their theoretical model; namely, that riskier banks are more likely to engage in standby letters of credit arrangements than safer banks and that securitised loans are generally safer than the loans in the same bank's asset portfolio. They found empirical support for both hypotheses. Baer and Pavel (1988) found empirical evidence that regulatory taxes and changes in bank risk had an impact on the growth of eurodollars and standbys. Their results are particularly interesting because, unlike earlier studies which were based on cross-sectional datasets for banks for a particular period, Baer and Pavel (1988) used a database of 33 banks for the years 1979–85, and thus their study was able to capture the effects of variations in regulatory taxes over time as well as across banks. Avery and Berger (1991b) examined the relationship between bank risk and standbys issuance. They found that standbys were positively related to risk for small banks, but negatively related to risk for large banks. Berger and Udell (1993) suggested that these results might indicate that the collateralisation hypothesis dominates for small banks and the market discipline hypothesis dominates for large banks. Koppenhaver and Stover (1994) and Hassan *et al.* (1994) have also found empirical support for the market discipline hypothesis in US commercial banks' issuance of OBS instruments.

The empirical evidence on the relationship between commitments and risk consistently (e.g. Berger and Udell, 1990 and Avery and Berger, 1988, 1991a, 1991b) reveals a negative relationship between bank risk and commitments for both used and unused commitments, consistent with the market discipline hypothesis (that is, the market valuation of these contingent claims encourages banks which issue them to increase their safety and/or offers relatively safer banks a comparative advantage in issuing these claims).

Perhaps the most comprehensive of these studies is the one by Berger and Udell (1993) in which they examined the relationship between several types of securitisation and numerous measures of risk and liquidity using over 400 000 quarterly observations on banks from 1983 to 1991. Their study has the advantage of including the three main types of securitisation—loan sales, standby letters of credit, and loan commitments—in the same regressions. Berger and Udell (1993) found empirical support for their 'monitoring technology hypothesis' which predicts that the growth in disintermediation-type securitisation (e.g. loan sales without recourse), due to changes in the technology of monitoring, is independent of bank risk and liquidity. The monitoring technology hypothesis argues that this type of securitisation may change the size of the banking sector but not the economic role of banks as holding risky, illiquid, information-problematic loans. This hypothesis, however, has no

empirical prediction about the relationship between off-balance-sheet securitisation (e.g. a loan sale with recourse, a standby letter of credit, or a loan
commitment) and risk.

In a more recent paper, Jagtiani *et al.* (1995) used the logistic model of
Mansfield (1961) to examine the diffusion of five off-balance-sheet financial
innovations (standby letters of credit, loan sales, swaps, options, and futures
and forwards) and assess the impact of regulatory changes on the growth of
these instruments. Their analysis was carried out at both the industry and
bank level and used aggregate dollar amounts as measures of diffusion. Their
results suggest that changes in capital regulation have had no consistent effect
on the adoption of these off-balance-sheet products. At the individual bank
level, they found that bank's size, capital ratios, and creditworthiness did not
explain the variation in adoption patterns across banks (except for standby
letters of credit). In the case of standby letters of credits (SLCs), they found that
creditworthiness factors had a positive impact on banks' decisions to issue these
claims, consistent with predictions of the market discipline hypothesis.

2.6 DEMAND FOR FINANCIAL INNOVATION

This part of the chapter focuses on the underlying factors that create demand
for new financial products. The BIS's (1986) *'Recent Innovations in International
Banking'* is the most influential study in this area. The framework analysed in
this study has been subsequently adopted in a number of studies of financial
innovation (e.g. Mayer and Kneeshaw, 1988; Llewellyn, 1992 and Kim, 1993).
The basic idea behind the demand-driven view of the financial innovation
process can be summarised as follows:

> Central to developing an economics of the innovation process is a taxonomy, or
> classification system, for financial innovations. A taxonomy establishes the important
> characteristics or functions of innovations. The demand for new instruments derives
> from the underlying demands for those characteristics or functions. The economics of
> the innovation process, then, can be expressed as propositions that relate the demand
> for those characteristics or functions to events of the global macro-economy. This is
> the essence of a demand-driven view of the innovation process.   BIS (1986, p. 172).

By specifying the general functions performed by a financial system, we can
classify innovations in relation to the specific function they enhance. The main
function of the financial system is to provide:

1. A mechanism for economic agents to transfer risk among themselves
2. Liquidity to the economy
3. Claims on the revenues of economic agents. These claims are either debt
   obligations or equity shares.

These functional distinctions lead to the following classification of financial innovations:

1. Risk-transferring innovations
2. Liquidity-enhancing innovations
3. Credit-generating (or debt-generating) innovations
4. Equity-generating innovations.

Table 2.8 classifies a list of selected major innovations according to the above functional distinction and distinguishes whether their use has direct balance-sheet implications or not. Certain innovations (e.g. swaps, NIFs, and securitised assets) serve more than one function.

From the 21 innovations appearing in Table 2.8, 8 are classified as price-risk transferring, 7 as credit-risk transferring, 7 as liquidity enhancing, 4 as credit generating, and only 1 as an equity generating innovation.

2.6.1 Demand-Driven Theory of Financial Innovation

The basic proposition of the demand-driven theory of financial innovation can be stated as follows:

- Price-risk transferring innovations are more likely to emerge the greater the perceptions of vulnerability of existing financial positions to the risk of asset price changes
- Credit-risk transferring innovations are more likely to emerge the greater the perception of vulnerability of existing financial positions to deterioration in creditworthiness
- Liquidity-enhancing innovations are more likely the greater the demand for liquidity in the economy
- Credit-generating innovations are more likely to emerge the greater the demand for credit generally or the stronger the demand for subclasses of credit, such as bond finance
- Equity-generating innovations are more likely the stronger the demand for equity finance.

2.6.2 Price-Risk Transferring Innovations

The demand for price-risk transferring instruments arose from the perceptions of the increased vulnerability of financial positions to asset price risk. Vulnerability in this context is the function of exposure and volatility of exchange rates and interest rates. Therefore, factors which induce more variability in these

Financial Innovation

Table 2.8   A classification of financial innovations by intermediation function

Innovations	Price-risk transferng.	Credit-risk transferng.	Liquidity-enhancing	Credit-generating	Equity-generating
A. On-balance-sheet					
Adjustable rate mortgages	✳				
Floating rate notes	✳				
Back-to-back loans	✳				
Asset sales without recourse		✳			
Loan swaps		✳			
Securitised assets		✳	✳		
Transferable loan con.cts.		✳	✳		
Sweep accounts and other cash management techn's.			✳		
Negotiable money-mkt instruments			✳		
Money-mkt Mutual Funds			✳		
Zero coupon bonds				✳	
'Junk' bonds				✳	
Equity participation financing				✳	
Mandatory convertible debentures					✳
B. Off-balance-sheet					
Futures	✳				
Options & loan caps	✳				
Swaps	✳			✳	
Forward rate agreements	✳				
Letters of credit		✳			
Note issuance facilities	✳	✳	✳		
Credit-enhancing gur. sec.		✳	✳		

Source: BIS (1986, p. 172).

rates cause increased demand for price-risk transferring instruments (mainly derivatives). In particular, the BIS (1986) report quotes the following underlying forces that create demand for price-risk transferring innovations:

- Higher variability in foreign exchange rates as a result of the adoption of floating exchange rates policies
- The removal of deposit rate controls meant that in periods of monetary stringency the effects have worked mostly through the price mechanism of

higher interest rates and less through the quantity mechanism of reduced credit availability

• The removal of deposit rate controls caused some financial institutions to face severe structural balance-sheet mismatches. This motivated them to innovate floating-rate instruments on their asset side and to utilise derivatives in hedging their price exposure (recall that price-transferring innovations consist of hedging and floating rate instruments).

2.6.3 Credit-Risk Transferring Innovations

Demand for credit-risk transferring innovations arise from the perceived vulnerability of existing financial positions to deteriorations in creditworthiness. The BIS (1986) cited two important factors; the collapse of the energy sector boom, and the LDC debt crisis. The creditworthiness of large international banks that were lenders to high risk customers was questioned, especially after the failure of Continental Illinois Bank in 1984. As a result, investors became less willing to deposit their money at banks, and a shift towards capital market instruments emerged. Banks themselves sought to benefit from this trend by pursuing asset securitisation and loan sales strategies, and by expanding their role as guarantors of capital market instruments.

2.6.4 Liquidity-Enhancing Innovations

Liquidity-enhancing innovations arise from increased demand for liquidity. Higher interest rates in the 1970s increased the opportunity cost of holding transactions liquidity in traditional forms. The increase in the demand for interest-yielding liquidity transactions explained the emergence of cash management accounts, money-market mutual funds, and new types of negotiable deposit accounts. More recent innovations are more geared to improving the liquidity of capital-market-type instruments. Specifically, the BIS (1986) report quotes two factors to justify increased demand for liquidity. First, there has been a loss of liquidity for investors as a consequence of the shift from bank deposits to capital-market instruments. The second factor is the increased leveraging in the United States as reflected by higher debt/income and debt/equity ratios for household and corporations, respectively.

2.6.5 Credit-Generating Innovations

Credit-generating innovations are designed to mobilise dormant assets to support new borrowings (e.g. leveraged buy-out financings and equity access accounts) or to tap new sources of credit either directly (e.g. junk bonds) or indirectly (e.g. liability-based interest rate swaps). The demand for credit-generating innovations increases as the overall demand for credit increases (e.g. due to demographic factors) or when there are broad shifts in the pattern of credit demand (e.g. shifts to capital market instruments or international financial markets). The BIS (1986) report shows that during the early 1980s

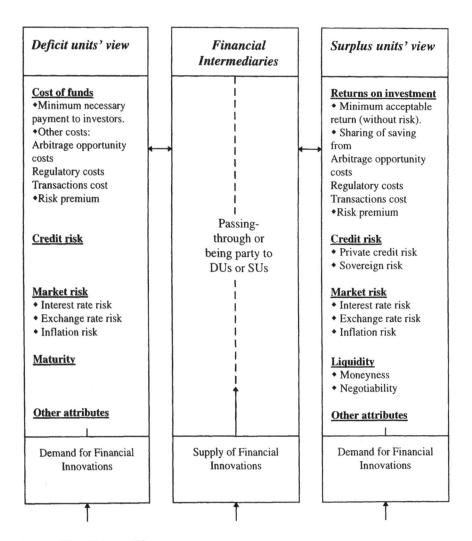

Source: Kim, 1993, p. 202.

Figure 2.11 Attributes of financial instruments and supply-demand for financial innovations

both trends were observable in the Unites States where financial innovation was most advanced.

2.6.6 Equity-Generating Innovations

The number of innovations that fall in this category is relatively small in comparison to other types of innovations. Examples of equity-generating innovations include variable rate preferred stock in the United States and perpetual floating rate notes in the United Kingdom. Commercial banks have made extensive use of both of these types of instruments. This can be attributed to regulators' demands for increased capitalisation in banking.

2.6.7 Demand and Supply of Financial Innovations: Deficit versus Surplus Units

An alternative approach to analyse the demand and supply of financial innovations is suggested by Kim (1993). Kim stresses that financial instruments may be characterised by a number of their attributes from the point of view of the economic deficit units (DUs) as well as that of the surplus units (SUs). Although there is a common set of major attributes regarded by both sides, there are some differences in emphasis by each side. Each side's demand for new instruments may imply the combination of different attributes or the same attributes but in different ways. Figure 2.11 summarises the main attributes that are generally considered by DUs and SUs.

2.7 CONCLUSION

This chapter examined the emergence of a number of financial innovations in international financial markets and reviewed the main structural trends prevailing in the financial services industry. The growth of financial innovation, reflected in the securitisation trend, is considered one of the most significant features over the last decade. Through the increased use of OBSAs, there has been a notable shift towards capital market instruments and away from bank loans. These instruments can be broadly divided into three groups, euromarkets (eurodollars, eurobonds, FRNs, NIFs, ECP, and EMTNs), contingent banking instruments (standby letters of credit, commitments, and backup facilities), and derivatives (swaps, forwards, futures, and options). In addition to these, securitisation has also been reflected in the increased marketability of banks' traditional assets, mainly loans through loan sales and loan sales without recourse (i.e. *bank asset securitisation*).

An important feature which emerges from our discussion of various financial innovations is that in many cases the *emergence* of some of these new financial instruments was due to certain changes in the regulatory environment. However, these instruments (e.g. eurobonds, ECP, zero-coupon bonds) continued to grow even after the crucial regulations had been removed or even reversed. That is, factors governing the growth of financial instruments are not necessarily the same as those which create opportunities for their introduction. This turns out to be an important observation as will be seen in Chapters 6, 7 and 8.

The chapter discussed a demand-driven theory of financial innovation related to the functions these innovations perform in the financial system. On the supply side, we examined the effects of technology, regulation, competition and globalisation. A clear understanding of the demand–supply factors associated with the wave of financial innovations that has appeared over the last twenty years is essential before any attempt is made to derive a theory of financial innovation.

There is no generally accepted theory of financial innovation. The analysis of this process is not as well developed as its counterpart in the real sector. This perhaps is due to the complexity and the large number of factors that should be incorporated into any model of financial innovation. Nevertheless, a number of theoretical approaches have been developed to explain financial innovation and these are reviewed in the next chapter.

ENDNOTES

1. The borrower will usually arrange for a back-up lines of credit but they will be separate arrangements from the ECP programme.
2. In December 1989, Merrill Lynch, a pioneer of the ECP market and one of its leading participants, withdrew from the market. In December 1990, CSFB, the fourth ranked dealer at the time, and SG Warburg pulled out (Euromoney, 1991a).
3. As an example, Citicorp and Ford have been issuing yen-denominated EMTNs and swapping back into US dollars; French banks have been issuing in Ecu and swapping Canadian dollars, and swapping into sterling to fund their UK branch assets (Euromoney, 1991b, pp. 62–3).
4. Sovereign lending, which dominated syndicated bank loans in the 1970s (as opposed to corporate lending which dominated in the 1980s), declined sharply in the early 1980s as a consequence of the LDC debt crisis (e.g. Mexican default in 1982).
5. Loan sales are a form of OBSA only if it is 'without recourse'. Loan sales with recourse, whereby the bank retains an obligation to assume the credit risk if the securitised asset (e.g. loan) defaults, cannot be taken off the balance sheet.
6. The nine money-center banks are Citibank, Chase Manhattan, Manufacturers Hanover, Morgan Guaranty, Bank of America, Chemical Bank, Bankers Trust, Security Pacific, and First Chicago.
7. The study used notional values as indicator of business size.
8. In November 1995 the Basle Committee on Banking Supervision (Basle Committee) and the Technical Committee of the International Organisation of Securities

Commissions (IOSCO) issued a joint report on the public disclosure of trading and derivatives activities of international banks and securities firms. The report noted improvements made by participants in 1994 by providing new information, particularly with respect to market and credit exposures and risk management practices. The report stressed, however, that some firms continued to disclose very little information. Consequently, the governors of the G-10 central banks endorsed a proposal to amend the 1988 Basle capital accord to include market risks in order to ensure an adequate degree of transparency and consistency of capital requirements across banks.

9. Rankings were based on GRV figures (Gross Replacement Value—the sum of positive replacement values) as a measure of market values. Notional amounts outstanding figures were also provided.

10. See the BIS (1986) report, pp. 149–53, for a discussion of relevant regulations in UK, France, Germany, Japan, and the US.

11. See Berger and Udell (1993) for a comprehensive review of these studies.

3

Theoretical Approaches Towards Financial Innovation

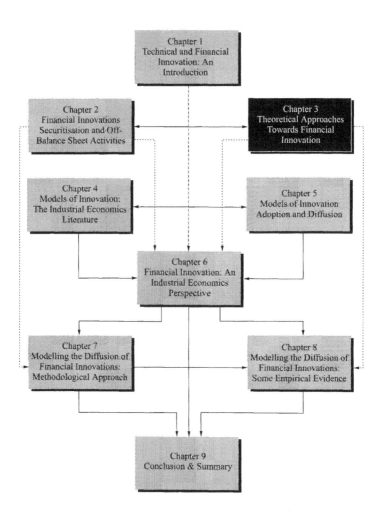

3
Theoretical Approaches Towards Financial Innovation

3.1 INTRODUCTION

The analysis of the process of financial innovation is not as well-developed as its counterpart in the real sector. There is no generally acceptable framework to employ in analysing the process of financial innovation. One reason might be that developments in the financial sector are not independent from the real sector. Schumpeter (1939), although not dealing explicitly with financial innovation, links financial change with technological and institutional development in the real sector. The development of the Eurodollar market in the 1960s, for example, was mainly due to political and international economic factors that influenced capital flows between nations (e.g. petrodollars, US balance of payment deficit, and former communist nations' desire to hold dollar-denominated deposits outside the US). As can be seen from the discussion in the previous chapter, the development of the Eurodollar market was instrumental in the subsequent development of a number of new financial products. On the other hand, developments in the real sector do not necessarily explain all changes in the financial sector. The UK, for example, experienced more innovations in finance but less economic growth than either Germany or Switzerland (Johnson, 1987, p. 7). Although there must be some connection between economic growth and financial innovation, it is difficult to capture the long-term relationship between the two. The link between financial innovation and economic growth is not straightforward. Podolski (1986) points out the difficulty of observing this relationship by stating that 'an intriguing aspect of financial innovations since the 1970s is that they have occurred in generally depressed economic conditions, but in the environment of structural and technological change, inflation and deregulation', Podolski (1986, p. 185).

Also the interaction of a large number of factors such as regulation, technology, globalisation, and volatility of interest and exchange rates, and a number of participants (issuers, investors, and intermediaries) makes it difficult to create a general framework which can explain financial innovation. According to the BIS (1986), an ideal theory of financial innovation should explain how changes in general economic conditions create specific profit opportunities for new instruments to emerge. It should explain all innovations and the order in which they arise. None of the theoretical approaches discussed in this chapter meet all these criteria. The BIS (1986) report's demand–supply view of financial innovation is probably the most comprehensive study of most factors causing financial innovation during the 1980s. There is also a number of studies which have made significant contributions in this regard, most notably those by Silber (1975, 1983) and Kane (1977, 1978, 1980, 1981, 1983, 1984a, 1984b). Recently, various studies model financial innovation within the context of the literature on security design and general equilibrium models in incomplete markets (e.g. Allen and Gale, 1988, 1991, 1994, Demange and Laroque, 1995a, Chen, 1995, and Rahi, 1995). Below we examine the various approaches that have been advanced to model the process of financial innovation.

3.2 THE CONSTRAINT-INDUCED HYPOTHESIS

One of the earliest contributions in this area is that of Silber (1975). Silber approaches the subject from the microeconomic point of view of a financial firm. The main hypothesis is that new financial instruments or practices are innovated to lessen the financial constraints imposed on firms. Firms maximise utility subject to a number of balance sheet constraints. These constraints are imposed both externally and internally. Government regulations are among the most prominent external constraints. The market places constraints on the firm's optimisation problem by defining the parameters of demand and supply for different financial instruments and simultaneously identifies the policy tools available to the firm. If market power exists, for example, then the firm sets prices or yields and accepts whatever volume of funds is offered. Alternatively, if the firm is a price taker, it can buy precisely the quantity of funds that maximises utility.

Silber (1975) also considers internally imposed constraints. Firms may impose constraints on their balance sheets such as target growth rates and liquidity constraints, and these would influence the optimisation problem. In the normal course of events, a firm maximises its objective function subject to existing constraints. That is, it will sell securities or accept deposits and invest the proceeds, all within the framework of existing parameters and constraints. Given this general framework, Silber (1975) explains the process of financial innovation as follows:

> New financial instruments or practices will be innovated when there is an exogenous change in the constrained optimisation of the firm that stimulates a search for new

policy tools. There are two types of changes that induce firms to undertake the search costs required to modify its traditional policy tools. In one case, exogenous changes in constraints force a reduction in the utility of the firm and the firm innovates in an effort to return to its previous levels of utility [...]. In the second case, innovation responds to an increase in the cost of adhering to a constraint.   Silber, 1975, pp. 65–6.

In a linear programming context, the 'shadow price' of a constraint represents the cost of adhering to that constraint (in terms of the potential increase in the objective function that would be gained if that constraint is removed). Silber (1975) gives the constraint-induced innovation hypothesis a time dimension by assuming that as the cost of adhering to a constraint rises over time (or the firm experiences continued decreases in utility over time) the firm will undertake or intensify the search for new financial instruments and/or practices. The sharper the rise in shadow price (or the reduction in utility) the greater will be the innovative effort. Silber (1983) defines the time-dimension of the constraint-induced innovation hypothesis by postulating that only a sustained increase in shadow prices over time will stimulate new product innovation. Given the constrained-induced hypothesis, one would expect that the time-series of shadow prices should rise prior to the introduction of a new financial instrument and drop immediately thereafter.

In a subsequent paper, Silber (1983) takes a less formal approach to evaluating the constraint-induced explanation of the emergence of 38 new financial products or practices during the 1970–82 period. In particular, he proposes five exogenous forces that influenced financial constraints during the 1970–82 period, and examines how many new financial products were stimulated by these forces. The study suggests that 19 of the innovations were due to inflation related factors, 13 of which were due to inflationary high levels of interest rates (other inflation related categories are general price level and tax effects); 15 to volatility of interest rates; 10 to technology, 11 to legislation, and two to internationalisation.[1] Silber's (1983) main conclusion is that the constraint-induced innovation hypothesis explains at least half of the new products and practices during the 1970–82 period. Silber (1983) also argues that, similar to technological innovations in the real sector which improve economic welfare through expanding physical output, financial innovations improve the financial system by:

1. Improving the ability to bear risk (e.g. futures markets)
2. Lowering transaction costs (e.g. ATMs), and
3. Circumventing outmoded regulations (e.g. money-market mutual funds and regulation Q).

An interesting aspect of the constraint-induced innovation hypothesis is that it can be tested empirically. This, however, requires a detailed dataset for long periods of time which may not be readily available. A formal test of this hypothesis is provided by Ben-Horim and Silber (1977). The model was simulated for the period 1952–72 using data from the First National City Bank and an aggregate of four large New York banks. The model should be able to show costs rising over time and then dropping after an innovation is introduced. They report that the results indicate that the model can explain the innovations of the 1960s and therefore support the constraint hypothesis. There is, however, a suspicion that with the benefit of hindsight, they found what they were looking for (Johnson, 1987, p. 15). Although Silber's theory of financial innovation represents a major contribution in what was a neglected area, the approach has its limitations. These are neatly summarised by Podolski (1986, p. 186):

> . . . Silber's 'general theory' of financial innovation is both too general and too specific. It is too general in the sense that it suggests, essentially, that financial firms innovate in order to maximise profits; the stress is mainly on 'adversity innovations', that is, on innovations when an externally imposed constraint, such as a state regulation, needs to be circumvented in pursuit of the highest attainable profit. It is too specific in the sense that it applies to firms and may not be suited to the study of innovation in the macroeconomic context dealing with the emergence of new markets, new firms or new monetary standards.

3.3 THE REGULATORY DIALECTIC

Regulation is perhaps the most often quoted force behind financial innovations. The relationship between regulation and financial innovation has been extensively studied by a number of researchers, most notably Kane (1977, 1978, 1980, 1981, 1984a and 1984b) for the US banking markets, and the Bank of England for the UK market (e.g. Bank of England, 1983a and 1983b). The regulatory dialectic view of financial innovation (Kane, 1978, 1981) uses a 'struggle model' to depict the ongoing battle between regulators and regulatees. This model portrays financial change as the outcome of continuing struggle between opposing economic (regulatees) and political (regulators) forces. Kane (1981, p. 357) makes the distinction between invention and innovation.[2] Invention is the act of finding new ways to do useful or profitable things—usually cheaper and more efficient ways of doing them. Innovation is the act of putting an invention into practice—that is the commercial application of an invention. Every invention makes one or more innovations feasible, but we can always identify an *innovation lag*. Kane's main argument is that the burden of bank regulation increases the rewards for doing things differently *per se*. This is because that, unlike an unregulated firm, banks may adopt innovations which are not necessarily technically advantageous, but which tend to render obsolete particular elements and concepts of pre-existing regulation. For this reason, regulating an industry tends to reduce its innovation lags, while ongoing acts of innovation tend to lengthen and exploit parallel *regulatory lags* that develop as regulators contemplate the unexpected problems created by specific innovations and decide what (if anything) to do about the situation. Innovation lags exist because before an innovation can be adopted commercially, the opportunities it opens up must promise enough after-tax profits to counterbalance the costs of overcoming institutional inertia and the management and the employee resistance associated with changing established ways of doing things. It is assumed however that innovation lags are shorter than *re-regulation lags* because there are no profit incentives associated with the latter.

Regulation circumvention typically occurs by acts of product *substitution* no more imaginative than installing parallel but formally different production processes and relabelling regulated products (Kane, 1981, p. 359). Because legal obligations can be defeated by relying on implicit distinctions, regulatees can substitute unregulated or (less regulated) products or practices for ones which are extensively regulated. Regulatees benefit from innovation as reregulation does not occur immediately and usually takes long periods of time. A political system is far more forgiving of excessive delay than it is of hasty and ill-considered action. Unless a regulatory crisis threatens, officials prefer to postpone a definitive regulatory response until a large body of information accumulates. The adoption of an innovation by a heavily regulated firm as a means to circumvent regulations would also attract the attention of less regulated firms to any profitable opportunities arising from the adoption of the innovation, thus facilitating the diffusion of that innovation. The participation of a large number of banks and their competitors in the new markets (or practices) is likely to shorten the reregulation lag. When reregulation finally takes place, it is likely that it would be introduced gradually and that it would impose less burdens on regulatees than the regulations that had applied to pre-innovation arrangements. Reregulation would then foster a new wave of innovations and so on.

The regulatory dialectic model envisions repetitive stages of regulatory avoidance and reregulation with stationary equilibrium virtually impossible. The adjustment process by each party can be disturbed by exogenous forces. In particular, two forces are stressed; accelerating inflation and technological advances. Accelerating inflation is important because by raising nominal rates of interest, it tends to increase the earning opportunities for banks and the opportunity losses associated with the government restrictions on banking (Kane, 1980, p. 9). These effects are particularly obvious for three major types of banking regulation: (i) reserve requirements, (ii) deposit rate ceilings, and (iii) branching and investment limitations. Exogenous technological change is important because it lowers the marginal costs of avoiding regulatory burdens. Diffusion of financial innovations is facilitated by the rising marginal benefits of avoidance activity (i.e. accelerated inflation) and decreasing marginal costs (i.e. technological advances). Accelerating inflation and exogenous technological change open up arbitrage opportunities for regulated institutions by enabling them to substitute innovative techniques, products, and organisational forms for more traditional counterparts. This tends to increase regulatees' after-tax income as they can earn much the same revenues while lightening their implicit tax burdens (Kane, 1981, p. 361).

Miller (1986) shares this view. In a discussion of the main financial innovations over the last twenty years, Miller finds that regulatory and tax factors have provided the major impetus for financial innovation. He describes *significant successful* financial innovations as 'seeds beneath the snow, waiting for some change in the environment to bring them about' (Miller, 1986, p. 38). Interestingly, this view of financial innovations, before their introduction, as *existing financial contracts but in zero-supply* seems to be influential in the current literature on financial innovation. Miller (1986) defines significant successful innovations as those which not only manage to survive but continue to grow even after the initiating forces have been removed. An example of this can be observed in the case of zero-coupon bonds. Zero-coupon bonds came to be widely used in the US in the early 1980s because of a tax loophole. Although the loophole was quickly closed when firms started to take advantage of it on a large scale, the market for zero coupons nevertheless continued as their payment characteristics were found to be desirable to investors because of the lack of reinvestment risk, and some tax advantages remained for Japanese investors (Allen and Gale, 1994, p. 20). Similar arguments can be made about the growth of the eurobond market and the re-emergence of the ECP market in the eighties, both of which seem to have been independent of the initial changes in the regulatory environment that led to their introduction (see Chapter 2). According to Miller (1986), the major impulses to successful financial innovation, financial futures in particular, come from regulations and taxes. While stressing that most of the critical tax and regulatory frameworks that supplied the motives for the financial innovations were put in place in the 1930s, Miller (1986) explains this delayed effect by general economic conditions. In Silber's terminology, it was not the imposition of these constraints but the cost (shadow price) of adhering to them that increased (abnormally) in the last twenty years or so, thus prompting circumventive innovations. This same phenomenon of delayed effects seems to have prompted some researchers to distinguish between two types of innovations.

Holland (1975) defines two types of innovations—circumventive and transcendental.[3] Circumventive innovations are a free market reaction by those who seek to avoid or circumvent the consequences of regulatory and monetary control. Transcendental innovation refers to all types of innovations unrelated to regulatory control. Holland cites the emergence of CDs and other money market instruments as examples of transcendental innovation. Goldfeld (1975), however, argues that these innovations and others provided by Holland (1975) hardly seem unrelated to regulatory control. According to Goldfeld (1975), it appears that an innovation is considered as circumventive if the banks try to get around it *quickly* but transcendental if they *meditate* about it for a while before doing something about it. This suggests that the distinction between the two types of innovation may not be that clear cut. Goldfeld takes a critical view on regulations which invite *and* permit substantial circumventive innovation. 'The appearance of substantial innovations of this sort indicates that either the regulators missed some fundamental truism about the way financial markets work or, that they knew what they were doing, but simply were not clever enough to close all the loopholes in the first place. Neither state of affairs seems to be particularly commendable' (Goldfeld, 1975, pp. 173–4).

Kane (1978, 1980, 1981) shows that the emergence of a large number of financial innovations can be traced to some regulatory restrictions in certain form on existing products or practices. In other words, Kane assumes that financial innovations are merely bank (or bank's competitors) substitutes for existing regulated items. Although this can be a fair description of a number of financial innovations (e.g. CDs as a substitute for demand-deposit accounts) it may not be sufficient to explain the emergence of other financial instruments (e.g. NIFs). In particular, financial innovations introduced in international capital markets are subject to a large number of forces which influence both the demand and supply of financial innovations. Moreover the regulatory dialectic model ignores demand-pull innovations.

The relationship between regulation and financial innovation seems to have been particularly important in the United States but this pattern is not necessarily representative of other countries' experiences. In Italy, for example, regulation seems to have had little impact on financial innovations. In a study of financial innovation in Italy, Caranza and Cottarelli (1987) examine the main causes of 20 innovations introduced between 1975 and 1984. They (subjectively) conclude that 'more binding regulation', 'lifting of regulation' and 'policy action', together with some other causes can explain the emergence of only six innovations. The emergence of 12 innovations is attributed to inflation and volatility of interest rates. In Japan, large-scale issues of government bonds, the development of open financial markets, inflation and interest rate volatility, increasingly active international capital flows under the floating exchange rate system, and technological innovations in electronic and telecommunications are seen as the major influences of financial innovation (Suzuki, 1987, p. 230). Even in the US, Van Horne (1985) lists 23 product and process innovations, only nine of which he attributes to regulatory effects, compared to 15 innovations attributed to volatile inflation and interest rates. For process innovations, the major cause seems to be technological advances. In fact, Van Horne emphasises that regulatory change prompted many a financial innovation in the early 1970s while deregulation was more influential in the late 1970s and 1980s. As a result of deregulation, boundaries that functionally separated financial institutions were lowered and, in some cases, removed altogether. When constraints are reduced, market participants enter new lines of business possessing previously unattainable profit and/or risk reduction possibilities (Van Horne, 1985, p. 623).

Dufey and Giddy (1981) list 22 international financial innovations, only four of which they consider due to existing regulations. It should be stressed here that these taxonomies are developed using subjective approaches. In some cases a certain financial innovation is attributed to different factors by different researchers. As Johnson (1987) points out, currency futures are allocated to internationalisation by Silber (1983); but to transfer of default risk by Dufey and Giddy (1981): 'they are probably both right, which demonstrates the difficulty of using taxonomies in this area of economics' (Johnson, 1987, p. 18). In general, we would expect the process of financial innovation to be a result of the interaction of many driving forces. Therefore, to explain the process of financial innovation using only one factor is to oversimplify the issue (Boreham, 1984). Nevertheless, regulatory taxes are frequently cited as the major factor in understanding a number of financial innovations. The literature in this area, however, concentrates on the US market. Examples include Judd (1979) for commercial paper, Koppenhaver (1986) for loan commitments, Benveniste and Berger (1986) for standby letters of credit, and Baer and Pavel (1988) for eurodollar and standby letters of credit. Most of these studies test the empirical relationship between the level of regulatory taxes and banks' participation in the new markets, with mixed results.

3.4 FINANCIAL INNOVATION AS A BUNDLING AND UNBUNDLING PROCESS IN INCOMPLETE MARKETS

An interesting aspect of financial innovations which distinguish them from innovations in the real sector is that in most cases financial innovations do not offer a *completely* new product but rather change, add, or eliminate a characteristic of an existing financial product. At its basic level, the financial instrument is a contract written on paper and potentially all possible financial contracts can be written without any technological barrier (Desai and Low, 1987, p. 115). In this sense, financial innovations are not new goods. They are implicitly always there, but in zero supply (Greenbaum and Heywood, 1973). Most financial products can be described by a number of specific characteristics such as yield, maturity, liquidity, exposure to price and credit risk, etc. Financial innovation can be viewed as the 'unbundling' of the separate characteristics and risks of individual instruments and their reassembly in different new combinations. Niehans (1983) argues that even the most complex financial arrangements can usually be described as 'bundles' of the three standard products or services offered by the financial system. One service consists in the exchange of present money against future money. Another is the bringing together of borrowers and lenders. The third is the execution (or facilitating) of payments on the behalf of customers. Dufey and Giddy (1981) argue that financial innovation largely consists in the development of new ways of bundling the basic services. While the bundling and unbundling exhibits an infinite variety, the basic products themselves have remained largely unchanged. As Niehans (1983, p. 538) puts it, 'Except for electronic technology, if an experienced banker from medieval Venice or Geneva came to life again, he could understand the operations of a modern bank in a matter of days'.

In addition to pricing, maturity and liquidity, other important characteristics of a financial product are (Llewellyn, 1992, p. 21):

- Price risk, i.e. the extent to which the price of an asset or liability may change
- Earning risk, e.g. the difference between equities and loan contracts
- Credit risk, i.e. the possibility of a default
- Country risk, i.e. the risk that a shortage of foreign currency in a country may inhibit debt-serving
- Pricing formula including, in the case of a floating rate facilities, differences in the base rate used, the frequency of changes and whether any upper or lower limits are imposed
- Conversion characteristics, i.e. the extent and circumstances in which the instrument can be converted into something else, e.g. convertible debentures
- Size of the facility
- Exchange rate risk
- Discretion, i.e. the extent to which the instrument allows either the issuer or holder to exercise discretion, e.g. an option contract
- Hedging facility, i.e. the extent to which an instrument enables risks to be avoided, e.g. forward contracts.

Llewellyn (1992) argues that the functions of a financial system must be the focus because the ultimate criterion when judging financial innovation is the extent to which it increases the efficiency of financial intermediation in particular and the functions of the financial system in general. The process of financial innovation enables the unbundling of risks so that each can be priced separately and redistributed to those who are more able and willing to absorb them. Van Horne (1985) takes a critical view of the process of financial innovation. He argues that for an idea to be viable as a financial innovation, it must make the market more efficient in an operational sense and/or more complete. A financial innovation may make the market more efficient by reducing the cost of financial intermediation to consumers of financial services. Financial innovation may as well fill gaps between the existing products or services and thus initiate movement towards market completeness. According to Van Horne, incomplete markets exist when the number and types of securities available do not span all contingencies in the world. In other words, there is an unfilled desire for a particular type of security on the part of an investor clientele (Van Horne, 1985, p. 622).

Desai and Low (1987) adopt the view of financial innovation as a means towards market completeness and express this view in a more formal setting. They propose a microeconomic model of financial innovation based on *location theory*. Location theory views goods as being a combination of various characteristics. Existing products (or firms) can be plotted on a characteristics space according to how they score on each of the characteristics. For simplicity, Desai and Low (1987) consider only two characteristics; return (yield) and access (liquidity). Figure 3.1 below is an example of such a characteristics space. Yield R is measured along the vertical axis and liquidity A is measured along the horizontal axis with assets being most liquid at zero and becoming more illiquid the farther away one goes from this point. If there were no other constraints, one should observe a continuous spectrum of assets from zero yield, zero illiquidity (ready cash) to the highest yield on the most illiquid instrument. Consumers with diverse tastes could choose their most preferred instrument along such a frontier depending on their marginal rate of substitution between the two characteristics.

Desai and Low (1987) use this theoretical framework to identify and measure gaps in the range of available products in the financial market which will indicate the potential opportunity for creating and launching new products. In Figure 3.1, x_1 and x_2 represent two existing financial products each with a

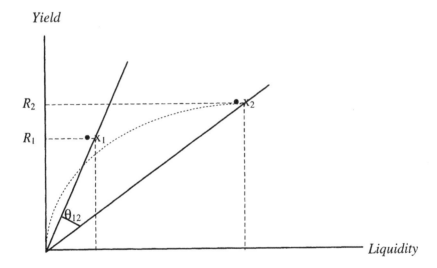

Source: Desai and Low (1987, p. 116)

Figure 3.1   A two-dimensional characteristic space of financial products x_1, x_2

specific combination of yield and liquidity. The opportunity for launching a new product is a function of the gap between existing products and can be measured by the angle θ_{12} between x_1 and x_2. Over time, new financial products with different combinations of yield and liquidity are introduced which will fill in the gaps between existing products. The change in θ_{12} over time can then be used as a measure of the innovativeness of the market. The more innovative a market is, the closer θ_{12} is to zero and the higher the rate at which it declines. When there are more than two products, the maximum θ between any two products can be used to measure the opportunity for innovation. When assets are crowded out in the two characteristic space, innovation can take place through opening up a new characteristic.

As indicated by Desai and Low (1987), the characteristic space model measures the opportunity for innovation rather than explaining why innovations occur. The model does not incorporate demand factors. Whether or not a certain gap will be filled by introducing a new product would depend on the demand for the individual characteristics and on the marginal rate of substitution between the two characteristics. To explain why financial innovation occurs we need to understand why an innovation has been introduced at a certain time (although the gap which that innovation fills existed before). In steady-state market equilibrium, it would not be possible to make the market more complete and/or efficient because all profitable exploitation through financial innovation would be exhausted. The environment must change for there to be exploitable opportunities and for financial innovation to occur (Van Horne, 1985). Changes in regulation, inflation, volatility of interest rates, technological advances, levels of economic activity, or advances in the academic finance literature alter marginal rates of substitution between existing characteristics, or open up new characteristics, and thus create demand for new combinations, which prompt financial innovation. An increase in the volatility of interest rates, for example, would cause a change in the marginal rate of substitution between yield and immunity to interest rate risk. Monetary policy and the level of interest rates can cause a change in the marginal rate of substitution between yield and liquidity.

Ross (1989) develops an agency-theoretic model in which financial innovations are viewed as means available for *institutions* to move back into their sets of acceptable portfolios. Institutions can be moved out of their acceptable sets by an unanticipated event that was not incorporated in the original acceptable set. His model is particularly interesting because it focuses on the role of institutions in financial markets and it also models the marketing cost structure for a financial innovation. This illustrates that there may be much to gain from an integration of marketing analysis and finance. Unlike innovations in the real sector, we know little about the cost structure associated with developing and introducing financial innovations. Understanding the relationships between cost structures and amounts sold (or bought) and/or the number of suppliers of a financial innovation can be vital if models from the industrial economic literature are to enhance our understanding of the process of financial innovation. We discuss this area in more detail in Chapter 6.

3.5 SECURITY DESIGN AND INCOMPLETE MARKET MODELS OF FINANCIAL INNOVATION

A recent trend in the literature has been to explain financial innovation using security design and general equilibrium models. Although the literature on security design and general equilibrium theory is not new (see for example, Walras, 1874, Arrow and Debreu, 1954 and Arrow, 1964), it is only recently that this framework has been used to explain the introduction of new securities and their optimal design.[4] One may view these models as formal presentations of the ideas discussed earlier in the chapter; specifically, that financial innovation is a bundling and unbundling process and a means by which gaps in the product space are filled and markets become more complete (i.e. the *spanning* role of financial innovation). In a series of articles on financial innovation and security design, Allen and Gale have examined the part of theory which deals with risk sharing and optimal security design (e.g. Allen and Gale (1989, 1990, 1991)). Recently, Allen and Gale (1994) collected their research on financial innovation and risk sharing in a text which includes an extensive survey of the topic. We review their theory below.

3.5.1 Risk Sharing

Allen and Gale (1994) propose an outline of a theory of financial innovation which concentrates on the risk-sharing aspects of this process. The following assumptions characterise the general setting of their model:

A.1. There are two dates $t = 1, 2$ with a single consumption good at each date. The consumption good serves as numeraire.
A.2. There is a finite set of states of nature $\Omega = (\omega_0, \omega_1, \ldots, \omega_w)$ which occur with probabilities $\mu_0, \mu_1, \ldots, \mu_w$.
A.3. There is a countable set of investors. There is a finite set of K types of investors. The difference between the types of investors arises from their random future incomes. The cross-sectional distribution of investor types is denoted by $\nu = (\nu_1, \ldots, \nu_K)$ with ν_1 denoting the proportion of investors who are of type 1. Investors are assumed to be risk averse and interested in consumption at both dates.
A.4. Investors have Von Neumann–Morgenstern utility functions $U(c_1, c_2) =$

$c_1 + V_k(c_2)$ where c_t is consumption at date t and U_k: $\Re^2 \to \Re$, so consumption can be negative. U_k is continuous, differentiable once, strictly increasing and strictly concave.[5]

A.5. Investors' income at date 1 are normalised to zero. Each investor has a random income $Y_k(\omega)$ in state ω at date 2.

A.6. There is no storage or investment technology for transforming consumption at date 1 into consumption at date 2.

A.7. A central planner (or government) can transfer resources directly between people at each date (through subsidies and taxes). At date 1 the transfer for group k is τ_k. At date 2 the transfer for group k is $\tau_k(\omega)$ in state ω. Transfers balance at every date and in every state so:

$$\sum_{k \in K} \tau_k = 0; \qquad (3.1)$$

$$\sum_{k \in K} \tau_k(\omega) = 0 \ \forall \omega \in \Omega. \qquad (3.2)$$

A Pareto optimal allocation of resources can be achieved by maximising the expected utility of one type, $k = k_0$, and holding the expected utilities of the other groups, all $k \neq k_0$, constant:

$$\underset{\tau_k, \tau_k(\omega)}{\text{Max }} EU_{k_0}(\tau_{k_0}, Y_{k_0}(\omega) + \tau_{k_0}(\omega)), \qquad (3.3)$$

subject to:

$$EU_{k_0}(\tau_{k_0}, Y_{k_0}(\omega) + \tau_{k_0}(\omega)) \geq \bar{U}_k, \quad \forall k \neq k_0, \qquad (3.4)$$

and the constraints in equations 3.1 and 3.2 (where $\bar{U}_k$ is the level of utility type k's attain in the allocation). At a Pareto optimum, the first-order conditions imply that marginal rates of substitution are equated:

$$\frac{\partial U_{k_0}/\partial c_2(\omega)}{\partial U_{k_0}/\partial c_1} = \frac{\partial U_k/\partial c_2(\omega)}{\partial U_k/\partial c_1} \ \forall k \neq k_0. \qquad (3.5)$$

In this allocation, risk sharing occurs through transfers from those individuals with relatively high incomes to those with relatively low incomes. Given that consumption is a function of income ± transfers, this implies that each individual's consumption in a particular state depends on the total income in that state. Consumption by individuals move in the same direction as aggregate income. Allen and Gale (1994, p. 63) present the following numerical example to explore requirements of optimal risk sharing. It is assumed that there are two dates $t = (1,2)$ and two states of nature $\Omega = \{\omega_0, \omega_1\}$. The states are equally likely, so $\mu_0 = \mu_1 = 0.5$. There are two types of investors; $K = \{k_0, k_1\}$, and they are equally distributed in the population, so $\nu_0 = \nu_1 = 1/2$. Each type has the same utility function:

$$U_k(c_1, c_2) = c_1 + V_k(c_2), \quad \forall k \in K, \qquad (3.6)$$

where V is continuous, differentiable once, strictly increasing, and strictly concave. Allen and Gale (1994) assume that investors are risk neutral at date 1 which implies that utility is transferable. That is: one unit of consumption at date 1 generates one unit of utility for everybody, $\partial U_k/\partial c_1 = 1$ for $k = k_0, k_1$. This assumption simplifies the welfare analysis because it allows welfare gains and losses to be measured in terms of consumer's surplus. The future income of the investors at $t = 2$ is:

$$Y_{k_0} = \begin{cases} 5 & \text{if } \omega = \omega_0 \\ 10 & \text{if } \omega = \omega_1 \end{cases}; \quad Y_{k_0} = \begin{cases} 10 & \text{if } \omega = \omega_0 \\ 5 & \text{if } \omega = \omega_1 \end{cases}. \tag{3.7}$$

Since $\partial U_k/\partial c_1 = 1$ for $k = k_0, k_1$, it follows from equation 3.5 that equating the marginal rate of substitution is equivalent to equating marginal utilities of consumption at date 2, $V'(c_2)$, in each state:

$$V'(Y_{k_0}(\omega) + \tau_{k_0}(\omega)) = V'(Y_{k_1}(\omega) + \tau_{k_1}(\omega)), \quad \forall \omega \in \Omega. \tag{3.8}$$

In state ω_0 type k_0's receive 5, while type k_1's receive 10. Since both have the same utility function, equating marginal utilities means they both consume 7.5. This requires a transfer of 2.5 from type k_1 to type k_0 so $\tau_{k_0}(\omega_0) = 2.5$ and $\tau_{k_1}(\omega_0) = -2.5$. Similarly in state ω_1, except the transfer is in the opposite direction, so $\tau_{k_0}(\omega_0) = -2.5$ and $\tau_{k_1}(\omega_0) = 2.5$. The possibility of trading thus enables investors to maximise utility through risk sharing. Securities, therefore, provide the means by which investors of one type can trade consumption in current periods for the future income of another type of investors. The role of securities in this context is examined below.

3.5.2 Securities and Risk Sharing

So far, it has been assumed that transfers take place through a central planner or government. The model can be extended to incorporate the role of securities as a means of resource allocation. In the absence of securities there would be no trade and each agent is forced to consume their endowment. In the absence of trade, the expected utility of type k is:

$$EU_k^* = EU_k(0, Y_k(\omega)). \tag{3.9}$$

Since income is random, each person bears some risk. Allen and Gale (1994) introduce securities into their model as a means to share risk. Let us return to our numerical example and assume that there is a security S with payoffs $(1, 0)$ in states $\{\omega_0, \omega_1\}$. The security is in zero net supply and is issued at date 0 in exchange for the consumption good. In equilibrium, two conditions must be satisfied:

- Every investor maximises their expected utility
- Markets clear.

Assume the security trades at price P_s at date 1. The demand of a type-k investor, S_k, is given by the solution to

$$\underset{S_k}{\text{Max}} - P_s S_k + EV(Y_k(\omega) + S_k), \tag{3.10}$$

where $EV(Y_k(\omega) + S_k)$ is the type-k investor's expected utility of consumption at date 2.

The first-order condition for an optimum is:

$$P_s = \frac{1}{2} V'(Y_k(\omega_0) + S_k), \quad \text{for each } k, \tag{3.11}$$

and the market-clearing condition is:

$$S_{k_0} + S_{k_1} = 0. \tag{3.12}$$

Thus, in the example, securities replace the central planner as the medium of transfers. The effectiveness by which investors can share risk by issuing securities depends on the *completeness* of securities markets.

3.5.3 Incomplete Markets

In the previous example trading securities S allows the two types of investors to share risk and equate marginal utilities of income in state ω_0. Numerically, $S_{k_0} = 2.5$, $S_{k_1} = -2.5$, and $P_s = V'(7.5)$. If S had payoffs of $(0, 1)$, then risk sharing would have improved in state ω_1. Securities of this type, which pay off in only one state, are known as *Arrow securities* or *pure securities*.[6] A pure security is defined as a security that pays \$1 at the end of the period if a given state occurs and nothing if any other state occurs. The concept of a pure security allows the logical decomposition of market securities into portfolios of pure securities. Thus every market security can be considered a combination of various pure securities (Copeland and Weston, 1988). Hence the view that financial innovations, before their introduction, are not new but existing products in zero net supply. The concept of pure securities links this literature to that reviewed earlier in the chapter (i.e. financial innovation as a bundling and unbundling process in incomplete markets). If there is an Arrow security for each state, then markets are complete and resource allocation will be efficient. If there are too few securities or securities have not been chosen appropriately, markets will be incomplete and an efficient allocation of risk will not be achieved. When markets are incomplete, there are unexploited gains from sharing risks. Introducing securities enables agents to share these risks and capture some of these gains.[7]

3.5.4 Optimal Security Design

When markets are incomplete, security design matters because it affects the opportunities for risk sharing.[8] Returning to our numerical example, if a security with payoffs (1, 0.5) was introduced, and this was the only security, investors will trade the security, but the efficient allocation of consumption will not be attained. Incomplete markets give rise to the question of optimal security design. Although a complete set of Arrow securities is sufficient for optimal risk sharing, it is not necessary. Allen and Gale (1994) show that, in the case of our simple example, we can achieve efficient allocation by introducing a single security whose payoffs are equal to the optimal transfers defined by equation 3.8. Suppose there is a security with price P_f which has payoffs $f(\omega)$ where:

$$f(\omega) = \tau_{k_0}(\omega). \tag{3.13}$$

That is, its payoffs are (2.5, −2.5). Each investor's decision solves:

$$\underset{Q_k}{\text{Max}} - P_f Q_k + EV(Y_k(\omega) + \tau_{k_0}(\omega)Q_k), \tag{3.14}$$

which gives the necessary and sufficient first-order condition:

$$P_f = E\tau_{k_0}(\omega)V'(Y_k(\omega) + \tau_{k_0}(\omega)Q_k). \tag{3.15}$$

In the case where:

$$Q_{k_0} = 1 \quad \text{and} \quad Q_{k_1} = 1, \tag{3.16}$$

and P_f is chosen to satisfy (3.15), both types of investors are maximising expected utility and the market for security S clears, so that both of the conditions for an equilibrium are satisfied. The levels of utility achieved by investors are given by:

$$EU_{k_0}^{**} = -P_f + EV(Y_{k_0}(\omega) + f(\omega)), \tag{3.17}$$

$$EU_{k_1}^{**} = P_f + EV(Y_{k_1}(\omega) - f(\omega)). \tag{3.18}$$

The above example is intended to show that when markets are incomplete an appropriately designed security can lead to an efficient allocation of resources. Redesigning securities or adding new ones can improve economic welfare. It should be noted however that the characteristics of optimal securities as explored above depend on the parameters of the model, which in this case are a bit restrictive. It is because there are only two types of investors that efficient allocation can be achieved with one security. Allen and Gale (1994) explore this issue further and derive an upper bound on the number of securities needed for efficient risk sharing. Without short sales and if there are K types of investor, no more than $K - 1$ securities are needed in general. See Allen and Gale (1988, and 1994, Chapters 4 and 6) for an in-depth analysis of optimal security design and an extensive review of the literature on this issue.

3.5.5 Equilibrium and the Incentives to Innovate

We have outlined the main components of the theory of financial innovation and risk sharing as developed by Allen and Gale (1994). The discussion so far has defined the setting of the economy, the role of securities in optimal risk sharing, and the investors' decision problem. By introducing firms into the analysis, Allen and Gale derive the conditions necessary for the existence of an equilibrium and its characteristics. They show that firms innovate to increase the market value of their assets by paying a fixed cost and introducing new securities. Choosing a complex financial structure can increase market value when *markets are incomplete* and agents have *different marginal valuations* of the securities issued. In effect, one is breaking the firm into pieces and selling the pieces to the clientele that value it most. It is the ability to increase the value of the firm that provides the incentive to innovate and allows the cost of the innovation to be covered (Allen and Gale, 1994, p. 73). Their conclusion seems to be consistent with the view of financial innovation as an 'unbundling' and 'bundling' process as discussed earlier in the chapter.

3.5.6 Extensions to the Basic Framework

Although the model developed above provides useful insights into the process of financial innovation, its implications are still limited by the underlying assumptions. In an extended version of their model, Allen and Gale (1994) allow firms to choose from the set of all possible financial structures rather than a finite subset. This is particularly useful for the purpose of characterising optimal securities and highlighting their *spanning role*. They show that the new securities span the old, so investors can obtain their existing consumption bundles by holding appropriate amounts of the new securities. They also relax the assumptions of no short sales and infinite number of firms. In an economy with a finite number of firms, competitive price-taking behaviour is no longer appropriate and the definition of equilibrium has to be altered to take into consideration the strategic interactions between firms. Allen and Gale (1994) model this situation by assuming that equilibrium in the assets markets at date 1 is achieved in two stages:

1. At the first stage, firms simultaneously choose their financial structures taking the choices of others as given
2. At the second stage, investors buy and sell the supply of securities determined at the first stage on a competitive auction market.

The equilibrium prices observed at the second stage depend on the choices made by firms at the first stage. When firms make their decisions at the first stage, they anticipate the prices that will result at the second stage. Therefore, firms are not price takers.

3.5.7 Innovation by Financial Institutions

We now focus on the role of financial institutions in the process of financial innovation. By that we mean financial intermediaries such as investment banks which undertake innovation on their own rather than assisting firms to issue securities. Allen and Gale (1994) first model the case of a monopoly investment bank which introduces a security to achieve optimal risk sharing. They assume that:

- There exists a monopoly investment bank. The owners only consume at date 1, so the objective of the investment bank is to maximise date 1 profits. There are costs C of issuing the security.
- There are two types of non-intermediary agent, A and B. Type A are investors and type B are issuers. They cannot trade directly but must use the investment bank.
- The investment bank charges a lump-sum fee, ϕ_k where $k = A, B$, irrespective of the amount purchased.

The investment bank has incentives to choose a security which leads to a Pareto efficient allocation of resources. Hence if it innovates in equilibrium it will choose the Pareto-efficient security $f(\omega_i)$ that maximises revenues and the fees it charges will be:

$$\phi_k = EU_k^{**} - EU_k^{**} \quad \text{for } k = A, B, \tag{3.19}$$

where EU_k^{**} is their utility when they can use the security without paying any fees and EU_k^* is their utility when they cannot use the security. The bank's profit will be:

$$\Pi = \phi_A + \phi_B - C. \tag{3.20}$$

Innovation will only occur in equilibrium when $C \leq \phi_A + \phi_B$. The resulting Pareto optimal depends crucially on the assumptions of monopoly and lump-sum fees which enable the bank to capture all the benefits of innovation and can weigh these against the costs of innovation as reflected in equation (3.20). These assumptions can be relaxed by introducing competition and a constant fee per dollar of a security that is sold which allows us to investigate the effect of competition through imitation. Allen and Gale (1994) further assume:

- There are three dates $t = 1, 2, 3$. One-period securities are issued at dates 1 and 2.

- Because we are focusing on short-term securities, for a given security, the inverse aggregate demand curve in terms of the fees charged can be represented by $\phi = \phi(Q)$.
- In order to supply a new security an investment bank must pay a development cost C. If another bank subsequently imitates the security, its development cost is zero. The innovating bank and its imitators must train staff to deal with the new security, and it is this that determines capacity. For a bank to develop capacity q costs $c(q)$.

The innovating bank is the only issuer at date 1. At date 2 other banks will imitate if it is profitable to do so. The innovating bank takes this into account when it chooses its capacity. Let the innovating bank be denoted by the subscript $i = 0$, and the other banks that enter can be denoted $i = 1, \ldots, N$. Suppose the discount rate is zero. The innovating bank will then solve:

$$\underset{q_0}{\text{Max}} \; \phi(q_0)q_0 + \phi\left(q_0 + \sum_{i=1}^{N} q_i\right)q_0 - c(q_0) - C, \tag{3.21}$$

taking $q_i, i = 1, \ldots, N$ as given. The imitator's problem is:

$$\underset{q_j}{\text{Max}} \; \phi\left(q_0 + \sum_{i=1}^{N} q_i\right)q_j - c(q_j), \tag{3.22}$$

taking $q_i, i = 1, \ldots, N, i \neq j$ as given.

The number of imitators is determined by the requirement that make non-negative profits. It is also necessary that the innovator make a non-negative profit for the innovation to occur. The first-order condition for the innovator is:

$$\phi''(q_0)q_0 + \phi(q_0) + \phi''\left(q_0 + \sum_{i=1}^{N} q_i\right)q_0 + \phi\left(q_0 + \sum_{i=1}^{N} q_i\right) - c'(q_0) = 0. \tag{3.23}$$

For the imitator it is:

$$\phi''\left(q_0 + \sum_{i=1}^{N} q_i\right)q_0 + \phi\left(q_0 + \sum_{i=1}^{N} q_i\right) - c'(q_0) = 0. \tag{3.24}$$

Provided $\phi(.)$ and $c(.)$ satisfy the standard conditions, so $\partial(MR - MC)/\partial q < 0$, it can be seen that $q_0 > q_i$ for $i = 1, \ldots, N$. That is, the innovator obtains a larger market share than imitators. It also implies that the fee charged initially will be higher than in subsequent periods. Allen and Gale (1994) compare their model with the empirical studies in the literature. Specifically, the study by Tufano (1989) is of particular interest as it examines the quantity and spread advantages of first-movers in the market for a new security. Using a database of 58 financial innovations from 1974 to 1986 Tufano examined how investment banks are compensated for their investment in developing new products. He found that investment banks that create new products do not charge higher prices in the brief period of monopoly before imitative products appear, and in the long run charge prices below, not above, those charged by rivals offering imitative products. This finding is consistent with Allen and Gale's (1994) model. The second finding of Tufano's (1989) study is that banks capture a larger market share of underwriting with innovations than with imitative products. Innovators continue to capture larger shares in subsequent years (Tufano, 1989, p. 232). He also found that the share captured by a particular bank as a pioneer is larger than the share won by the same bank when it offers an imitative product. This is also consistent with the model above.[9]

The model of Allen and Gale (1994) does not explain which banks innovate and which imitate. It is not clear how external factors such as regulation and market conditions fit into the model. Other limitations of the model which are pointed out by Allen and Gale (1994, p. 101) are:

- In practice, the demand function will be uncertain, both because the innovator cannot be sure of what issuers and investors want and because issuers and investors are not familiar with the characteristics of the new product
- The model ignores the role of banks as market monitors searching for missing opportunities for sharing risk
- The model ignores the role of banks' networks as a tool for marketing new products. Its ability to identify potential issuers and investors and persuade them of the advantages of the new product is crucial to its success. This depends on the bank's existing business and customer base.

As stated by Allen and Gale (1994, p. 101), 'the emphasis on uncertainty, information, and networking suggests that the market for new securities will be much more complex than the analysis in this section has allowed ... but much research remains to be done'. A more important limitation of their model is that it focuses only on risk sharing as a motivation for financial innovation. Other important factors include reduction of transaction costs, corporate control, and information. Nevertheless, the work of Allen and Gale (1989, 1990, 1991) Allen and Gale (1990) and their extensive survey in Allen and Gale (1994) has greatly enhanced our understanding of the process of financial innovation and security design in incomplete markets. Their research has also filled a considerable gap in the literature. The theoretical literature covering these issues is relatively young but it is growing quickly.

In a review of recent literature on security design models of financial innovation, Duffie and Rahi (1995) classify the models into two main groups—general equilibrium models (e.g. Elul, 1995; Chen, 1995 and Pesendorfer, 1995) and security design models in an exponential-normal setting (e.g. Rahi, 1995; Ohashi,

1995; Bhattacharya *et al.*, 1995; Demange and Laroque, 1995a and 1995b, and Hara 1992 and 1995). We review both separately below.

3.6 GENERAL EQUILIBRIUM MODELS OF FINANCIAL INNOVATION

General equilibrium models concentrate on the opportunities and incentives for innovating new securities. Innovators in these models are generally assumed to be investment banks. An investment bank can innovate by acting as an intermediary to a new derivative security or through its underwriting business acting as a design consultant and marketing agency for firms which will issue new financial products. Most models assume that innovators maximise the utility of the proceeds of the sale of the new issue as in Chen (1995), Demange and Laroque (1995b) and Pesendorfer (1995). Other models assume that the innovator acts only as an intermediary which profits from the provision of transactions services, as in Hara (1995) and Ohashi (1995).

The literature on financial innovation and security design is growing rapidly. A number of papers on financial innovation have appeared in a special issue of *Journal of Economic Theory*, February 1995, '*Symposium on Financial Market Innovation and Security Design*'. Most of the studies published in this issue are concerned with the problem of security design and financial innovation in a general-equilibrium setting. In the introductory article, Duffie and Rahi (1995) present a standard model of general equilibrium in a given set of security markets, and use it to discuss some of the ideas in the articles appearing in the same issue which use a similar framework. Below, we review the standard model as formulated by Duffie and Rahi (1995, p. 12):

Models of financial innovation often begin with a standard setup for general equilibrium in incomplete markets where there is a finite set of $\{1, \ldots, \Omega\}$ of states of nature, with trading at time 0 of L commodities and a finite number of securities, and trading at time 1, in each given state of L commodities. The consumption set $C \subset \Re^L \times (\Re^L)^\Omega$ contains an element c representing an initial commodity bundle $c_0 \in \Re^L$ and a state-contingent commodity bundle $c_\omega \in \Re^L$ at time 1 in state ω. Each agent h in some set H of households has preferences over C represented by a utility function $u^h \colon C \to \Re$. The initial distribution of consumption to agents is given by a function $e \colon H \to C$.

There is a set R of potential financial structures. Each financial structure R in R is a finite subset of $\Re^\Omega$, a collection of $\#R$ securities each characterised by a vector in $\Re^\Omega$ of state-contingent payoffs in terms of a fixed numeraire commodity. For each financial structure R there is an associated admissible set $\Theta(R) \subset \Re^{\#R}$ of portfolios. Given a price vector $p \in \Re^L \times (\Re^L)^\Omega$ for spot consumption and a price vector $q \in \Re^{\#R}$ for securities, a budget-feasible choice for agent h is a pair $(c, \theta) \in C \times \Theta(R)$ such that:

$$p_0 \cdot (c_0 - e(h)_0) + q \cdot \theta \leq 0 \tag{3.25}$$[10]

and

$$p_\omega \cdot (c_\omega - e(h)_\omega) \leq \theta \cdot R_\omega, \quad \omega \in \{1, \ldots, \Omega\}, \tag{3.26}$$

where R_ω denotes the vector of payoffs of the securities in state ω. For each agent h, given prices (p, q), a budget-feasible choice (c, θ) is optimal if there is no budget-feasible choice (c', θ') such that $u^h(c') > u^h(c)$. A market equilibrium, given parameters $(u, e, R, \Theta(R))$, consists of (p, q) and allocation $c : H \to C$ and $\theta : H \to \Theta(R)$ of consumption and securities such that, for all h the choice $(c(h), \theta(h))$ is optimal for agent h given these prices, and such that markets clear:

$$\sum_{h \in H} c(h) - e(h) = 0;\tag{3.27}$$[11]

where $\sum_{h \in H}$ denotes summation when H is finite, and otherwise denotes integration, with suitable measurability and integrability conditions on c, e, and θ, taking H to be a particular measure space.

The parameter of particular interest in a study of innovation is the financial structure R. Although most models in this area use a similar framework to the one shown above as presented by Duffie and Rahi (1995), the particular assumptions and aims of the study requires certain modification or differences in the methodology. Elul (1995) examines the welfare effects of financial innovation in incomplete market economies with several consumption goods. He shows that it is possible to arbitrarily perturb the equilibrium utilities by introducing the appropriate assets making, for example, all agents worse off. This result is in contrast to the traditional intuition that innovation—in so far as it fulfils a demand by agents for increased opportunities to manage risk in suboptimal incomplete market economies—should increase the welfare of everyone in the economy in incomplete markets. Elul's (1995) results are conditional on the assumption that markets are *sufficiently incomplete*. Generally, one should not interpret the results of Elul's study as suggesting that some innovations are good and others are bad. 'Rather, it is meant to highlight the rich variety of behaviour which would be expected as soon as one moves away from a simple-minded single-commodity paradigm, and to suggest that greater sophistication, and perhaps greater oversight, is needed in dealing with this problem, both from a theoretical and from a practical point of view' (Elul, 1995, p. 73).

Pesendorfer (1995) develops a model of financial innovation, in which intermediaries can issue new financial securities against collateral in the form of standard securities. Examples of this type of financial innovation include collateralised and stripped mortgage obligations and stripped treasury securities. There is a single commodity and N types of financial intermediaries. The model considers the following forces behind financial innovation:

1. A demand for opportunities for risk-sharing, risk-pooling, hedging, and inter-temporal or spatial transfers of wealth that are currently not available.
2. The lowering of transaction costs.

A financial intermediary can purchase a portfolio of securities and issue a collection of financial products against the returns of this portfolio. Like Allen and Gale (1988, 1991), Pesendorfer (1995) models an equilibrium in which all consumers maximise utility, intermediaries optimise and markets clear. While Allen and Gale (1988, 1991) assume that firms innovate to maximise profits, in Pesendorfer's (1995) two-period model, intermediaries purchase securities to create new financial products. Intermediaries have to market their innovations and marketing is costly. Intermediaries behave optimally along two dimensions: first they choose an optimal production and marketing plan given the set of innovations, and second they choose an optimal set of innovations. Due to the costs of marketing, financial intermediaries will try to create instruments that enable households to economise on the number of securities traded and on the volume of trade in each security, which leads to 'redundancies'. Pesendorfer shows that the equilibrium asset structure may exhibit 'redundancies' as frequently observed in financial markets; i.e. new securities may be linear combinations of other securities but nevertheless be utility-improving for households.

Chen (1995) models financial intermediaries that create new securities collaterised by old securities. When decomposing existing securities and opening new markets, innovators serve important economic functions, such as allowing investors to obtain consumption at lower costs, enabling investors to achieve better risk sharing, and making the fundamental value of more payoffs observable. Chen (1995) shows that innovators serve these functions even when they introduce redundant securities that are not yet issued. That is, these are innovations which do not change the span of the available instruments but rather make it cheaper for traders to make the desired transaction (Pesendorfer, 1995, p. 93). Short sales constraints imply that, even when the linear span of existing securities is complete, innovation may be profitable because it can reduce the cost of market frictions, in this case, short sales. Some of this reduction in costs is captured by profit-maximising innovators' constraints (Duffie and Rahi, 1995, p. 18). Chen (1995) adopts the *rational conjecture condition* defined by Hart (1979) and Allen and Gale (1988) which states that: the price that an investor expects to receive upon issuing a security is equal to the maximum amount that any investor is willing to pay to hold a small quantity at the margin. In frictional economies, the equilibrium price function, as defined by the rational conjecture condition, is sublinear and thus there will be incentives to innovate. This aspect of Chen's (1995) model is particularly significant, given the failure of the 'incomplete market' view of financial innovation to explain the introduction of redundant securities. According to this view, financial innovation helps bring an incomplete market closer to being complete. But this fails to explain why redundant securities are sometimes introduced (Chen, 1995, p. 118).

3.7 SECURITY DESIGN IN A LINEAR FRAMEWORK

Models in this category adopt a standard linear framework for the analysis of security market innovation. Although the assumptions underlying this type of framework are quite restrictive, they have the advantage of admitting closed-form solutions (Duffie and Rahi, 1995, p. 23). This allows us to compare the impact of alternative financial structures on risk-sharing opportunities in asset markets. It is generally assumed that securities are designed and introduced by either an exchange (e.g. Duffie and Jackson, 1989; Cuny, 1993; Rahi, 1995), or a risk-averse entrepreneur (e.g. Rahi, 1993; Demange and Laroque, 1995a) to maximise a certain utility function; that is, these are optimal securities from the point of view of the innovator. If the expected reduction is large, the exchange decides not to innovate a new contract. In the case of security innovation by an exchange, it is generally assumed that the exchange innovates new security contracts (e.g. new futures contracts) to maximise its transaction fee revenue (or its proxy) (Ohashi, 1995, pp. 198–9).

Most models in this category assume a single-good economy with uncertainty, asymmetric information, and a variable financial structure and constant absolute risk aversion. Rahi (1995) uses such a framework to compare alternative incomplete asset structures in a productive economy, focusing on the role of assets in allocating risk and transmitting private information. Asset structures are constrained efficient in terms of both risk-sharing and information-transmission. Rahi (1995) develops specific optimality criteria that are used to evaluate innovation by volume maximising futures exchanges. In this model, futures contracts serve as hedging instruments for producers. Futures also serve as risk-reducing instruments since the risks these producers face arise from the stochastic nature of production. Thus futures prices guide investment decisions by revealing privately held information about production returns. Rahi (1995) finds that it is possible to choose the parameters determining future payoffs in such a way as to independently control the efficacy with which these assets perform the above mentioned functions (i.e. hedging and price discovery).[12] Given the optimality criteria and using certain conditions, Rahi (1995) also shows that (i) the optimal choice of one futures exchange innovating a single contract is both hedging-efficient and informationally-efficient, and that

(ii) the market structure determined by a number of competing exchanges is informationally-efficient.

Hara (1995) develops a framework which assumes assets are created by a single party, *the designer*, which can create any number of assets and charge commission fees as long as the total number of types of asset does not exceed some exogenously determined constant. The designer's objective function is to maximise its commission revenues. The designer is the only agent which can create new assets, and the number of types of asset is endogenously determined by the designer to maximise its objective function. Using this setup, and some more assumptions, Hara (1995) shows that when the designer can create at most two assets, a commission-revenue maximiser always exists; if the designer can create more than two assets, it may not.

An important assumption that underlies Rahi's (1995) model is that there are *too few* futures, not enough to allow for complete risk-sharing or full revelation of information. Ohashi (1995) develops a model of contract innovation by futures exchanges in which the exchange can create up to a given number of contracts costlessly, with the number of futures contracts being endogenously determined. As assumed by Rahi (1995), the exchange's objective function is to maximise the expected trading volume of the contracts. In this model, however, the upper bound on the number of contracts can be large enough to attain Pareto-optimal risk sharing. Thus, Ohashi (1995) studies the determination of the number of futures contracts created by an exchange. Ohashi finds that the existence of an upper bound on the number of contracts depends crucially on the nature of information that investors have. If investors have symmetric information, then the exchange creates as many contracts as possible. Given that there is unhedged risk, it is always possible to create an additional contract so as to obtain the additional trading for the unhedged risk and to increase the expected trading volume. In the case of asymmetric information, however, there can be endogenously determined upper bounds on the number of contracts that the exchange is willing to create, even when innovation is assumed to be costless. This arises from the possibility that new contracts may diminish the demand or trading volume of existing ones. The innovation of a new contract, while capturing the additional liquidity and hedging transaction, transmits additional information, which may make the investors' information symmetric and, therefore, decrease the volume of transactions due to differential information.

3.8 CONCLUSION

This chapter reviewed the literature on theoretical models of financial innovation. Most of the early literature is descriptive in nature and attempts to highlight the factors responsible for the emergence of specific financial innovations. The main factors often quoted in the literature as causes of financial innovation are regulation, volatile interest and exchange rates, competition, globalisation, and technology. A prominent trend in the literature is to view financial innovation as a *bundling* and *unbundling* process whereby new financial products just simply represent changes in the combinations of certain general attributes of financial instruments (e.g. liquidity, maturity). This is motivated by the observation that financial innovation rarely creates completely new products but often modifies certain characteristics of existing instruments. More recent literature attempts to formalise the view of financial innovation as a bundling and unbundling process by modelling the process of financial innovation in the context of general equilibrium theory. In this setup, it is assumed that there is an exogenously given set of assets traded in the market and the transaction of those assets are the only way to exchange risky future incomes. Each consumer maximises utility by forming a portfolio of assets under a budget constraint. Equilibrium assets prices are determined by, and the final allocation of risky future incomes results from, the liquidation of an equilibrium assets allocation. Using this framework, questions such as optimal securities design, the role of securities in risk-sharing and information transfer, and the relationship between financial structures and equilibrium properties can be examined in the context of new assets formation. Although more attention is now being paid to the study of financial innovation as a process, there is still no generally accepted and unified theory of this process. In comparison with its counterpart in the real sector, financial innovation remains an under-researched phenomenon.

The long established industrial economic literature on innovation, innovation adoption, and innovation diffusion provides a number of interesting theories that could further explain innovation in financial markets. The following two chapters examine this literature.

ENDNOTES

1. The total of these numbers exceeds 37 as more than one cause can be attributed to an innovation.
2. This distinction is mainly adapted from the industrial economics literature which distinguishes between invention, innovation, and diffusion.
3. Another classification of financial innovations was proposed by Niehans (1983). He classifies innovations as either adaptive or technological. Adaptive innovations are 'entrepreneurial adaptations to changing market conditions'. They are reversible in the sense that if the underlying conditions disappear, they will in due course disappear as well.
4. See Cornwall (1984) for an introduction to the use of general equilibrium analysis.
5. Von Neumann and Morgenstern (1947). See Roberts and Schulze (1973, ch. 3) for a discussion of the Von Neumann–Morgenstern system of utilities.
6. Also known as Arrow–Debreu securities since Arrow (1964) and Debreu (1959) set forth their original specifications.

7. The view that financial innovation helps bring an incomplete market closer to being complete fails to explain why redundant securities are sometimes introduced (Chen, 1995, pp. 117–8). See Chen (1995) and Pesendorfer (1995) discussed later in the chapter.

8. Modigliani and Miller (1958) show that capital structure, i.e. the debt/equity ratio, has no effect on a firm's value if capital markets are complete and perfect and no taxes are in effect. With taxes in effect, Modigliani and Miller (1963) show that firms should use entirely debt finance. This result is contradicted by empirical evidence and was challenged by proponents of bankruptcy and liquidation costs theory. Recently, many studies in the literature have taken the approach of examining the *optimal securities* that should be issued rather than the *optimal debt equity ratio* (e.g. Freeman and Tabellini, 1991 and Anderson and Sundaresan, 1993). See Allen and Gale (1989) for a discussion of the 'optimal capital structure' versus 'optimal security design' debate.

9. It can be shown that $q_0 > q_i$ for $i = 1, \ldots, N$, which implies that the innovator captures a larger market share than imitators.

10. Note that at time 0, for surplus agents $c_0 - e(h)_0 > 0$ and for deficit agents $c_0 - e(h)_0 < 0$. Equation 3.25 states that a surplus agent with savings of $c_0 - e(h)_0$ (total initial wealth minus spot consumption) valued at $p_0(c_0 - e(h)_0)$ can invest in no more than θ securities priced at q. For a deficit unit equation 3.25 can be rewritten as $q \cdot \theta \geq -p_0 \cdot (c_0 - e(h)_0)$ which, since $c_0 - e(h)_0 < 0$, states that the agent has to issue (i.e. borrow) a minimum θ of securities at market price q to cover for a spot deficit consumption of $c_0 - e(h)_0$. By the same token, equation 3.26 characterises agents' consumption and investment opportunities at time 1.

11. That is, total lending equal total borrowing and demand equal supply in both commodities and securities markets.

12. Hedging-efficiency implies that the hedging quality of futures contracts cannot be improved for one agent without reducing it for another. Similarly, information-efficiency implies that the informational content of futures prices cannot be increased for one agent without decreasing it for another.

4

Models of Innovation: The Industrial Economics Literature

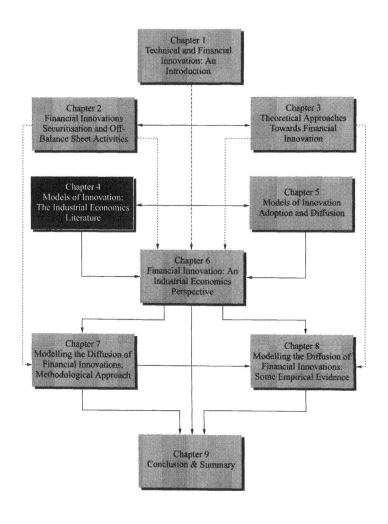

4
Models of Innovation: the Industrial Economics Literature

4.1 INTRODUCTION

The importance of technological progress has been recognised by researchers for a long time. Economists are well aware of the role of technological progress in improving welfare. It may not be surprising that the introduction of new products and processes is usually regarded as responsible for much of the improvement in standards of living (Ferguson, 1988). The relationship between technological advances and economic growth is important and economists have argued for a long time that it is critical that we understand the dynamics of the process of technological change. Traditionally, particular emphasis in the economic literature has been placed on examining the relationship between market structure and the level of inventive activity. The seminal work of Schumpeter (1934, 1942), which suggested a positive relationship between monopoly power and size on the level of inventive activities, stimulated an increasing interest in this area. The hypotheses of Schumpeter were particularly controversial, given that western economies are based on the notion of free and competitive markets as the most efficient way towards economic progress. A wave of studies have appeared in the literature investigating the relationship between market structure and the incentive to innovate.

Following the early work by Schumpeter, the literature distinguishes three stages in the process of change—invention, innovation, and diffusion. Invention relates to the generalisation of a new idea and its subsequent development to the point where its implementation becomes feasible. Innovation refers to the *commercialisation* of an invention by an entrepreneur. Diffusion refers to the spread of the use of an innovation among the population of potential adopters over time (i.e. inter-firm diffusion). The literature tends to focus on the last two stages by concentrating on the D component of the R&D and taking the R component as given. That is, most models assume that the entrepreneur is faced with a list of *known* but as yet unexploited inventions from which they may select one for development as an innovation. The economics of decision making associated with the introduction of an innovation are different from those associated with adopting an existing innovation, and so are the factors, both innovation and firm-specific factors, that influence these decisions. This explains why innovation and diffusion are usually examined separately. It is clear that for an invention to have its impact on economic growth both stages, innovation and diffusion, are necessary. This chapter concentrates on the literature on innovation and the following chapter focuses on diffusion processes.

The progress of the literature on innovative activities can be summarised as follows:

- Schumpeterian hypotheses on market structure and innovative activity.
- Macroeconomic studies of the incentives to innovate. Stimulated by Arrow's (1962) pioneering work, a number of papers appeared to examine the relationship between market structure and innovation in a more formal way and these include the studies by Demsetz (1969), Kamien and Schwartz (1970), and Needham (1975).
- Individual firm decision-theoretic models of *timing of innovation*. Models in this category deal with the influence of various factors on the innovating firm's choice of the speed of development once the project has started (i.e. timing of innovation). Profit-maximising firms consider the effects of the rewards for innovation and imitation, the development cost function, and the intensity of rivalry as given exogenous parameters in their optimisation problem. In selecting the optimal development schedule and introduction date, cost savings from postponement of the introduction date are balanced against the opportunity cost of lost potential profits during that period of delay. This approach enables researchers to examine the effects certain parameters of the model (e.g. rivalry as a measure of market structure) have on the speed of development and allocation of resources and compare the results to what would be *socially optimal*. From the standpoint of a social planner (e.g. government), efficient allocation of resources calls for selection of the introduction date of the innovation such that the marginal social cost of accelerating development just matches the discounted marginal social benefits of earlier introduction. This approach was initially explored by Barzel (1968) but advances in this area are mainly due to the extensive research undertaken by Kamien and Schwartz (1972, 1974a, 1974b, 1976, 1978a, 1978b, 1980), later summarised in Kamien and Schwartz (1982).
- Aggregate market game-theoretic models of timing of innovation. Similarly to the previous approach, firms are assumed to maximise their expected profits. The trade-off is between a declining development cost function of time and the larger profits realised from the earlier introduction of the innovation (and the difference in profit flows on an innovating versus an imitating product). Unlike the previous approach, however, the intensity of

rivalry is an endogenous variable in this analysis. This approach was pioneered by Scherer (1967) and was then extended and refined by Loury (1979), Reinganum (1979), Lee and Wilde (1980), and Dasgupta and Stiglitz (1980).

The following chapter provides a more detailed exposition of the above approaches.

4.2 BASIC DEFINITIONS

4.2.1 Product versus Process Innovation

It is customary to distinguish in the literature between product and process innovations. This is usually done to facilitate the analysis of the incentives to innovate. The benefits of introducing a new product are generated by abnormal returns during the temporary monopoly an innovator enjoys in the market for the new product. For process innovations, innovators benefit from either decreased costs and thus higher profit margins (if prices are constant) or from larger market shares (if prices are reduced). The distinction between the two is not always clear cut. The production of new products usually requires some modification to existing production techniques and thus may be said to include process innovation. On the other hand, new techniques for producing existing products are likely to alter at least some of these products' characteristics. Nevertheless, the distinction between product and process innovations makes it easier to model the profits implications associated with introducing innovations. As Blaug (1963, p. 13) puts it, 'In principle, novel ways of making old goods can be distinguished from old ways of making novelties. Since the index-number problem has so far doomed all theoretical analysis of innovations which alter the quality of final output, the refusal to discriminate between product- and process-innovations would close the subject of technical progress to further analysis.'

4.2.2 Types of Innovation

In analysing technical change, most economists tend to focus upon the introduction of new products and processes which incorporate technological advances. But innovation-related technical progress can be achieved in other forms as well. Schumpeter (1934), for example, identifies five types of innovation:

1. The introduction of a new product or service, or an improvement in the quality of an existing product or service

2. The introduction of a new method of production
3. The development of a new market
4. The exploitation of a new source of supply
5. The reorganisation of methods of operation.

It is clear that Schumpeter's broad definition of innovation covers most of the ways in which the efficiency of resource allocation can be enhanced. In spite of the appropriateness of the above definition most models reviewed in this chapter tend to focus narrowly on process and product innovations. The modelling of the innovator as a profit maximising firm necessitates a clear and direct link between his/her profit and the innovative activity so that the incentives to innovate can be identified. This link is relatively easy to establish when focusing on process and product innovations. This is not necessarily the case for other types of innovations, which makes the modelling of such situations more complicated. It is not clear whether or not most of the welfare effects of technical change can be attributed to process and product innovation but, nevertheless, it does not seem unreasonable to focus primarily on these two types of innovation as is the case with the bulk of the literature on technical change.

4.2.3 Uncertainty and the Assumption of Perfect Information

Entrepreneurs with a list of inventions face a resource-allocation-under-uncertainty problem. To generate innovations, entrepreneurs have to allocate resources to their development programmes, and compare the expected return on these programmes with the expected return on other activities. The entrepreneur cannot know in advance whether his/her innovation will succeed. Uncertainty is an important aspect to be incorporated into models of innovation. Models which assume perfect information are inadequate to explain the process of change. With the assumption of perfect information, imitation will be instantaneous, and innovators will generate no abnormal profits that compensate them for the cost they incur during the development period, with the result that no innovation will be introduced. Assuming that changes are undertaken to maximise profits, it is then necessary to assume barriers to entry for models of perfect information to explain technical change. There are various ways to incorporate uncertainty into the analysis of technical change as will be shown in later parts of this chapter. But first we should identify the major sources of uncertainty associated with the process of innovation. Firms face uncertainty regarding the continued success of their current products; uncertainty about competing innovations; and uncertainty about the profitability of their innovations. Moreover these uncertainties are interdependent. As Kamien and Schwartz (1982, p. 24) state, 'continued success of its current products and also the profitability of its own innovation both depend on the nature and timing of competing innovations. The profitability of its innovations depends also on the technical difficulties and the cost of overcoming them'. Specifically, Kamien and Schwartz (1982, pp. 109–110) identified two major sources of uncertainty:

1. Technical uncertainty: refers to uncertainty regarding the development cost function (both cost- and time-wise). Technical uncertainty can be incorporated into models of R&D rivalry by assuming that development cost is a stochastic (as opposed to deterministic) function of time
2. Market uncertainty: refers to uncertainty about the expenditure level of rivals on the development of a substitute innovation, or whether or not, and when, a rival innovation will appear. Market uncertainty can be incorporated into R&D rivalry models by expressing the benefits to firms as a probability-weighted average of the rewards to innovators and the rewards to imitators (where usually the former is assumed to be larger than the latter).

4.2.4 Demand-Pull versus Technology-Push Hypotheses

The literature identifies two hypotheses to explain the forces driving the process of technical change; demand-pull and technology-push hypotheses. The former is attributed to the extensive work of Schmookler (1966) on the role of demand forces in stimulating innovation. The second is mostly associated with Nelson (1959) and Phillips (1966). The difference between the two hypotheses lies in the assumption regarding the direction of the flow of ideas between a firm's research staff, its production staff and its marketing staff. The technology-push hypothesis views a firm's research staff as the initiator of innovations. Advances and breakthroughs in scientific knowledge are brought to the attention of the marketing staff for possible commercialisation. In the demand-pull hypothesis, the interaction is between a firm's marketing staff (for product innovation) or production staff (for process innovation) on one hand and its research staff on the other hand. The marketing and production staff identify potential profit improving opportunities and the research staff seek feasible solutions.

The important implication of both hypotheses is that firms with larger research and marketing departments are more likely to scan a wider range of profitable innovational opportunities and to find solutions more quickly and effectively, time and cost wise. In the technology-pull hypothesis, the pace of innovative activity will depend on the advance in scientific knowledge implying that innovative activity tends to be slower in areas where the underlying scientific base is stationary than in those areas where it is growing. The demand-pull hypothesis, on the other hand, stresses the role of growing industries in creating profit opportunities which can be tapped by innovative firms. The state of scientific knowledge will probably act as a ceiling to the number and type of potential profitable innovations. The number of ideas that a firm's marketing staff can come up with is only limited by their imagination but those posed to the research staff must fall within the realms of technological advances. As pointed out by Kamien and Schwartz (1982, p. 36), technology-push and demand-pull hypotheses may be viewed as complementary rather than competing explanations of innovation, with the former being more of a long-run theory and the latter, a short-run theory. A more formal definition of these two hypotheses is proposed by Scherer (1967) and is discussed later in the chapter. Demand-pull and technology-push hypotheses should be taken into consideration when examining the Schumpeterian hypotheses regarding market structure and innovation. We comment further on this point in the next section.

4.3 SCHUMPETERIAN HYPOTHESES

The view of technical change as an *economic activity* can be traced back to the writings of Schumpeter who in three books, *The Theory of Economic Development* (1934), *Business Cycles* (1939), and *Capitalism, Socialism and Democracy* (1942), examined the role of economic agents in the process of change. In *The Theory of Economic Development* (1934), Schumpeter examined the typical European industrial structure of the late nineteenth century characterised by many small firms. The pattern of innovative activity is characterised by technological ease of entry in an industry and by a major role played by new firms in the innovative activity. New entrepreneurs enter an industry with new ideas, new products or new processes. They launch new enterprises which challenge established firms and thus continuously disrupt the current ways of production, organisation and distribution and wipe out the quasi rents associated with previous innovations (Malerba and Orsenigo, 1995, p. 47).

Schumpeter's somewhat revised view of the dynamics of the innovative activity, and the one now most associated with him, is found in his *Capitalism, Socialism and Democracy* (1942) which was inspired by the American industry of the first half of the twentieth century. Emphasis, according to this view, is on the institutionalisation of innovative activity, the industrial R&D laboratory for technological innovation and the key role played by large firms. According to this view, the pattern of innovative activities is characterised by the prevalence of large established firms and by relevant barriers to entry for new innovators. Large firms' advantages stem from their accumulated stock of knowledge in commercially-critical technological areas, economies of scale and economies of scope in large scale R&D projects, and from their distributional and financial superiority.

Schumpeter criticised mainstream economics for failing to realise that capitalism consists of *change* and cannot be analysed in static terms; 'capitalism, then, is by nature a form or method of economic change and not only never is but never can be stationary', Schumpeter (1942, p. 82). Static analysis of welfare economics shows perfect competition as a welfare maximising system. It may however be necessary to sacrifice short-term efficiencies to gain long-term welfare maximum, a hypotheses that cannot be examined by static analysis. As Schumpeter (1942, p. 83) put it, 'a system—any system, economic or other— that at *every* given point of time fully utilises its possibilities to the best advantage may yet in the long run be inferior to a system that does so at *no* given point of time, because the latter's failure to do so may be a condition for the level or speed of long-run performance'.

Innovation, as Schumpeter's broad definition suggests, is the 'fundamental impulse that sets and keeps the capitalist engine in motion'. Mainstream economic theory has focused on price competition, but according to Schumpeter it is competition in the innovative activity market that matters. '[I]t is not that kind of competition [price competition] which counts but the competition from the new commodity, the new technology, the new source of supply, the new type of organisation—competition which commands a decisive cost or quality advantage and which strikes not at the margins of the profits and the outputs of the existing firms but at their foundations and their very lives' (Schumpeter, 1942, p. 84). Capitalism, according to Schumpeter, is a process of *creative destruction* that incessantly revolutionises the economic structure from within, incessantly destroying the old one, incessantly creating a new one (Schumpeter, 1934, p. 83). It is through this concept of *competition through innovation* that the two hypotheses mostly associated with Schumpeter emerged. Before discussing these two hypotheses it is important to note that the competition Schumpeter describes is not solely confined to competition which exists between rivals in one industry but it also exists in the form of an ever-present threat. A firm may innovate to deter potential competition in existing markets. A model of a profit-maximising entrepreneur may fail to explain a firm's decisions to innovate if profitability of innovation is measured without taking into account the effects of potential rivalry.

Schumpeter's work regarding the relationship between market structure and innovation can be summarised in two hypotheses:

1. There is a positive relationship between innovation and monopoly power
2. Large firms are more than proportionately more innovative than small firms.

Before discussing the justifications for these two hypotheses, it should be noted that Schumpeter claimed that these hypotheses hold, *all others being equal*. Two things that may not be equal are the level of scientific knowledge (e.g. stationary vs growing) and the industry's growth rates and profit opportunities. In other words, among others, market-pull and technology-push hypotheses have to be controlled for in estimating the effects of monopoly power and firm size on the pace of innovation.

4.3.1 Monopoly and Innovation

The relationship between monopoly and innovation runs both ways. Firstly, an innovating firm must enjoy a period of monopoly over its innovation long enough for the internalised revenues to cover development cost. As argued before, immediate imitation by rivals eliminates any potential profits while costs remains. Therefore, the anticipation of a temporary monopoly is essential if firms are to invest in R&D activities. On the other hand, a firm that has a monopoly power over its present products may be able to extend that power to its new products (e.g. through monopolisation of channels of distribution). Also, to the extent that R&D activities, due to their riskiness, have to be financed internally, a monopolist earning extraordinary profits is more likely to be able to finance R&D projects than a firm earning only normal profits. Put in other words, a monopolist is more able to finance a larger number of parallel R&D projects so as to reduce technical uncertainty associated with these activities. A firm with limited internal resources will be reluctant to invest heavily in a single R&D project which may fail in terms of generating an innovation.

4.3.2 Firm Size and Innovation

The second hypothesis associated with Schumpeter, and developed more fully by Galbraith (1952), relates to the relationship between innovation and firm size. This hypothesis states that larger firms are more than proportionately more innovative than smaller ones. Arguments put forward to support this hypothesis can also be used to further support the first hypothesis to the extent that monopoly power is associated with large firms. The advantages larger firms enjoy over smaller ones stem from the development cost associated with R&D activities, the expected benefits generated by the innovation, and the interaction between these two. As is the case with a monopolist, larger firms will typically allocate more resources to R&D activities enabling them to increase the expected number of successful projects (by running multiple projects for a number of potential innovations), and the probability of success for a given project (by running parallel projects to achieve the same innovation). Economies of scale and scope in R&D activities, if any, suggest that larger firms might incur relatively smaller total development cost per R&D project than smaller firms. On the benefits side, firms with larger market share are likely to benefit more from the adoption of a new cost-reducing process innovation than firms with relatively smaller market shares. Larger firms also have more incentives to innovate a new product if they are able to build on their penetration of existing markets (e.g. through brand name, channels of distribution, experienced marketing staff, etc). Nelson (1959) argued that a larger firm may be better equipped to exploit the innovation of an unforeseen product because it can more easily establish a new market, given its reputation. The cost and benefits of innovations cannot be examined separately for it is the difference between these two that determines the profitability of innovations.

For an innovation to be profitable the sale of the new product or the output produced using the new process must exceed the break-even output level (i.e. the output level at which the benefits of the innovation equals the development cost). Because the cost of innovation development is generally independent of output size larger firms are likely to consider a greater number of potential innovations as profitable than relatively smaller firms or are more likely to consider a given innovation as profitable than smaller firms. This is the case even if we assume an equal break-even output level for all firms, even though the arguments stated above regarding the development cost suggest a lower break-even output level for larger firms (i.e. due to lower development cost).

4.4 THE INCENTIVE TO INNOVATE

4.4.1 The Arrow Model

The first formal model of the incentive to innovate under different market structures was developed by Arrow (1962). In this paper the incentives to innovate are represented by the profit potential that an innovator can earn. The potential returns to an invention of a new process for a using industry is compared under the assumption that the using industry is either competitive or monopolistic. Both are then compared with what is socially optimal. The using industry is characterised by Figure 4.1 below. The using industry faces demand curve DD and pre-invention constant average costs CC. If monopolised, the monopolist user will price where marginal revenue equals costs (i.e. the intersection between CC and MR) and will therefore supply quantity Q_m at price P_m and earn profit π_A. If the industry is competitive, however, it will supply Q_C and P_C and earn zero profit. Now let us assume that an entrepreneur from outside the industry introduces a cost-reducing innovation which will lower production costs to $C'C'$. If the innovator charges the competitive using industry a royalty rate r per unit of output, the competitive price after the invention will be $P' = C' + r$ but this has to be lower than C for firms to adopt

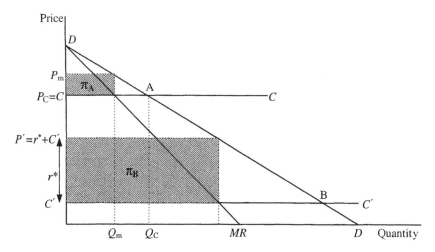

Figure 4.1 The incentive to invent

the innovation. The inventor selling to a competitive industry sets the royalty rate r so as to maximise the size of the rectangle π_B in Figure 4.1 (i.e. maximise rQ with respect to r subject to $r \leq P_C - C'$). This can be achieved by choosing a value for $r = r^*$ such that the quantity demanded is where marginal revenue, MR, is equal to $C'C'$. The returns to the innovation are represented by the area π_B in Figure 4.1. Therefore an entrepreneur will be willing to invest so long as the cost of developing the innovation is less than π_B.[1]

We next consider the incentives to innovate when the using industry is a monopoly. The inventor in this case can be assumed to be either from outside the industry or the monopolist itself leading to the same conclusions. Let us consider the former case. The innovator charges the monopolist a lump sum rather than a per unit royalty since the latter would cause the monopolist to restrict output. The most the innovator can charge is the monopolist's increase in profits between pre- and post-innovation periods. As in the pre-innovation situation, the monopolist will continue to price its output where marginal revenue equals average costs, C' in the post-innovation situation. The post-innovation profits of the monopolist is equal to π_B while the increase in profits will be equal $\pi_A - \pi_B$. So, even assuming that the innovator is able to claim the entire increase in profits from the monopolist, his/her incentives to innovate (i.e. $\pi_B - \pi_A$) is less than those that can be obtained by innovating for a competitive industry (π_B). The innovator selling to a competitive industry would be willing to innovate if his/her cost is less than π_B while an innovator selling to a monopolist (or the monopolist) would be willing to innovate only if the cost is less than $\pi_B - \pi_A$. Therefore, Arrow (1962) concludes that the incentive to innovate is larger in the competitive case than in the monopoly case. The key to this result lies in the fact that the innovator is able to extract the full profit potential resulting from the lower cost curve from the competitive industry but not from the monopolist where profits were already being made in the pre-innovation period. As Davies (1989, p. 198) puts it, 'this conclusion may be likened to the somewhat vague assertion sometimes made that monopolists may be less motivated to innovate precisely because they are able to earn super-normal profits in the first place'. This implies that competitive markets will attract more research and inventive activity than monopolistic markets. The reason behind this being that some inventions would never proceed to innovation because costs exceed returns for the innovator given a monopolistic using industry, while they would not if the using industry were competitive.

The second important issue that Arrow's paper deals with is the divergence between private and social benefits due to the adoption of the innovation. The social benefits in this analysis are computed as the increase in the sum of producer and consumer surplus. This surplus is equal to the triangle $p_C AD$ in the pre-innovation situation and $P'ED$ in the post-innovation period. This generates an increase in surplus equal to the trapezium $P_C AEP'$. If the market was managed by a social planner, however, it would be optimal for price to be equated to the new lower costs curve $C'C'$. This would have generated an increase in surplus equal to the trapezium $CABC'$ which is always larger than $P_C AEP'$ for any $r > 0$. Moreover, since $CABC'$ is larger π_B, it is clear that the private benefits are less than the potential for social benefits. The implications of this result is that some innovations will never take place under either structure because the costs exceed the private benefits, even though these costs are smaller than the social benefits. Based on the above analysis, Arrow (1962) concludes that competitive markets will attract more research and inventive activity than will monopolistic industries, and that both will lead to under-investment in innovation development programmes when compared with what is socially optimal.

4.4.2 The Arrow–Demsetz Model

Demsetz (1969) argues that Arrow (1962) compares monopoly and competition on unequal terms. Specifically, Demsetz (1969, p. 16) points out two extraneous issues which he argues influence Arrow's analysis:

1. The innovator is assumed to possess a monopoly power which enables him/her to discriminate in the royalty charges he/she sets for the two industries
2. Arrow (1962) ignores the differences in the size of the output of both

industries. Although Arrow (1962) assumes that both industries face identical demand and cost conditions, the output under monopoly is smaller than under competition.

Demsetz (1969) argues that the analysis should take into consideration the fact that a monopolist will use less of all inputs, including an innovation, because he/she produces less output. The demonstration of any *special* effect of monopoly on the incentive to invent requires that adjustments be made for this normally restrictive monopoly behaviour. The restrictive effect of monopoly on output can be removed by equating the pre-innovation outputs of the two hypothetical industries. In terms of Figure 4.1, Demsetz (1969) suggests that *MR* be defined to be the demand curve facing the competitive industry. Under this scenario, and ignoring any adjustments to royalties charges, Demsetz shows that Arrow's (1962) conclusions are reversed. That is; the development of a monopoly invention with price discriminating power will receive greater rewards from a buying industry that is a monopoly.

The apparent contradiction of the results of the works by Arrow (1962) and Demsetz (1969) stimulated further research on market structure and the incentives to innovate. Kamien and Schwartz (1970) show that in the context of the Arrow–Demsetz model differences in demand elasticities can matter. They follow Demsetz's (1969) model in comparing industries of equal initial output size. Their comparisons involved variation of industry structure (monopoly and competition) and variation of industry demand elasticity. Specifically, they show that the more elastic the industry demand curve is, the greater the incentives to invent regardless of the internal structure of the industry. In comparing a competitive industry with a monopoly, they found that the monopoly will have greater incentives to innovate provided that the industry demand curves are equally elastic.

Demsetz's (1969) requirement of equal pre-innovation output levels of a monopolistic and a competitive industry leads to the assumption that the demand conditions confronting the two industries are different; in fact that demand is twice as great at any price under monopoly than under competition. Ng (1971) shows that this assumption implies that the post-innovation output level is twice as great under monopoly than under competition, and that is the main reason why Demsetz (1969) is able to produce contradicting results to Arrow's (1962) findings. He further shows that when *both* the pre-innovation and post-innovation output levels in the two industries are equal, Arrow's (1962) main conclusion remains valid. The inappropriateness of Demsetz's (1969) model for policy purposes is neatly summarised by Kamien and Schwartz (1970, p. 243): 'For even though we can draw our diagrams to equalise the outputs of a competitive industry and a monopolistic industry, it does not follow that we can achieve the same results in the real world, or indeed that we would want to do so. The fact that reorganisation of an industry will cause output to expand should make a difference in determining antitrust policy.' This view is further shared by Clarke (1985) who points out that the standard of comparisons used by Arrow (1962) seems to be the more appropriate for policy issues concerning the monopolisation or deconcentration of *existing* industries.

4.4.3 Schumpeter versus Arrow

The last two sections discussed two seemingly contradictory views of the relationship between market structure and the innovative activity; namely those of Schumpeter and Arrow. In this section we re-examine Arrow's (1962) theory with the Schumpeterian hypotheses in mind. The discussion is mainly centred around the monopoly effects on innovative activity with the implicit assumption that monopoly power is associated with large firms. First we consider the hypotheses that monopoly is more conducive for innovation compared with competition. The following arguments can be put forward to support this hypotheses:

1. Higher profit potential: a monopoly with a large market will gain more, in absolute terms, as a result of a cost-reducing process innovation
2. Cost advantage: to the extent that monopoly is associated with 'bigness' and that there are economies of scale in R&D activities, the cost of developing an invention is lower for larger firms
3. Interaction between 1 and 2 above: as innovation development costs tend to be independent of the output level (i.e. fixed-costs) while the returns on the innovation are dependent on the output level, firms with larger market shares will consider a larger number of potential R&D projects than firms with relatively smaller market share
4. Smaller discount rate due to the absence of uncertainty regarding rivals' reactions: the discount rate used to compute the present value of the expected returns on R&D projects (returns-cost) will depend on the uncertainty associated with these returns. Clearly, in a competitive industry rivalry will increase the probability of the innovation being imitated or superseded by competitive innovations
5. Ability to finance R&D projects: to the extent that R&D are financed internally (i.e. retained earnings) because of their riskiness, smaller firms will consider a smaller number of R&D projects than firms with larger profits flows
6. Diversification due to economies of scope: larger firms can reduce the riskiness of R&D activities by running multiple projects at the same time. A larger firm is more able to absorb the potential losses associated with failing projects.

With the above arguments in mind, Arrow's (1962) model can be re-examined from a new perspective. This helps us to appreciate the significance of some of the implicit assumptions underlying Arrow's (1962) model:

1. Monopoly of the innovative activity: as pointed out by Needham (1975), Arrow (1962) assumes that the innovation itself is monopolised. This assumption tends to exaggerate the profit potential for an innovator who is one of the firms in the industry, since according to Arrow's formulation the rewards to innovate are a function of the *industry's total output* as opposed to the innovator's market share. Also, in the absence of rivalry in the inventive activity, Arrow's (1962) model ignores the differences in the uncertainty associated with R&D projects as should be reflected in the discount rate
2. Equal costs: by focusing solely on the returns on a single innovation as a measure of the incentives to innovate it is implicitly assumed that the development costs are equal whether the innovator is a monopolist or one of the firms in a competitive industry. We know however that one argument favouring monopoly is economies of scale and scope in R&D processes leading to lower aggregate development costs for a monopolist
3. Equal resources: by ignoring the costs of innovation development, Arrow's (1962) model rules out the possibility of a longer list of innovations available to larger firms as opposed to firms in a competitive industry. That is, assuming that R&D budgets are largely financed internally, Arrow's (1962) model ignores potential financing advantages that a monopolist may have over firms in a competitive industry.

To summarise, the main limitations of Arrow's (1962) model are that it ignores competition in the inventive process and that it does not incorporate the cost of developing inventions into the analysis. The discussion in the previous section suggests that more specific models of individual-firm decision making are needed to deal with the question of market structure and innovative activity. Neither Schumpeter's informal hypotheses nor Arrow's general model is regarded as adequate to provide a comprehensive analysis of this issue. As pointed out by Davies (1989), some of the theoretical literature discussed in the next three sections can be viewed as attempts to meet such criticisms.

4.5 PACE OF DEVELOPMENT AND TIMING OF INNOVATION

The literature on the process of innovation discussed in the previous sections ignored an important aspect of this process, namely the speed of innovation with rivalry among potential innovators. This aspect of innovation has attracted considerable attention in the theoretical literature throughout the 1970s and 1980s. Competition among potential innovators is thought of as a race to be first in introducing an innovation. The introduction date, or completion date, is a function of the amount of resources an innovator devotes to the development of a new product or process, in either a deterministic or stochastic way. There is a monetary reward for being first which is usually higher than that of being second. The innovator enjoys a period of monopoly of the innovation until rivals imitate. An imitator may diminish the reward to the innovator. The main questions addressed at the firm level are how profits and costs determine the speed of development of an innovation, and how the optimal pace of innovation is affected by the competitive environment in which the firm operates. At the industry level, the main questions are how the intensity of rivalry affects the pace of innovation, do monopolistic and oligopolistic industries innovate more rapidly than competitive ones, and how do they compare with what is socially optimal.

A review of modern theories of market structure and innovation should begin with the work of Scherer (1967) and Barzel (1968). The influence of these two papers can be observed in most of the subsequent literature on innovation and market structure. This section discusses the basic approaches adopted in these two models. The next two sections review the development of the subsequent literature.

4.5.1 Scherer's Model

Scherer (1967) analyses the phenomenon of research and development rivalry in a dynamic profit maximisation framework based on predictions about which type of market structure is most conducive to rapid technological progress. In this model, a profit-maximising firm will conduct its R&D projects so as to maximise the surplus of expected revenues over expected costs, each stream discounted to present value. The revenues from successful R&D projects depend on the completion date, the customer demand, and the reactions of rivals. The costs depend upon the state of technology, the quality of the end product, and the speed of development. It is assumed that when time is saved by increasing the rate of spending the total cost of development increases. Scherer (1967) puts forward the following arguments in favour of this inverse time–cost relationship:

1. R&D is a heuristic process where each sequential step provides knowledge useful in the next step. Saving time by overlapping steps means more and more actions (or steps) are taken with less amount of prior knowledge, resulting in more costly mistakes

2. R&D often involves significant uncertainties about feasible solutions. Expected time to successful solution can be reduced by running technical approaches concurrently, but this increases the expected value of project cost because more approaches which will ultimately prove unnecessary will be run
3. Development time can be compressed by allocating more and more technical personnel to each task, but this will increase total expected costs because of diminishing returns to inputs.

Based on these arguments, Scherer (1967) argues that the relationship between the expected value of development time and the expected value of total development cost is generally convex to time and cost coordinates. As time is compressed, total development cost increases $(\partial C/\partial T < 0)$ at an increasing rate $(\partial^2 C/\partial T^2 > 0)$. This characterisation of the time–cost relationship has dominated the subsequent literature in this area. The functional relationship between development time to product introduction T and total expected cost C, given quality objective Q, can be written as:

$$C = \int_0^T c(t, T, Q) \, dt \qquad (4.1)$$

Assuming development effort begins at time $t = 0$. Confronted by a time–cost trade-off, a firm must decide how rapidly to execute its development project. The optimal schedule depends upon the payoffs from saving time in introducing the innovation. Assuming for the moment that this is a game against nature situation (i.e. no rivalry), then the firm must estimate the stream of quasi-rents flowing from the innovation, $\nu(t)$, and discount them to present value at the rate r. The discount rate r reflects the opportunity cost of committing scarce R&D resources to the project and perhaps also a premium for uncertainty. Assuming that the development project is initiated at time $t = 0$, is brought to the point of commercialisation in T years, and that the end product becomes obsolete at time $t = H$, the total expected benefits flowing from the project can be given by:

$$V = \int_T^H \nu(t) e^{-rt} \, dt \qquad (4.2)$$

The firm's problem is then to maximise the surplus π of discounted expected returns V over discounted expected development costs C with respect to the length of development period T. The first order condition for a maximum gives:

$$\nu(T) e^{rt} = -\frac{\partial C}{\partial T} \qquad (4.3)$$

Equation 4.3 implies that the discounted increase in quasi-rents due to introducing the product one period earlier must at the optimum equal the discounted increase in cost due to completing the development effort one period earlier. Before the analysis is extended to account for rivalry, certain simplifying assumptions are needed. The first is that only one new product quality level is considered by all firms. All firms share a single quality objective. Second, it is assumed that rivals have identical time–cost trade-off functions. Third, it is assumed that $t = 0$ when at least one of the firms begins development. That is, t is neutralised to zero whenever, or for whatever reason, a new product rivalry begins.

Scherer (1967) considers two main types of product innovation rivalry: the introduction of product improvements which, if not matched, leads to changes in participants' market shares within a market of a given size; and the introduction of completely new products. The formulation of the profitability of innovations will differ in these two cases. Let us first consider the case where the innovation is a completely new product (as opposed to an improvement in existing products). In what follows, we consider a two firms industry. Let the potential quasi-rents attainable from the sale of the new product be estimated at V per year. Further, assume that the profit making potential of a new product is likely to decline over time due to exogenous technological obsolescence at a rate of 100σ per cent per year. The discounted quasi-rent potential for year t will therefore be Ve^{-pt}, where $p = r + \sigma$.

The proportion of the potential profits that an innovator will actually realise will depend on the rate at which the new market is being cultivated and won, and the ability of the innovator to overcome consumers' resistance to change. Let the 'penetration coefficient' γ indicate the proportion of the unexploited quasi-rent potential captured each year, then this gradual penetration process can be represented by letting the innovator's *discounted total quasi-rent realisations* in the absence of imitation be written as:

$$V_L = \int_{T_L}^{\infty} [1.0 - e^{-\gamma(t-T_L)}] V e^{-pt}\, dt, \tag{4.4}$$

where the firm (the leader) starts receiving profit flows at time T_L. The gradual penetration process is reflected in the $e^{-\gamma(t-T_L)}$ term which will approach zero as t (time) increases resulting in a 100% realisation percentage. The larger the penetration coefficient γ is, the faster the actual market realisation will approach the potential one, and the larger the innovator's total discounted quasi-rent will be. Now we can consider the effect of imitation. Assume that an imitator's quasi-rents depend on its 'target' share, S_F^*, of the new market and the rate at which it can build up sales to reach that target share (100μ per cent each year following imitation). S_F^* will depend primarily upon the firm's share of related markets, the strength of its distributional organisation, its advertising coverage, *et cetera*. The imitator's total quasi-rent realisations V_F can be written as:

$$V_F = \int_{T_F}^{\infty} [S_F^* - S_F^* e^{-\mu(t-T_F)}] V e^{-pt}\, dt, \tag{4.5}$$

where the imitator moves towards full realisation of its share at a rate of 100μ per cent each year following imitation. The larger the value of μ is, the sooner the imitator will realise his full target market share, and the larger his total discounted quasi-rent will be.[2] The imitator's total quasi-rent realisations V_F can be modified to account for the possibility that the imitator will not achieve its target share due to delay in imitating. This can be represented by letting the imitator's target share decay 100ε per cent for every year of imitation lag:

$$V_F = \int_{T_F}^{\infty} [S_F^* e^{-\varepsilon(T_F - T_L)} - S_F^* e^{-\varepsilon(T_F - T_L) - \mu(t - T_F)}] V e^{-pt} \, dt, \qquad (4.6)$$

where the follower starts receiving profit flows at time T_F and $T_F > T_L$ (i.e. the leader innovates earlier than the follower). Equation (4.6) is identical to equation (4.5) when $\varepsilon = 0$; that is, for the special case of no permanent market share erosion due to delay in imitating. The innovator's quasi-rent equation becomes:

$$V_L = \int_{T_L}^{\infty} [1.0 - e^{-\gamma(t - T_L)}] V e^{-pt} \, dt$$

$$- \int_{T_F}^{\infty} [S_F^* e^{-\varepsilon(T_F - T_L)} - S_F^* e^{-\varepsilon(T_F - T_L) - \mu(t - T_F)}] V e^{-pt} \, dt. \qquad (4.7)$$

Now consider the market-sharing rivalry model. During its period of technological leadership an innovator in a market-sharing game captures more and more of its rival's market share. Part of this won market share is temporary and is won at a rate of δ per cent per year of leadership and recovered at a rate of β per cent per year by the imitator after imitating. The rest of the market-share winnings are permanent and this is expressed by the permanent market-share erosion coefficient ε (the percentage erosion of imitator's market share for each year of delay in imitating). The innovator's quasi-rent in a market-sharing case is:

$$V_L = \int_{T_L}^{T_F} [S_F - S_F e^{-\delta(t - T_L)}] V e^{-pt} \, dt + \int_{T_F}^{\infty} [S_F - S_F e^{-\varepsilon(T_F - T_L)}] V e^{-pt} \, dt$$

$$+ \int_{T_F}^{\infty} [-S_F e^{-\delta(T_F - T_L)} + S_F e^{-\varepsilon(T_F - T_L)}] e^{-\beta(t - T_F)} V e^{-pt} \, dt, \qquad (4.8)$$

where S_F is the imitating firm's original market share. Note that in a market-sharing case, and given a constant market size, the only source of the innovator's quasi-rent from the sale of the improved product is the rival's original quasi-rents; that is, this is a zero sum game. What is won by an innovator must be lost by a rival who eventually becomes an imitator. The first term in equation (4.8) is the innovator's gain during its leadership period, the second its gain following imitation due to the permanent erosion of its rival's market share, and the third its temporary gain following imitation before the imitator fully recovers its new permanent share. As time passes after the imitation, the term $e^{-\beta(t-T_F)}$ approaches zero and the innovator earns no more quasi-rent due to temporary erosion of the imitator's market share. The larger the value of β, the sooner this happens. Since the innovator's gain must be the imitator's loss in a pure market-sharing rivalry, the imitator's quasi-rent equation is simply the negative of equation (4.8). When the rivals have identical product introduction dates ($T_L = T_F$), no change in market shares occurs and $V_1 = V_F = 0$.

Scherer (1967) derives a Cournot-reaction equilibrium in which each firm is assumed to maximise its own profit with respect to its own development time taking its rival's development time as a parameter. In the general case in which an innovating firm leads the way, he shows that for both market-sharing and new product innovation:

1. The deeper the potential stream of quasi-rents at stake is, the shorter an innovating firm's optimal time of development will be, *ceteris paribus*
2. The larger its rival's actual or target market share is, the stronger an innovator's incentive to conduct its development project rapidly. This suggests that smaller firms have more to gain by rapid innovations than larger firms. Note, however, that the incentive to conduct development project rapidly is only considered from the point of view of an innovator
3. The permanent share erosion coefficient ε has a critical influence on innovator reactions to changes in rival's schedule changes. The higher ε is, the more likely aggressive reactions to rival's accelerations are, and the stronger the reactions will be.

The analysis above assumes that the innovator's sales growth is dependent mainly upon the amount of unexploited market potential. This ignores the possibility that firms may be unable to tap sales growth fully because physical and organisational bottlenecks constrain the rate at which they can expand production and sales. Small firms may have an advantage in innovating but they are usually disadvantaged in terms of their production and marketing capabilities. As Scherer (1967) argues, a small innovator's market penetration may be governed by internal growth limits initially, and by unexploited market potential only when a certain critical level size is attained. By limiting the market share growth rate per year, Scherer (1967) finds that the larger the innovator's market share (the smaller the rival's market share), the stronger its incentive to conduct the development rapidly. This is a reversal of the earlier conclusion in favour of relative smallness. 'Thus, we find that relatively small firms subjected to sales growth constraints are not nearly the innovative tigers they are when their penetration into dominant firm positions is limited only by customer loyalties and similar friction summarised in the takeover coefficient δ or the penetration coefficient γ. Whether this or our earlier conclusion describes the actual position of small firms is an empirical question (Scherer, 1967, p. 388).

Finally, Scherer (1967) considers the more realistic case of an industry with N firms. Using certain simplifying assumptions, he finds that the greater the number of potential new market entrants, the stronger the incentive an innovating firm will have to develop its new product quickly and to accelerate its development effort in response to rival accelerations. An increase in the number of firms beyond that value which permits all participants to anticipate earnings profits could discourage vigorous research and development. An overcrowded new market may encourage firms to redirect their R&D resources into less competitive fields. The higher the market's overall quasi-rent potential is, the higher N can be without having this adverse impact.

Scherer (1980) summarised his earlier work using the diagram depicted in Figure 4.2. The V and C curves represent the benefits and development cost of a product innovation confronting a would-be innovator. The horizontal axis measures the introduction time of the innovation (and not time). That is, Figure 4.2 depicts a *static* situation where a would-be innovator can choose the optimal introduction time which would maximise his expected surplus of benefits over development cost. Initially, let us assume that the benefits and development costs facing the firm are V_1 and C, respectively. A profit maximising firm would choose optimal introduction time T_1 at which marginal losses from a moment's delay equals marginal benefits.

Scherer (1980) argues that the competitive environment affects the location

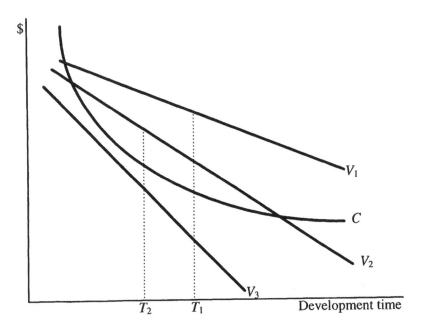

Figure 4.2 Optimal speed of new product development

of the V curve in two ways; its slope and its location. V becomes steeper and lower as market concentration declines. The justification for this is that as the number of rivals increases, the portion the innovator gets to enjoy during its term of leadership increases. A monopolist can benefit from no market share effect and increased revenues can only come from expanding the total market or charging higher prices for the improved product. The time dimension in this model is reflected in shifts that occur to either the V or the C curve. Scherer (1980) refers to changes in the slope of the V curve due to increased rivalry as the *stimulus factor*. This is shown in Figure 4.2 (from V_1 to V_2) where the profit maximising introduction date is now T_2. This increase in rivalry has the effect of compressing development time and increasing benefits. An increase in rivalry also shifts the benefits function down and to the left (V_3). Scherer (1980) refers to this effect as the *market room factor*. This is the case because after imitation takes place the innovator will find itself dividing up the market's total profit potential with more rivals and enjoying a smaller share itself, all else being equal. Also, a large number of rivals may lead to a breakdown in pricing discipline causing not only the innovator's share of the profit pie, but also the pie itself to shrink. An increase in rivalry that leads to a shift in the V_1 curve to V_2 in Figure 4.2, for example, means that the innovation will never be profitable and the firm will not introduce it.

This model can be useful in defining demand-pull and technology-push innovations. Let us assume that initially the firm faces the V_3 and C curves. For the firm to introduce the innovation, the C curve must fall below the V_3 for at least some values of T. This can happen as a result of two factors. On the one hand, population growth or a rise in *per capita* income may shift the benefits curve in a north-easterly direction. On the other hand, advances in basic knowledge may cause either a smooth continuous or a sudden downward shift to the C curve to the point that it would lie at least partially below the benefits curve. Demand-pull innovations are rendered attractive by rising demand (upward shifts in the V curve). Technology-push innovations are induced by advances in knowledge (downward shifts in the C curve). Usually both supply and demand conditions are changing, and innovation may be induced by a combination of both forces. It should be recalled that the analysis is considered from the point of view of individual firms, and therefore for an innovation to be introduced it is sufficient that at least one firm's C curve lies below that firm's V curve for some introduction time T.

To summarise Scherer's (1967, 1980) conclusions, rapid innovation is likely where the number of sellers is greater, and concentration is lower (the stimulus effect), but beyond some lower limit on concentration, the stimulus to innovation may be killed off by fears that the innovation's returns can not be internalised long enough to compensate potential innovators for the development cost (the market room). The work by Scherer has been very influential in the subsequent literature on *game-theoretic* models of innovation.

4.5.2 Barzel's Model

The main goal of Barzel's (1968) model is to demonstrate the effects of rivalry on the introduction time of innovation as compared to what would be socially optimal. He argues that innovations are introduced when their present value is positive rather than waiting until the profits are maximised. Specifically, Barzel (1968) assumes that innovations can be introduced by investing a once-and-for-all amount of resources in R&D activities. Innovations are introduced when they are profitable. If the economy is stationary, no innovations are introduced since an innovation which is profitable today would have been profitable all along and would have been introduced earlier. When the economy is not stationary, the output of a commodity affected by the innovation is expanding over time, and the innovation will become progressively more profitable. This is because the cost of introducing the innovation is independent of the output affected while the revenues are proportional to the output. Formally, Barzel (1968) assumes the following:

1. The capital cost of developing an innovation is constant and equal to I dollars
2. The innovation, adopted without a delay by the entire industry, reduces the cost of each unit of output by k dollars without affecting its quality.
3. The demand for the competitively produced output is X_0 in the initial period ($t = 0$) and it grows at a continuous rate p. Hence, demand at time t will be given by the exponential function $X_t = X_0 e^{pt}$.
4. The royalty rate is set at $h = k$ dollars per unit of output. If the innovation is being applied at the initial period, total royalty earnings are $hX_0 = S_0$.
5. Only one innovator is associated with a given innovation.
6. The instantaneous and constant rate of discount is r.
7. The parameters of the system are widely and accurately known.

Assumption 4 enables us to measure social saving by solving for the innovator's profit since no benefits are passed to consumers and the only beneficiary is the innovator himself. The profitability of the innovation is measured by its net present value, R_0. The present value of an innovation is the difference between the discounted stream of benefits that grow at the rate p per period and the discounted value of the investment in the innovation. If the stream of benefits begins when the innovation investment is completed, at time t, the present value of the innovation is:

$$R_0 = \int_t^\infty S_0 e^{-(r-p)\tau} \, d\tau - Ie^{-rt}, \qquad (4.9)$$

where

$$r < p, \qquad (4.10)$$

and

$$R_0 = \frac{S_0 e^{-(r-p)t}}{r-p} - Ie^{-rt}. \tag{4.11}$$

The value of t, $t(m)$, which will maximise the present value of the innovation, is:

$$t(m) = \frac{\ln r + \ln I - \ln S_0}{p}, \tag{4.12}$$

where[3]

$$0 < p < r. \tag{4.13}$$

From equation (4.12), we can see that the higher the initial benefits (S_0), and the faster the rate at which they grow, (p), the smaller is $t(m)$ and the earlier is the introduction date for maximum present value. *Conversely*, the larger the investment required (I) and the higher the discount rate (r), the later the maximising introduction date.

From equation (4.11) we can obtain the point in time at which the net present value of the innovation will be zero:

$$t(z) = \frac{\ln(r-p) + \ln I - \ln S_0}{p} \tag{4.14}$$

Comparing equation (4.14) with (4.12) we see that $t(z) < t(m)$ since $p > 0$, and the point of zero present value will be reached earlier than the point of maximum present value. Figure 4.3 depicts the behaviour of revenues and costs as a function of the time lapsed after the introduction of the innovation. Both curves are declining exponentially. The revenues curve declines more slowly due

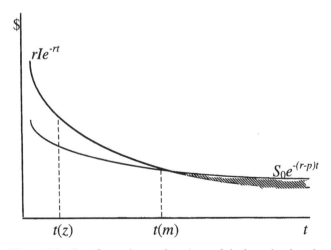

Figure 4.3 Benefits and costs functions of the introduction time

to the positive rate of growth in output. The cost curve reflects the interest rate that would have been earned had I not been invested in innovation development. The two curves intersect when introduction time is equal to $t(m)$. Earlier than this date, the innovator's costs per unit of time will be larger than his benefits and the innovator will be better off to wait. On the other hand, at any date later than $t(m)$ the benefits per unit of time will be larger than the costs, and the innovator could have increased his profits by advancing the date of his investment activity. At $t(m)$ benefits are equal to costs, and this is the profit maximising date.

The shaded area between the two curves to the right of $t(m)$ in Figure 4.3 represents the net present value of the innovation if it is introduced at time $t(m)$. If the innovation is introduced at time $t(z)$, the net present value will be zero, since the present value of losses between $t(z)$ and $t(m)$ is equal to the present value of profits beyond $t(m)$. If the innovation is introduced after $t(z)$ but before $t(m)$, the net present value will be positive but will not be maximised.

In the absence of competition, the innovator will introduce the innovation at time $t(m)$ so as to maximise the present value of the investment. Under the stated conditions, maximum private value is identical with maximum social present value. If, however, the invention was not monopolised as was assumed above, then each firm realises that other firms can earn positive profits by introducing earlier than $t(m)$ and the introduction date will be pushed all the way back to $t(z)$. Threat of entry thus will drive profits, and social saving, to zero.

Barzel (1968) extends the previous analysis by relaxing some of the assumptions stated above. Two cases are worth noting. Firstly, the innovator's profit may diverge from the social benefits if the royalty rate h' charged by the innovator is less than k, cost saving per unit of output. Table 4.1 summarises the effects on social and private benefits of different market structures (monopoly versus competition) and different values of h ($h = k$ and $h < k$). Secondly, I was assumed to be constant in the previous analysis. A breakthrough in basic knowledge may be viewed as reducing the investment required to introduce a given innovation. If this occurs, i.e. a downward shift in the cost curve in

Table 4.1 Market structure and timing of innovation

	State of competition in innovational activity	
	Monopoly	Competition
$h < k$	Optimal social timing Maximum private PV Maximum social PV	Introduction date too early Zero private PV Zero social PV
$h = k$	Introduction date too late Maximum private PV Positive social PV	Introduction date intermediate Zero private PV Positive social PV

Figure 4.3, the profitability and the timing of the innovation will be affected (and $t(m)$ and $t(z)$ will be relatively smaller). Notice that in Barzel's (1968) model, monopoly and competition are characteristics of the innovative activity rather than the using industry. Competition is shown again to push the introduction date to the modified $z(t)$ and the advancement in basic knowledge is economically wasted.[4]

According to Barzel's (1968) model, the amount of resources devoted to innovating activity is in general not optimal because of two factors. Firstly, competition between potential innovators tend to make this amount too large (*the competition column in Table 4.1*). Secondly, the inability of innovators to capture all the benefits tends to make the amount too small (the $h < k$ row in Table 4.1). The amount of resources devoted to innovating activity is optimal only when the activity itself is monopolised and the innovator is able to capture all the benefits. The work by Barzel (1968) has motivated other researchers to extend his decision-theoretic approach to allow for uncertainty with explicit treatment of strategic interactions between firms.

4.6 DECISION-THEORETIC MODELS OF INNOVATION

Although Barzel's (1968) model deals with more issues than Arrow's (1962), such as competition in the innovating activity and the cost function, it remains vague in its treatment of other issues. The model assumes that the parameters of the system are widely and accurately known. For example, it is not clear how firms' expectations of rivals' actions lead to equilibrium. More importantly, uncertainty is not incorporated explicitly into the model. Moreover, the cost function is assumed to be independent of the length of the development period (Ie^{-rt} is decreasing with t but not I itself). In a series of papers in the 1970s (Kamien and Schwartz, 1972, 1974a, 1974b, 1976, 1978a, 1978b, 1980), later summarised in Kamien and Schwartz (1982), the authors set out to extend Barzel's (1968) model into a more general framework which explicitly specifies how each firm takes into account the presence of rivals. The main theoretical difference between Kamien and Schwartz's (1982) model in comparison to that of Barzel (1968), is that the former expresses the return to an innovation as the weighted average of returns to the innovator and returns to imitators. This allows us to incorporate uncertainty in the innovating activity. That is, the probability of a competitor introducing the innovation before a certain time is incorporated explicitly into the model in computing expected returns. To facilitate a clear discussion of Kamien and Schwartz's (1982) model, let us use the following notation:

$r \equiv$ flow of profits on current good

$p_0 \equiv$ flow of profits on a new good

$P \equiv$ capitalised value of a stream of receipts on a new good

$g \equiv$ the growth (or decline) rate of the market.

The analysis can be simplified by looking at things from the point of view of a single firm. Let r have a subscript 0 or 1 with 0 indicating that no rival's innovation has been introduced, 1 indicating that a rival's innovation has been introduced. Let P have a subscript of 1 or 2, with 1 indicating that our firm has introduced its innovation prior to rivals and 2 indicating otherwise. Then we have:

$r_0 \equiv$ the profit flow to our firm when no innovation has been introduced,

$r_1 \equiv$ the profit flow to our firm when a rival has introduced an innovation and our firm did not,

$P_1 \equiv$ capitalised value of a stream of receipts on a new good when both firms introduced the innovation but our firm did so first,

$P_2 \equiv$ capitalised value of a stream of receipts on a new good when both firms introduced the innovation but our firm did so second.

Letting T and ν be the times our firm and a rival respectively introduce their new products, the receipts can be summarised as follows:

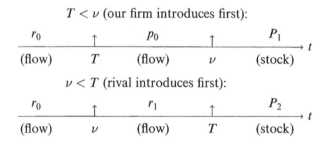

$T < \nu$ (our firm introduces first):

$v < T$ (rival introduces first):

with all receipts multiplied by e^{gt}. All these profits are nonnegative with $r_0 \geq r_1$ (i.e. rival innovation does not increase our firm's profits from an existing good). The rewards to a firm as a monopolist includes all returns from the innovation, whether the firm uses or markets the innovation itself or licenses it to others. The values of P_1 and P_2 may depend on the lags $\nu - T$ and $T - \nu$ respectively. This is not unreasonable since early adopting firms can achieve competitive advantages in terms of larger and more loyal customer bases, distribution channels, and experienced personnel. From the point of view of our firm, and assuming $T < \nu$, the later a follower appears, the greater the foothold we shall have established in the marketplace, so the derivative $P_1' \geq 0$ typically. On the other hand, if $\nu < T$, the greater our lag in following, the smaller is the remaining market, so the derivative $P_2' \leq 0$ typically. To summarise, by accelerating the introduction date, a firm increases its expected profits in two ways; increasing the period during which its profit flow equals p_0 as opposed to r_0 or r_1 in the short run, increasing the probability of earning P_1 as opposed to P_2 in the long run, and increasing the absolute value of P_1 and P_2 if it innovate or imitates, respectively.[5]

Each firm is aware that competing products may appear from a large number of sources including current rivals, firms in other related markets, or new entrants. The intensity of rivalry is characterised by each firm using a single subjective probability distribution over the introduction date of any rival product. Let $F(t)$ be the firm's assessment at time $t = 0$ of the probability that the composite rival will have introduced innovation by time t. Then, the probability density that the composite rival will introduce its innovation in the next moment, given that it has not done so prior to time t, is represented using the hazard function:[6]

$$H(t) = F'(t)/(1 - F(t)) \tag{4.15}$$

Alternatively, Kamien and Schwartz (1982) write the hazard rate as a non-decreasing hazard function $u(t)$, multiplied by a hazard parameter h:

$$H(t) = hu(t) \tag{4.16}$$

This allows us to examine later the effect of the parameter h on the speed of development. An increase in the hazard parameter h results in a constant proportionate increase in the hazard rate. Given equation (4.15), it can be seen that the h is a parameter of the $F(t)$ probability distribution which can be used to measure the intensity of rivalry where larger values of h indicate faster expected rival innovation.

Discounting future profits at rate i, the firm's expected profit stream if it introduces its new product at time T is:[7]

$$W(t) = \int_0^T e^{-(i-g)t}[r_0(1 - F(t)) + r_1 F(t)]\,dt$$

$$+ \int_T^\infty e^{-(i-g)t}[p_0(1 - F(t)) + P_1(t - T)F'(t)]\,dt$$

$$+ \int_0^T e^{-(i-g)T} P_2(T - t)F'(t)\,dt \tag{4.17}$$

In equation (4.17) we simply weight each possible outcome by the probability of its occurrence to arrive at the firm's expected profit stream. The net value of introducing the innovation at time T will depend on the rewards as expressed in equation (4.17), but also on the costs of development. Kamien and Schwartz (1982) adopt the inverse time-cost trade-off introduced by Scherer (1967). In this formulation, the costs of introducing the innovation at time T, $C(T)$, is an inverse function of the length of development time. In support of this formulation, Kamien and Schwartz (1982) argue that the more rapid spending associated with delaying T involves overtime and premiums for more intensive use of factors of production and may involve greater use of parallel rather than sequential lines of enquiry. The second characteristic of the cost function is that as T decreases, i.e. development time is compressed, $C(T)$ increases at a increasing rate. Both classical diminishing returns tendencies and the uncertain features of the R&D process lead to diminishing returns to time compression of research. Therefore,

$$C(T) > 0, \quad C'(T) < 0, \quad C''(T) > 0 \quad \text{for all } T > 0. \tag{4.18}$$

It is further assumed that $C(T)$ is so large that immediate entry is not worthwhile. The difference between the expected rewards from introduction at T and the cost of doing so is:

$$V(T) = W(T) - C(T) \tag{4.19}$$

The components specifying the problem facing the firm are now clear. The firm wishes to maximise $V(T)$ subject to equations (4.17), (4.18), and (4.19). In doing so, the firm decides on the optimal introduction time that maximises equation (4.19), and solves for the amount of resources it has to devote to R&D activities according to a time-cost function described by equation (4.18). For each possible introduction date T there exists a corresponding development cost $C(T)$. This relationship is assumed deterministic, and therefore no technical uncertainty is incorporated into the model. The choice of development time also affects expected rewards $W(T)$, but in a stochastic way. Market uncertainty is reflected in this relationship. The date of rival innovation is unknown but there is sufficient information for precise probabilities to be attached to different possibilities. The choice of the optimal introduction time, T^* involves balancing the marginal gains from a moment's delay (the reduction in $C(T)$), against the marginal cost from doing so (reduction in $W(T)$). While the source of marginal gains due to a moment's delay is clear, the marginal cost is less straightforward. The marginal loss depends on whether or not a rival has already innovated by time T. If no rival's innovation has appeared, then the firm gives up the innovational reward (p_0) in favour of the return on the existing good (r_0) for the period of delay (i.e. marginal loss is reflected in $p_0 - r_0$). In addition, the delay reduces the expected lag between the firm's innovation and rival's imitation if the firm innovates first and increases the expected lag between the rival's innovation and the firm's imitation if the rival innovates first and the firm imitates later. This may reduce the rewards of innovation after a rival's imitation or the rewards of imitation after a rival's innovation if these rewards depend on the length of the lag (i.e. reduced P_1 and P_2). Finally, the delay increases the probability of the rival's innovation before the firm, in which case the firm loses the reward stream to the innovator with followers and gets instead the stream to the follower (i.e. marginal loss reflected in $P_1 - P_2$).

If a rival's innovation has already appeared, then the firm gives up the imitational reward (P_2) in favour of the now reduced receipts on the existing good (r_1) during the delay period. Also, the delay increases the lag between rival's innovation and the firm's imitation which may decrease the total reward stream from imitation (P_2). Kamien and Schwartz derive the following predictions from comparative static analysis of the solution:

The firm will choose to innovate more rapidly (i.e. devote more resources or select a lower T):

1. The greater are the post-innovational profits p_0 and P_1. These rewards stimulate innovations for offensive reasons
2. The smaller are the profits from existing goods, r_0 and r_1. Current profits are lost upon innovation, thereby reducing the net gain from innovation. A new good that does not supplant an existing one marketed by the firm will appear more rapidly than one that replaces a current product, all others being equal. Likewise, other things being equal, the incentive to bring out a new good is greater for a firm that is new to the industry than for an incumbent. However, other things may not be equal because an incumbent may have other advantages not possessed by the new entrant (e.g. customer base, brand name, and marketing experience)[8]
3. The greater the potential loss $r_0 - r_1$ from rival precedence.[9] This potential loss stimulates defensive innovations. This motive is particularly interesting because Kamien and Schwartz (1982) show that large potential losses due to rival precedence may cause firms to develop a less profitable good than the current one.

Conditions 1 and 3 above capture the 'carrot' and 'stick' effects for innovation. Firms innovate to capture high profits rates (carrot effect) or to protect against loss of current profits (stick effect). The carrot effect is stronger the lower are current profits. Firms with small market share in current markets (including new entrants with zero market share) are more likely to innovate the stronger is the carrot effect. Firms with dominant market share (including a monopolist) are more likely to accelerate development the stronger is the stick effect. To solve for the relationship between the intensity of rivalry as measured by the hazard rate h and the speed of development requires further assumptions. Firstly, $P_1 > P_2$ (i.e. having followers is preferable to being a follower). Secondly, these rewards are independent of the lag between innovation and imitation (i.e. $P_1' = P_2' = 0$). Under these assumptions, Kamien and Schwartz (1982) show that there are just two cases. First, the optimal development period may increase with the intensity of rivalry h. In this case, pure monopoly (i.e. $h = 0$) yields the fastest development and thereby the maximum inventive activity. In the second case the optimal development period decreases with increasing rivalry up to a point h^* after which increases in h lead to a lengthening of the development period. In this case, maximum inventive activity, or minimum development period, occurs at an intermediate level of h between competition (h approaches infinity) and monopoly ($h = 0$). Within this framework it is not possible to specify the circumstances under which each alternative holds. By relaxing the assumption that R&D is unalterable in response to the actions of rivals, Kamien and Schwartz (1982) were able to characterise the circumstances under which each alternative will hold. In the modified form of their model, if a firm innovates, rivals may change their development pace, accelerating or decelerating their own efforts as a consequence. Under this condition, they found that pure monopoly will be most conducive to innovation activity for projects offering moderately good improvements in rewards. One the other hand, minimum development time will occur with intermediate levels of rivalry for projects offering a large increase in expected receipts. Moreover, by making more assumptions, they found that the more attractive the project is, the larger will be the development period minimising the degree of rivalry and the shorter will be that minimum development period.

In comparing a nonrivalrous solution with no imitation possible with the firm's optimal introduction date T^* as derived in the previous analysis, Kamien and Schwartz (1982) confirmed Barzel's (1968) result that T^* may be premature or belated compared with the nonrivalrous solution T^*. However, they show that under the strict assumptions imposed by Barzel (e.g. winner takes all, no existing good is being supplanted, and no diminishing returns to compression of the development period), the firm's optimal introduction date is always later than the zero profit introduction date that Barzel (1968) expects. They also show that in a perfectly competitive industry (i.e. zero profit rate on current goods, immediate imitation, no innovational rivalry anticipated, and little innovational rewards after imitation) firms will not undertake development at all. This is not a surprising result because, as noted earlier, models of perfect information with immediate imitation and no barriers to entry cannot explain technical change. The carrot and stick effects tell us that for innovation to take place, there have to be either positive profits on existing goods or potential innovational rewards, both of which are ruled out in perfect competition.

Finally, Kamien and Schwartz (1982) extend the model described above to investigate the effects of a number of factors. These include modifications of the model to address issues such as the existence of a range of innovations, the effects of self-financing, the contractual nature of costs, new product pricing, impossible imitation and costless imitation. Their work has filled a considerable gap in the literature and managed to address issues previously untackled. One area, however, which their work ignores is the game-theoretic aspects of the process of technical change. In focusing on the individual firm's decision, one ignores certain game-theoretic aspects which could alter the results considerably. Consider for example Davies's (1989, p. 204) arguments of how significant the implications of a game-theoretic approach can be:

> ... suppose there is an industry of n identical firms each making the development decision simultaneously, and each knowing how much its rivals intend to spend. Since all firms are identical, all would presumably plan to innovate by the same time. But this will significantly reduce the returns from the new product and each firm might be tempted to spend a little more than its rivals to ensure being first (on Cournot conjectures). However, if all firms act in this way they will all be frustrated and probably incur losses. In fact so long as all these firms perceive this to be the case *ex ante*, none will consider it worthwhile to incur R&D expenditures and no innovation will occur, even though for the individual firm taken in isolation it would appear that innovation is profitable. (This argument is analogous to Scherer's case in which the V-curve lies anywhere below the C-curve.)

Game-theoretic models deal with this issue by explicitly taking into account the interaction between firms' R&D decisions in solving for an equilibrium in which all firms optimise. The late 1970s and post 1980s literature on modelling R&D and innovation decision making is predominantly game-theoretic. The next section discusses developments in this literature.

4.7 GAME-THEORETIC MODELS OF INNOVATION

4.7.1 Winner-Take-All Games of Innovation

While the 1970s literature focused on decision-theoretic models, especially the work of Kamien and Schwartz, game-theoretic models have dominated recent literature on the timing of innovation. The main weakness of decision-theoretic models is that they are partial equilibrium analyses which examine the behaviour of an individual firm that views market conditions, including rival's decisions, parametrically. As Loury (1979, p. 396) points out, 'in a given industry, every firm is the rival of every other firm. Thus, the likelihood of rival precedence depends on the R&D strategies chosen by other market participants, and cannot be treated as a parameter when analysing changes in those decisions'. An individual firm's behaviour (e.g. over-investment versus under-investment) does not necessarily represent the aggregate industry behaviour. Lower investment by all firms, for example, may be outweighed by an increase in the number of firms resulting in over-investment by the industry as a whole.

The general game-theoretic approach avoids the above mentioned limitations by formulating the decision to innovate as a Cournot game. Each firm takes account of other firms' expected behaviour in formulating its optimal strategies, but believes that its strategy will not cause rivals to alter their plans. The first such model was developed by Scherer (1967) and was discussed earlier in the chapter. Scherer's (1967) model assumed a deterministic development cost function where a firm's choice of an R&D intensity level ensures the firm an introduction date T. Recent game-theoretic studies build on Scherer's (1967) work but they model the introduction date of an innovation as a stochastic function of R&D spending. Each firm invests in R&D under both technical and market uncertainty. Market uncertainty implies that firms cannot be certain about a rival's possible innovation date. Technical uncertainty implies that firms, given their spending on R&D projects, cannot be certain about their innovation introduction date (i.e. stochastic cost–time relationship). Most game-theoretic models further assume that the winning firm wins a constant, known, and perpetual flow of rewards V that will become available only to the first firm that introduces an innovation. It is commonly assumed that no resources are committed until all firms make their bid and the winner is determined. Only the winner will spend the budget it has assigned for developing the innovation and all other firms commit no resources. Without this assumption, it may be impossible to derive an equilibrium.[10]

Loury (1979) used such a framework to model the pace of innovation in a given industry consisting of n firms. It is assumed that firm i, by making a contractual commitment to R&D with an implied present value of cost x_i, in effect purchases a random variable $\tau(x_i)$, which represents the uncertain date at which the R&D project will be successfully completed. Loury (1979) assumes the following technological relationship where $\tau(x_i)$ is exponentially distributed:

$$\Pr[\tau(x_i) \le t] = 1 - e^{-h(x_i)t}, \tag{4.20}$$

with an expected time of introduction given by:

$$E\tau(x) = h(x)^{-1}. \tag{4.21}$$

That is, an R&D expenditure at present valued at x buys a firm a probability $h(x)$ that the innovation will be perfected at any subsequent moment. $h(0)$ is assumed to be twice continuously differentiable, strictly increasing, and satisfying:

$$h(0) = 0 = \lim_{x \to \infty} h'(x) \tag{4.22}$$

and

$$h''(x) \ge (\le)0 \quad \text{as} \quad x \le (\ge)\bar{x} \tag{4.23}$$

Equation (4.22) states that there is a point after which $h(x)$ does not increase with increased expenditure x. Equation (4.23) states that there is initially increasing returns to scale in R&D investment up to a point $\bar{x}$ after which diminishing returns are encountered (for $\bar{x} > 0$, Figure 4.4A). Continuous increasing returns to scale are represented by $\bar{x} = 0$ (Figure 4.4B). In Figure 4.4 below, $\tilde{x}$ denotes the point where $h(x)/x$ is greatest.

Loury (1979) incorporates market uncertainty regarding rivals' introduction date by defining $\hat{\tau}_i$ as the random variable representing this unknown date. $\hat{\tau}_i$ is related to the behaviour of other firms as follows:

$$\hat{\tau}_i = \min_{1 \leq j \neq i \leq n} \{\tau(x_j)\} \tag{4.24}$$

Assuming that the random variables $\hat{\tau}_i, i = 1, 2, \ldots, n$, are independent, then:

$$\Pr[\hat{\tau}_i \leq t] = 1 - \exp\left(-t \sum_{i \neq j} h(x_i)\right) = 1 - e^{-a_i t}, \tag{4.25}$$

where

$$a_i \equiv \sum_{i \neq j} h(x_j). \tag{4.26}$$

Let r be the rate at which firms discount future receipts. At any time $t \geq 0$ the ith firm earns revenue flow V in the event that $\tau(x_i) \leq \min(\hat{\tau}_i, t)$. A firm's problem is to choose a spending level x_i, given a_i, r, and V to maximise expected discounted profits. It can be shown that the expected benefit of investing in R&D is given by:

$$\frac{V h(x)}{a + h(x) + r} \tag{4.27}$$

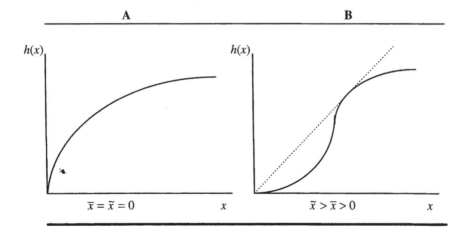

Source: Loury (1979, p. 398)

Figure 4.4 Benefits and costs and the introduction time

Loury (1979) examined the effects of rivalry on firm's equilibrium R&D spending and found that as the number of firms in the industry increases, the equilibrium level of firm investment declines. Moreover, increasing the number of competitors in the industry is shown to reduce the expected time that society has to wait for the innovation despite the fact that each competitor invests less in R&D.

The analysis above examined the optimal firm investment in R&D with a given market structure, (n). Loury (1979) examined the effects of entry on optimal investment decisions using the zero-profit condition; that is, in the absence of barriers to entry, new firms will enter the race as long as expected profits are strictly positive. It is shown that with costless entry and an active zero-profit condition, more firms will enter the race than is socially optimal. The long-run industry equilibrium when there is an initial range of increasing returns and zero expected profits always involves 'excess capacity' in the R&D technology. Firms invest more in R&D than would be socially optimal because they do not take account of the parallel nature of their efforts. In doing so each firm considers only its marginal benefit from investment and does not take into account the reduction it imposes on the expected value of other firms' investment. According to Loury (1979), social welfare can be maximised by appropriately limiting entry and firm investments with licensing fees and finite patent life.

As stated by Loury (1979), the results of the model have been bought at some cost. The implicit assumption of infinite patent life (i.e. no imitation) and therefore no imitation is not very realistic. Although imitation does not affect the socially optimal allocation, it reduces private rewards. If that is the case, and imitation is taken into consideration, firms may not overinvest. Moreover, with imitation, the zero expected profit may be reached with fewer firms, and thus the result that entry barriers can improve welfare may fail. Finally, Loury (1979) assumed that the random variable $\tau(x)$ is purchased by paying x at $t = 0$. This formulation does not allow for firms to adjust their R&D expenditures (e.g. cease investment altogether) if and when the firm or one of its rivals perfects the innovation.

Lee and Wilde (1980) investigated the effect of an alternative specification of R&D spending on the results obtained by Loury (1979). Their models follow that of Loury (1979) (equations (4.20) to (4.27)), but depart from Loury's in their specification of the costs of R&D. They assume that $\tau(x)$ is purchased by paying a fixed cost of F and incurring a flow cost of x. The expected costs (EC) can be written as:

$$EC = \frac{x}{a + h(x) + r} + F \qquad (4.28)$$

Where the first term represents the expected variable cost and F is the fixed cost. The firm maximises the expected profits, $E\pi$, which is equal to the expected benefits (equation (4.27)) minus expected costs (equation (4.28)):

$$E\pi = EB - EC = \frac{Vh(x) - x}{a + h(x) + r} - F \tag{4.29}$$

The firm will continue to pay the flow cost until it, or one of its rivals, perfects the innovation. Expected introduction date is a stochastic function of x only. One may interpret F as entry cost; that is, fixed costs that have to be incurred to enter a new market (or a new R&D race). Recall that Loury (1979) assumed that development costs are contractual; that is, the same amount is spent on R&D whether or not the firm wins the race. Lee and Wilde (1980) showed that Loury's conclusion regarding the effects of an increase in the number of competing firms on a firm's R&D investment level are sensitive to his formulation of R&D costs. When fixed cost is incorporated into the model, Loury's conclusion is reversed; as the number of firms in the industry increases, the equilibrium investment in R&D increases. This finding holds despite the fact that Lee and Wilde (1980) confirmed Loury's (1979) results of decreased expected profits and an earlier expected industry introduction date as a result of an increase in the number of competing firms. As long as expected profits are positive, firms enter, increasing investment levels in R&D and decreasing expected profits. Lee and Wilde compared these results with a situation in which a monopolist controls the industry, but may wish to invest in number of parallel R&D projects. This is analogous to the role that can be played by a social planner, and therefore enables us to analyse investment in R&D which would be socially optimal. They concluded the following:

1. Given a fixed market structure, firms' investment in R&D projects will be, in industry equilibrium, more than is socially optimal.
2. With initial increasing return to scale in the R&D technology, competitive entry leads to a larger number of firms than is socially optimal.

Reinganum (1989) observed that Lee and Wilde's (1989) results regarding the impact of an increased n does not necessarily contradict those of Loury (1979). She stated that one should compare total expected investment in Lee and Wilde's model with total lump-sum investment in Loury's model. She argues that no general ranking emerges from this comparison, and that these results are consistent. The two models however, lead to different conclusions relating the effect of n on each firm's expected innovation date. In Loury (1979), success by any one firm is delayed on average by an increase in n, while in Lee and Wilde (1980) it is hastened. However, as mentioned before, the first success date (i.e. the expected industry introduction date) is hastened by an increase in n in both models. Reinganum (1989) concluded that 'normative prescriptions' are essentially the same for both models; restrict entry to the optimal number of firms, then adjust the patent value to eliminate over-investment. This recommendation is however based on the assumption of winner-take-all (i.e. no imitation).

In the models discussed so far, the focus has been on a single invention where investment in R&D determined how quickly it takes to transform this known invention into an innovation. Knowledge acquired during the development period only affected the rewards attainable from the perfection of that single invention and was not allowed to influence the rewards firms can gain from potential future innovations which in some way could be based on the same R&D projects. Dasgupta and Stiglitz (1980) proposed a model where innovation and R&D are viewed as continuous activities with the effect of pushing the cost curve downward for process innovations.[11] Their model is an extension of Arrow's (1962) with the major addition of incorporating rivalry in R&D activities. The greater the investment in R&D, the greater the shifts in the cost curve are. This approach utilises the concepts of demand elasticity in a similar way to the analysis of advertising budgets in the industrial economics literature. Perhaps one of the most interesting conclusions reached by Dasgupta and Stiglitz (1980) is related to their characterisation of 'effective competition'. They found that high degrees of concentration are by themselves not an evidence of lack of effective competition (Dasgupta and Stiglitz, 1980, p. 288). This is a somewhat formal presentation of Schumpeter's earlier arguments that the number of firms in an industry is not necessarily a measure of effective competition. As Dasgupta and Stiglitz (1980, p. 277) put it, 'equilibrium is maintained not by entry, but by firms spending more on R&D to forestall entry (essentially by spending all of their profits on R&D)'.

An important distinguishing feature of Dasgupta and Stiglitz's (1980) model from previous work is their treatment of market structure as an endogenous factor. That is, they stressed that both market structure and the nature of inventive activity are endogenous and thus jointly determined. If that is the case then the pace of innovative activity must be traced neither to the degree of concentration, nor to the degree of monopoly in the industry in question, but to more basic ingredients such as demand conditions, R&D technology, the nature of capital markets, etc.

Dasgupta and Stiglitz (1980) found that in a market economy with free entry there may be excessive duplication of research efforts reflected in (i) larger industry-wide R&D expenditure than is socially optimal, even though (ii) cost-reduction is lower than is socially optimal. Davies (1989, p. 209) noted that the 'model is stacked against more competitive market structures by construction; the assumption that each firm must undertake its own research to achieve the same process innovations as its competitors (i.e. each firm is perfectly protected by its own patent) makes duplication inevitable'. He suggests that a more realistic situation is where firms can achieve partial imitation of its rivals' innovations. Alternatively, one may argue that the productivity of rivals' R&D activities may increase when a firm's process innovation is introduced. Given that R&D and innovation are viewed as continuous activities in this approach, then it is quite reasonable to assume that the amount of investment in R&D activities required to achieve a certain downward shift in the cost curve is smaller today than it was few years ago. Scientific knowledge is a public property and this limits the extent to which patents can protect innovators from imitation.

4.7.2 The Effects of Imitation on the Innovative Activity

Reinganum (1981a, 1982) generalised the decision-theoretic work of Kamien and Schwartz (1972) to include explicit game-theoretic interactions among rivals using a dynamic model. Previous work by Scherer (1967), Loury (1979), Lee and Wilde (1980), and Dasgupta and Stiglitz (1980) are static in the sense that firms choose the amount to invest in R&D research at the outset; they choose an investment strategy from a subset of R^+. Reinganum (1982), following Kamien and Schwartz (1972), employs a dynamic formulation of investment strategy in which each firm chooses a function, a time path of spending on R&D. This function determines how much to invest in R&D at each instant of time until successful development by the firm or one of its rivals. More significantly, Reinganum (1982) considers the case of imperfect patent protection, an area ignored in earlier studies.

Assume that the date of successful completion is influenced by firm's investment in knowledge acquisition. Firm i acquires knowledge at rate μ_i. The knowledge accumulates according to the differential equation $\dot{z}_i(t) = \mu_i(t, z(t))$, where $z_i(t)$ denotes firm i's knowledge stock at t. The date of successful innovation is a random function of the amount of accumulated knowledge. Reinganum (1982) assumes the probability of success given a knowledge stock of z or less is:

$$F(z) = 1 - \exp\{-\lambda z\} \tag{4.30}$$

That is, the amount of knowledge needed to succeed is exponentially distributed with mean $1/\lambda$. Since the stock of knowledge $z_i(t)$ is a function of time, given the rate of acquisition $\mu_i(t)$, then the probability that firm i succeeds at or before t is:

$$\Pr\{t_i \leq t\} = F_i(z_i(t)) = 1 - e^{-\lambda z_i(t)} \quad t \in [0, T], \tag{4.31}$$

and the conditional probability density of success, given no success to date is:

$$\Pr\{t_i \in [t, t + dt] | t_i > t\} = \lambda \mu_i(t) \, dt, \quad t \in [0, T]. \tag{4.32}$$

Where t_i is the time at which firm i succeeds, and T is the time at which the firms abandon the project entirely if they have not yet perfected the innovation. Equation (4.32) indicates that the conditional density of success depends only upon the current investment. The firm can determine the probability of successful completion by any date through its choice of the pace of accumulation of knowledge. It is assumed that P_L is the present value of the innovation to the innovator and P_F is the present value of the reward to imitator. Further it is assumed that $P_F \leq P_L$, and that both are independent of the date of success and thus constant in present value terms. Therefore, the incentives to invest are focused upon the possibility of a rival's prior success. The discounted cost of additional knowledge μ_i acquired at t is given by $e^{-rt}c_i(\mu_i)$, where $c_i(\mu_i) = (1/2)(\mu_i)$. Development costs are assumed to cease the moment the race to innovate has been won.

Using sophisticated differential-game solution concepts, Reinganum (1982) derived a Nash equilibrium whereby each firm maximises its own payoff, taking its rivals' strategies as given. She showed that an increase in the payoff to the innovator stimulates firms to invest at a faster rate, while an increase in the payoff to imitation causes the firm to reduce its equilibrium rate of knowledge acquisition. All other things being equal, firms invest at a higher rate as time progresses. Also, firms generate knowledge at a uniformly higher rate when patent protection is perfect than when protection is imperfect. If $P_F = P_L$ (i.e. patent protection is ineffective), and in the absence of technical uncertainty, Nash equilibrium fails to exist with each firm preferring to imitate rather than innovate. In the presence of technical uncertainty there remains a positive probability that no rival will succeed within the planning horizon, and firms therefore have to pursue the payoff actively, rather than simply to wait for a rival to succeed and then reap the reward of imitation. The amount of knowledge required to perfect an innovation, given the perfection/imperfection of patent protection, can also affect the rate at which firms generate knowledge. If the innovation is sufficiently highly rewarded relative to imitation, then firms will invest at a uniformly higher rate in projects which (on average) require less knowledge. In the extreme case where patent protection is completely ineffective firms would invest at a higher rate on a project requiring (on average) more knowledge.

Reinganum (1982) addressed the question of whether or not competition is conducive to technical advance and compared the results obtained using her model to those of Kamien and Schwartz (1972, 1976), Loury (1979), and Lee and Wilde (1980). The number of firms is used as a measure of rivalry. In the case of perfect patent protection, as assumed by Loury (1979) and Lee and Wilde (1980), the results confirm those of Lee and Wilde (1980) that an increase in the number of Nash rivals results in an increase in each firm's individual equilibrium investment in R&D activities. In the case of imperfect patent protection, more precise assumptions regarding the determination of $P_L(n)$ and $P_F(n)$ are required to generate unambiguous results. Depending upon the payoff structure, increased rivalry in this case may accelerate or delay innovation. If, for example, rewards are completely nonappropriable; $P_L = P_F$, the same results are obtained as in the perfect patent case. This contradicts the

Kamien and Schwartz (1976) results that innovation will be unambiguously delayed by an increase in the number of rivals. Finally, Reinganum (1982) found that it is not worthwhile investing in R&D activities for any individual firm in a *perfectly competitive* industry (i.e. $P_L(n)$ and $P_F(n)$ both approach zero as n approaches ∞). This coincides with Kamien and Schwartz's (1972) results that in a perfectly competitive industry firms will not undertake development at all.

Stewart (1983) considered the case of imperfect patent protection by incorporating a 'share parameter', σ, describing the manner in which profits are divided among rivals when one firm is successful. This model follows those of Loury (1979) and Lee and Wilde (1980) in formulating the probability distribution of successful innovation by time t from the individual firm's point of view (equations (4.20)–(4.26)), and the model of Lee and Wilde (1980) in formulating the expected cost function (equation (4.28)). Stewart (1983) departs from Lee and Wilde (1980) in formulating an expected discounted return to successful innovation, EB which can be shown to be:

$$EB = \frac{V(\sigma h + (1 - \sigma)a/(n - 1))}{a + r + h},\tag{4.33}$$

and the expected profit:

$$E\pi = EB - EC = \frac{V(\sigma h + (1 - \sigma)a/(n - 1)) - x}{a + r + h} - F.\tag{4.34}$$

Note that for $\sigma = 1$ (no imitation), equation (4.34) reduces to equation (4.29). That is, this model is a straightforward generalisation of the Lee and Wilde's (1980) formulation. A Cournot-type behaviour by firms is assumed, in which each firm takes its rivals' investment rates as given and chooses the value of x, its constant investment rate, that maximises (4.34). The effects of rivalry can now be evaluated for given levels of patent protection, σ, and the results compared with earlier studies. The effect of rivalry on firms' investment in R&D depends on the magnitude of σ, and can be examined in two ways; the reaction of the firm to an increase in rival's investment rates, and the effect of an increase in the number of firms on the firm's optimal investment strategy. We consider the former case first. For $\sigma = 1$ the results are identical to those reached by Lee and Wilde (1980). Stewart (1983) showed that there is a critical value of σ, $\sigma^* < 1$, such that changes in rivals' investment rate will have no effect on firm's optimal investment strategies. For $\sigma > \sigma^*$, increased rivals' spending will hasten technical advances, while for $\sigma < \sigma^*$ firms will decrease their investment as a result of an increase in rivals' investment rate. Thus the effects of rivalry are crucially dependent on the innovation's rewards (i.e. the extent to which innovation rewards are protected from imitation).

The effect of an increase in the number of rivals is identical to that observed by Lee and Wilde for $\sigma = 1$, namely that an increase in the number of firms stimulate firms to accelerate their investment in R&D. For $\sigma = \sigma^* < 1$, however, Stewart (1983) showed that the net effect of an increase in the number of firms is a reduction in the equilibrium investment rate. Interestingly, Stewart (1983) showed that the equilibrium would prevail when $\sigma = \sigma^*$; that is, σ^* maximises expected industry profits by guiding noncooperative oligopolists to choose the profit-maximising investment rate. Moreover, it is shown that $\sigma = \sigma^* < 1$ leads to an investment rate identical to that which would be chosen by a jointly managed cartel.

4.7.3 Asymmetric Models and Pre-emptive Innovations

A strand of the literature has focused on the role of small and new firms in stimulating change as direct sources of innovation, but more specifically as spurs to existing firms in the industry. Models of pre-emptive patenting examine the situation where an incumbent firm innovates to deter potential entry. Gilbert and Newbery (1982) showed that under certain conditions a firm with monopoly power has an incentive to maintain monopoly power by patenting new technologies which sometimes are neither used nor licensed to others, which are referred to as *sleeping patents*. A monopolist protected from entry would not invest resources to produce a sleeping patent. Yet a sleeping patent may occur as the consequence of pre-emptive patenting by a monopolist. Consider the following simplified version of Gilbert and Newbery's (1982) auction model. A monopolist is faced with potential entrants who also compete for the same innovation. To win the innovation each firm i must bid the maximum amount that the firm will spend on research and development, x_i. The firm which bids most wins and spends the amount of its bids. If the incumbent ties with one or more potential entrants, then the patent is awarded to the incumbent. The rewards to winning are summarised as follows; the incumbent receives $P^m e^{rT(x_i)} - x_i$ in present value terms, where $T(x_i)$ is the date of completion and P^m is the capitalised value of the innovation if the relevant product market is monopolised. If a potential entrant wins the bid then the market for the new product is shared with the entrant receiving $P^e e^{-rT(x_e)} - x_e$ and the incumbent receiving $P^i e^{-rT(x_e)} - x_e$, where x_e is the amount of the potential entrant's winning bid.

Gilbert and Newbery (1982) show that if $P^m \geq P^e + P^i$ (i.e. there is some dissipation of rents when the market is noncooperatively shared rather than monopolised), then the current incumbent will win the bidding game with a bid of x^*, where x^* is the largest solution of:

$$P^e e^{-rT(x)} - x = 0. \tag{4.35}$$

Potential entrants will bid up to x^*, and if the incumbent bids x^* or more it will win the bidding game. If it does, the incumbent would receive $P^m e^{rT(x^*)} - x^*$, and if it does not it would receive $P^i e^{-rT(x^*)} - x^*$. The incumbent will match potential entrants' bid if and only if $P^m e^{rT(x^*)} - x^* \geq P^i e^{-rT(x^*)} - x^*$. This reduces to $[P^m - (P^i + P^e)]e^{-rT(x^*)} \geq 0$. Thus, the incentive for pre-emptive patenting and persistent monopoly depends on the extent of dissipation of industry profits, $[P^m - (P^i + P^e)]$, due to the noncooperative behaviour that is associated with less concentrated markets. When there is dissipation of industry profits, a firm can maintain a monopoly through pre-emptive activity despite the potential of entry. Gilbert and Newbery (1982, p. 524) argue that the undesirable consequences of pre-emptive activity are evident in situations where they lead to a 'sleeping' patent; that is, when the monopolist does not use the innovation and also denies society the use of these technologies. The costs of sleeping patents to society are reflected in three ways; the resources spent on the development of new technologies, the inefficiencies due to the use of inferior technologies, and any inefficiencies associated with maintained monopoly.

Reinganum (1983) develops an asymmetric model of innovation in an industry where the incumbent faces a challenge from potential entrants. The model is a straightforward extension of that of Lee and Wilde (1980) which distinguishes between the incumbent firm and the potential entrant in terms of both their current and post-innovation profit flows.[12] This model captures both ways in which potential entrants stimulate innovation; as a spur to existing firms, and also as a direct source of innovation. She showed that the incumbent firm (the winner of the previous innovation) invests less on a given project than does the potential entrant, and thus is less likely to be the innovator than is the challenger. The asymmetry in this model is reflected in a positive flow of profits that the incumbent (and not the potential entrant) receives so long as no one has succeeded. This period is of random length, but is stochastically shorter the more the incumbent (and the potential entrant) invests. The incumbent has relatively less incentive than the potential entrant to shorten the period of its incumbency.

Reinganum (1985) extends this model to an arbitrary number of firms and a sequence of innovations to describe the Schumpeterian 'process of creative destruction'. This model highlights the 'competition through innovation' aspects of the dynamic evolution of markets. Since it invests at a lower rate, the incumbent is least likely to win the current race. Thus, the industry is characterised by a turnover of the technological leadership rather than a single increasing leadership. Vickers (1986) found that the latter is more likely in very competitive industries and the former when industries are not very competitive. In comparison with models discussed previously, the models developed by Vickers (1986) and Reinganum (1985) are particularly useful in depicting the Schumpeterian 'process of creative destruction' because of their dynamic nature. It should be noted, however, that these conclusions are based on the assumption that the incumbent enjoys no advantage which is due to incumbency *per se*. For example, the incumbent may invest more, and thus becomes more likely to innovate, if it enjoys a sufficiently large marginal cost advantage in the conduct of research.

Katz and Shapiro (1987) examine pre-emption in a general two-firms industry which may include a monopolist and a potential entrant. Their model possesses two unique aspects in comparison with other pre-emption models. Firstly, a firm may benefit from an innovation even if that innovation is developed by a market rival. Secondly, they assume an exogenous decline in the cost of developing an innovation due to ongoing and freely available basic research. Let π_0^i denote the firms' current profit flow where $i = 1, 2$. If firm 1 develops the innovation its profits become π_1^1 and firm 2 earns π_1^2. If firm 2 develops the innovation its profits become π_2^2 and firm 1's profits become π_2^1, where subscripts denote the firm in question and superscripts denote the identity of the innovating firm (and is zero if neither firm innovates). Let $\pi_i = \pi_i^i + \pi_i^j$ denote industry profits when firm i innovates, and assume that $\pi_1 \geq \pi_2$ (that is, post-innovation industry profits are at least as large when firm 1 innovates as they are when firm 2 does so).

Two sources of incentive to innovate are identified. *Stand-alone incentive* refers to the increase in profits due to innovation (i.e. $\pi_i^i \geq \pi_0^i$). *Pre-emption incentive* refers to the incentives to win and avoid losing because the rewards are assumed higher when a firm innovates than when a rival wins (i.e. $\pi_1^1 \geq \pi_2^1$). In the absence of rivalry the firm will be driven by its stand-alone incentive only. If each firm suffers a reduction in profits when its rival innovates, the pre-emption incentives are larger than the stand-alone incentives (i.e. $\pi_i^i - \pi_j^i > \pi_i^i - \pi_0^i$ if $\pi_0^i > \pi_j^i$). In this case the winner must be the firm with the greater pre-emption incentive and the R&D competition takes the form of a race to be the innovator. The models of Gilbert and Newbery (1982) and Reinganum (1982) assume this setting. If, however, profits from losing (attainable through imitation) are larger than current profits (i.e. $\pi_j^i > \pi_0^i$) then stand alone incentives exceed pre-emption incentives and the nature of R&D competition may become that of a waiting game rather than a race. Katz and Shapiro (1987) show that in such cases the existence of rivalry in R&D activity has no effect on the date of development. If firm 1 has both a larger stand-alone incentive and a larger pre-emption incentive, then firm 1 will win. If firm 2 has the larger stand-alone incentive and firm 1 has the larger pre-emption incentive then either firm may innovate. To compare this model with previous literature, Katz and Shapiro (1987) derive some specific predictions about the pattern of innovation in an industry composed of small and large firms. They predict that for markets in which patent protection is strong, major innovations will be made by industry leaders. If patent protection is imperfect and imitation is easy, industry followers or potential entrants are more likely to perfect major innovations.

Reinganum (1989, p. 876) uses Katz and Shapiro's (1987) definition of the incentive to innovate to explain why the auction model of Vickers (1986) provides opposite results from the stochastic models of Gilbert and Newbery

(1982), and Reinganum (1983, 1985). Her comments neatly summarise the significant differences between the two approaches:

> In the deterministic model, so long as the stand-alone incentive is non-negative, the incentive to pre-empt dominates the firm decision (and an incumbent monopolist has a greater incentive to pre-empt than does a challenger). But when the date of rival success is drawn from a continuous distribution as in the stochastic racing model, concern about pre-emption is much less acute. Moreover, for drastic innovations, the pre-emption incentive is the same for both firms (both get monopoly profits if successful and nothing if unsuccessful), while the stand-alone incentive is greater for the challenger. Even for less drastic innovations, in which the pre-emption incentive is greater for the incumbent, the fact that pre-emption is only probabilistic means that both incentives come into play, with the result that for some less than drastic innovations, it is the greater stand-alone incentive for the challenger which carries the way.

In the asymmetric models of Gilbert and Newbery (1982), Reinganum (1983, 1985), and Vickers (1986), the asymmetry does not confer any strategic advantages upon one firm or another. That is, although these models distinguish between incumbents and potential entrants in terms of their incentives to innovate (i.e. profit flows before and after innovation), and thus generate *ex post* advantages, all firms are equally likely to become the winner, *for a given level of investment in R&D*, and the differences among firms do not confer any *ex ante* advantages upon any particular firm. In multi-stage single innovation models a firm's position at any stage affects the effectiveness of its R&D activities in subsequent stages. Fudenberg *et al.* (1983), for example, develop such a model of a multi-stage patent race, but with limitation on firms' abilities to vary their research intensities. Lippman and McCardle (1988) extended this model to allow for intermediate stages of the R&D process. Harris and Vickers (1985) allowed for continuous choice of research efforts by firms in their deterministic race model. Judd (1985) allowed for progress in the context of stochastic competition. His model assumes that strategic advantages are acquired endogenously over time through acquired knowledge and intermediate successes. The applicability of the model is however restricted by the assumption that the winner's prize is of arbitrarily small value. Grossman and Shapiro (1987) analyse a two-stage innovation model which captures the dynamic aspects of R&D rivalry in a two-firms industry without any of the restrictions imposed by previous models. Their model follows that of Lee and Wilde (1980) in adopting a stochastic structure but allows for progress during the R&D process. The two stages can be referred to as *research* and *development*. The firm has to complete both stages to perfect an innovation. Each firm is fully informed about the state of progress of its rival. Analysing the game from the point of view of one firm (i.e. our firm), at any point of time and before the innovation is introduced, there are four distinct possibilities; none of the firms completed the first stage, our firm completed the first stage and the rival did not, the rival completed the first stage and our firm did not, and finally that both firms completed the first stage.[13] Let x_{00}, x_{10}, x_{01}, and x_{11} denote the equilibrium investment levels associated with the possibilities specified above, respectively. Let V_{00}, V_{10}, V_{01}, and V_{11} denote the Nash equilibrium profits. The symmetric equilibrium to the sub-game that results in each case can be derived as follows. If both firms have completed the first stage but neither completed the second stage, this reduces to the situation modelled by Lee and Wilde (1980), and the payoff to each firm can be written as:

$$V_{11}(x,a) = \frac{h(x)P - x}{r + h(x) + a} \qquad (4.36)$$

The second (and conversely the third) case is where firm 1 has finished the first stage but firm 2 has not. The payoff structure for firm 1 and 2, respectively:

$$V_{10}(x,a) = \frac{h(x)P + aV_{11} - x}{r + h(x) + a}, \qquad (4.37)$$

and

$$V_{01}(x,a) = \frac{h(x)V_{11} - x}{r + h(x) + a}. \qquad (4.38)$$

And the final case is where neither firm has completed the first stage, and each firm's payoff is given by:

$$V_{00}(x,a) = \frac{h(x)V_{10} + aV_{01} - x}{r + h(x) + a}. \qquad (4.39)$$

Grossman and Shapiro (1987) conclude that the leader always devotes more resources to R&D than the follower. If the follower catches up, however, both firms intensify their efforts, and the leader's spending in this case exceeds that when only one firm has succeeded. That is, the rate of expenditures on R&D activities when both firms have succeeded with the first stage is higher than that when neither has succeeded. When only one firm has succeeded with the first stage it is still possible for either or both firms to speed up or slow down, although numerical simulations conducted by Grossman and Shapiro (1987) over a wide range of parameter values suggest that perhaps the most typical outcome is one where the firm that succeeded with the first stage intensifies its efforts while its rival reduces its rate of spending.

Clemenz (1992) develops a model of cost-reducing process innovations where R&D projects are assumed to yield new production processes characterised by the unit costs of the output. The main theoretical difference between this model and that of Grossman and Shapiro (1987) is that the former incorporates uncertainty not only as far as the timing of the innovation is concerned but also with respect to the quality of the innovation, while Grossman and Shapiro (1987) assume that in each period there exists exactly *one type of innovation* (i.e.

an exact new cost level) which may or may not be introduced. Vickers (1986) allows for a sequence of unit cost levels but assumes that the unit cost level which can be reached in each period is exogenously determined. Moreover, Vickers's (1986) model does not incorporate technical uncertainty. The model by Clemenz (1992) allows for a more realistic environment and examines not only the timing aspect of R&D competition but also the target levels and uncertainty associated with the quality of innovations. Clemenz (1992) analyses the results obtained under two possible market structures; either a pure monopoly or a Bertrand-oligopoly. He finds that both pure monopoly and Bertrand competition generate too little R&D compared with what would be socially optimal. The main reason for this divergence is that firms consider only the expected increase of their profits due to R&D, but not the benefits enjoyed by consumers.

A recent approach to this question has been to explain Schumpeter's early hypotheses in the context of the industry life cycle (e.g. Klepper, 1992). According to this view, in the early history of an industry, when technology is changing very rapidly, uncertainty is very high and barriers to entry very low, new firms are the major innovators and are the key elements in industrial dynamics. By the time the industry develops and matures, however, economies of scale, learning curves, barriers to entry, and financial resources become important in the competitive process and large firms with monopolistic power come to the forefront of the innovation process.

Malerba and Orsenigo (1990, 1993, 1995) argue that the Schumpeterian 'widening' and 'deepening' patterns of innovative activities are related to the key features of the 'technological regime' which characterise an industry. A widening pattern of innovative activities is related to the innovative base which is continuously enlarging through the entry of new innovators and the erosion of the competitive and technological advantages of the established firms in the industry (i.e. technological turnover). A deepening pattern of innovation, however, is related to the dominance of a few firms which are continuously innovative through the accumulation over time of technological and innovative capabilities (i.e. increasing dominance). Malerba and Orsenigo (1990, 1993, 1995) have defined technological regimes in terms of *opportunity* (ease and potential for innovation of each technology), *appropriately* (ability to protect innovations from imitation), *cumulativeness* (the fact that existing innovators may continue to be so in the future with respect to non-innovators), and *properties of the knowledge base* (the number and type of basic and applied sciences necessary to innovative activities).

Malerba and Orsenigo (1993) define widening patterns of the innovative process to be determined by high opportunity and low appropriately conditions, which favour the continuous entry of innovators in the industry, and by low cumulativeness conditions, which do not allow the persistence of monopolistic advantages in the industry. In contrast, deepening patterns are determined by high opportunity, appropriately, and cumulativeness conditions which allow innovators to accumulate technological knowledge and capabilities continuously and to build up innovative advantages over non-innovators and potential entrants. Malerba and Orsenigo (1995) find that '*stability*' is another important feature of the patterns of innovative activity, 'technological performance is strongly associated with the emergence of a stable group of innovators, who innovate consistently and continuously over time, rather than the concentration of firm size. This result holds both in deepening and in widening technological classes.' The important implication of this work is that the answer to the question of what industry structure is more conducive to innovation (e.g. competitive versus monopolistic, small firms versus large firms) depends on the specific features of the relevant technology regime. For example, Malerba and Orsenigo (1995) find that widening patterns of innovative activities are characteristics of the mechanical sector. Deepening patterns, on the other hand, are associated with chemical, electrical, and electronics industries. In the former, labelled as Schumpeter Mark I technological classes, an industrial structure in which innovators are of small size is more conducive to technological performance than an industrial structure in which innovators are of larger size. The opposite is true in Schumpeter Mark II technology classes.[14]

The most recent studies in the literature tend to focus on the strategic technology adoption in an environment of continuous technological progress and fixed adoption costs (e.g. Vickers, 1986, Beath *et al.* 1987, Delbono, 1989, Budd *et al.* 1993, and Riordan and Salant, 1994). Models of new technology adoption build on the earlier work of Gilbert and Newbery (1982) and Vickers (1986). Firms in this environment face recurring adoption decisions and must weigh the sunk cost of each adoption against the benefits of lower production costs or higher demand prices. The strategic aspects of this problem is reflected in the fact that the benefits a firm derives from the adoption of new technology are reduced when it or one of its rivals adopt an even newer technology. The problem is still of timing, but these models focus on the timing of the adoption of new technologies rather than on the R&D race to perfect a specific innovation.[15] (Innovation adoption and diffusion is the subject of the next chapter.)

4.8 SUMMARY OF THE LITERATURE

Table 4.2 below summarises the main contributions reviewed in this chapter. The fact that emerges from examining these models is that there is no single answer to most of the questions addressed in the literature. The findings of these models depend crucially on the assumptions they make regarding a number of factors. These factors can be summarised as follows:

Table 4.2 Development of the industrial economics literature on market structure and technical change

Studies of economic growth and technological change
⇓
Schumpeterian hypotheses
⇓
Macroeconomics models of the incentives to innovate
Arrow (1962), Demsetz (1969), Kamien and Schwartz (1970), and Ng (1971)

Scherer (1967)	Using a deterministic game-theoretic model of R&D rivalry, Scherer found that an increase in the number of firms competing to perfect a given innovation leads to an increase in the firm and industry equilibrium investment rate, up to a point after which further increases in the number of firms causes firms to reduce their investments.
Barzel (1968)	Competition in R&D leads to zero social benefits from technical change and causes firms to overinvest in R&D compared to the socially optimal level. The amount of resources devoted to R&D is optimal only when this activity is monopolised *and* the innovator is able to capture all the benefits.

Decision-Theoretic Models

Kamien and Schwartz (1972) (1974a) (1974b) (1976) (1978a) (1978b) (1980) and (1982)	These studies develop the earlier work of Barzel (1968) to analyse individual firm behaviour. Their models specify how each firm takes into account the presence of rivals by incorporating market uncertainty in the R&D activities of firms. Their main findings are that, depending on the profitability of the innovation, either a pure monopoly or an intermediate level of rivalry is most conducive to innovative activity. They find that under perfect competition, as characterised by Barzel's (1968) model, firms will not undertake development at all. They also find that competition leads to overinvestment compared to a nonrivalrous with no imitation case. Finally, Kamien and Schwartz extend their analysis to investigate the effects of a number of factors including the existence of a range of innovations, the effects of self-financing, the contractual nature of costs, new product pricing, impossible imitation, and costless imitation.

Game-Theoretic Models

Loury (1979)	A stochastic model of R&D race which incorporates both technical and market uncertainties. The main finding is that firms overinvest in R&D activities and that free entry leads to a larger number of firms than is socially optimal. An increase in the number of firms competing to perfect an innovation causes a reduction in the individual firm's investment level, but leads to an earlier expected introduction date of an innovation. These results are based on the assumption of no imitation.
Lee and Wilde (1980)	Adopts the framework developed by Loury (1979) with the exception that development costs consist of a fixed component and a flow component. The main finding is that an increase in the number of firms leads to an *increase* in the individual firm's investment rate, otherwise their study confirms the results obtained by Loury (1979).

(*Continued overleaf*)

Table 4.2 *Continued*

Game-Theoretic Models, continued

Dasgupta and Stiglitz (1980)
Model R&D activity as a continuous process with the effects of pushing the firm's demand curve outwards for product innovation (e.g. Needham, 1975) or its cost curve downwards for process innovations. Their main finding is that firms overinvest in R&D and achieve less cost reduction compared with what would be socially optimal.

Reinganum (1981a) and (1982)
Generalises the decision-theoretic work of Kamien and Schwartz (1972) to include explicit game-theoretic interactions among rivals using a dynamic model. She shows that an increase in the payoff to the innovator stimulates firms to invest at a faster rate, while an increase in the payoff to imitation causes the firm to reduce its equilibrium rate of knowledge acquisition. All other things being equal, firms invest at a higher rate as time progresses. Also, firms generate knowledge at a uniformly higher rate when patent protection is perfect, compared with when protection is imperfect. In the case of either perfect patent protection or completely ineffective patent protection, an increase in the number of rivals leads to an increase in each firm's individual equilibrium investment in R&D activities, confirming the results of Lee and Wilde (1980) in the former case and contradicting the results of Kamien and Schwartz (1976) in the latter case.

Stewart (1983)
A generalisation of Lee and Wilde's (1980) model with imitation. The effects of an increase in the number of firms depends on the effectiveness of patent protection.

Multi-Innovation Asymmetric Models of Pre-emption

Gilbert and Newbery (1982)
Distinguishes between firms (incumbent/monopolist versus potential entrant). When there is dissipation of industry profits a monopolist can maintain monopoly through pre-emptive activity which can lead to 'sleeping patents'.

Fudenberg *et al.* (1983)
A model of multi-stage patent race with limitation on firms' abilities to vary their research intensities as firms suffer from information lags regarding the research activities of their rivals.

Reinganum (1983)
An asymmetric version of Lee and Wilde's (1980) model. Found that the incumbent (winner of last R&D race) spends less on R&D and thus is less likely to be the winner of the next R&D race. This means that the industry is likely to be characterised by a technological turnover rather than increasing dominance as can be the case in Gilbert and Newbery (1982).

Reinganum (1985)
Extended Reinganum (1983) to an arbitrary number of firms and a sequence of innovations and confirmed the result that technological turnover is more likely than increasing dominance.

Vickers (1986)
Showed that an 'action–reaction' (i.e. technological turnover) is more likely in very competitive industries and an increasing dominance pattern is more likely in uncompetitive industries.

Katz and Shapiro (1987)
Examines pre-emption in a general two-firm industry with an exogenous decline in the cost of development. They define two incentives to innovate; stand-alone incentive and pre-emption

incentive, and they characterise the conditions under which one of these incentives will dominate. Specifically, their model predicts that for markets in which patent protection is strong, major innovations will be made by industry leaders. But if imitation is easy, industry followers or entrants will make major discoveries. For minor innovations, the industry leader will typically be the innovator regardless of whether or not patent protection is effective.

Grossman and Shapiro (1987)	A two-stage-innovation generalisation of Lee and Wilde's (1980) stochastic model. Concludes that the leader always devotes more resources to R&D than the follower. The rate of investment in R&D when both firms have succeeded with the first stage is higher than that when neither has succeeded. Numerical simulations conducted by Grossman and Shapiro suggest that when only one firm succeeds with the first stage it intensifies its efforts while its rival reduces its rate of spending on R&D.
Lippman and McCardle (1988)	Extends the model by Fudenberg et al. (1983) to allow for intermediate stages of the R&D process.
Clemenz (1992)	A model of cost-reducing process innovations with uncertainty regarding the quality of the innovation (i.e. the extent of cost reduction) as well as the timing of introduction. Found that pure monopoly and Bertrand competition generate too little R&D compared with what would be socially optimal.
Malerba and Orsenigo (1990) (1993) and (1995)	Define the relationship between market structure and the innovative activity in terms of characteristics of the relevant *technology regime*. A widening pattern of innovative activities, or *technological turnover*, is associated with technology regimes characterised by high opportunity, low appropriately, and low cumulative conditions. A deepening pattern, or *increasing dominance*, is associated with high opportunity, appropriately, and cumulative conditions. Thus the contribution of small or new firms (widening pattern) and large or incumbent firms (deepening pattern) to the innovative activities is a function of characteristics of the relevant technology regime.

1. Game versus decision theoretic approach. Although decision-theoretic models provide interesting insights of R&D determinants at the firm level, they fail to explain the industry's aggregate behaviour. Game-theoretic models are more appropriate for policy purposes since they consider industry-wide implications of changes in market structure. Decision-theoretic models are particularly useful in cases where potential competition in the R&D race can come from different sources and when the number of firms involved in the race cannot be identified.

2. Deterministic versus stochastic models. Models which assume a stochastic relationship incorporate technical uncertainty and seem to be more appropriate in explaining firms' decisions regarding their R&D investment levels (the R component in the R&D activity). Deterministic models are

appropriate in cases of new product development in which any technical uncertainties have already been resolved (the D component in R&D).

3. Asymmetric versus symmetric models. Asymmetric models distinguish between firms in terms of their pre-innovation and/or post-innovation profit flows (incumbent versus potential entrant) while symmetric models do not distinguish between firms (assume a homogeneous firms population). Asymmetric models are more appropriate in examining the relationship between firm size and market structure and the level of the innovative activity.

4. Single innovation versus multi-innovation models. Single innovation models assume that there is a given single invention and R&D is undertaken in order to perfect that invention into an innovation. With the technical characteristics of the innovation known in advance, the amount of investment in R&D only determines the length of time that it takes for the transformation to take place (in either a deterministic or stochastic way). Multi-innovation models, on the other hand, view the innovative activity as a continuous process where investment in R&D is not directly related to perfecting a specific innovation but rather determines the *innovativeness* of the firm. Multi-innovation models are more appropriate in examining industries where advances in R&D are likely to spur the development of a series of related innovations.

5. Single-stage versus multi-stage models. Multi-stage models have the advantage of allowing firms to adjust their investment rates in R&D according to how they stand in the technological race with their rivals. Multi-stage models provide probably a more accurate characterisation of real life R&D competition and are better suited to examine firm's reactions to changes in their rivals' spending on R&D activities. Single-stage innovation models are appropriate in cases where firms are not likely to be aware of the progress of their rivals' R&D programmes.

Finally, models falling in the above categories can be further classified according to their assumptions regarding development cost functions:

6. Contractual versus non-contractual development cost. Models which assume contractual development cost functions view investment in the R&D activity as a continuous process where firms can accelerate, decelerate, or cease investment at any moment. These focus primarily on the research stages of the R&D process. Models which assume a non-contractual development cost are appropriate when the innovative activity involves investing a pre-determined amount in a new technology once the research stage is completed.

4.9 CONCLUSION

This chapter reviewed the literature on market structure and innovative activity. The bulk of the literature can be characterised as models of R&D competition focusing on the timing and intensity of investing in R&D to perfect a given single innovation. In these models the firms must select the optimal amount to spend on R&D where either the timing or value of the innovation is random. The decision theoretic formulations solve for the optimal rate of R&D spending for a single firm and evaluate the effects of parameter changes on that rate. The game theoretic formulation compare the socially optimal number of research projects with the amount of research performed by firms in a noncooperative game. The conclusions drawn in both formulations focus upon the effects of market structure on the amount of R&D spending. A common finding of these models is that firms' spending on R&D diverges from the level that is socially optimal. The main reason for this divergence is that firms only consider the marginal benefits that they derive from investing in R&D and do not take into account the reduction in expected benefits that they impose on other firms. This result, however, depends crucially on the assumption of effective patent protection, which makes duplication of efforts inevitable. At the industry level (i.e. game-theoretic models), and allowing for market uncertainty, the following two conclusions emerge:

1. An increase in the number of competing firms leads to an earlier expected industry introduction date of an innovation, and (with fixed development cost) to a higher level of equilibrium investment rate at the firm level.
2. Competitive entry leads to a larger number of firms than is socially optimal.

An important implication of these studies is that the strategic interactions between firms (i.e. each firm takes into consideration the actions of its rivals in making its own decisions) can have significant effects on the eventual equilibrium that prevails at the industry level. This can be seen clearly from the conflicting conclusions obtained by researchers assuming a decision-theoretic versus game-theoretic framework. In focusing on the individual firm's decision, taken in isolation from that of other firms, one ignores certain important game-theoretic considerations.

The more recent literature focuses on new technology adoption by firms in a given industry. Asymmetric adoption models address the question of which firm is more likely to adopt a new technology (incumbent or monopolist versus a potential entrant) and which pattern of technological leadership (action–reaction versus increasing dominance) is more likely to emerge and under which conditions. The findings of these studies are summarised in Table 4.2.

Although the above literature examines the determinants of R&D spending under many different conditions, its usefulness for policy purposes is still limited. This is mainly for two reasons. Firstly, there is a lack of descriptive studies which relate the findings of the literature to any specific application. As noted before, the implications that can be derived from the literature can vary considerably depending on the assumptions underlying the specific models. The assumptions underlying a particular model (e.g. ease of imitation) can describe one industry but not another (e.g. the software industry but not the chemical industry), and thus the usefulness of the model depends on the specific application that a researcher is concerned with. Secondly, there is a lack of testable models of either firm or industry equilibrium behaviour. The predictions of theoretical models can only be confirmed by empirical testing, especially in cases where models with the same underlying assumptions but different formulations lead to contradictory predictions. Most models reviewed in this chapter do not lend themselves to an obvious testable form.[16] Finally, the models reviewed in this chapter do not (directly) examine the diffusion patterns of innovations. An important empirical observation regarding the adoption of innovations is that, once an innovation has been perfected, adoption is usually delayed and all firms do not adopt an innovation simultaneously. Instead, innovations *diffuse* into use over time. The next chapter reviews the literature on innovation adoption and diffusion models.

ENDNOTES

1. Assuming the cost of developing the innovation is the same for all firms, then the results of the analysis are still the same if the innovator is one of the firms in the competitive industry.
2. Note that equation (4.5) expresses the imitator's profit as a proportion of the *potential* quasi-rents attainable from the sale of the new product rather than as a proportion of the actual quasi-rents given the level of market penetration as defined by equation (4.4). Under this formulation, for given values of the parameters, the imitator may end up earning more than what an innovator with no imitators would have earned; that is, more than the total quasi-rents attainable given the level of market penetration. This effect is not significant when t is very large (i.e. when actual quasi-rents approach potential quasi-rents), but nevertheless points out an inconsistency in the definitions employed.
3. Equation (4.3) is indeterminate for $p = 0$. For $p < 0$, when output is declining, $t(m)$ is negative, indicating that the innovation should have been introduced in the past.
4. This is based on the assumption that the breakthrough in basic knowledge occurs before $t(z)$.
5. That is assuming that P_1 and P_2 depend on the lag between innovation date and imitation date.
6. Let $f(t) = F'(t)$ be a probability density function reflecting the probability of period of time during which event X does not occur, and let $F(t)$ be the cumulative density of t, then a hazard function is the conditional density function (Kennedy, 1994, p. 246):

$$\lambda = \frac{f(t)}{1 - F(t)} \rightarrow \lambda\Delta t = \frac{f(t)\Delta t}{1 - F(t)}$$

$$= \text{Prob } [X \text{ occurs in } (t, t+1)|X \text{ has not occurred in } (0, t)].$$

λ is called the *hazard rate*. The term originated in survival analysis and is applied in economic applications such as firm survival analysis and employment duration (Amemiya, 1985, p. 435).

7. See Kamien and Schwartz (1982), pp. 114–16, for a mathematical derivation and interpretation of equation (4.17).

8. By assuming all firms face an identical cost function, the analysis does not allow for incumbents to enjoy cost advantages in producing the new product. Although it is likely that a new product will require new production techniques, it is reasonable to assume that at least part of the production processes of existing products can be utilised in the production of the new product. This however will require further assumptions to characterise new entrants and the extent to which the entry decision is separate from innovation decisions.

9. Recall that all profits are assumed to be positive. Losses do not mean negative profits but a decrease in profit rates.

10. Riordan and Salant (1994, pp. 248–49) argue that an alternative interpretation of this assumption is that patented innovations are developed by independent entrepreneurs who license their inventions to the highest bidder. On this interpretation, argue Riordan and Salant (1994), these are models of new innovation adoption rather than of R&D competition. Models of innovation adoption are discussed in Chapter 5.

11. Focusing on the demand side, Needham (1975) models product innovation as a continuous activity with the effects of pushing the demand curve upward.

12. In a sense, this model is the asymmetric version of Lee and Wilde's (1980) symmetric model.

13. To facilitate the comparison of this model to previous models, we use the terminology proposed by Reinganum (1989, pp. 880–81).

14. One might also argue that smaller firms are more conducive to the level of *inventive* activities while large firms are more conducive to the level of *innovative* activity; that is, the successful and efficient commercialisation of inventions.

15. Riordan and Salant (1994) criticise earlier R&D race studies for assuming that the loser incurs no R&D expenses and argue that a reasonable interpretation of this assumption is that patented innovations are developed by independent entrepreneurs upstream who license their inventions to the highest downstream bidder, in which case models in this category are of new technology adoption rather than of R&D competition.

16. See Isaac and Reynolds (1988) for a laboratory experimental test of a stochastic model of R&D investment.

5
Models of Innovation Adoption and Diffusion

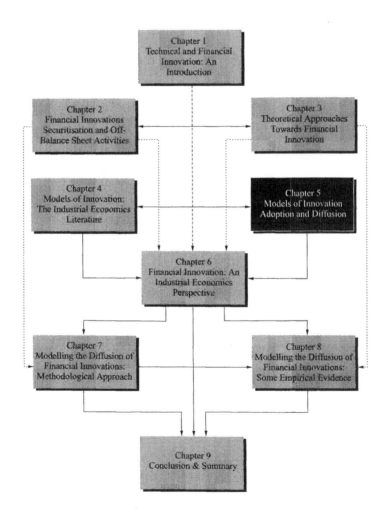

5
Models of Innovation Adoption and Diffusion

5.1 INTRODUCTION

An important empirical observation regarding the adoption of innovations is that adoption is typically delayed and that firms do not adopt the innovation simultaneously. Instead, innovations 'diffuse' into use over time (Reinganum, 1989, p. 893). The last chapter focused on the strategic and competitive aspects of R&D competition with emphasis on the impact that market structure has on the timing of innovation and the level of investment in the inventive activity. Research alone, however, is not sufficient for progress; innovations yield no benefits until they are employed. The incentives for adopting an innovation are as important as the incentives for their discovery and development. This chapter focuses on the adoption of innovations and their diffusion patterns among firms. That is, given that an innovation has been introduced by one or more firms, what determines the adoption decision of other firms in the industry? The last chapter focused on the supply side of the new technology where firms are viewed as being in a race to innovate, with the 'winner-take-all' benefits of the innovation. This view is consistent with, and derives from, the entrepreneurial theory of innovation developed by Schumpeter (McCardle, 1985, p. 1373). This chapter focuses on the demand for innovations. Studies modelling the demand for innovations drop the 'winner-take-all' premise, for it precludes adoption of the innovation by the firms which do not win the race to innovate.

Metcalfe (1988, p. 3) clarified the distinction between adoption and diffusion. 'Adoption analysis considers the decisions taken by agents, typically organisations such as firms, to incorporate a new technology into their activities. It is concerned with the process of decision making, and leads to the propositions linking the nature and timing of adoption decisions to specified characteristics of adopters, e.g. the size of firms, or their sociometric position within a communication network. By contrast, diffusion analysis is concerned with how the *economic significance* of a new technology changes over time. Economic significance may be measured in a number of ways, e.g. by the share of the market held by a product innovation or by the fraction of industry output produced with a process innovation [...] The relation between the adoption pattern and the diffusion pattern depends upon a complex of factors, including differences in intra-firm rates of adoption, and time lags between the decision to adopt and the implementation of that decision.'

So while adoption models focus on the decision-making process of individual firms, diffusion models examine the aggregate behaviour of the industry as a whole and analyse the time-pattern structure of the diffusion process. Adoption models are based on the assumption of a heterogeneous population of adopters regarding at least one firm-specific characteristic affecting the benefits of adoption to firms (e.g. differences in firm size). Adoption models can be extended to explain why innovations *diffuse* by making appropriate assumptions regarding the distribution of these characteristics across the population of potential adopters, and changes in these characteristics (or their impact on the benefits of adoption) over time. The literature on diffusion models, however, seems to have emerged independently (and earlier than) the literature on innovation adoption models. This chapter discusses models of innovation adoption by individual firms and the literature on empirical models of innovation diffusion at the aggregate industry level.

5.2 RATIONAL-EFFICIENCY MODELS OF INNOVATION ADOPTION

Adoption models analyse situations in which an innovation is announced which is relevant to the operation of a specific number of potential adopters, e.g. firms. The innovation can be developed and introduced by a firm from either outside or within the using industry. Most models assume that the technical characteristics of the innovation are known with certainty at the time the innovation is announced. Each firm in the industry has to decide whether or not to adopt the innovation. Adoption decisions are based on firms' assessments of the costs and benefits of adoption. At any point of time, the firm has two options: it can adopt the innovation, where adoption is irreversible, or it can wait. If the firm waits, then it updates its assessment of the innovation and faces the same decision at the start of the next period. A firm's adoption decision, based on its assessment of the innovation, is thus influenced by:

1. The unique cost/benefit characteristics of the innovation
2. Relevant firm-specific characteristics that affect the profitability and cost of adoption
3. Tendency by firms to acquire information and their information-processing capabilities.

The above three factors determine firms' *initial* assessments of the innovation's benefits and costs, or its net profitability. If the assessment is high enough in comparison with a certain critical level, the firm will adopt the innovation. If not, the firm will wait until it updates its assessment of the innovation's desirability. Sources of changes in firms' updated assessments of the innovation can be:

4. Changes in the characteristics of the innovation
5. Changes in firms' characteristics or changes in the critical level for adoption
6. New information acquired by firms.

The general pattern for economic models of diffusion is described by David (1969, p. 10):

> whenever or wherever some stimulus variate takes on a value exceeding a critical level, the subject of the stimulation responds by instantly determining to adopt the innovation in question. The reasons such decisions are not arrived at simultaneously by the entire population of potential adopters lies in the fact that at any given point of time either the 'stimulus variate' or the 'critical level' required to elicit an adoption is described by a distribution of values, and not a unique value appropriate to all members of the population. Hence, at any point in time following the advent of an innovation, the critical level has been surpassed only in the cases of some among the whole population of potential adopters. Through some exogenous or endogenous process, however, the relative positions of the stimulus variate and critical response level are altered as time passes, bringing a growing proportion of the population across the 'threshold' into the group of actual users of the innovation.

Factors 1–3 above determine the initial stimulus and the firm-specific critical level required for immediate adoption. Factors 4–6 define the sources of changes in the stimulus variate and the critical response level over time. This process of change can be endogenous or/and exogenous, depending on the extent to which the number of early adopters impact on other firms' updated assessments of the innovation. That is, the literature distinguishes between diffusion processes which are driven by changes in external events, and those which are driven by endogenous change from within. The models in the literature differ in their assumptions of critical characteristics defining the heterogeneity in the population of potential adopters and in their assumption of the sources of changes in firms' assessments of the innovation's desirability.

5.2.1 Heterogeneous Population of Potential Adopters

An early contribution in this area is the model developed by Davies (1979) which can be used as an example to illustrate how the various factors highlighted above can be incorporated in an economic model of decision-making under uncertainty. Using a probit approach, Davies (1979) assumes that firms use yardstick or target payback/rates of return when deciding whether or not to adopt an innovation. The adoption decision may be formulated using the following two definitions (Davies, 1979, p. 67):

> *Let ER_{it} be firm i's expectation of the pay-off period associated with adoption at time t (that is, its expectation of the period elapsing before the initial outlay will be recouped from increased net earnings), and let R_{it}^* be a yardstick or target which it gives as the maximum pay-off period acceptable.*

Then denoting the state of firm i having adopted the innovation by time t as $q_{it} = 1$ and the state of not having adopted as $q_{it} = 0$, it is assumed that:

$$q_{it} = 1 \quad \text{if } ER_{it} \leq R_{it}^* \text{ for some } \tau \leq t,$$
$$q_{it} = 0 \quad \text{if } ER_{it} > R_{it}^* \text{ for all } \tau \leq t. \tag{5.1}$$

The condition for $q_{it} = 1$ states that there must have been some time τ before the present (i.e. t) during which ER_{it} was less than R_{it}^*. Conversely, the condition for $q_{it} = 0$ implies that there was never a time before the present such that ER_{it} was less than R_{it}^* (or that ER_{it} was always larger than R_{it}^* for all time τ before the present).

The expected pay-off ER is an inverse measure of the profitability of the innovation. It reflects not only the innovation's actual profitability of adoption, but also the availability of information and the firm's differential information-processing capabilities. Based on the assumption that information quality improves with time and prior research on the determinants of innovation profitability, Davies (1979) assumes that ER varies between firms and over time as follows:

$$ER_{it} = \theta_1(t) S_{it}^{\beta(1)} \varepsilon_{1it}, \tag{5.2}$$

$$\varepsilon_{1it} = \prod_{j=1}^{r} X_{ijt}^{\gamma(j)} > 0, \tag{5.3}$$

where θ_1, $\beta(1)$, and $\gamma(j)$ are parameters of the model, ε_{1it} is a multiplicative error term, X_{ijt} is a set of unspecified firm characteristics affecting ER_{it}, r is the number of these characteristics, and

$$\theta_1(t) > 0; \quad (d\theta_1/dt)/\theta_1 < 0 \quad \text{for all } t \tag{5.4}$$

Thus, the heterogeneity imposed here is through measuring the pay-off period from adoption as a function of firm size, S_{it}, and r other unspecified characteristics of the firm, X_{ijt}, which reflect the differences between firms, and in the stimulus variate. Firms also differ in their target or critical pay-off period against which adoption is assessed (the critical level). This is represented in a similar mathematical formulation:

$$R_{it}^* = \theta_2(t)S_{it}^{\beta(2)}\varepsilon_{2it}; \tag{5.5}$$

$$\varepsilon_{2it} = \prod_{j=1}^{u} Y_{ijt}^{\phi(j)} > 0, \tag{5.6}$$

where θ_2, $\beta(2)$, and $\phi(j)$ are parameters of the model, ε_{2it} is a multiplicative error term, Y_{ijt} is a set of certain unspecified firm characteristics affecting ER_{it} (which may or may not be the same as X_{ijt}), u is the number of these characteristics, and

$$\theta_2(t) > 0; \quad (d\theta_2/dt)/\theta_2 > 0 \quad \text{for all } t. \tag{5.7}$$

Davies (1979) incorporates the effects of exogenous factors by assuming that the pay-off period (as a measure of firms' assessment of the profitability of adoption) declines monotically with time (equation (5.4)). This is due to the strong likelihood that incoming information will tend to improve most firms' views of the profitability of adoption and to the possibility of post-innovation improvements which increases the profitability of adoption over time (factor 4). It is also assumed that the critical pay-off period, R^*, increases with time, reflecting relaxation of risk premium and the effect of competitive pressures (equation (5.7), factor 5). Using certain simplifying assumptions, the adoption problem facing the firm (equation (5.1)) can be reformulated as:

$$q_{it} = 1 \quad \text{if } S_{cit} \leq S_{it} \quad \text{for } \beta > 0$$
$$q_{it} = 1 \quad \text{if } S_{cit} \geq S_{it} \quad \text{for } \beta < 0 \tag{5.8}$$

where

$$S_{cit} = (\theta_t \varepsilon_{it})^{-1/\beta} \tag{5.9}$$

$$\beta = \beta_2 - \beta_1 \tag{5.10}$$

and

$$\varepsilon_{it} = \varepsilon_{2it}/\varepsilon_{1it} > 0 \tag{5.11}$$

S_{cit}, which defines the critical firm size, will vary between firms depending on the host of factors (other than size) which influence each firm's adoption decision as reflected by ε_{it}. By analysing the distribution and specification of ε_{it} across firms, the model can move from prediction of the probability of adoption at the firm level, to predictions concerning the behaviour of the industry in aggregate; namely, the industry *diffusion* curve, which describes the growth in the proportion of firms having adopted the innovation.[1]

Other applications of the probit approach in adoption models include David (1969), Bonus (1973), and Stoneman and Ireland (1983). David (1969) offers both theoretical and empirical support for the use of firm size as a determinant of firms' adoption. Stoneman and Ireland (1983) build on the work of David (1969) by incorporating long-run optimising behaviour on the behalf of the innovation supplying industry given the demand curve and the size distribution of the using industry. In their model, firms decide to adopt a cost-saving process innovation when the cost savings stemming from reduced labour exceeds the capital cost of adoption. Since the cost reduction from adoption is a function of the output level of the firm, the critical size of adoption can be defined using the firm size, the cost of adoption, and wage growth rate. With labour cost growing at an exponential rate, they show that an increasing proportion of firms will find the new technology profitable, and the innovation will diffuse among firms given their size distribution.

Jensen (1982) uses differential initial assessments of the innovation's profitability as a source of heterogeneity in his decision theoretic model of innovation adoption under uncertainty. In this model, firms begin with varying initial assessments of the unknown profitability of an innovation and costlessly update their assessments based on new freely gathered information. If the firm's initial assessment is high enough, it adopts the innovation which involves a fixed cost and is irreversible. Otherwise, the firm will wait one more period during which it receives new information updating its assessments of the innovation's profitability in a Bayesian fashion, and it forgoes for one period potential profits of adoption. Given differential initial assessments of the innovation's profitability, firms will typically reach the critical level of assessed profitability at different times, and the innovation will diffuse into use, even though firms receive identical information and possess identical information processing capabilities. Jensen (1984c) considered the case of asymmetry in information processing capabilities. Jensen (1984a, 1984b) and McCardle (1985) generalised the model to include explicit costs of information gathering and also considered alternative cost function specifications.

5.2.2 Strategic Interactions and Innovation Adoption

Reinganum (1981b) models a situation in which each firm perceives the impact of other firms' adoption decisions upon its own profits. She showed that even in a world free of uncertainty and where all potential adopters are identical, innovations will be adopted sequentially. In her model, firms maximise the present value of adoption in a game-theoretic framework; that is, bearing in mind the behaviour of rivals with the profitability of adoption being greatest for early adopters and adoption cost dropping sharply as adoption is delayed. Reinganum (1981c) extends her earlier two-person game model to incorporate the case of an infinite number of firms. She shows that if the value of adopting a cost-reducing, capital-embodied process innovation declines with the number of firms which have already adopted it, then the same phenomenon persists (i.e.

diffusion or sequential adoption as opposed to immediate adoption by all firms) even in the limiting case of infinitely many firms. This diffusion results from purely strategic behaviour; there are no imperfections of information nor are there any assumed differences between firms (Reinganum, 1981c, p. 624).

Reinganum (1981b, 1981c) shows that the effects of strategic behaviour can be as important as imperfect information and/or heterogeneity of potential adopters in understanding the mechanics of diffusion. This model assumes that firms are committed to their adoption date, regardless of any subsequent information they might receive regarding the actions of rivals.

Fudenberg and Tirole (1985) examine situations in which firms will be able to respond to the actions of rivals in the absence of time or cost constraints. Fudenberg and Tirole's (1985) work enables us to examine the effect of pre-emption in games of timing. Pre-emption adoption refers to situations where firms will adopt sooner in order to prevent or delay adoption by their rivals. Fudenberg and Tirole (1985) find that when the gain to pre-emption is sufficiently low then the optimal *symmetric* outcome is an equilibrium which contrasts with Reinganum's (1981b, 1981c) results that in a precommitment equilibria there must be diffusion. A more critical evaluation of Reinganum's (1981b, 1981c) conclusions is provided by Quirmbach (1986) who analyses the key elements which combine to generate diffusion. Quirmbach (1986) finds that declining incremental benefits for later adoption and declining adoption costs create *ex post* heterogeneity which generates diffusion. That is, even though there is no *ex ante* heterogeneity among firms, these characteristics of the adoption problem lead to diffusion of innovations. The asymmetric outcome here is thus the result of asymmetries not among the players, but in the payoffs themselves (Quirmbach, 1986, p. 42). Strategic behaviour is inessential to the result; the patterns of incremental benefits and adoption costs are the key, with or without strategic behaviour.

Building on earlier work by Jensen (1982), McCardle (1985) models a single firm's adoption decision in the absence of strategic considerations regarding an exogenous technological innovation of unknown profitability. The model is a generalisation of Jensen's (1982) model which includes explicit costs of information acquiring. The firm continues to gather information sequentially, thus updating its assessment of the innovation's profitability in a Bayesian fashion. McCardle (1985) shows that this will reduce to a waiting game, where at the beginning of each period, the firm has to decide whether to adopt the innovation, gather more information, or stop and reject the innovation. The main results of the model are summarised in Figure 5.1. The firm starts with a given amount of information and an estimate p of profitability on the vertical axis. As the firm continues to gather information, it moves rightward in the direction of increasing information in Figure 5.1, favourable information causing an upward shift and unfavourable information causing a downward shift. The firm will continue to gather information as long as it remains in region II. If the

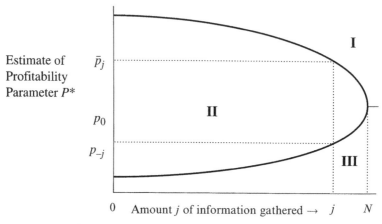

Source: McCardle (1985, p. 1374)

Figure 5.1 Information acquisition and adoption of innovation

firm arrives in region I, it stops and adopts the innovation. If the firm arrives in region III, it stops and rejects the innovation. Given that firms' initial information is modelled by a prior probability distribution of profitability and the costly sequential nature of information gathering, the model can explain situations where managers who behave *optimally* adopt unprofitable technologies and reject profitable ones. Mamer and McCardle (1985) extend McCardle's (1985) work into a two-firm game theoretic model with costly information signalling between adopters.

5.3 BANDWAGON THEORIES OF INNOVATION ADOPTION

5.3.1 Positive Network Externalities

Researchers in the area have long recognised that increases in the number of firms that adopt an innovation influence the number of remaining firms that will subsequently adopt this innovation (Mansfield, 1961). The impact of early adopters on other firms can take different forms. Rational-efficiency theorists argue that as the number of firms that have adopted an innovation increases, adoption cost decreases (Reinganum, 1981b and 1981c, and Quirmbach, 1986) or its return increases (Katz and Shapiro, 1985, and Farrel and Saloner, 1985), causing more firms to adopt the innovation. Incomplete-information theorists state that as more firms adopt the innovation, the more knowledge revealing the innovation's true characteristics is generated and disseminated from adopters to nonadopters (Mansfield, 1961; Rogers, 1962; Oren and Schwartz, 1988; and Chatterjee and Eliashberg, 1989). For profitable innovations, this information transfer either reduces the risk premium demanded by nonadopters (thus reducing the critical level for adoption) or improves the firm's assessment of the innovation. The influence of the number of adopters on subsequent adoption is an implicit element of the models discussed in the previous section. This section, however, focuses on models which explicitly model this influence.

A number of papers in the literature have addressed the question of free-rider and pre-emption problems associated with innovations with positive externalities. Unlike innovations which exert negative externalities on rival firms, these innovations suffer from firms' unwillingness to adopt unilaterally; expectations about whether others will follow are crucial to the behaviour of initial adopters (Reinganum, 1989). The phenomenon of 'positive network externalities' arises when the utility that a user derives from consumption of a good increases with the number of other agents consuming the good. This is referred to as positive *consumption* externalities. The consumption externalities may be generated through a direct physical effect of the number of purchasers on the quality of the product. The utility a consumer derives from purchasing a telephone, for example, depends on the number of others that have joined the telephone network, and with whom that consumer can make contact. Other sources of externalities include after-sale services where the number and variety of services available for a certain good (from independent suppliers) will depend on the number of consumers who purchase that particular good (i.e. the potential market size for complementary products). The amount and variety of software that will be supplied for use with a given computer, for example, will be an increasing function of the number of hardware units that have been sold. Cheaper prices of complementary goods arising from economies of scale enjoyed by the producing industry is another source of positive network externalities. In all of these cases, the utility that a given user derives from the good depends upon the number of others who are in the same 'network'. The above discussion can be linked to modelling adoption and diffusion of innovations by examining situations where an industry with old standards contemplates introducing new improved ones. Network externalities can play a crucial role in the context of success of innovations if consumers form expectations regarding the size of competing networks, and when these expectations affect the decision by firms to introduce new standards.

Katz and Shapiro (1985) develop a static model of oligopoly to analyse markets in which consumption externalities are present. They examine two sets of issues. The first is concerned with the effect of consumption externalities on competition and the form of market equilibrium. Using a notion of rational (or fulfilled expectations) equilibrium, they find that consumption externalities give rise to demand-side economies of scale, which will vary with consumer expectations. For some sets of expectations only one firm will produce the output, while for other sets of expectations there will be several firms in the market. Katz and Shapiro (1985, p. 425) state that these equilibria verify the intuition that 'if consumers expect a seller to be dominant, then consumers will be willing to pay more for the firm's product, and it will, in fact, be dominant'.

The second area that Katz and Shapiro (1985) explore is more in line with the literature we previously covered and deals with the incentives firms have to produce compatible goods or services. Comparing private and social incentives to produce compatible products, they find that firms with good reputations or large existing networks will tend to be against compatibility, even when welfare is increasing. In contrast, firms with small networks or weak reputations will tend to favour product compatibility, even in cases where the social costs of compatibility outweigh the benefits. Viewing firms as a collective decision maker, they find that the firm's joint incentives for product compatibility are lower than social incentives.

Farrel and Saloner (1985) examine markets in which there are positive net benefits from standardisation or compatibility of products. They examine the conditions under which the consumption network externalities mentioned above are outweighed by social costs of standardisation. Apart from the reduction in variety, social costs of standardisation arise when it causes firms to move extremely reluctantly to a new and better standard. That is, benefits from standardisation can 'trap' an industry in an obsolete or inferior standard when there is a better alternative, and thus reduce the incentives to adopt efficient innovations. Farrel and Saloner (1985) study the possibility that this 'excess inertia', the threat of losing the benefits of standardisation or compatibility, impedes the collective switch from a common standard or technology to a potentially superior new standard or technology. They show that with complete information and identical preferences among firms to switch, then all firms will switch. That is, there is no excess inertia impeding the switch to the improved standards. Both unanimity and complete information, however, are necessary conditions for this all-switch equilibrium. Allowing for uncertainty (in the form of incomplete information about other firms' preferences) yields a richer set of possibilities which we explore below.

Farrel and Saloner (1985) assume a two-period two-firm industry. Each firm can switch at time 1 or time 2 or not at all. Firms which switch at time 1 have no further decisions to make. The second-period move is conditioned on the players' own characteristics and the opponent's first-period move. Firms differ in their benefit functions and incentives to switch to the new technology or to stick with the old one. The firm's type is denoted by i where i measures firm's 'eagerness' to switch, and is distributed uniformly on the unit interval $[0, 1]$. Higher values of i indicate stronger preferences for the switch from technology X to technology Y. The benefits to the firm depend on whether it has adopted the new standard or not, and what its opponent does. Specifically, let $B^i(1,k)$ denote the benefits to the firm of type i from maintaining the standard k alone, and let $B^i(2,k)$ denote the benefits to the firm of type i from having the industry standardised at k, for $k = X$ or Y. The benefits to a firm from switching to the new standard Y are the net benefits relative to its benefits if all firms stick with X and maintain the *status quo*. In other words, status quo profits are normalised to zero so that the firm will be *in favour* of a change by the entire industry if and only if $B^i(2, Y) > 0$ and favour a switch on its own with its opponent sticking to standard X if and only if $B^i(1, Y) > 0$.[2] Now the assumption that all firms are better off using the same standard (whether X or Y) as opposed to using two different standards can be formalised as follows:

The basic assumptions of positive network externalities states that $B^i(2,k) > B^i(1,k)$ for both firms (regardless of type, i) and for $k = X$, Y. $B^i(2, Y)$ and $B^i(1,k)$ are continuous and strictly increasing in i.

Thus a *bandwagon strategy* for a firm can be defined by a pair $(i^*, \bar{i})$ with $i^* > \bar{i}$ such that:

(i)   If $i \geq i^*$, the firm switches at time 1
(ii) If $i^* > i \geq \bar{i}$, the firm does not switch at time 1, and then switches at time 2 if and only if the other firm switched at time 1
(iii) If $i < \bar{i}$, the firm never switches.

A '*bandwagon equilibrium*' is defined to be a perfect Bayesian Nash equilibrium in which each firm plays a bandwagon strategy. Symmetric bandwagon equilibria are those for which $(i^*, \bar{i})$ is the same for each player. Farrel and Saloner (1985) show that a unique symmetric bandwagon equilibrium exists and that there are no equilibria that are not bandwagon equilibria. For group (i) above, the incentives to switch are so great that it is worthwhile to take the risk of not being followed (because recall that both firms are always better off using the same technology than different ones). Firms in group (ii) are willing to switch only if their rivals do so before. For firms in group (iii), the prospects of switch are so bad that the firms prefer to stay alone using the old standard. Several features of the model can now be analysed:

(i)   There are some firms with $i < i^*$ for whom nonetheless $B^i(2, Y) > 0$. If both firms are of types that fall in this region, the switch will not be made, although it would have been made in a world of complete information and although both firms would then be better off. This *symmetric excess inertia* results from lack of co-ordination and communication, or as Farrel and Saloner (1985, p. 78) put it 'both firms are fencesitters,

happy to jump on the bandwagon if it gets rolling but insufficiently keen
to set it rolling'.

(ii) In addition, there is also *asymmetric excess inertia* where one firm may be
of the kind discussed in (i) ($i < i^*$ and $B^i(2, Y) > 0$), but the other firm
may have $B^i(2, Y) < 0$. Here again the switch will not be made even
though the sum of the benefits is positive, for there will *always* exist some
cases where $B^i(2, Y) + B^{i'}(2, Y) > 0$ and $i, i' < i^*$.

(iii) It is also possible that the switch will be made even though the sum of benefits is negative $(B^i(2, Y) + B^{i'}(2, Y) < 0)$. This occurs when one of the
firms favours the switch $(B^i(2, Y) > 0)$ and, although the other opposes it
strongly $(B^{i'}(2, Y) < 0)$, the latter prefers unilateral switching rather than
remaining alone with the old technology $(B^{i'}(1, X) < B^{i'}(2, Y) < 0)$. This
'*excess momentum*' will not always exist, but can occur for appropriately
specified benefit functions. Katz and Shapiro (1985) obtained similar
results where firms with small networks or weak reputations will tend to
favour product compatibility, even in cases where the social costs of
compatibility outweigh the benefits, equivalent to this equilibria of Farrel
and Saloner's (1985) model.

(iv) There are some types in the region $i^* > i > \bar{i}$ for which $B^i(2, Y) < 0$.
These firms will switch if the other firm switches (because
$B^i(1, X) < B^i(2, Y) < 0$), but would have preferred that the new technology had not come along at all. In such cases, the firm has to face a
reduction in benefits whether or not it follows. Following a leader,
however, is less disastrous than sticking alone with the old standard.[3]

(v) Finally, there are some types just above i^* for which $B^i(1, Y) < 0$. These
types start the bandwagon rolling, but if it turns out that the other firm
was of a type below $\bar{i}$ (so that their lead is not followed), they regret their
decisions *ex post*. That is, these firms sufficiently favour technology Y that
they risk starting the bandwagon even though they know with positive
probability that they are up against an 'intransigent' with type less than $\bar{i}$
and will end up worse off if this turns out to be so (Farrel and Saloner,
1985, p. 79).

This model is particularly interesting since it provides a theoretical background to the mathematical diffusion models discussed later in this
chapter. Specifically, it shows that there are generally two groups of firms;
the first consists of firms which always adopt an innovation regardless of
what their rivals do (firms with $i \geq i^*$, and equilibria (v) above), and the
second consists of firms whose adoption decision is influenced by their
rivals (equilibria (i), (ii), (iii), (iv)). Firms in the first group can be referred to
as *external* adopters and firms in the second group can be referred to as *internal*
adopters.[4]

5.3.2 Competitive and Institutional Bandwagon Pressures

Another branch of the literature has focused on situations where the sheer number of firms that have adopted the innovation can cause bandwagon pressure, prompting other firms to adopt this innovation. In these models, bandwagons are defined as diffusion processes whereby firms adopt an innovation, *not because of their individual assessments of the innovation's efficiency or return*, but because of a bandwagon pressure caused by the sheer number of firms that have already adopted the innovation (Abrahamson and Rosenkopf, 1990). In the models discussed above, the number of firms that adopt an innovation impact on other firm's *assessment* of the innovation's efficiency or returns, but firms are still characterised by rational optimising behaviour. Bandwagon theorists, however, argue that in some instances bandwagon pressure created by the number of firms that have adopted an innovation can cause other firms to adopt (reject) an innovation even though they consider it as inefficient (efficient). Adoptions can take place in latter stages even if non-adopters are unaware of updated information about the innovation's efficiency or return.

The information-transfer aspects of the rational-efficiency models assume that information about the innovation's efficiency or returns flow from early adopters to nonadopters. For this to happen, there must exist (Abrahamson and Rosenkopf, 1993, p. 490) (i) information, (ii) channels, (iii) a propensity by adopters to disseminate this information, and (iv) a propensity of nonadopters to be influenced by it. There are many situations where these conditions are not met. In many competitive markets adopters may not wish to disseminate information about the innovation to nonadopters. Even if some information is disseminated, its impact on nonadopters' decisions can be limited by differences between firms (e.g. differences in current business and customer bases, long-term strategic planning, or cost functions). Finally, firms may not risk waiting for information (from either adopter's experiences or their own research) because they fear that early adopters will have sizeable first-mover advantages in the new market. Moreover, the rational-efficiency hypothesis cannot explain situations in which firms reject an innovation even though the innovation is desirable at the firm level.

Bandwagon theories attempt to explain the diffusion patterns of innovations where one or more of the assumptions underlying the rational-efficiency hypothesis are not met. Two types of bandwagon pressures can be identified (Abrahamson and Rosenkopf, 1993); institutional bandwagon and competitive bandwagon. The former refers to pressures on organisations arising from the threat of lost legitimacy and lost shareholders' support. The increase in the number of firms adopting the innovation make firms that do not use the innovation appear abnormal or illegitimate to their shareholders. These firms adopt the innovation, not based on their individual assessment of its efficiency or returns, but because of pressures on them to demonstrate to the industry and shareholders that they are keeping pace with their competitors in terms of innovatory developments.

Competitive bandwagon refers to pressures on organisations to adopt the innovation arising from the threat of lost competitive advantage. Abrahamson and Rosenkopf (1990) developed a model in which firms will seek to avoid the worst-case scenario of being at a great competitive disadvantage by performing far below the average industry performance. The larger the number of adopters the worse is the firm's relative performance if the firm does not adopt and the innovation succeeds. By adapting a utility schema in which firms' perceived threat of a competitive disadvantage (if the firm does not adopt and the innovation succeeds) far outweighs the perceived value of an equally large competitive advantage (if the firm does not adopt and the innovation fails), Abrahamson and Rosenkopf (1990) show that adoption can become more attractive, as a means to reduce uncertainty, the larger the number of adopters. This is so because adopters' performance will approach the industry's average whether the innovation succeeds or fails.

Abrahamson and Rosenkopf (1993) develop a theoretical model of a bandwagon-effects-driven diffusion process. They argue that in the early stage of diffusion, certain organisations assess returns too low to adopt the innovation. These organisations may adopt the innovation in later stages, however, because of an added bandwagon pressure to adopt caused by the sheer number of early-stage adopters. Therefore, they model organisations' adoption decisions by summing their individual assessment of the innovation's return and the bandwagon pressure. The strength of bandwagon pressure in their model increases with the number of adopters, but this relationship is moderated by the level of ambiguity. The intuition behind this formulation is that social factors are more likely to have a significant impact on firms' adoption decisions the higher the uncertainty associated with the innovation's profitability. In the extreme case where information is complete and there is no uncertainty, firms base their adoption decisions solely on the innovation's profitability, and their optimising behaviour can be described by rational-efficiency models. It is the presence of uncertainty, however, which causes competitive and institutional bandwagon pressures to exist. When decisions to adopt cannot be based fully on economic considerations such as technical efficiency or returns, social considerations, such as bandwagon pressures, play a role in the occurrence of bandwagon processes.[5] Thus, the greater the ambiguity, the greater the bandwagon pressures on organisations to adopt an innovation that are generated by a given number of adopters.

Therefore, Abrahamson and Rosenkopf (1993) model bandwagon pressure as the product of ambiguity and the number of adopters. In sum, assessed returns (for initial assessments), ambiguity, and the number of adopters influence organisation's decisions to adopt an innovation according to the equation: $B_{i,k} = I_i + (A_i \cdot n_{k-1})$, where $B_{i,k}$ is organisation i's 'bandwagon assessment' of the innovation in bandwagon cycle k. I_i and A_i denote, respectively, organisation i's individual assessment of the innovation and ambiguity about this innovation. The bandwagon pressure during k is denoted by the product of the level of ambiguity, A_i, and the proportion of adopters, n, after $k - 1$ cycles. The number of organisations that must adopt in order to prompt organisation i's adoption is such that the bandwagon assessment, $B_{i,k}$, exceeds the adoption threshold. Implicit in this formulation is the assumption of *no* information transfer from early to late adopters regarding the innovation's profitability, or that transferred information is so ambiguous that it does not lead them to reappraise their individual assessment of the innovation (i.e. I_i remains constant over k). Assuming that individual assessments of organisations (I_i) are normally distributed, the proportion of organisations that have adopted in cycle k of a bandwagon can be derived analytically from this model. Two important assumptions underlie the model. First, each organisation's adoption gives an equal impetus to the bandwagon. That is, the number of adopters rather than their identity is the key factor. The second assumption is that innovation diffusion neither eliminates organisations from the adopting group nor attracts new organisations to the adopting group. These turn out to be two common assumptions of most of the models reviewed in the remainder of this chapter.

It should be clear that heterogeneity in organisation's initial assessments is the key factor leading to '*diffusion*' in this model. If the distribution of organisations' individual assessments is such that certain organisations assess returns from adopting above the adoption threshold, these organisations adopt the innovation. This does not imply that these organisations adopt simultaneously in the early stage, but rather they adopt the innovation because of their individual assessment of the innovation's returns. Organisations that did not adopt in the early stage now consider the sum of their assessed return and bandwagon pressure. If there does not exist a nonadopter whose bandwagon assessment of the innovation, $B_{i,k}$, exceeds the adoption threshold, then the diffusion process terminates. If such a nonadopter exists, then it adopts the innovation. The bandwagon process may not stop at this point. Bandwagon adoption can animate a cycle in which growing bandwagon pressures prompt bandwagon pressures to grow. The number of process cycles depends on ambiguity and assessed returns. Table 5.1 summarises the factors influencing firms' adoption of innovations that have been highlighted in the chapter so far.

5.4 EMPIRICAL MODELS OF DIFFUSION

The models discussed above offer interesting insights into the determinants of innovation adoption and the factors influencing the diffusion patterns of

Table 5.1   Factors affecting adoption of innovations

Firms adopt an innovation when the *stimulus variate* exceeds the firm-specific *critical level*.

The *stimulus variate* is initially determined by:
- The innovation's true return/cost characteristics
- Firm's differential access to information and their information-processing capabilities
- Relevant firm-specific characteristics affecting cost and benefit of adoption

and over time are influenced by:

- Changes in the true cost/benefit of the innovation. Can be due to number of firms that adopted the innovation (e.g. increase or decrease in expected benefits due to positive or negative externalities of adoption by one firm. A decrease in cost of adoption due to fixed-cost component paid by early adopters).
- Updated assessments of the innovation's cost/benefit based on new information from either external sources or from early adopters.

The *critical level* is initially determined by:
- Firm-specific characteristics (e.g. firm size, other potential investment opportunities, targeted customer base, long-term planning, etc . . .).
- Industry-specific factors (e.g. expected future growth rate, competition, etc . . .).

- Strategic factors can cause a firm to adopt an innovation not based on its assessment of the innovation's profitability but because of the threat of lost competitive advantage (competitive bandwagon effects).
- Bandwagon effects may cause firms to require less risk premium thus reducing critical levels required for adoption (institutional bandwagon effects).

innovations. There is, however, a lack of testable models of industry equilibrium behaviour. Theoretical economic models of individual firms' decision making do not generally lend themselves to an empirically testable format. The alternative is to develop models of aggregate industry diffusion patterns with less emphasis on the determinants of an individual firm's behaviour. The purpose of such models is to measure the diffusion rate of innovations by depicting the successive increase in the number of adopters or adopting units over time. By doing so, a diffusion model permits prediction of the continued development of the diffusion process over time as well as facilitating a theoretical explanation of the dynamic process in terms of general characteristics (Mahajan and Peterson, 1985, p. 10). Table 5.2 shows a number of diffusion studies and the innovations whose diffusion patterns have been modelled. Although the application of diffusion models extends over a large number of industries, only three studies that we are aware of, model innovations in the banking industry.

Table 5.2 Applications of diffusion models

Study	Innovations modelled
Griliches (1957)	Hybrid corn
Fourt and Woodlock (1960)	New grocery products
Mansfield (1961)	Innovations in the railroad, coal, steel, and brewery industries.
Coleman *et al.* (1966)	New drugs
Bass (1969)	Consumer durables (e.g. black and white and colour televisions)
Mahajan and Peterson (1978)	Membership in the United Nations
Kalwani and Silk (1980)	New packaged goods
Easingwood *et al.* (1981)	CAT head scanners and CAT body scanners
Lilien, Roa, and Kalish (1981)	New ethical drug
Sharif and Ramanathan (1981)	Oral contraceptives
Easingwood *et al.* (1983)	Consumer durables (e.g. air conditioners, dish washers, black and white and colour televisions)
Horsky and Simon (1983)	Telephone-based banking services
Mahajan *et al.* (1983)	New ethical drug
Skiadas (1987)	Diffusion of tractors in Spain
Alpar (1992)	The spread of automation of business functions in banks
Lavaraj and Gore (1992)	The spread of innovation of cross-breeding of goats
Sharma *et al.* (1993)	Consumer electronics
Jagtiani *et al.* (1995)	Off-balance-sheet activities

5.4.1 Basic Models

Most models in the literature are a special form of the fundamental model proposed by Mahajan and Schoeman (1977):

$$\frac{\partial N(t)}{\partial t} = g(t)[\bar{N} - N(t)], \tag{5.12}$$

where:

$N(t)$ = cumulative number of adopters at time t

$\bar{N}$ = Total number of potential adopters in the social system at time t

$\dfrac{\partial N(t)}{\partial t}$ = rate of diffusion at time t

$g(t)$ = coefficient of diffusion.

The above deterministic model posits that the rate of diffusion of an innovation at any time t is a function of (that is, is directly proportional to) the gap or difference between the total number of possible adopters existing at that time and the number of previous adopters at that time $[\bar{N} - N(t)]$. A consequence of this model formulation is that as the cumulative number of prior adopters, $N(t)$, approaches the total number of possible adopters in the social system, $\bar{N}$, the rate of diffusion decreases.

The form or nature of the relationship between the rate of diffusion and the number of potential adopters existing at time t, $[\bar{N} - N(t)]$, is represented or controlled by $g(t)$, the coefficient of diffusion. The value of $g(t)$ depends on innovation-specific characteristics such as the nature of the innovation, distribution of critical firm characteristics, communication channels employed, and other external factors which affect the desirability of the innovation. In addition $g(t)$ can be interpreted as the probability of adoption at time t. If this interpretation is used, then $g(t) \times [\bar{N} - N(t)]$ represents the expected number of adopters at time t, $n(t)$.

Two distinct approaches have been used to represent $g(t)$. One has been to represent $g(t)$ as a function of time; the other has been to represent $g(t)$ as a function of the number of previous adopters. $g(t)$ has been typically formulated as either:

$$g(t) = a, \qquad \text{External-influence} \quad \frac{\partial N(t)}{\partial t} = a[\bar{N} - N(t)], \qquad (5.13)$$

$$g(t) = b\,N(t), \text{ or } \quad \text{Internal-influence} \quad \frac{\partial N(t)}{\partial t} = b\,N(t)[\bar{N} - N(t)], \qquad (5.14)$$

$$g(t) = (a + b\,N(t)), \text{ Mixed-influence} \quad \frac{\partial N(t)}{\partial t} = (a + b\,N(t))[\bar{N} - N(t)]. \quad (5.15)$$

In the external-influence model it is assumed that the fraction of potential adopters, $[\bar{N} - N(t)]$, at time t who will adopt the innovation during time t is equal to 'a' which is defined as an index or coefficient of external influence emanating from the outside the social system. In general 'a' can represent any influence other than a prior adoption. Frequently 'a' is interpreted as representing the effect of mass media communication on the diffusion process. Thus the model does not attribute any diffusion to interaction between prior adopters and potential adopters. Examples of external-influence models include Fourt and Woodlock (1960) and Coleman et al. (1966).

In complete contrast to the external-influence model the internal-influence model is based on a contagion paradigm that diffusion occurs only through interpersonal contacts. The rate of diffusion is treated solely as a function of social interaction (or bandwagon pressures) between the prior adopters and potential adopters in the social system. Interpersonal communication or social interaction is represented by $N(t)[\bar{N} - N(t)]$ (i.e. prior adopters $\times$ potential adopters). Hence this model can be considered as a pure imitation diffusion model. The constant b is defined as an index of imitation or internal influence because it reflects the interaction of prior adopters with potential adopters. The most well-known internal-influence model is that of Mansfield (1961) and Griliches (1957).

The mixed-influence model subsumes both of the previous models by incorporating parameters representing external as well as internal influences.

As such, it is the most widely used and most general of the three fundamental diffusion model versions because it accommodates the assumptions of the other two. The first application of a mixed-influence model is due to Bass (1969).

Except for the external-influence model, it can be shown that the other models result in an S-shaped diffusion curve. A stream of empirical research has found that the typical pattern of diffusion follows an S-shaped curve, and has sought to explain this typical pattern in terms of communication channels and various characteristics of the potential adopter population (Freeman, 1988, p. 42).

One explanation of the S-shaped diffusion curve (for technological-substitution models) is that all relevant firms are aware of the innovation, but differences in the vintage of each firm's capital stock leads to differences in the optimal time to imitate (Ferguson, 1988, p. 93). Another explanation is provided by likening the diffusion process to the spread of epidemics. For a disease to spread requires people without immunity to the disease to be exposed to those with the infection. Initially there will be few people suffering from the disease so the rate of infection will be slow, even with a large number of uninfected people in the population. As the number of those infected grows, the epidemic spreads more rapidly until it reaches a maximum. Beyond this the spread of the epidemic slows because, although there are many infected people, there are fewer people left to catch the disease. Translations of such arguments to the diffusion of technical innovations are presented by Mansfield (1968). He explained the *slowness* of innovation adoption by all members of the population of potential adopters by considering demand side factors and stressing uncertainty regarding the value of the innovation and the rate at which that uncertainty is reduced as key determinants of the rate of diffusion. Rosenberg (1976) accounts for the S-shaped pattern of innovation diffusion by examining supply side considerations such as the continual improvements to the innovation, institutional barriers, need for changes in complementary industries, and the improvements that the new technology may force upon incumbent technologies.

Examples of an S-shape growth curve are: the logistic curve by Mansfield (1961), the generalised logistic curve by Bass (1969), and the normal distribution by Stapleton (1976). Other functions such as the lognormal distribution, the Poisson and the chi-distribution are also available and give rise to an S-shaped growth curve (Skiadas, 1987, p. 79). The next section discusses: the basic internal-influence models of Griliches (1957), Mansfield (1961); external-influence model of Fourt and Woodlock (1960); and the mixed-influence model of Bass (1969). Subsequent literature can be viewed as an effort to overcome the limitations of these basic models and these are covered in the remainder of this chapter.

5.4.2 The Mansfield (1961) Model

One of the earliest applications of the internal-diffusion model is due to the work of Griliches (1957). He studied the factors responsible for the wide cross-sectional differences in the historical rates of use of hybrid seed corn in the United States, in what can be considered the first formal application of an internal-influence diffusion model. Logistic growth functions were fitted to data for 31 states and for 132 crop reporting districts within these states. The logistic growth curve is defined by $P = K/1 + e^{-(a+bt)}$, where P is the percentage planted with hybrid seed, K the ceiling or equilibrium value, t the time variable, b the rate of growth coefficient, and a the constant of integration which positions the curve on the time scale. One feature of this curve is that the rate of growth is proportional to the growth already achieved and to the distance from the ceiling. It is this property that makes the logistic curve useful for modelling diffusion processes.

To estimate the parameters of the logistic, the function can be transformed into an equation linear in a and b. By dividing both sides of the logistic by $K - P$ and taking the logarithm, we get its linear transformation, $\log_e[P/(K - P)] = a + bt$, allowing us to estimate the parameters directly by least squares. Using this procedure, Griliches succeeded in reducing a large mass of data to three sets of variables—*origins* (a), *slopes* (b), *ceilings* (K). Economic interpretation of the differences in the estimated coefficients among the different districts was developed using regression analysis. Variations in the date of origin were identified with supply factors, variations in slopes with factors affecting the rate of acceptance by farmers, and variations in ceilings with demand factors affecting the long-run equilibrium position. The lag in the development of adaptable hybrids for particular areas and the lag in the entry of seed producers into these areas (differences in *origins*) were explained on the basis of varying profitability of entry, 'profitability' being a function of market density, and innovation and marketing cost. Differences in the long-run equilibrium use of hybrid corn (*ceilings*) and in the rates of approach to that equilibrium (*slopes*) were explained, at least in part, by differences in the profitability of the shift from open pollinated to hybrid varieties or corn in different parts of the country.

Mansfield (1961) investigated the factors determining how rapidly the use of a new technique spreads from one firm to another. He presented a model to help explain the differences among innovations in the rate of imitation. Let $\bar{N}_{ij}$ be the total number of firms that introduced the jth innovation in the ith industry ($j = 1, 2, 3; i = 1, 2, 3, 4$). Let $N_{ij}(t)$ be the number of these firms having introduced this innovation at time t, π_{ij} be the profitability of installing this innovation relative to that of alternative investments, and S_{ij} be the investment required to install this innovation as a percentage of the average total assets of these firms. Let $\lambda_{ij}(t)$ be the proportion of 'hold-outs' (firms not using this innovation) at time t that introduce it by time $t + 1$, i.e.

$$\lambda_{ij}(t) = \frac{N_{ij}(t + 1) - N_{ij}(t)}{\bar{N}_{ij} - N_{ij}(t)}. \tag{5.16}$$

The model is based on the following assumption. The proportion of 'hold-outs' at time t that introduce the innovation by time $t + 1$ is a function of (i) the proportion of firms that already introduced it by time t, $N_t / \bar{N}$, (ii) the profit-ability of installing it, π_{ij}, (iii) the size of the investment required to install it, S_{ij} and (iv) other unspecified variables. Allowing the function to vary among industries, then:

$$\lambda_{ij}(t) = f_i\left(\frac{N_{ij}(t)}{\bar{N}_{ij}}, \pi_{ij}, S_{ij}, \dots\right). \tag{5.17}$$

Before testing the function empirically, Mansfield provides a theoretical expectation about the relationship between the variables in the function. A positive relationship is expected between $\lambda_{ij}(t)$ and the proportion of firms already using the innovation. As more information and experience accumulates, it becomes less risky to introduce the innovation. Competitive pressures mount and 'bandwagon' effects occur. Where the profitability of using the innovation is very difficult to estimate, the mere fact that a large proportion of its competitors have adopted it may prompt a firm to consider it more favourably.

Second, the profitability of installing the innovation would also be expected to have an important influence on $\lambda_{ij}(t)$. The more profitable this investment is relative to others that are available, the greater is the chance that a firm's estimate of the profitability will be high enough to compensate for whatever risks are involved and that it will seem to be worthwhile to install the new technique rather than to wait.

Third, for equally profitable innovations, $\lambda_{ij}(t)$ should tend to be smaller for those requiring relatively large investment. Firms tend to be more cautious before committing themselves to such projects and they often have more difficulty in financing them.

Finally for equally profitable innovations requiring the same investment, $\lambda_{ij}(t)$ is likely to vary among industries. It might be higher in one industry than in another because firms in the former industry have less aversion to risk, markets are more keenly competitive, the attitude of the labour force towards innovation is more favourable, or because the industry is healthier financially.

Assuming that the number of firms having introduced an innovation can vary continuously rather than assuming only integer values, then $\lambda_{ij}(t)$ can be approximated adequately within the relevant range by a Taylor's expansion that drops third and higher order terms, and that $(N_{ij}(t)/\bar{N}_{ij})^2$ in this expansion is zero, equation (5.17) can then be rewritten as:

$$\lambda_{ij}(t) = a_{i1} + a_{i2}\,\frac{N_{ij}(t)}{\bar{N}_{ij}} + a_{i3}\pi_{ij} + a_{i4}S_{ij} + a_{i5}\pi_{ij}\,\frac{N_{ij}(t)}{\bar{N}_{ij}} + a_{i4}S_{ij} + a_{i6}S_{ij}\,\frac{N_{ij}(t)}{\bar{N}_{ij}}$$

$$+ a_{i7}\pi_{ij}S_{ij} + a_{i8}\pi_{ij}^2 + a_{i8}S_{ij}^2 + \cdots, \tag{5.18}$$

where additional terms contain the unspecified variables in equation (5.17). Thus,

$$N_{ij}(t+1) - N_{ij}(t) = [\bar{N}_{ij} - N_{ij}]\left[a_{i1} + a_{i2}\frac{N_{ij}}{\bar{N}} + \cdots + a_{i9}S_{ij}^2 + \cdots\right], \quad (5.19)$$

which, assuming that time is measured in fairly small units, can be approximated by the differential equation:

$$\frac{dN_{ij}(t)}{dt} = [\bar{N}_{ij} - N_{ij}(t)]\left[Q_{ij} + \phi_{ij}\frac{N_{ij}(t)}{\bar{N}_{ij}}\right] \quad (5.20)$$

the solution of which is given by:

$$N_{ij}(t) = \frac{\bar{N}[e^{l_{ij}+(Q_{ij}+\phi_{ij})t} - (Q_{ij}/\phi_{ij})]}{1 + e^{l_{ij}+(Q_{ij}+\phi_{ij})t}} \quad (5.21)$$

where l_{ij} is a constant of integration, Q_{ij} is the sum of all terms in equation (5.18) not containing $N_{ij}/\bar{N}_{ij}$, and $(\phi = a_{i2} + a_{i5}\pi + a_{i6}S_{ij} + \cdots)$. By imposing the boundary condition that $\lim_{t \to -\infty} N_{ij} = 0$, equation (5.21) reduces to:

$$N_{ij}(t) = \bar{N}_{ij}[1 + e^{-(l_{ij}+\phi_{ij}t)}]^{-1}. \quad (5.22)$$

where time t is measured by the number of years that have elapsed since the introduction of the innovation. Thus, the growth over time in the number of firms having introduced an innovation should conform to the S-shaped logistic growth function. Equation (5.22) implies that the rate of imitation is governed by only one parameter—ϕ_{ij}. Assuming that a_{i2}, a_{i5}, and a_{i6} do not vary among industries, then we have:

$$\phi_{ij} = b_i + a_{i5}\pi_{ij} + a_{i6}S_{ij} + z_{ij}, \quad (5.23)$$

where b_i equals a_{i2} in equation (5.18) and z_{ij} is a random variable with zero expected value. Hence the expected value of ϕ_{ij} in a particular industry is a linear function of π_{ij} and S_{ij}. The empirical test of the model is carried out in two steps: (i) by estimating ϕ_{ij} and l_{ij} and determining how well equation (5.22) fits the data, and (ii) by seeing whether the expected value of ϕ_{ij} seems to be a linear function of π_{ij} and S_{ij}. To carry out the first step, and if the model is correct, it follows from equation (5.22) that:

$$\ln\left[\frac{N_{ij}(t)}{\bar{N}_{ij} - N_{ij}(t)}\right] = l_{ij} + \phi_{ij}t. \quad (5.24)$$

To carry out the second step, we rewrite equation (5.23) as:

$$\hat{\phi}_{ij} = b_i + a_5\pi_{ij} + a_6 S_{ij} + z'_{ij}, \quad (5.25)$$

where $\hat{\phi}_{ij}$ is the estimate of the ϕ_{ij} derived above. b_i in equation (5.25) is a measure of the internal-influence, or rate of imitation, and is assumed to be industry-dependent. Other factors that influence the speed of diffusion are the profitability of the innovation, π_{ij}, and the size of the investment required, S_{ij}.

Mansfield (1961) estimated equation (5.24) using data on the number of the firms that have adopted 12 innovations in four industries (Table 5.3). Equation (5.24) was estimated for each innovation. Mansfield (1961) reported a 'good' fit for all innovations in the sense that the correlation coefficient between the dependent variable and time, r_{ij}, in Table 5.3 below, exceeds 0.89 in all cases. Judging by the r_{ij} values (and by visual comparison between expected and actual values of the number of adopting firms), Mansfield (1961, p. 751) concludes that 'ϕ_{ij} is generally reliable as a measure of the rate of imitation'.

The rate of diffusion as measured by ϕ_{ij} varied significantly between innovations ranging from 0.11 for *centralised traffic control* (CTC) to 2.4 for *tin containers* (TC). The coefficient ϕ_{ij} can be interpreted in two ways. Firstly, it measures the 'speed' of diffusion of an innovation. In this sense, CTC and TC witnessed the fastest and slowest diffusion rates, respectively. Figure 5.2 depicts the diffusion pattern of these two innovations. Note that to construct these values we only needed to know the respective values of ϕ_{ij} and l_{ij}.

Table 5.3 Parameter estimates for 12 innovations—Mansfield (1961)

Innovation	l_{ij}	ϕ_{ij}	r_{ij}
Railroads Industry			
Diesel locomotive	−6.64	0.20	0.89
Centralised traffic control	−7.13	0.19	0.94
Car readers	−3.95	0.11	0.90
Iron and Steel Industry			
Continuous wide strip mill	−10.47	0.34	0.95
By-product coke oven	−1.47	0.17	0.98
Continuous annealing	−8.51	0.17	0.93
Bituminous Coal Industry			
Shuttle car	−13.48	0.32	0.95
Trackless mobile loader	−13.03	0.32	0.97
Continuous mining machine	−24.96	0.49	0.98
Brewing Industry			
Tin container	−84.35	2.40	0.96
High-speed bottle filler	−20.58	0.36	0.97
Pallet-loading machine	−29.07	0.55	0.97

Note: l_{ij} and ϕ_{ij} are the intercept and the coefficient of time as estimated from equation 5.24. r_{ij} is the correlation coefficient between the dependent variable and time. Larger values of r_{ij} indicates better fit. The time-series regression analysis is in the form of $\ln(N_t/\bar{N} - N_t) = l_{ij} + \phi_{ij}t$. The coefficient of time, ϕ_{ij}, is used as a measure of the speed or rate of diffusion. Larger values of ϕ_{ij} indicates faster diffusion.
Source: Mansfield (1961, p. 749).

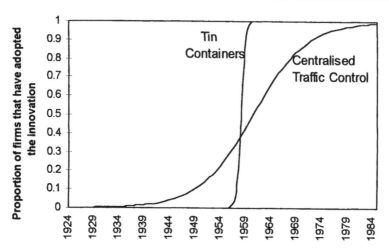

Figure 5.2   The diffusion rates of two innovations

The diffusion patterns of these innovations in Figure 5.2 were calculated using the formula $N_t/\bar{N} = [1 + e^{-(l_{ij}+\phi t)}]^{-1}$ where $l_{ij} = -7.13$ and $\phi_{ij} = 0.19$ for the CTC and are equal to $l_{ij} = -84.35$ and $\phi_{ij} = 2.4$ for the tin containers. Time, or t in the above equation, is equal to the number of years that have elapsed since the introduction of the innovation (i.e. $t = 1, 2, 3, \ldots$), and is measured by the horizontal axis. The vertical axis measures the proportion of firms which have introduced the innovation at each period of time t and is given by $N_t/\bar{N}$ for each innovation ij. In the data sample used by Mansfield (1961) all firms have eventually adopted the innovation and $\bar{N}$ was therefore assumed to be equal to the total number of firms in the industry and $N_t/\bar{N}$ is equal to one as t gets larger. As can be seen from Figure 5.2, according to the model predictions, it took less than five years for all firms in the brewing industry to adopt the tin containers innovation (1955–59) whereas it took more than 50 years for all firms in the railroads industry to adopt the CTC innovation (1934–84). This corresponds to a ϕ_{ij} value of 2.4 for a tin container compared to 0.19 for CTC (see Table 5.3).

Alternatively, one may interpret ϕ_{ij} as a measure of the bandwagon pressure exerted by adopters of innovation i on non-adopting firms. Table 5.3 indicates that the pressures exerted on firms to adopt an innovation by the adoption of their rivals, i.e. ϕ_{ij}, varies significantly from one industry to another, and between innovations within the same industry. That is, ϕ_{ij} depends on both industry-specific and innovation-specific factors. The second part of Mansfield's (1961) empirical work aimed at identifying these factors. Mansfield (1961) uses the resulting 12 ϕ_{ij} from the first part as the dependent variable in a cross-section regression analysis of the speed of diffusion based on equation (5.25). He includes dummy intercept variables to represent the four industries concerned. The results of this regression analysis are summarised below:

$$\phi_{ij} = \left\{ \begin{array}{c} -0.29 \\ -0.57 \\ -0.52 \\ -0.59 \end{array} \right\} + \underset{(0.015)}{0.530\pi_{ij}} - \underset{(0.014)}{0.027S_{ij}} \quad (r = 0.997), \qquad (5.26)$$

where the top figure in the brackets pertains to the brewing industry, the next to coal, the following to steel, and the bottom figures pertain to the railroads. The coefficients of π_{ij}, and S_{ij} have the expected signs (indicating that increases in π_{ij}, and decreases in S_{ij} increases the rate of imitation), and both are statistically significant. Equation (5.26) also reveals that there are significant inter-industry differences, the rate of imitation, for given values of π_{ij} and S_{ij}, being particularly high in the brewing industry. Mansfield (1961, p. 753) argues that 'these differences seem to be broadly consistent with the hypothesis often advanced that the rate of imitation is higher in more competitive industries', which, all others being equal, seems to reject the Schumpeterian hypothesis discussed in Chapter 4.

The pioneering work of Mansfield helped to fill a significant gap in the literature on technical change. It also motivated several researchers to extend Mansfield's analysis to other industries and to pursue other approaches to modelling innovation diffusion processes. As pointed out by Davies (1989, p. 221), 'Mansfield, his followers and others, have shown beyond much doubt that diffusion curves *are* invariably S-shaped'.

In spite of the significant impact it had on the literature, Mansfield's (1961) work has been criticised by a number of researchers (Davies, 1979, Stoneman and Ireland, 1983, and Abrahamson and Rosenkopf, 1993). On the empirical side, Mansfield (1961) uses a relatively small data sample, especially for the cross-section analysis which is based on only 12 observations. The major theoretical limitation of Mansfield's (1961) approach is its lack of any underlying model of decision making under uncertainty. Because the model focuses on the aggregate behaviour of firms, it does not offer any reason why some firms adopt earlier than others. On more specific issues, and given that it is a pure imitation model, the model does not explain what starts the diffusion process when no firms have adopted the innovation yet (i.e. $N_t \equiv$ cumulative number of adopters $= 0$). The underlying assumptions of the model also restricts its applicability. It is assumed, for example, that the pressure exerted on non-adopters by adopters is constant over the diffusion span and independent of the level of adoption. That is, the nth adopter impacts equally as the first or second adopter on nonadopters. Also, the model assumes that the innovation can be adopted only once by an adopting unit. Many innovations, however, are repeat- or multiple-adoption innovations meaning that they can be adopted more than once by an adopting unit. The subsequent literature can be viewed as an attempt to meet these criticisms of the Mansfield (1961) model.

5.4.3 Estimation of the Internal-Influence Model

Subsequent literature derives the internal-influence model directly from:

$$\frac{N(t+1) - N(t)}{\bar{N} - N(t)} = \beta \frac{m(t)}{\bar{N}}, \tag{5.27}$$

replacing discreet time by continuous time and integrating shows that an internal influence diffusion model will follow the logistic curve:

$$\frac{N(t)}{\bar{N}} = [1 - \exp\{\alpha + \beta t\}]^1, \tag{5.28}$$

where β is known as the coefficient of internal influence. To estimate β and α numerically, equation (5.28) is transformed as follows:

$$\log\left(\frac{N(t)}{\bar{N} - N(t)}\right) = \alpha + \beta t, \tag{5.29}$$

where time t is measured in number of time periods (e.g. years, months) that have elapsed since the adoption of the innovation by at least one firm (or adopting unit). Equation (5.29) can be estimated using ordinary least squares regression analysis, and the values of β and α can then be used to calculate the expected number of adopters. Examples of the application of the internal-influence models to other industries include Metcalfe (1970), Romeo (1977), Alpar (1992), and Jagtiani et al. (1995).

5.4.4 The Bass (1969) Model

While Mansfield's model implicitly assumes a homogeneous social system, Rogers (1962) suggests a criterion for adopter categorisation based on the adopter's innovativeness; the degree to which an individual is relatively earlier to adopt new ideas than other members of his social system. The efforts to explain the typical S-shaped diffusion curve, such as the one shown in Figure 5.3 below, in terms of various characteristics of the potential adopter population led to the classification of adopters as 'pioneers or innovators', 'early adopters', 'late adopters', and 'laggards' (Freeman, 1988, p. 43). A general explanation of the S-shaped curve in terms of adopters' characteristics is provided by Freeman (1988, p. 45):

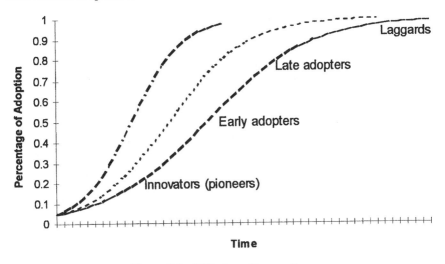

Figure 5.3 Diffusion of innovations

Sociologists tended to ascribe the supposed prevalence of this pattern to the combination of information dissemination with the social characteristics of various groups of the adopter population: the small number of pioneering, risk-taking innovators, the larger number of those who adopted only after convincing demonstration effects or advice from 'opinion leaders' and the tail of rather conservative (and in some accounts older) laggards. The 'pioneers' correspond to the first 'infected' individuals in the epidemic model; as their number increased, information became available to much larger numbers of people until only a few 'healthy' resistant or isolated individuals did not succumb.

The distinction of the different adopter categories motivated Bass (1969) to develop a growth model for consumer durables which considered these different categories explicitly in its structure. In the mathematical formulation of the model, however, the first three groups above are aggregated and defined as *imitators*. Imitators, unlike innovators, are influenced in the timing of adoption by the decisions of other members of the social system.

The model's basic assumption is that *the probability (p) that an initial purchase will be made at T given that no purchase has yet been made is a linear function of the number of previous buyers*. Thus, $P(t) = a + (b/\bar{N})N_t$, where a and $(b/\bar{N})$ are constants, N_t is the number of previous buyers, and $\bar{N}$ is the number of potential buyers in the population. At time $t = 0$, $N_t = 0$, and the constant a is the probability of an initial purchase and its magnitude reflects the importance of innovators in the social system. Since the parameters of the model depend upon the scale used to measure time, it is possible to select a unit of measure for time such that a reflects the fraction of all adopters who are innovators. The Bass (1969) model thus explicitly explains what starts the diffusion process. The product $(b/\bar{N})N_t$ reflects the pressures operating on imitators as the number of previous buyers increases. Note that replacement sales are excluded by restricting the analysis to that interval of time during which repurchase of the product by the same member of the social system is improbable. Therefore, the unit sales of the product will coincide with the number of initial purchases during the time interval under investigation.

Let $f(t) = F'(t)$ be a probability density function reflecting the probability that an innovation is adopted at time t, and let $F(t)$ be the cumulative density of t, then the likelihood of adoption (i.e. purchase of the new product) at time T, given that no purchase has yet been made, is given by the conditional density function:

$$f(t)/[1 - F_t] = \left[a + \frac{b}{N}N(t)\right] = a + bF(t), \qquad (5.30)$$

where $f(t)$ is the likelihood of purchase at time T and:

$$F(T) = \int_0^T f(t)\, dt, \quad F(0) = 0. \qquad (5.31)$$

Since $f(T)$ is the likelihood of purchase at T and $\bar{N}$ is the total number purchasing during the period for which the density function was constructed,

$$N(T) = \int_0^T S(t)\, dt = \bar{N}\int_0^T f(t)\, dt = \bar{N}F(t) \qquad (5.32)$$

is the total number purchasing in the $(0, T)$ interval. Therefore, sales at T:

$$S(T) = \bar{N}f(T) = p(T)[\bar{N} - N(T)] \qquad (5.33)$$

$$= \left[a + b\int_0^T S(t)\, dt/\bar{N}\right]\left[\bar{N} - \int_0^T S(t)\, dt\right], \qquad (5.34)$$

where $p(t) = f(t)/[1 - F_t]$. Expanding this product we have:

$$S(T) = a\bar{N} + (b - a)N(T) - b/\bar{N}[N(T)^2]. \qquad (5.35)$$

Bass (1969) summarises the behavioural rationale for his mixed-influence model in the following two points:

1. Initial purchases of the product are made by both 'innovators' and 'imitators', the important distinction between an innovator and an imitator

being the buying influence. Innovators are not influenced in the timing of their initial purchase by the number of people who have already bought the product, while imitators are influenced by the number of previous buyers. Imitators *learn*, in some sense, from those who have already bought

2. The importance of innovators will be greater at first but will diminish monotically with time. The growth rate resulting from the Bass model is depicted in Figure 5.4. Since for successful new products the coefficient of imitation will ordinarily be much larger than the coefficient of innovation, sales will attain the maximum rate at about the time that cumulative sales are approximately one-half $\bar{N}$, the initial purchases.

In this model, a is referred to as the coefficient of innovation and b as the coefficient of imitation. In subsequent literature a and b became known as the coefficient of *external influence* and coefficient of *internal influence*, respectively. We adopt this terminology in the remainder of this book.

To test the model, Bass (1969) developed regression estimates of the parameters of the model using annual time series data for eleven different consumer durables (Table 5.3). The discreet analogue of the model in the form of:

$$S_T = q\bar{N} + pN_{T-1} + cN_{T-1}^2, \tag{5.36}$$

where S_T = sales at T, and $N_{T-1} = \sum_{t=1}^{T-1} S_t$ cumulative sales through period $T - 1$. Note that the sales data more or less reflect the number of households that purchased the innovation because the period of the study was restricted in

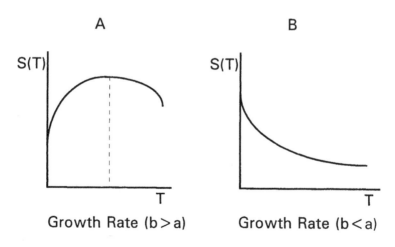

A

B

Growth Rate (b > a)

Growth Rate (b < a)

Source: Bass (1969), p. 461

Figure 5.4 Sales growth in the Bass model

every case to include only those intervals in which repeat purchasing was not significant. Once the least squares estimates of the parameters in equation (5.36) are obtained, these can be converted into estimates of a, b, and $\bar{N}$.[6] Table 5.4 displays the regression results. The R^2 values indicate that the model describes the growth rate behaviour rather well. Using visual presentations of the expected versus the actual sales data for the eleven products, Bass (1969, p. 464) states that 'the regression equations describes the general trend of the time path of growth very well'. For all products, the ratio of (b/a) is more than one suggesting that the internal influence (the so-called *word-of-mouth effect* for innovations whose adopters are consumers as opposed to firms) dominated the diffusion rates of these products. The relative contribution of external influence (e.g. mass media and advertisement) was largest for black and white TVs $(b/a = 9.0)$ and smallest for electric refrigerators $(b/a = 9.0)$. The fact that internal influence dominated external influence for all products (i.e. $b > a$) indicates that the growth curves of these products follow the pattern depicted in Figure 5.4A where sales attain their maximum value at about the time that cumulative sales are approximately one-half $\bar{N}$.

One of the more important contributions derived from the regression analysis is the implied estimate of the total number of initial purchases (i.e. excluding repeat purchases) to be made over the life of the product ($\bar{N}$ in Table 5.4 expressed in terms of units sold). The model provided 'reasonable estimates of $\bar{N}$, ranging from 5 793 000 for water softeners to 96 717 000 for black and white TVs.

Table 5.4 Parameter estimates for 12 innovations—Bass (1969)

Innovation	Period covered	a	b	b/a	$\bar{N}$(000s)	R^2
Electric refrigerators	1920–40	0.002516	0.21566	85.71542	40 001	0.903
Home freezers	1946–61	0.018119	0.17110	9.443126	21 973	0.742
Black-and-white TVs	1946–61	0.027877	0.25105	9.005632	96 717	0.576
Water softeners	1946–61	0.017703	0.29695	16.77399	5 793	0.919
Room air conditioners	1946–61	0.010299	0.41861	40.64569	16 895	0.911
Clothes dryers	1948–61	0.017206	0.35688	20.7416	15 092	0.896
Power lawnmowers	1948–61	0.009183	0.33790	36.79625	44 751	0.932
Electric bed coverings	1949–61	0.005876	0.24387	41.50272	76 589	0.976
Auto. coffee makers	1946–61	0.017135	0.30145	17.59265	58 838	0.883
Steam irons	1949–60	0.028632	0.32791	11.45257	55 696	0.828
Record players	1952–61	0.024796	0.65410	26.37925	21 937	0.899

a: Time period one is defined as that for which sales equal or exceed $a\bar{N}$ for the first time.
b: Interrupted by war.
Source: Bass (1969, p. 467).

5.4.5 Estimation of the Mixed-Influence Model

The Bass (1969) model is usually referred to as the mixed-influence diffusion model, and has the general form:

$$\frac{\partial N(t)}{\partial t} = (a + bN_t)(\bar{N} - N(t)), \tag{5.37}$$

where a and b are the coefficients of external and internal influence respectively. To estimate the model, a discreet analogue of equation (5.37) is derived:

$$N(t+1) - N(t) = a\bar{N} + (b\bar{N} - a)N(t) - bN^2(t), \tag{5.38}$$

or

$$N(t+1) - N(t) = \beta_1 + \beta_2 N(t) + \beta_3 N^2(t) + e(t). \tag{5.39}$$

The βs can then be estimated using ordinary least squares regression analysis. Once these values are obtained, a, b, and $\bar{N}$ are obtained as follows:

$$\bar{N} = \frac{-\beta_2 \pm \sqrt{\beta_2^2 - 4\beta_1\beta_3}}{a\beta_3}, \tag{5.40}$$

$$b = -\beta_3, \tag{5.41}$$

$$a = \frac{\beta_1}{\bar{N}}. \tag{5.42}$$

One such application of the mixed-influence model in the banking industry was provided by Alpar (1992) who evaluated data on the number of US banks that had automated 17 certain banking functions (e.g. safe deposits, commercial loans, investments). The data covered the period 1979–86 and concentrated on 175 US commercial banks. The results obtained indicate some evidence of external influence but the internal influence was significant in only one case (real estate mortgage loans). The significance of the coefficient of internal influence for real estate mortgage loans indicates that the automation of this function by one bank exerts competitive pressures on its rivals to follow suit. Overall, the results for all banking functions examined suggest that the automation of banking functions by one bank exerts no competitive or institutional band-wagon pressures on its rivals. Alternatively, Alpar (1992) argues that these results may be due to shortcomings of the basic diffusion models. We discuss these shortcomings and review extensions to these models in the rest of this chapter.

5.4.6 External-Influence Models

A third category of diffusion models fits an exogenously determined mathematical function to depict the successive increase in the number of adopters.

Much of the early popularity of such *external-influence* models is due to the work of Coleman *et al.* (1966), who used these models to investigate the diffusion of a new drug by US medical practitioners. The model results in a decaying or modified exponential diffusion curve. Diffusion processes with such a functional form are hypothesised as only being driven by information from a communication source external to the social system (Mahajan and Peterson, 1985), with the rate of diffusion dependent only on the potential number of adopters. Fourt and Woodlock (1960) develop a model for early prediction of market success for new grocery products. Experience with a large number of earlier new products is used to determine the general functional form or shape of the cumulative penetration (diffusion) as a function of time. Observations of penetration for the particular new product are then used to determine its unique constants. By examining numerous cumulative 'penetration' curves, Fourt and Woodlock (1960) observed the following:

1. Successive increments in these curves decline
2. The cumulative curve seems to approach a limiting penetration which is less than 100%.

A simple model with these properties states that the increments in penetration for equal time periods are proportional to the remaining distance to the limiting ceiling penetration. That is, in each time period the ceiling is approached by a constant fraction of the remaining distance. Figure 5.5 depicts an example of the two-parameters modified exponential function proposed by Fourt and Wood-lock (1960).

The model is then adjusted by assuming that increments of penetration approach a small positive increment k, rather than zero. The value of k is estimated empirically as one-half the increment of new buyers during the fourth average purchase cycle. Fourt and Woodlock (1960) extend their analyses to include predictions for repeat buying. The type of data required to implement their method is shown in Table 5.5 below. The first column shows the number of purchases made during the year classified according to the buyers' order of purchasing; new buyers, first repeaters, second repeaters, etc. The fourth column showing purchases are observations through somewhat shorter periods. While 6021 new purchases were made in the first year, only 4472 had been made 4.82 (2×2.41) months before the end of the year.

Purchases in the first column tend to underestimate the number of customers who will ever make a repeat purchase because some customers have not yet had an opportunity to repeat. Therefore, the fourth-column purchases are used in calculating the repeat ratios shown in the fifth column. The first repeat ratio, 0.485, is obtained by dividing 2170, the number of first repeat purchases, by 4472, the number of repeat purchases who had adequate opportunity to make a first repeat purchase.

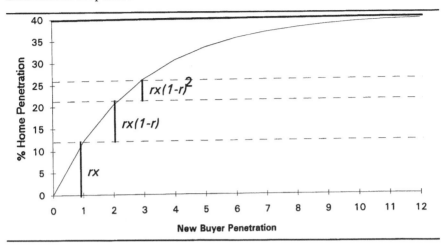

New Buyer Penetration

Example: $x = 40\%$, $r = 0.3$
Increments in Penetration

Time Period	Formula	Numerical Example
1	$r(x - 0) = rx$	$0.3(40) = 12$
2	$r(x - rx) = rx(1 - r)$	$0.3(40)(0.7) = 8.4$
3	$rx(1 - r)^2$	$0.3(40)(0.7)^2 = 5.9$
i	$rx(1 - r)^{i-1}$	$0.3(40)(0.7)^{i-1}$

Source: Fourt and Woodlock (1960, pp. 32–33)

Figure 5.5   The modified exponential function

Fourt and Woodlock (1960) emphasise two marketing considerations to be considered once estimates are obtained:

1.   Is the total volume predicted sufficient for profitable operation?
2.   Is a sufficient part of that volume expected to come from repeat customers?

The second question is particularly important because new buyer volume can be expected to deflate substantially through time. Repeat buyer volume is the ultimate determinant of success or failure.

Despite its useful diagnostic powers, the model of Fourt and Woodlock (1960) is constrained by several assumptions. These assumptions are that distribution, promotional expenditures, price, the product or the package, or competitive activities will not differ strikingly. In other words, the forecast obtained by the model should not influence the management's decisions if these forecasts are to be accurate. The assumption that distribution will not shift greatly, for example, implies that the analysis does not take into consideration

Table 5.5 Derivation of repeat ratio

Repeat Buyer type ratio	No. of purchases during observation period (000's)	Average interval until next purchase (months)	No. of cycles in lag	No. of purchases in observation period less lag
New Buyers	6021	2.41	2	4472
1st repeaters 0.485	2170	1.72	1	1932
2nd repeaters 0.559	1076	1.43	1	917
3rd repeaters 0.645	591	1.20	1	550
4th repeaters 0.593	326	1.19	1	282
5th repeaters 0.797	223	1.19	1	190
Over time 3.300	627	—	—	—

Source: Fourt and Woodlock (1960, p. 36)

the possibility of entering new geographical markets. Markets however grow by entering new areas. Thus, this assumption of constant distribution has the double burden of meaning steady availability in the old areas and also of warning that the introduction of products into new areas must be estimated separately (Fourt and Woodlock, 1960, p. 35).

Finally, it should be noted that the theoretical aspects of the Fourt and Woodlock (1960) model, as well as of most external-diffusion models, are not clear. The model implicitly assumes that the diffusion process is entirely innovative (i.e. no imitation effects). In general, the external-influence model is appropriate when members of the social system are isolated with no inter-personal communication. This limits the applicability of external-influence diffusion models, which may be the reason why few extensions or refinements to this category of diffusion models have been attempted in the literature.

5.4.7 Assumptions Underlying the Fundamental Model

The basic diffusion models discussed earlier are based on several assumptions. For the most part they are simplifying assumptions designed to facilitate analytical solutions to the model. These assumptions must be taken into consideration before applying these models or before the results can be interpreted. The basic models assume the following:

- The diffusion process is binary. Members of the social system either adopt or do not adopt the innovation. Therefore stages in the adoption process are not taken into account (e.g. awareness, knowledge, etc.).
- There is a distinct and constant ceiling, $\bar{N}$, on the number of potential adopters in the social system, and that this ceiling is either known or can be estimated.
- Except for the external-influence diffusion model by Fourt and Woodlock (1960), basic diffusion models assume only one adoption by an adopting unit. Multiple adoptions by an adopting unit (e.g. repeat purchasing of a product) are not permitted.
- In the internal-influence and mixed-influence models, the term $N(t)[\bar{N} - N(t)]$ implies that there is complete mixing of social system members. Furthermore it is implicitly assumed that the effect of interaction between prior adopters and potential adopters (as reflected by the coefficient of internal influence b) is identical, regardless of time of adoptions and time of interaction.
- The innovation itself does not change over time. In the case of new technology, for example, modifications would not take place during the diffusion process. Moreover, the innovation is assumed to be independent of other innovations. Thus adoption of an innovation does not complement, substitute for, detract from, or enhance the adoption of any other innovation (and *vice versa*).
- Finally, when applying the basic diffusion models, a global assumption is that all relevant information about the diffusion process have been captured by the model. Thus when forecasting the sale of a product, for example, it is assumed that all relevant information as to marketing strategies employed, activities of competitors, and the like is represented in the model, usually through the term $N(t)$. Generally speaking, application of the basic diffusion models requires the common forecasting assumption that the past can be used to predict the future.

These limitations of the basic models have motivated several researchers to develop more flexible models which are not constrained by the assumptions discussed above. These extensions are discussed in the remainder of this chapter.

5.4.8 Flexible Models

Because of lack of flexibility of the basic diffusion models several attempts have been made to develop alternative models. These models are more flexible in the sense that their adoption function exhibits a greater variety of shapes than basic models, which provide these models more freedom in adjusting to mirror the adoption function of a particular innovation, rather than forcing this function to adjust to a predetermined shape. Mahajan and Peterson (1985) compare six flexible models with regard to their symmetry and their point of inflection. Let $F = N_t/\bar{N}$, where N_t is the cumulative number of adopters and $\bar{N}$ is the number of potential adopters in the population. The coefficient of external influence is denoted by a, the coefficient of internal influence by b, and σ, δ, θ, and γ are constants. Below is a summary of the mathematical expressions of these models:

Floyd (1968)

$$bF(1 - F)^2 \qquad (5.43)$$

Sharif and Kabir (1976)

$$\frac{bF(1 - F)^2}{1 - F(1 - \sigma)} \qquad (5.44)$$

Jeuland (1981)

$$(a + bF)(1 - F)^{(1+\gamma)} \qquad (5.45)$$

Non-Uniform Influence (NUI)
(Easingwood *et al.*, 1983)

$$(a + bF^\delta)(1 - F) \qquad (5.46)$$

Non-Symmetric Responding
Logistic (NSRL)
(Easingwood *et al.*, 1981)

$$bF^\delta(1 - F) \qquad (5.47)$$

Von Bertalanffy (1957)

$$\frac{b}{1 - b} = F^\theta(1 - F^{(1-\theta)}) \qquad (5.48)$$

The non-uniform influence (NUI) and non-symmetric responding logistic (NSRL) models can both accommodate symmetric as well as non-symmetric diffusion patterns. In addition, the point of inflection can occur at any time during the diffusion process. The advantage of these models with comparison to other flexible models is related to their treatment of the effect of internal influence over time. Floyd, Sharif-Kabir, and Jeuland implicitly assume the following representations for the effect of the internal influence, $W(t)$ (Mahajan and Peterson, 1985, p. 33):

Floyd:

$$W(t) = b(1 - F), \qquad (5.49)$$

Sharif-Kabir:

$$W(t) = \frac{b(1 - F)}{(1 - F(1 - \sigma))}, \qquad (5.50)$$

Jeuland:

$$W(t) = b(1 - F)^\gamma. \qquad (5.51)$$

In all of these models the effect of internal influence can only decrease with time. For the Sharif-Kabir model, differentiation of $W(t)$ with respect to F gives:

$$\frac{dW(t)}{dF} = \frac{-b\sigma}{(1 - F(1 - \sigma))^2}. \qquad (5.52)$$

Because b is positive and $0 \leq \sigma \leq 1$, $dW(t)/dF$ is negative and hence $W(t)$ must decrease with time. The same is true for the Jeuland model, because

$$\frac{dW(t)}{dF} = -b\gamma(1 - F)^{\gamma-1}, \qquad (5.53)$$

and so the effect of internal influence must decrease with time. Moreover, for all three models the internal influence effect becomes zero when F reaches unity. For the NUI or NSRL model, though,

$$\frac{dW(t)}{dF} = b(\delta - 1)F(t)^{\delta-2} \qquad (5.54)$$

is less than zero for $0 \leq \delta \leq 1$, equal to zero for $\delta = 1$, and greater than zero for $\delta > 1$. Because $dF/dt \geq 0$, the effect of internal influence can increase over time (when $\delta > 1$), remain constant (when $\delta = 1$), or decrease over time (when $0 \leq \sigma \leq 1$); its value at complete saturation (i.e. when $F = N_t/\bar{N} = 1$, all members of the population have adopted the innovation) is b. Hence, the time-varying nature of the internal influence is described by a family of curves given by $bF^{\delta-1}$. In addition, values of δ between 0 and 1 cause an acceleration of influence leading to an earlier and higher peak (i.e. dF^*/dt) in the level of adoptions. Values of δ greater than one reflect less internal influence and result in later and lower peaks. Unfortunately, despite their advantages, the NUI and NSRL models are not amenable to simple explicit solutions for F. The NUI model is explained in more detail in the next section.

The above models achieve their flexibility by requiring estimation of an additional parameter (all parameters can be estimated by means of nonlinear or maximum likelihood procedures). As a consequence of their flexibility, though, it is possible to develop a taxonomy of diffusion patterns because the models produce diffusion curves that mirror, rather than 'force' the shape of the underlying diffusion data.

5.4.9 Extensions and Refinements

The extensions to the basic models can be divided into two categories: models with time-varying parameters and repeat-adoption models. Table 5.6 summarises the attributes of the main models reviewed in this chapter.

Table 5.6 Empirical models of innovation diffusion

Work by	Coefficient of internal influence	Coefficient of external influence	Total number of potential adopters
Basic models			
Fourt and Woodlock (1960)	0	Constant	Constant
Mansfield (1961)	Constant	0	Constant
Bass (1969)	Constant	Constant	Constant
Time-varying parameter models			
Easingwood *et al.* (1983)	Constant	f(number of adopters)	Constant
Robinson and Lakhani (1975)	f(price)	Constant	Constant
Horsky and Simon (1983)	Constant	f(advertising)	Constant
Lilien and Roa (1978)	Constant	f(personal selling)	Constant
Repeat-adoption diffusion models			
Dodson and Muller (1978)	0	Constant	f(advertising and word-of-mouth)
Kalwani and Silk (1980)	0	Constant	Constant
Lilien *et al.* (1981)	Constant	f(promotion activities)	Constant
Mahajan *et al.* (1983)	Constant	f(number of adopters)	Constant
Dynamic-population diffusion models			
Mahajan and Peterson (1978)	Constant	Constant	f(all relevant variables)
Sharif and Ramanathan (1981)	Constant or 0	Constant or 0	Various exogenously determined mathematical functions

5.4.10 Diffusion Models with Time-varying Parameters

The basic diffusion models of new product growth, i.e. modified exponential curve, logistic curve, generalised logistic, and Gompertz curve, assume constant parameters in their formulation. Given the interpretation of these parameters, this implies that the effectiveness of the marketing programme of a company and other exogenous factors (e.g. mass media) remain constant over the entire life of the product growth. This is obviously a restrictive assumption especially in later stages of the diffusion process. Flexible models discussed in the previous section relax this assumption. These models (except for NUI and NSRL), however, assume *a priori* the direction of change in the value of the parameters.

Specifically, these models can only be applied when it is known *a priori* that the internal-influence is going to decrease with time. This obviously limits their applicability. Therefore, various extensions have been proposed to relax this assumption. Easingwood *et al.* (1983) argue that the coefficient of imitation should be allowed to systematically change over time while being represented as a function of penetration. That is,

$$w(t) = b\left[\frac{N(t)}{\bar{N}}\right]^\alpha \tag{5.55}$$

where α is a constant and $w(t)$ represents the time-varying coefficient of imitation. Fitting that into a mixed-influence diffusion model yields:

$$\frac{dN}{dt} = a[\bar{N} - N(t)] + b\left[\frac{N(t)}{\bar{N}}\right]^\alpha \frac{N(t)}{\bar{N}}[\bar{N} - N(t)] \tag{5.56}$$

$$= a[\bar{N} - N(t)] + b\left[\frac{N(t)}{\bar{N}}\right]^\delta [\bar{N} - N(t)] \tag{5.57}$$

or given that $F = N_t/\bar{N}$, we have:

$$\frac{dF(t)}{dt} = a[1 - F(t)] + bF(t)^\delta[1 - F(t)] \tag{5.58}$$

where $\delta = \alpha + 1 \geq 0$ and

$$w(t) = b\left[\frac{N(t)}{\bar{N}}\right]^{\delta-1} = bF(t)^{\delta-1}. \tag{5.59}$$

The Non-Uniform Influence model (NUI) can, therefore, be written as:

$$\frac{dF(t)}{dt} = [a + bF(t)^\delta](1 - F(t)). \tag{5.60}$$

With $\delta = 1$, the model will be reduced to the Bass (1969) uniform mixed-influence diffusion model. When the coefficient of innovation is equal to zero, $a = 0$, the NUI gives the non-uniform model for the Mansfield (1961) model, $dF/dt = bF(1 - F)$. The special case of the NUI model when $a = 0$ has been termed the Non-symmetric Responding Logistic (NSRL) model.

In order to illustrate the generality of the NUI model, Easingwood *et al.* (1983) have applied it to sales data for five consumer durables. The durables included were black and white televisions, clothes dryers, room air conditioners and dishwashers. The time series were restricted to the early years of sales growth to avoid repeat purchases. Thus the sales data correspond to the number of households that bought the products, which is consistent with the model being structured around the number of adopters (i.e. households in this case). Furthermore, in order to assess the relative performance of the NUI model, these durables were also analysed by using the Bass and Sharif-Kabir models. Using the sales data, the associated parameters of the models were computed by using a non-linear programming algorithm. In each case the algorithm searched for the parameter values that most closely approximated the actual diffusion curve, and the corresponding deterministic model that best fitted the data was obtained.

Table 5.7 displays the NUI model results obtained by Easingwood *et al.* (1983). The results confirm the Bass (1969) finding that internal influence *b* dominates the growth rates of consumer durables. That is, the interaction between early adopters and non-adopters plays a much more significant role than do mass media and advertisements. Except for dishwashers, the fitted values of the non-uniform influence factor, δ, of the NUI model were less than 1.0 for all of the five products, indicating high initial influence that decreases with penetration. The NUI estimates of the time-varying internal influence (i.e. $w(t) = b(N_t/\bar{N})^{\delta-1}$) vary considerably over the time periods analysed. The ratio of initial period to final period estimate of the coefficient of imitation is 28.5 black and white televisions, 4.5 for colour televisions, 3.9, and 62.4 for room air conditioners. The larger this value is, the faster is the decay of the effectiveness of the interaction between adopters and non-adopters or internal influence (for room air conditioners, for example, the effectiveness of internal influence has been much more effective in the early stages of the diffusion process than in later stages; for colour TVs, however, the internal influence seems to have been relatively uniform throughout the diffusion span). For dishwashers, the only product with an increasing internal influence ($\delta > 1$), final period value is 6.0 times initial period value.

The NUI model also produced meaningful estimates of total population of potential adopters ($\bar{N}$) in the US for the respective product category (48.1 million for black and white televisions, 41.6 million for colour televisions, 17.2 million for clothes dryers, 22.4 million for room air conditioners, and 9.98 million for dishwashers).[7] Using three measures of goodness of fit (variance

Table 5.7 Parameter estimates for 5 innovations—Easingwood *et al.* (1983)

Parameters	B&W television	Colour television	Clothes dryer	Room air conditioners	Dishwasher
a	0.000 021	0.010 610	0.008 794	0.000 168	0.018 380
b	0.2805	0.4121	0.2494	0.2134	0.3717
$\bar{N}$(000)	48 096	41 678	17 233	22 389	9987
δ	0.3000	0.6000	0.7179	0.4954	1.5437

Source: Easingwood *et al.* (1983, p. 284).
a, the coefficient of external influence measures the effects of mass media and advertisements.
b, the coefficient of time-varying internal influence, measures the effects of interaction between adopters and non-adopters. $\delta < 1$ indicates decreasing internal influence and $\delta > 1$ indicates increasing internal influence.

explained-adjusted, mean absolute error, and mean squared error), Easingwood *et al.* (1983) report that the NUI model provides a better fit than the other two models for each of the five consumer durables. Similar results were obtained when assessing the models' forecasting accuracy.[8]

Easingwood *et al.* (1983) concludes that the NUI model fits the actual data well and by means of the flexibility introduced by the non-uniform influence factor allows the model to respond to the diffusion process. Given that the flexibility offered by the NUI model is determined by the NUI factor δ, some work has been undertaken to develop a taxonomy of diffusion patterns based on δ and the coefficient of imitation. Lawrence and Lawton (1981), for example, have found that the coefficient of imitation is lower for consumer durables than for industrial products.

In the representation and applications of the NUI model presented above, it was assumed that for a particular innovation the internal influence can either increase, decrease or remain constant over the diffusion span. However, Easingwood *et al.* (1983) state that it is highly likely that for certain innovations the word of mouth effect may have a pattern where the effect increases in certain periods and decreases or remain constants in other periods. They state that the proposed model is capable of capturing such behaviour. However, this would require usage of time-varying estimation procedures such as feedback approaches to estimate the NUI model parameters. However, interpretation of the parameters of such models must take place entirely outside the model, and hence may be difficult. Although the current form of the model limits the model's ability to respond to the data, Easingwood *et al.* (1983) argue that the freedom of movement has been lost for gains in interpretability '... another approach to allow the diffusion model coefficient to change over time is to introduce the factor causing the change into the diffusion model (e.g. Robenson and Lakhani 1975). The advantage of this approach is that the relationship is made explicit and can be measured and tested. However many new product diffusions are characterised by the simultaneous interplay of several factors. It would, in such cases, be difficult, if not impossible, to statistically estimate these relationships, especially as there are usually few data points available for diffusion modelling'.

A straightforward approach to obtaining time-varying parameters is to explicitly incorporate the variables believed to affect these parameters into the model. Once the factors that represent the external-influence and internal-influence coefficients are identified, these coefficients can be written in terms of a function of the specified factors. The most commonly used factors are marketing decision variables of the firm such as advertising and price. The advantage of such models is that they enable managers to observe the effect of their decisions on the diffusion pattern of their new products. The question of which factors (e.g. price) represent which coefficients (a, b, or $\bar{N}$) has been handled differently by the various extensions proposed.

Robenson and Lakhani (1975), for example, argue that innovators are only a dominant factor in the marketplace during the short period required to achieve the first several percent of market penetration. Therefore, if the coefficient of internal influence (imitation) is developed as a function of marketing decision variables such as advertising and price, the diffusion model will enable management to evaluate the effect of a certain marketing programme on the growth of the product.

Horsky and Simon (1983) argue that the primary effect of advertising is to be a direct tool for disseminating information about the existence of the new product. They suggest that a correct specification of a diffusion model should express the coefficient of external influence as a function of advertising expenditures (i.e. advertising cause innovators, rather than imitators, to try the product, and its effects are independent of the number of adopters that already purchased the product). In applying their model to a new telephonic banking system, Horsky and Simon (1983) assume the following values of the external-influence coefficient a:

$$a(t) = a_1 + a_2 A(t) \qquad (5.61)$$

where a_1 and a_2 are constants and $A(t)$ is the level of advertising expenditures. This results in the following mixed-influence model:

$$\frac{dN(t)}{dt} = (a_1 + a_2 \ln A(t) + bN(t))(\bar{N} - N(T)) \qquad (5.62)$$

Horsky and Simon (1983) analysed the diffusion of a telephone banking service in five different *Standard Metropolitan Statistical Areas* (SMSAs) in the United States. The telephone banking service was introduced by national savings banks between October 1974 and April 1975. Adopters in this study are *customers* who opened accounts at these banks, and thus $N(t)$, the number of adoptions or adopters at time t, measures the number of newly opened accounts. To estimate their model, Horsky and Simon derive the following discreet analogue of their model:

$$N(t+1) - N(t) = a_1(\bar{N} - N(t)) + a_2 \ln A(t)(\bar{N} - N(t)) + bN(t) - (\bar{N} - N(t))$$

$$(5.63)$$

Advertising outlay $A(t)$, measure total expenditures on advertising by banks. Its influence on the number of newly opened accounts is captured by a_2. The coefficient a_2 captures the effects of banks' publicity independent of their advertising expenditure. The above discreet model is then estimated using ordinary least squares. $\bar{N}$ in this study is treated as a constant, and was varied to obtain the highest R^2 for each area. Table 5.8 below displays the results obtained by Horsky and Simon (1983). The results show that the effectiveness in advertising varies significantly from one area to another both in magnitude and significance (e.g. a_2 is 2.99×10^{-3} for SMSA A compared to 0.15×10^{-3} for SMSA E). Unlike findings of studies of consumer durables (e.g. Bass, 1969; Easingwood et al. 1981) the coefficient of internal influence b, is smaller than that of external influence (publicity or advertisement). In SMSA B, for example, b is 2.08×10^{-5} compared to $a_2 = 1.32 \times 10^{-3}$ and $a_1 = 0.64 \times 10^{-3}$).[9] Moreover, areas with higher advertising coefficients tend to have higher internal-influence coefficients and lower market potential (as measured by $\bar{N}$).

A similar model was proposed by Lilien and Roa (1978) who examine the effect of a firm's promotional activities on the growth rates of a new product innovated by the firm. However, they express the external-influence coefficient a as a function of the company's promotional activity, while expressing a switching coefficient as a function of rivals' spending on their new competitive products.

To relax the assumption of a constant ceiling of the potential population, Mahajan and Peterson (1978) developed a model which treated $\bar{N}(t)$ as a function of exogenous variables such as general economic conditions, technological change, government actions, etc. Similarly, Dodson and Muller (1978) suggest that since $\bar{N}(t)$, the eventual number of buyers at time t, represent the number of potential buyers who are aware of the product, it is $\bar{N}(t)$ which should be expressed as a function of advertising expenditure. In the formulation of their model they assume two ways in which unaware individuals become aware of the product; word-of-mouth communication between product-aware and unaware individuals, and advertising. Sharif and Ramanathan (1981) proposed a diffusion model with a dynamic population of potential

Table 5.8 Parameter estimates of telephone banking diffusion model

SMSA	Market potential $\bar{N}$	Promotional effects Publicity $(a_1 \cdot 10^{-3})$[a]	Advertising $(a_2 \cdot 10^{-3})$	Word of mouth $(b \cdot 10^{-5})$	Goodness of fit (R^2)	Number of months
A	1700	1.52 (4.1)	2.99 (1.77)	3.64 (1.29)	0.66	14
B	3600	0.64 (0.17)	1.32 (0.35)	2.08 (0.32)	0.91	16
C	6200	0.57 (0.19)	0.89 (0.21)	1.28 (0.61)	0.82	20
D	21 500	1.53 (0.70)	0.23 (0.10)	0.40 (0.11)	0.74	21
E	22 800	1.17 (0.43)	0.15 (0.04)	0.29 (0.07)	0.82	13

a: Values in parentheses are standard errors
Source: Adapted from Horsky and Simon (1983)

adopters. In their model, $\bar{N}$ varies over time according to some alternative predetermined mathematical functions of time. Another approach to overcome the limitation of the basic models (in terms of their assumptions of a fixed $\bar{N}$) is suggested in Skiadas (1987) in which he proposed a diffusion model with no 'upper limit' parameter for the early and middle stage prediction of innovation diffusion.

Bretschneider and Mahajan (1980) propose another approach to time-varying parameter diffusion models. Their approach employ feedback estimation procedures to develop an adaptive technological substitution model. The whole idea behind the adaptive approaches to estimation of coefficients is to use information provided by a forecast error $e(t)$ between the actual number of adopters $(N(t))$ and the predicted number of adopters $(\hat{N}(t))$ to update the models' coefficient parameters. Thus, unlike the polynomial and exponential approach to model the time-varying parameter, feedback estimation requires no *a priori* assumptions about the time path of the parameters, nor knowledge about the nature or cause for time variation in the parameters. However, if factors affecting time variations in the parameters are known and are included in the model, this approach assists in studying the time effectiveness of such factors—see Bretschneider *et al.* (1977) and Makridakis and Wheelwright (1977) for applications of adaptive filtering to time-series analysis, Cooley and Prescott (1973) for a theory and application of varying parameter regression, Swamy *et al.* (1989) for a survey of random coefficient models, and Harvey (1990) and Kennedy (1994) for an introduction to models with changing parameter values.

Finally, Lavaraj and Gore (1992) propose an external-influence model with a time-varying adoption function decreasing with time. Consider the following differential equation:

$$\frac{\partial N_t}{\partial t} = \frac{\bar{N} - N_t}{a + t},$$

where a is the coefficient of external influence and t is time that elapsed since the introduction of the innovation. This equation represents a situation in which adopters do not affect others, but a fraction of the remaining population adopts the innovation in every unit of time. The fraction goes on decreasing progressively. In other words, this is an external-influence model with an effectively decreasing coefficient of external influence given by $1/(a + t)$. Solving the model, we have: $-\ln(\bar{N} - N_t) = \ln(a + t) + c$, and using the initial condition $N_0 = 0$, we get:

$$N_t = \frac{\bar{N}t}{a + t}.$$

It should be noted, however, that the above model assumes *a priori* the pattern and direction of variation in the parameter of the model. Thus, it is only applicable to situations where it is known *a priori* that external influence will decrease with time.

5.4.11 Multi-adoption Diffusion Models

As mentioned before, the objective of a diffusion model is to depict the successive increase in the number of adopters. In a product-innovation context, however, the successive increase in the number of adopters may consist of first-time buyers as well as repeat buyers of an innovation. Because a great many product-innovations that are introduced into the market-place are re-purchasable, sellers of these innovations are interested in number of adopters due to repeat purchase even more than the number of first-time buyers.

A number of repeat-purchase models have been developed to forecast sales for product-innovation. For a comprehensive review of these models, see Wind *et al.* (1981). In this section we focus on the most well-known repeat-purchase models. One of the early repeat-purchase models is that of Fourt and Woodlock (1960).[10] Kalwani and Silk (1980) develop a model which focuses on the structure of repeat buying for new packaged goods. Their analysis follows the work of Fourt and Woodlock (1960) and Eskin (1973).

Lilien *et al.* (1981) developed a model which helps managers develop effective detailing policy (i.e. personal selling). Figure 5.6 below outlines the two-state repeat-purchase model proposed by Lilien *et al.* (1981). In their modelling of the diffusion of new ethical drugs among doctors, they consider two classes of doctors, prescribing or not prescribing. The flow between these classes is controlled by the company's own and competitive promotional spending, and product experience, positive or negative.

Mahajan *et al.* (1983) propose another model for repeat-purchase innovation diffusion. Unlike the other repeat-purchase models discussed above, this model explicitly incorporates the non-uniform nature of the word-of-mouth effect. In doing so, the model relaxes two of the assumptions underlying the generalised model; a constant word-of-mouth effect over the entire diffusion span and a single adoption by the adopting units.

In their modelling of the adoption of an ethical drug by doctors, Mahajan *et al.* (1983) assume that the number of doctors prescribing at time $(t + 1)$ is equal to:

1. A fraction of the doctors who were prescribing at time t and who will continue to prescribe at time $(t + 1)$, i.e. repeaters
2. A fraction of the doctors who were not prescribing in period t but will prescribe in period $(t + 1)$ because of promotion or other marketing mix elements, i.e. triers due to company efforts

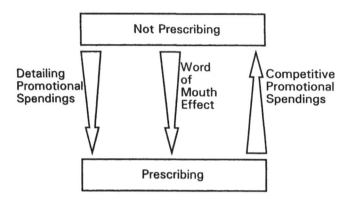

Source: Lilien *et al.* (1981), p. 496

Figure 5.6 Simplified flow model describing the process

3. A fraction of doctors who were not prescribing in period t but will prescribe in period $(t + 1)$ because of the word of mouth effect, i.e. triers due to word-of-mouth.

In order to facilitate the formal development of the model, let:

$n(t)$ = number of doctors prescribing at time $t, t = 1, 2, \ldots$,

$\bar{N}$ = number of doctors in prescribing class who will eventually prescribe the drug

$F(t) = n(t)/N$ = fraction of potential number of doctors prescribing at time t

$\bar{N} - n(t)$ = number of doctors not prescribing at time t

c = coefficient of retention

a = coefficient of innovation

δ = non-uniform influence factor, $\delta \geq 0$

b = coefficient of imitation when $\delta = 1$

$w(t)$ = time-varying coefficient of imitation, $w(t) \geq 0$.

The repeat-purchase model of Mahajan *et al.* (1983) is:

$$n(t + 1) = cn(t) + a(\bar{N} - n(t)) + b\left(\frac{n(t)}{\bar{N}}\right)^{\delta} (\bar{N} - n(t)), \qquad (5.64)$$

or in terms of the fraction of potential number of adopters:

$$F(t+1) = cF(t) + a(1 - F(t)) + bF(t)^{\delta}(1 - F(t)). \qquad (5.65)$$

Note that single-adoption diffusion models discussed earlier in the chapter employed the *cumulative* number of adopters, $N(t)$, as their dependent variable. This is different from repeat adoption models (equation (5.64)) which use the number of adopters at any period of time t, or $n(t)$, as the dependent variable. Whereas the cumulative number of adopters $N(t)$ can only increase over time, the number of adopters during a given period of time $n(t)$ can be larger, smaller, or equal to the number of adopters in the previous period or periods. This distinction arises because an adopting unit (e.g. firms) can adopt an innovation at time t but not at time $t+1$. In this case $n(t)$ will include that firm but not $n(t+1)$.

Note that the model proposed by Mahajan *et al.* (1983) is a direct extension of the NUI model discussed above. Assuming a constant population of potential adopters ($\bar{N}$), the first term in equation (5.64), $cn(t)$, indicates the number of adopters in period t who continue to adopt in period $(t+1)$ (repeaters). The second term, $a(\bar{N} - n(t))$, represents the number of first-time adopters at time $(t+1)$ due to external influence (e.g. the company's promotional efforts), and the third represents first-time adopters due to internal influence.

It is the third term in equation (5.64) that captures the non-uniform internal effect over time. It is assumed that the doctors prescribing at period t interact with the non-prescribing doctors at period $t-1$ and the effectiveness of this interaction is reflected in the time-varying coefficient of imitation given by:

$$w(t) = b(F(t))^{\delta-1} \qquad (5.66)$$

In order to test their proposed model, Mahajan *et al.* (1983) applied the model to data on the number of doctors prescribing a new ethical drug.[11] The model was estimated using a Marquardt-type non-linear programming algorithm. The results indicate that the model does fits the data very well (variance explained $= 0.99$). The forecasting capability of the model was also tested. The model produced an estimate of δ of 0.1606 which is less than 1, indicating that the time-varying internal influence, $w(t)$, declined over time. This result is consistent with the findings of Coleman *et al.* (1966) and Easingwood *et al.* (1983) who also found that internal influence eventually lost importance.

Finally, Mahajan *et al.* (1983) uses the parameter estimates produced by the non-linear regression to investigate the relative contributions of the various diffusion model components to the total number of prescriptions. As expected, contributions of the first time adopters due to either external or internal influence to the total sales decline over time whereas the contribution by repeaters increases over time.

5.4.12 Evaluation of Diffusion Models

With the large number of diffusion models in the literature, an obvious question that a researcher has to answer is which one is appropriate in our case for investigating the diffusion pattern of a particular innovation, or financial innovations. There is no consensus as to the optimal characteristics of appropriate models, and there is a need for criteria for evaluating diffusion models. An obvious and most important criterion is the model's actual performance, that is, the accuracy of its forecast. Yet often this criterion is of limited practical value since most models are claimed, by their developers, to provide an extremely high level of accuracy (Wind, 1981, p. 13). Kumar and Kumar (1992) compare the performance of 13 diffusion models in forecasting the diffusion of the oxygen steel process. Their results show that all models provide 'good fit' to the data. Kumar and Kumar (1992, p. 167), however, stress that the 'model suitability may not be judged by the predictions only, since they give little information for the "predictability" of the model'.

Young (1993) proposes an empirical-oriented criterion to choose a diffusion model for a specific application. Using 50 innovation-diffusion time series, Young (1993) estimates nine alternative model specifications (e.g. the logistic Mansfield model, the Bass, the Gompertz and linear Gompertz, and the NSRL) for each data set, and compares these models' forecast accuracy. The alternative formulations of the diffusion models are grouped in four general categories; cumulative data with known upper limit $\bar{N}$ (e.g. the Mansfield (1961) logistic curve), cumulative data with unknown upper limit (e.g. linear Gompertz model), rate of change with known upper limit (NSRL model),[12] rate of change with unknown upper limit (e.g. the Bass (1969) and NUI model).[13] The lack of a clear definition of 'forecast accuracy' makes the choice among diffusion models on empirical grounds difficult since different measures of forecast accuracy yield different rankings of these models in terms of their accuracy. Young, for example, employs more than three measures of forecast accuracy and his ranking of the models is summarised in seven tables, from which no clear conclusions emerge.[14]

Assuming that two models can predict equally well, the question is: what other criteria can be used in evaluating alternative forecasting models? Wind (1981) suggests several criteria for this purpose which are summarised in Table 5.9 below.

The relative importance of the factors suggested by Wind et al. (1981) will depend on the purpose of the analysis. The diagnostic power of the model is of special importance when the analysis is aimed at shedding light on the factors affecting the pattern of diffusion for an innovation. In such cases, expressing the parameters of the model in terms of other variables can be very useful. This, however, requires a limited number of parameters whose value can easily be

Table 5.9   Criteria for evaluating new-product forecasting models

Predictive Accuracy
Short and long term
Ability to identify turning points
Economic versus statistical evaluation

Ability to Develop and Implement the Model
Technical (mathematical, statistical, and programming) skills required
Management acceptance
Data required—type, timing, and cost
Time required for model development, implementation, and maintenance
Cost of model development, implementation, and maintenance

Diagnostic Power
Forecast for defined market segment(s)
Forecast under defined marketing efforts
Forecast under defined competitive and environmental conditions
Assessment of uncertainty

Source: Wind (1981, p. 14)

interpreted. This is also required when comparison between the patterns of diffusion for certain innovations is the aim of the analysis.

5.5 CONCLUSION

This chapter has covered the literature on modelling innovation adoption and diffusion in the industrial economics literature. Adoption models explain diffusion by assuming a heterogeneous population of potential adopters. *Ex ante* heterogeneity stems from differences in firms' characteristics which are critical to the adoption decision (e.g. firm size). *Ex post* heterogeneity stems from either exogenous factors including declining incremental benefits for later adoption and declining adoption costs or endogenous factors such as band-wagon effects where the sheer number of firms that adopt the product creates a pressure on non-adoption firms (competitive and institutional bandwagon effects).

Empirical diffusion models are general mathematical functions which focus on the aggregate industry diffusion rate by depicting the successive increase in the number of adopters or adopting units of an innovation over time. Adopters can be firms (e.g. a new production technique) or consumers (e.g. a new product). The most basic of these is a mixed-influence diffusion model which distinguishes between two categories of adopters, internal and external adopters. Internal adopters are firms (or consumers) which are influenced in the timing of their initial adoption by the number of firms (or consumers) that have already adopted the innovation. External adopters, on the other hand, are influenced in the timing of their initial adoption by any exogenous factors other than the number of early adopters. In relation to models of adoption, external influence can be viewed to represent the influence of exogenous factors which leads to the initial introduction of the innovation. The differences in the timing of external adopters are due to the *ex ante heterogeneity* in firms' (or consumers') characteristics which affect the optimal timing of adoption. Internal influence, on the other hand, captures the effects of bandwagon pressures, and changes in the return/cost characteristics of the innovation that are related to the number of firms (or consumers) that have already adopted the innovation. That is, it captures the *ex post heterogeneity* generated by, or related to, the number of firms that have already adopted the innovation.

Basic diffusion models can be extended to include time-varying parameters to allow for the effects of external factors on the internal influence, the external influence, and/or the population of adopters to be incorporated either directly or indirectly into the model. The analysis can also be extended to incorporate repeat adoption. This chapter has reviewed the most-widely used diffusion models in the literature. The mathematical derivations as well as the practical application of several models have been discussed. Whenever possible, relationships between the various models have been highlighted and comparison of their mathematical and theoretical aspects was made. Although a large number of diffusion models exist in the literature, the knowledge of the relationships among models helps researchers narrow down choice. Furthermore, knowledge of the motivation behind the respective models, including the underlying assumptions, need also to be taken into consideration when formulating new model specifications. When the user ends with more than one model that meets the unique characteristics of the innovation in question, empirical tests of these models might be the only guideline that leads him/her to the appropriate choice.

The last two chapters have examined the industrial economics literature covering the process of innovation, innovation adoption, and innovation diffusion. In the few instances where the diffusion patterns of innovations in the banking industry have been modelled, the studies lack any theoretical justification for the motivation of empirical analysis. In addition, these studies are also isolated from the theoretical literature on innovation adoption. The next chapter, therefore, uses the industrial economics literature reviewed in this and the previous chapter, and the finance literature reviewed in chapters two and three, to develop a theoretical framework of the adoption and diffusion of financial innovations. This framework motivates the empirical analysis carried out in the final chapters.

ENDNOTES

1. Davies (1979) shows that, assuming a lognormal firm size distribution, the diffusion of innovations using his model will follow a skewed, cumulative lognormal S shape, which is consistent with earlier empirical findings.

2. Note however that the firm will still decide to switch even if the opponent switches to standard Y and $B^i(2, Y) < 0$ if $B^i(2, Y) > B^i(1, X)$. That is, the firm will switch to minimise losses but would wish that the new standard was never introduced.

3. It should be clear that when $B^i(1, X)$ and $B^i(2, Y) < 0$ does not necessarily mean the firm gets negative returns in absolute terms. This is only a simplification conditioned on the assumption of normalised benefits to status quo. If the firm's status quo benefits are positive, then a $B^i(1, X)$ and $B^i(2, Y) < 0$ simply implies a net reduction in benefits as compared to the status quo.

4. Or internal disadopters. Note that $\bar{N}$ in the diffusion models discussed later in this chapter will include only firms for which $i > \bar{i}$.

5. The assumption that the greater the ambiguity, the more social, as opposed to economic, considerations govern the adoption of innovation may seem at odds with models of rational optimisation under uncertainty. This, however, is justified by defining ambiguity as (Abrahamson and Rosenkopf, 1993): (i) ambiguity of goals, (ii) ambiguity of means–ends relations, and (iii) ambiguity of environments. In other words, it is implicitly assumed that the ambiguity surrounding the innovation's characteristics and relevance makes it difficult to model the adoption decision as an expected-profit maximising problem.

6. We have three identities with three unknowns: q estimates $a\bar{N}$, p estimates $b - a$, and c estimates $-b/\bar{N}$. See Bass (1969, p. 462) for the exact equations.

7. The data of the study was obtained from the *Statistical Abstracts of the United States*, and thus the $\bar{N}$ estimates relate to the US market only. These respective estimates of $\bar{N}$ by Bass (1969) in millions of units are 96.7 for black and white TVs, 22.3 for room air conditioners and 15.0 for clothes dryers. The large discrepancy between the two models' estimates for black and white TVs may be explained by the emergence of colour TVs. Interestingly, the combined NUI estimates for black and white and colour TVs is 89.6 million compared to 96.7 for black and white TVs only by Bass (1969).

8. This is achieved by removing the last two periods for short time series and the last four periods for longer ones, and fitting the models to the truncated data. Forecasts are then produced for these periods by extrapolating the fitted models, and the obtained values are compared to the actual ones.

9. This however does not necessarily imply that the number of adopters due to external influence exceeds the number of adopters due to internal influence since the latter is given by $\sum bN_t(\bar{N} - N_t)$ and the former by $\sum (a_1 + a_2 \ln A(t))(\bar{N} - N_t)$.

10. See also Dodson and Muller (1978) who developed a multi-stage repeat-adoption model. Although they provide interesting theoretical insights into the different stages of a diffusion process, Dodson and Muller do not explain how their model can be applied empirically.

11. Although the data set used in the study covers the number of prescriptions filled, Mahajan *et al.* (1983) make certain assumptions to convert these data into the number of doctors prescribing the new drug.

12. Recall that the NSRL model is a special case of the NUI model when the coefficient of internal influence a is equal to zero. See equations (5.56) to (5.60).
13. Rate of change models uses ΔN_t as their unit of analysis where N_t is the *cumulative* number of adopters up to and including time period t and ΔN_t is the number of adopters *during* time period t.
14. For each measure of forecast accuracy, the rankings depend on the assumed length of the data set, whether the upper limit is known or not, and whether rate of change or cumulative data is used.

6
Financial Innovation: An Industrial Economics Perspective

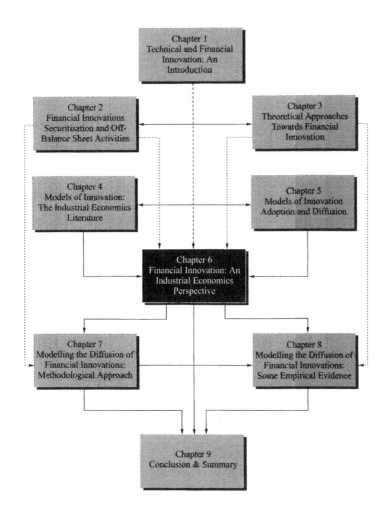

6

Financial Innovation: An Industrial Economics Perspective

6.1 INTRODUCTION

The two previous chapters highlighted the importance that the incentives to innovate and innovation adoption and diffusion processes have received in the industrial economics literature. The application of such models to financial innovation, however, seems to have attracted little attention. Indeed, there is a lack of any systematic and comprehensive studies which examine the implications of the literature reviewed in the last two chapters to the financial industry. This chapter aims at developing a general theoretical framework that relates this literature to the adoption of financial innovations by banks. The first part of the chapter compares the process of innovation in the real and the financial sectors and the academic literature in both fields. We analyse models of the process of financial innovation which, though based on the industrial economics literature, takes into account the unique characteristics of financial products and markets. The chapter also examines the empirical characteristics of innovation in financial markets and the empirical diffusion patterns of OBSAs. Based on the above, the final part of the chapter discusses a general theoretical framework for analysing the adoption and diffusion of innovations in financial markets and links this framework to mathematical models of innovation diffusion discussed in the previous chapter.

6.2 COMPARISON OF THE INDUSTRIAL ECONOMICS AND THE FINANCE LITERATURE

Harrington (1992) compares the literature on financial innovation with that found in the industrial economics literature. He argues that the financial literature approaches the topic in a different way:

1. In the financial literature, there is concern to describe and to classify what exactly has been going on. Innovations are listed frequently and distinguished from each other according to one criterion or another.
2. There has been a lot of work to explain why financial innovations occur. Instead of a microeconomic model of profit-maximising firms as often encountered in the industrial economics literature, studies of financial innovation have often sought more specific causes, such as the avoidance of regulations. The unique characteristics of the financial industry seems to have resulted in a literature characterised by descriptive studies examining the specific factors affecting the emergence of a particular financial innovation rather than attempting to model financial innovation *as a process*.
3. There has been relatively little concern with the influence of industry structure on innovation. Even though a number of writers have referred to increased competition as being one casual factor of innovation, the subject has not been central to the discussion, as it has been with industrial economists.

There are a number of reasons that may explain the fact that finance researchers have relied little on the insights from the literature on technical innovation in explaining financial innovation. Firstly, the cost factor of innovation development and adoption is central to the discussion of technical innovation. The cost of developing or adopting an innovation, however, seems to play a much less crucial rule in the financial industry. This is especially the case for product innovation. Tufano (1989) estimates the cost of developing a new financial product to range between $50 000 and $5 000 000. Secondly, industrial economics models of innovation and adoption usually assume that decisions are irreversible. While there is strong justification for this assumption in cases of technology substitution, there is less support for this assumption in the financial industry. Financial institutions can exit or cease unprofitable areas of business without facing high sunk costs. Thirdly, strong patent protection (i.e. no imitation) is an important implicit assumption in many models of R&D competition. The innovating firm has to guarantee a period of monopoly long enough to compensate for the R&D costs associated with developing new products. Financial markets, however, are characterised by ease of imitation. Petruzzi *et al.* (1988) argue that most financial products cannot be patented.[1]

So although the industrial economics literature has explored many of the basic theoretical problems of innovation, the differences between the financial industry and manufacturing industry seem to have limited the applicability and usefulness of these models in understanding financial innovation. This makes the methodology and approach employed in these models more useful than the specific conclusions reached. The unique aspects of the process of financial innovation and the specific characteristics of the financial industry should provide useful guidelines as to how these models, and the assumptions underlying them, can be adjusted to explore basic theoretical problems of financial innovation. As we have already covered in Chapter 3, Allen and Gale (1994), for example, observed that there are two important incentives to innovate in the financial markets that do not have direct counterparts in the manufacturing industry; changes in the value of pre-existing assets and the risk-sharing benefits of innovation. They developed models of financial innovation which explicitly reflects these incentives to innovate.

Even withstanding the unique characteristics of financial innovation, the industrial economics literature still offers a large number of studies whose results are applicable to the financial industry. The assumptions underlying some of these studies can be justified in financial markets though they would require alternative interpretation. In fact, careful inspection of the industrial economics literature reveals that certain features of innovation competition which have been explored extensively by economists are particularly important in the financial industry. Positive externalities aspects of innovation adoption are particularly interesting in the context of innovation in financial markets. Two sources of positive externalities can be identified in financial markets; informational and network externalities. The former refers to situations where there is information transfer from early adopters to late adopters. In such circumstances late adopters have the advantage of basing their adoption decision on more accumulated information regarding the innovation's profitability, which increases the probability of adopting successful innovations and rejecting unprofitable ones. Informational externalities give rise to the 'free-rider' problem, where late adopters can benefit from their rivals' early adoption of an innovation. As will be shown later in this chapter, the presence of free-rider problems in an innovation-diffusion setting may in some cases lead to a situation where profitable innovations (privately and socially) are not adopted by any firm in the industry.

Two studies, closer in spirit to the industrial economics literature have analysed the presence of informational externalities in financial markets. Anderson and Harris (1986) developed a model of the incentives to innovate applied to new products in the financial industry. Their model is similar to that of Fudenberg and Tirole (1985) discussed in Chapter 5. The model can be distinguished from those reviewed in the last two chapters in terms of its explicit treatment of unique characteristics of the financial industry such as the importance of liquidity and absence of patent protection.

6.3 MODELS OF INNOVATION WITH APPLICATION TO THE FINANCIAL INDUSTRY

6.3.1 Anderson and Harris (1986)

Anderson and Harris (1986) assume a hypothetical industry composed of two exchanges which can add a new financial instrument to their portfolio of traded instruments. The exchanges are assumed to be identical and so are the products they innovate. At any time an exchange may decide to introduce the new product by incurring a fixed cost C to cover development costs including product design, marketing, legal work, and regulatory procedures. Once the exchange decides to innovate it has to wait a period of length N before offering the product which reflects time for development including possible regulatory lag. Both C and N are assumed to be independent of time or the actions of either of the exchanges, and are identical for both exchanges. Once the product is introduced it will generate net revenues at the constant rate R for the industry as a whole indefinitely into the future.

The total revenues generated from introducing the product are assumed to be independent of the number of exchanges which have introduced it. If only one exchange offers the product, it captures all the net revenues. If two exchanges offer the product they will split the market with the market share of the leader, who innovates earlier, higher than that of a follower. Let $S(M)$ be the market share of an exchange that has offered the product a period of length M before the other exchange with $M < 0$ for the leader. Thus $S(-M) = 1 - S(M)$. The assumption that the follower's share is decreasing in the length of the lag between the leader's and the follower's innovation reflects the advantage which liquidity effects bestow on the exchange that innovates first. If both exchanges introduce the product at the same time then they will share the market equally; $S(0) = 0.5$. It is further assumed that $dS/dM < 0$, that $S(\infty) = 0$, and that $1 > S > 0$ for all M. Demand for the product is uncertain before it is on the market, but R can take on two possible values R^H and R^L with probabilities p and $(1 - p)$ respectively, where $1 > p > 0$ and $R^H > R^L \geq 0$. That $R^L \geq 0$ reflects the assumption of costless possible exit which may be a feature of certain financial markets.

The model incorporates positive externalities as follows. The leader which innovates first produces an externality by revealing the level of demand for the new product. The follower benefits from this externality. Thus the model has the feature that first-movers have both an advantage (market share) and a disadvantage (lack of information) relative to the follower. Under the assumptions of the model, it follows that if an exchange chooses to copy an innovation it will do so immediately because waiting results in a loss of revenue because potential market share falls with increasing delay. Similarly, it may be verified that if an exchange decides to introduce an innovation before observing demand (rather than imitate once the demand is known) then it will do so immediately. The analysis of the model can then be summarised in terms of three possible scenarios: monopoly where one exchange innovates at time 0 (and thus introduce at time N) and the other exchange never does; market sharing where both exchanges decide to introduce the innovation at time 0; or a competition where one exchange innovates at time 0 and the other exchange imitates at time N a successful innovation. (Note that the imitator has to wait until a period of length N has passed before the innovation is introduced by the innovator and the demand level is revealed. If the demand level suggests that the innovation is profitable given the delay of adoption in terms of lost market share, then the exchange will have to wait until time $2N$ before it can introduce its imitating product). The payoffs to both exchanges in either of the three scenarios outlined above are summarised in Table 6.1 below, where r is the discount rate, R^H is the flow of net revenues if demand is high, R^L is the flow of net revenues if demand is low, and $\bar{R}$ is the expected value of the flow of revenues and is given by $\bar{R} = pR^H + (1 - p)R^L$.

Anderson and Harris (1986) then show that equilibrium always exists. Furthermore, in equilibrium,

(i)   If $\pi_1 < 0$ then neither exchange ever innovates. For $\pi_1 > 0$, then:
(ii) If, in addition, $\max\{\pi_2, \pi_3\} < 0$ then only one exchange ever innovates, and it does so immediately;
(iii) If $\pi_2 > \max\{\pi_3, 0\}$ then both exchanges innovate at once;
(iv) If $\pi_3 > \max\{\pi_2, 0\}$ and $\pi_4 > 0$ then one exchange innovates immediately and the other innovates at time N if the level of demand is high;
(v)   If $\pi_3 > \max\{\pi_2, 0\}$ but $\pi_4 < 0$ then neither exchange ever innovates.

Table 6.1 Profit flows under monopoly, market sharing, and competition

Scenario	The payoff to exchange A	The payoff to exchange B
Monopoly	$\pi_1 = -C + e^{-rN}\bar{R}/r$	Zero

Exchange A innovates at time 0 and introduces the innovation at time N, and exchange B never imitates. Exchange A thus captures all profits from time N onward and exchange B receives nothing.

Market Sharing	$\pi_2 = -C + e^{-rN}S(0)\bar{R}/r$	$\pi_2 = -C + e^{-rN}S(0)\bar{R}/r$

Both exchanges decides to innovate at time 0 and introduce the innovation at time N. Each receive a fraction $S(0) = 0.5$ of the final profit flow from time N onward.

Competition

$$\pi_4 = -C + e^{-rN}(1 - e^{-rN})\bar{R}/r \qquad\qquad \pi_3 = p(-e^{-rN}C$$
$$+ e^{-2rN}(p(1 - S(N))R^H + (1 - p)R^L)/r \qquad\qquad + e^{-2rN}S(N)R^H/r)$$

Exchange A innovates at time 0, receive profits from time N to time $2N$, and then either shares the market with profit flow of $p(1 - S(N))R^H$ if the demand is high or continues to monopolise the market with expected profit flows $(1 - p)R^L$ if the demand is low. Exchange B innovates at time N and thus introduces the innovation at time $2N$ if demand is high. It will then receive a share of the profit $S(N)R^H$ from time $2N$ onwards. If the demand is low, exchange B will never imitate and will receive nothing.

The equilibria of cases (i) and (iv) are asymmetric, both in respect of the actions taken by the exchanges and the payoffs they receive. By assuming identical exchanges, however, the model does not explain which exchange will innovate and which will imitate. The equilibria cases (i) to (v) provide interesting insights into certain strategic behaviour in financial markets. Firstly, case (i) states that if the innovation is not profitable even when it is monopolised (i.e. $\pi_1 < 0$), then neither exchange will introduce it. Case (ii) states that if the innovation is only profitable when it is monopolised (i.e. if $\pi_1 > 0$) but not if it is either shared or imitated (i.e. both π_2 and $\pi_3 < 0$), then only one exchange will introduce it because it had the edge, and the other exchange will find it unprofitable to either introduce it in a market-sharing situation or to imitate when the level of demand is revealed. This case may arise if costs are high relative to average demand, and if a high level of demand is insufficient to compensate the market share lost due to entering with a delay of N.

Thirdly, if market sharing is profitable ($\pi_2 > 0$), and more so than copying a successful innovation ($\pi_2 > \pi_3$), then simultaneous innovation will occur. This might happen if average demand is high relative to costs, but the loss of market share $S(0) - S(N)$ due to a delay of N is also very large. If the opposite is true, however, and copying a *successful* innovation (i.e. when demand is revealed to be high) is profitable (i.e. $\pi_3 > 0$) and more so than engaging in a market sharing (i.e. $\pi_2 < \pi_3$), then one exchange will innovate and the other will follow suit with a delay of N if the innovation is successful. This might happen if average demand is low relative to costs, but R^H is considerably greater than R^L. Then there are two possibilities; either that the competition through imitation of a successful innovation may not be sufficient to render the initial risk not worthwhile ($\pi_4 > 0$ as in case (iv)), perhaps because the delay or lag between the innovator and the imitator enables the innovator to establish a sufficiently large market share, in which case one exchange decides to innovate at time 0, and the other exchange follows suit if demand is high at time N. Alternatively the knowledge that competition through imitation will make the profits negative and thus will render the risk of innovation not worthwhile ($\pi_4 < 0$ as in case (v)), in which case neither exchange innovates. Although Anderson and Harris (1986) explain the conditions under which each equilibrium will prevail qualitatively, they do not provide any quantitative analysis of these conditions in terms of the parameters of the model.

Note that in both cases (i) and (v), neither exchange introduces the new product, but for different reasons. In case (i), neither exchange introduces the innovation simply because it is unprofitable to do so even under monopoly.[2] In case (v), however, neither exchange will innovate for strategic reasons even though the innovation under monopoly may be profitable, $\pi_1 > 0$, and thus the availability of the innovation will be socially optimal. Case (v) implies that an exchange would not take the risk of innovating on its own if this action caused a loss if its rival imitated after a delay (i.e. $\pi_4 < 0$). This, however, can only happen if imitation yields positive expected profits for the rival, and thus the condition that $\pi_3 > 0$.

This case of equilibrium is particularly interesting since it describes the *free-rider* problem that can be encountered in situations involving positive externalities. The positive externalities in this instance do not stem from information transfer regarding the demand level, but from leading the way by introducing an innovation (unprofitably, as $\pi_4 < 0$) while rivals which could not obtain any profit flows before the innovation is initially introduced, can now imitate (profitably as $\pi_3 > 0$) and earn a positive flow of profits. Note also that the equilibria in state (iv) and (v) have been derived irrespective of the relationship between π_3 and π_4. Specifically, will the equilibrium in state (iv) still exist if $\pi_3 > \pi_4$; i.e. copying is more profitable than undertaking the initial innovation? Clearly if $\pi_3 > \pi_4 > 0$, then each exchange will prefer to introduce the innovation than not ($\pi_4 > 0$ and $\pi_3 > 0$), *and* to follow than to lead (because $\pi_3 > \pi_4$).

The model of Anderson and Harris (1986) offers interesting insights into a previously unexplored area. A number of extensions of their work can be visualised. Firstly, the model can be extended to an *n*-number of exchanges. This should make the conclusions more reliable. It should also allow the authors to examine the resulting diffusion patterns as well as the relationship between market structure and the innovative activity in financial markets. Secondly, the model can be easily adjusted to model competition between investment banks or other financial intermediaries. A different interpretation of the liquidity condition (i.e. $dS/dM < 0$) will be needed in this case. Tufano's (1989) work, for example, suggests that financial intermediaries gain first mover advantage in new financial markets, which justifies the liquidity condition assumed by Anderson and Harris (1986) though for different reasons. Thirdly, some of the assumptions underlying the model can be relaxed to represent more accurately the unique characteristics of financial markets and institutions. The assumption of constant profit flow R, for example, rules out the possibility that total market revenues can increase with the number of banks joining the market because of enhanced liquidity and the expanded customer base.

The Anderson and Harris (1986) model only takes into account one type of positive externality, the informational externality, which leaders bestow on followers. Liquidity of the overall market for the new instrument is another important positive externality which followers bestow on leaders in financial markets. Finally, the model can be extended by relaxing the assumption of identical firms. Incorporating heterogeneity into the model may enable the authors to evaluate questions such as which firms are more likely to innovate (or imitate) than others, and what firm-specific characteristics affect firm's incentives to innovate. This will also allow the relaxation of the assumption of equal C and N for all firms (recall that, once a firm decides to innovate, C is the fixed cost incurred to cover development costs and N is the period of time that the firm has to wait before offering the product). Imitators, for example, are likely to be able to introduce the innovation cheaply and within a shorter period of time (i.e. smaller C and N for imitators), which can add a further dimension to the optimal timing question, and will bring the model more in line with previous literature on technical change. Nevertheless, the work of Anderson and Harris (1986) shows how models of innovation in the industrial economics literature, and the insight they provide into this process, can be adjusted to take into consideration factors unique to the financial industry.

6.3.2 Kapadia and Puri's (1995) Model

The second contribution in this area is the model by Kapadia and Puri (1995). Their model focuses on optimal costly-information acquisition strategies in financial markets. The framework of the model is built around an industry composed of multiple identical risk-neutral firms and multiple new and potentially profitable products waiting to be discovered.[3] To reduce uncertainty regarding the profitability of a potential product innovation, the firm can acquire new information to update its priors in a Bayesian fashion. This process, however, is costly. Moreover, firms can avoid incurring this cost by waiting until a rival invests in information acquisition and observe the same information (i.e. a free-rider problem). Under such a scenario, all firms may wait and no innovation will take place.

Kapadia and Puri (1995) argue that empirical observations of recent spurs in financial innovation reveal two features: (i) many of the innovations have been developed simultaneously, and (ii) that different firms, rather than a single firm, have introduced these innovations even though the innovations have been related. These two observations suggest that there exist some circumstances under which it is optimal for firms not to free-ride, that is; even though there is a positive cost of information acquisition, the firm might prefer to incur this cost rather than costlessly observe the leading firm's information. Using reverse deduction, Kapadia and Puri (1995) specify the conditions under which it is always optimal to free-ride, and given the empirical observations, conclude that these are not features of financial markets. The two counterexamples they provide are a situation where either information is perfectly correlated or when uncertainty is completely resolved by the newly acquired information. The former refers to a situation where the information observed from other firms is as valuable as information directly acquired as a result of the firm's own investment in information acquisition. This can happen when the potential products of all firms are identical and information transfer is perfect. Under these conditions then the direct (and costly) observation through own investment is more informative and therefore is worth more to the firms than an indirect (though free) observation through information transfer. The second counterexample is a situation in which the new acquired information completely resolves any uncertainty regarding the profitability of the innovation. Since this information cannot be held proprietary, all the other firms in the industry also share this information. Kapadia and Puri (1995) show that under either of these situations, it will always be optimal for the second firm to free-ride on the first firm's investment in information acquisition. Thus, the industry structure will see only one firm innovating. The other firms in the industry will imitate the innovator's investment in the product if the product proves to be profitable.

Kapadia and Puri (1995) show that both residual uncertainty and imperfect correlation may be necessary for firms to consider investment in information, and that under such circumstances it may be optimal for different firms to simultaneously innovate in new products in an uncertain environment than for a firm to wait and free-ride on information generated by other firms. This result, however, does not necessarily mean that information transfer reduces the incentives to innovate. In fact Kapadia and Puri show that under certain conditions, the rate of information acquisition might be positively affected by the rate of information transmission between firms. The intuition behind this result is that although information-transfer from one firm to another can create an incentive to free-ride, it can also allow one firm to learn from the experience of another. This is true to the extent that potential products are related. The value of information in this context stem from decreasing the probability of pursuing an unprofitable innovation or abandoning a profitable innovation. The value of information to the individual firm depends on the extent to which information regarding current potential innovations are correlated with information regarding future potential innovation (and the extent to which potential innovations for one firm are correlated with those of another). Thus, the public nature of information, and the absence of patent or copyright protection, may increase the overall incentive for innovation.

6.4 EMPIRICAL ASPECTS OF THE INNOVATION PROCESS IN FINANCIAL MARKETS

Another factor that may limit the relevance of findings of industrial economics literature is the lack of studies of empirical features of innovation in the financial industry. The results obtained from industrial economics models of individual firm and aggregate industry behaviour can vary considerably under different sets of assumptions underlying these models. Economists have benefited from a substantial empirical literature on innovation and market structure in formulating their theoretical models of technical innovation. The finance literature, however, offers only limited and isolated studies of the relevant empirical features of innovation in the financial industry. This has tended to limit the ability to relate the findings of industrial economics literature to the finance industry, or to develop models that are specifically attuned to describe innovation in the financial world.

A recent survey by Drew (1995) investigates the factors affecting financial firms' decisions regarding new product development periods. He finds 'speed-to-market' is becoming crucial to securing competitive advantage for financial firms. Pressures for increased speed of development arise from the base of innovation in computer technology, rapid changes in industry regulation and fast-changing customer needs. Accelerated new product development can (potentially) contribute to improvements in organisational performance in various ways, including enhanced profits, greater market share, reduced time-to-break-even, and improved competitive advantage, image, and reputation (Drew, 1995). There are costs and barriers, however, to accelerated development periods. Based on case studies, interviews, and a mail survey to new product development managers in North American banks, Drew (1995, p. 16) finds that faster product development was a major strategic priority in all sectors, 'reasons for speed included the need to retain existing customers, competitive market pressures and changing customer needs. Few managers believed that major increases in market share or revenues would result, since most businesses are at the mature stage of the life cycle. However, all felt that firm reputation, image, and customer loyalty would be heightened by faster innovation. Most felt they had no choice but to accelerate development since the customer was demanding greater responsiveness and had alternate sources of supply. Many mentioned the ease of copying by competition and entry of new types of competitors into their markets. This posed dilemmas of business strategy. As illustration, one retail banker concerned with electronic home banking products questioned: *Should I bring out a shoddy new product now because a competitor may be faster to market—or can I wait and deliver a quality service?'*.

Table 6.2 summarises the key factors affecting new product development (NPD) in the banking sector. The important implications of this study is the importance of strategic behaviour in financial innovation development.

6.5 EMPIRICAL DIFFUSION PATTERNS OF OBSAs

There have been limited applications of mathematical diffusion models (reviewed in Chapter 5) to the study of financial innovations. The most notable example are studies by Jagtiani *et al.* (1993, 1995) in which they analyse the diffusion pattern of five OBSAs; swaps, options, futures and forwards, loan sales, and standby letters of credit (SLCs). Using a sample of 86 large US commercial banks, they model OBS activity i as a financial innovation subject to the following logistic diffusion adoption pattern:

$$\ln\left[\frac{n_{it}}{(\bar{N}_i - n_{it})}\right] = \alpha_i + \beta_i(t) + \mu_{i1}(DUM1) + \cdots + \mu_{i3}(DUM3)$$
$$+ \mu_{i4}(t.DUM1) + \cdots + \mu_{i6}(t.DUM3), \qquad (6.1)$$

Table 6.2 Factors affecting new product development period (NPD)

Area	Importance of faster NPD	Reasons for faster development	(1) Barriers and (2) Means of acceleration
1. Corporate banking	Very high.	Customer relations and loyalty. Changing needs. Revenues.	(i) Slow internal systems development. (ii) Use of outside resources.
2. Corporate banking	Very high. Support from the top	Competitive forces.	(i) Culture, slow systems development, bureaucracy. (ii) Outsourcing.
3. Corporate banking	Very high	Maintaining revenue stream. Product differentiation.	(i) Internal mainframe systems. (ii) Use of outsiders. Re-engineering.
4. Corporate banking	Essential	Must deliver new types of products. Customer demands.	(i) Culture. (ii) Stream-lining and fast-tracking product development.
5. Retail banking	Very high. Top management insisting.	Competitive pressures. Staying as leader in innovation.	(ii) Use of advanced technology. New approaches to IT.
6. Retail banking	High.	Competitive pressures. Customer requests.	(i) Difficulty of changes in large branch network. Lengthy approval processes. (ii) Teamwork.
7. Mid–small business banking	Very high.	Keeping existing customers. Increased customer sophistication.	(i) Size of institution, slow bureaucracy. (ii) Process re-engineering.
8. General insurance	Very high, key part of strategy.	Product differentiation to support niche strategy.	(i) Industry culture. (ii) Use of advanced technology.
9. Life insurance	Very high. President very concerned.	Rapidly shifting customer needs. Need to react to new competitors.	(i) Internal systems. (ii) Radical redesign of business.
10. Credit card services	Very important	Need to provide differentiated products.	(i) Bureaucracy, systems, slow decision making. (ii) Cross functional teams.

Source: Drew (1995), p. 17

where n_{it} is a measure of diffusion of innovation i at time t and $\bar{N}_i$ is the equilibrium level for n_{it}. Two measures of diffusion (i.e. n_{it}) are employed:

1. Number of banks that engaged in OBSA i where n_{it} = number of banks in the sample that engage in activity i at time t divided by the number of all banks in the sample and $\bar{N}_i = 1$ assuming that all banks in the sample will engage in activity i at $t = \infty$, and

2. Dollar volume of OBSA i where n_{it} = aggregate dollar amount of OBSA i issued by all banks in the sample at time t divided by the aggregate dollar amount of total assets plus OBSA i offered by all banks in the sample at time t, and $\bar{N}_i = \text{Max}(n_{it}) + \sigma(n_{it})$ or $= \text{Max}(n_{it}) + 2\sigma(n_{it})$ or $= 1$, where σ is the standard deviation of n_{it} and $\text{Max}(n_{it})$ is the maximum value of n_{it} during the period of the study.

The dummy variables in equation (6.1) are incorporated to measure the impact of changes in capital requirements during the period January 1984 (June 1985 for swaps) to September 1991 (31 quarters and 26 quarters for swaps). Using the 1984:I–1985:II base period, DUM1 captures the 1985 increase in capital requirements and equals one for the period 1985:III–1988:II. DUM1 is expected to have a positive coefficient because banks had to maintain fewer capital ratios the more they used OBSA instead of traditional on-balance sheet items. DUM2 captures the post-announcement, pre-implementation of risk-based capital requirements (RBC) and equals one for the period 1988:III–1990:II. Finally DUM3 captures the post-implementation of RBC and equals one for the period 1990:IV–1991:III. DUM2 and DUM3 are expected to have negative coefficients since the respective changes in capital requirements removed the advantages of switching to OBSA that were brought about by the 1985 changes (i.e. opposite to the 1985 changes, the move from a non-RBC to a RBC requirement removes any capital-requirements-related advantages from issuing OBSA). Note that while DUM1, DUM2, and DUM3 are intended to capture regulatory effects on the intercept, the $t \times \text{DUM1}$, $t \times \text{DUM2}$, and $t \times \text{DUM3}$ capture the effects on the slope.

In their earlier extended working paper, Jagtiani et al. (1993) used both measures of diffusion (i.e. n_{it}); the number of banks that issued the OBS item i, and the percentage of the output of the industry reflecting the innovation (i.e. aggregate dollar amount of the OBS activity i issued by banks in the sample divided by the aggregate dollar amount of total assets plus OBS activity i issued by banks in the sample). Jagtiani et al. (1995) adopt only the second measure of diffusion.[4] The analysis is carried out at both the industry level (aggregate values for all banks in the sample) and at the bank level (i.e. inter-firm diffusion). The former allows the authors to test for the effects of regulatory changes on the overall diffusion of the innovation and the latter allows the investigation of bank-specific factors that affects the speed at which individual banks adopt the innovation (as a proportion of its overall business activities).

Tables 6.3 and 6.4 below show the results obtained by Jagtiani *et al.* (1995). The speed of adoption is positive and highly significant for all OBSAs except standby letters of credit (SLCs) and loan sales. The coefficient of DUM1 is negative (unexpected) for OBSA derivatives but significantly positive for loan SLCs and weakly significant for loan sales. This suggests that SLCs and loan sales may have been used by banks as OBSA substitutes for traditional lending to avoid the increase in capital requirements imposed in 1985:III and until the 1988:II period. The coefficients of DUM2 are significantly negative for options and futures and forwards suggesting that the RBC requirements may have reduced the adoption of options, futures, and forwards to a level below that expected by the logistic curve, while having no significant impact effect on other OBSAs. Overall, Jagtiani *et al.* (1995, p. 654) conclude that the results suggest that the RBC requirements appear to have had little effect in discouraging banks from engaging in OBSAs both during the 'phase-in period' before the actual implementation and after the actual implementation.

In the second part of their empirical analysis, Jagtiani *et al.* (1995) investigated the bank-specific factors that influence banks' adoption of OBSAs (Table 6.4). The speed of diffusion coefficient b_{ij} was estimated for each bank j in the sample for every OBS activity i (Panel A of Table 6.4). These values were then treated as independent variables in a cross-sectional regression analysis (Panel B in Table 6.4) and the variations in them across banks were explained in terms of capital adequacy, bank size, creditworthiness, and international presence.

Table 6.3 OBSAs diffusion patterns for the banking industry

Variable	SLCs	Loan sales	Swaps	Options	Fut & Fwd
K	0.1098	0.2470	0.8045	0.5757	0.6515
Intercept	17 609**	−13 852**	−26 746**	−11 996**	−21 098**
	(0.0001)	(0.0001)	(0.0001)	(0.0001)	(0.0001)
Time	−0.040*	0.018	0.050**	0.142**	0.066**
	(0.0342)	(0.3853)	(0.0001)	(0.0001)	(0.0001)
DUM1	0.676**	0.549†	n/a	−2.980**	−0.699**
	(0.0043)	(0.0876)	—	(0.0001)	(0.0005)
DUM2	0.724†	0.765	0.066	−3.434**	−0.742
	(0.0720)	(0.1107)	(0.1616)	(0.0001)	(0.0096)
DUM3	1.103*	−0.033	0.015	−3.367**	−0.664†
	(0.0383)	(0.9574)	(0.8151)	(0.0002)	(0.0545)
No quarters	31	31	26	31	31
R^2	0.389	0.788	0.993	0.876	0.956
R^2-adjusted	0.294	0.755	0.992	0.857	0.949

Notes: *P*-values are reported in parentheses. Significance at the 1, 5, and 10% level is indicated by **, *, and † respectively. *Source*: Adapted from Jagtiani *et al.* (1995, p. 653)

Financial Innovation

Table 6.4 Factors determining variations in diffusion patterns across banks

PANEL A	SLCs	Loan sales	Swaps	Options	Fut & Fwd
Mean of β_i	0.0128	0.0213	0.1170	0.2724	0.0536
Std. dev.	0.0553	0.1380	0.1639	0.5950	0.3583
Minimum	−0.2332	−0.3872	−0.7350	−0.4844	−1.3979
Maximum	0.1252	0.3680	0.6089	3.8351	2.4384
Average adj. R^2	0.607	0.376	0.697	0.491	0.452
Coeff. of variation	4.32	6.48	1.40	2.18	6.68
Significant at 5%	49/86	31/86	67/86	29/82	32/86
PANEL B	SLCs	Loan sales	Swaps	Options	Fut & Fwd
Intercept	0.036*	0.004	0.088	0.340	−0.005
	(0.0212)	(0.9284)	(0.1092)	(0.1083)	(0.9519)
CAPITAL	0.017*	−0.020	0.021	0.131	0.024
	(0.0130)	(0.2813)	(0.3728)	(0.1656)	(0.5376)
PROFIT	−0.005	0.010	−0.062	−0.570	−0.013
	(0.8634)	(0.8985)	(0.5358)	(0.1423)	(0.9365)
NPLOAN	−0.019†	−0.005	−0.004	0.025	0.022
	(0.0622)	(0.8522)	(0.9102)	(0.8599)	(0.7077)
FGDEPO	0.0002	−0.0001	0.003	−0.005	0.002
	(0.7052)	(0.9723)	(0.1372)	(0.4758)	(0.5859)
RISKWGT	0.111	0.291	0.272	−0.509	0.305
	(0.1399)	(0.1734)	(0.3015)	(0.6418)	(0.4819)
ASSETS	−0.012**	−0.005	−0.021	−0.019	−0.026
	(0.0092)	(0.7165)	(0.1901)	(0.7724)	(0.3184)
R^2-(adjusted)	0.194	0.048	0.070	0.080	0.041
	(0.135)	(−0.021)	(0.001)	(0.002)	(−0.032)

Source: Adapted from Jagtiani *et al.* (1995, p. 656)

The independent variables included log of total assets (ASSETS), foreign deposits as a percentage of total deposits (FGDEPO) and the following items as a percentage of total assets: non-performing loans (NPLOAN), net income (PROFIT), equity capital (CAPITAL), and risk-adjusted assets (RISKWGT).

For swaps, options, futures and forwards, and loan sales, none of the independent variables are significant. In the case of SLCs, the creditworthiness factors proxied by CAPITAL and NPLOAN have positive and negative effects respectively on the speed of adoption. This implies that more creditworthy banks were quicker in adopting SLCs, which is consistent with the market discipline hypothesis (that is, the market valuation of these contingent claims encourages banks which issue them to increase their safety and/or offers relatively safer banks a comparative advantage in issuing these claims). The coefficient of ASSETS is significantly negative for SLCs, which is inconsistent with the notion that larger banks are perceived as more credible sellers of guarantees because they are 'too-big-to-fail'. Overall, Jagtiani *et al.* (1995,

p. 655) conclude that the results 'seem to suggest that banks' decision to adopt various OBSA products are generally related to purely technological and learning factors'.

6.6 A FRAMEWORK FOR MODELLING INNOVATION ADOPTION IN FINANCIAL MARKETS

Chapter 2 outlined the main reasons why banks engage in OBSAs. A number of interesting hypotheses have emerged and have been empirically tested. These include the *market discipline hypothesis*, Boot and Thakor (1991) and Koopenhaver and Stover (1991); the *collateralisation hypothesis*, Benvensite and Berger (1986, 1987); the *moral hazard hypothesis*, Thomas and Woolridge (1991); and the *comparative advantage and regulatory tax hypotheses*, Pavel and Phillis (1987), Pennacchi (1988), and Carlston and Samolyk (1995). These studies have adopted a static framework which provides a useful insight into the determinants of an individual bank's adoption decisions, yet ignores a number of important factors. Innovations are often developed and diffused among banks in a dynamic environment where the presence of uncertainty makes the interaction among rival firms impact strongly on the individual firm's adoption decisions. Such strategic, competitive, and informational interactions between firms impact on the timing of adoption of innovations and on the number of firms that will eventually adopt the innovation. There has been little or no systematic analysis of such interactions among firms in the financial industry.

Chapters 4 and 5 have shown that these and similar questions have long been raised in the industrial economics literature which by now offers an extensive and long-established study of the innovation process. Surprisingly, there has been little effort made to relate the findings of this literature to the area of financial innovation. It seems that it is implicitly assumed that differences between real and financial products limit the applicability of the industrial economics literature to the financial sector. It is often argued, for example, that innovations in the financial industry do not involve large development costs and that they can be developed within a short period of time, thus the trade-off between innovation introduction time and development costs becomes of little significance. Another important difference is the lack of patent protection on new financial products. Studies which assume that innovators can monopolise the markets for their inventions long enough to compensate for the development cost of the innovation, therefore, cannot be directly applied to competition in the innovative activity in the financial industry. Finally, one may argue that the introduction of new financial products involves relatively small sunk costs which makes it less of a consideration to introduce new products, since their failure would not cause substantial financial losses.

All the above arguments should be taken into consideration when trying to derive the implications of the industrial economics literature to the financial sector. They do not, however, imply that studies of real innovations cannot shed light on the determinants of innovation in the financial sector. The industrial economics literature has extensively examined many different scenarios some of which meet the unique characteristics of the financial industry. The characteristics of the process of financial innovations is also changing. The arrival of *'rocket engineers'* to the banking industry shows that banks are now actively investing resources to develop new products which they can market to their customers. Drew's (1995) study shows that the development period (and thus the introduction date) of an innovation is a major consideration for financial institutions. Banks have to adjust quickly to meet the changing demands of their customers. This has been fostered further by the increased competition between financial institutions and markets and by the removal of traditional barriers between different financial institutions. Globalisation and deregulation have also contributed to the institutionalisation of the innovation process, bringing it closer to its counterpart in the real sector. The study by Tufano (1989) which used a dataset of 57 innovations has also shown that even in the absence of patent protection, financial institutions have motivation to develop successful new products because they gain, on average, a larger market share in the markets in which they have developed new products compared with those in which they follow. On the other hand, banks risk their reputation if the products they innovate fail. All these factors make the strategic and competitive aspects of the adoption and diffusion of financial innovations an important issue. The findings of studies of competition in innovative activity in the industrial economics literature has therefore become more relevant and useful to the financial industry.

The aim of the remainder of this chapter is to develop a general diffusion-related approach to examine the adoption of financial innovations by banks. This approach is largely based on studies in the industrial economics literature covered in Chapters 4 and 5 which have not been related to the banking industry. The framework discussed forms the basis for the later empirical analysis.

The theoretical background of our approach can be explained as follows. Due to some exogenous factor or factors (initial stimulus) an innovation becomes desirable for a specific group of banks (*external adopters*). We refer to the initial stimulus as *external influence*. Banks in this group do not adopt the innovation in the same time because the *stimulus variate* or the *critical level* required to elicit an adoption is described by a distribution of values, and not a unique value appropriate to all firms in the population. This heterogeneity can be incorporated in a number of ways, such as firm size, differential access to information, or differential initial estimates of the profitability of the innovation. Under appropriate conditions, innovations can also be shown to diffuse (as opposed to being adopted instantaneously by the whole population) even when one assumes identical firms and perfect information.

In the absence of any strategic and competitive factors, all banks in that group will adopt the innovation with the timing of adoption being determined by bank-specific characteristics, and banks outside that group would not adopt the innovation. The presence of strategic, competitive, and informational factors, however, can impact on the number of banks that will eventually adopt the innovation in two ways: either a proportion of banks affected by the initial stimulus would reject the innovation due to these strategic and competitive factors, *or* these factors will cause a number of banks outside the initial group to adopt the innovation (internal adopters or adopters due to internal influence). Ignoring internal diffusion rules out any element of bandwagon effects and information transfer as explanations of innovation adoption (that is, the appraisal by firms of an innovation's desirability is complete the moment the innovation is announced, and delay in adoption can only be the result of objective circumstances).[5] Given banks' initial assessments of the innovation's desirability, however, the adoption by one or more banks of the innovation can make it either more or less desirable for other banks to adopt.[6] Internal influence captures the dynamics of how innovations diffuse among banks and allows us to assess how innovation adoption by one bank makes it more or less desirable for other banks to adopt the innovation. Banks adopt or reject an innovation due to internal influence because of either their updated assessment of the innovation's returns (rational-efficiency hypothesis) or competitive and institutional bandwagon effects (bandwagon hypothesis). In the former case, innovation adoption by one bank favourably affects other banks' updated assessments of the innovation's profitability (i.e. banks which previously rejected the innovation). In the latter case, banks adopt the innovation due to bandwagon pressures created by the number of their rivals that have adopted the innovation, and not based on these banks' individual assessments of the innovation's profitability.[7]

Figure 6.1 depicts the framework of our theoretical approach. The vertical axis measures the initial assessment of an innovation's profitability from the point of view of an individual firm. If the initial assessment is positive, the firm will adopt the innovation. For negative assessments, the firm will wait one more period after which it will update its assessment. Sources of changes in the firm's assessments are: increase or decrease in R, r, or C, where R is the mean estimate of the innovation's profitability, r the discount factor reflecting the uncertainty regarding R, and C the total adoption costs. Any changes in either of these parameters can be either related to or independent of the number of firms which have adopted the innovation (internal influence and external influence, respectively). Figure 6.2 summarises the main factors that can cause a change in a firm's assessment of the innovation's profitability.

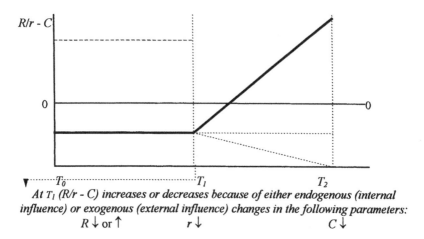

At T_1 $(R/r - C)$ increases or decreases because of either endogenous (internal influence) or exogenous (external influence) changes in the following parameters:
$$R \downarrow \text{ or } \uparrow \qquad r \downarrow \qquad C \downarrow$$

Figure 6.1 Initial and updated assessments of innovation's profitability

6.6.1 Rational-Efficiency as an Explanation of Innovation Diffusion

The rational-efficiency hypothesis states that subsequent adoptions of an innovation by firms which did not adopt earlier are based on these firms' updated assessment of the innovation's profitability. Firms which did not adopt earlier change their assessment of the innovation's profitability due to (initial) exogenous or endogenous factors. In the former case changes in the environment in which these firms operate may cause a decrease in the expected cost of adoption or an increase in expected return prompting firms to view adopting the innovation more favourably. The cost/return characteristics of the innovation can also change with the increase in the number of earlier adopters. Return can increase due to positive externalities associated with the number of earlier adopters. Adoption costs can fall for earlier adopters because of the fixed costs component associated with the development of new markets and promotional activities to overcome customers' resistance to change.

Incomplete information theorists argue that, for profitable innovations, the larger the number of firms that have adopted the innovation, the more information about the innovation's true cost/returns characteristics is available and disseminated from adopters to nonadopters, and the greater the number of subsequent adoptions by firms. In the case of incomplete information, firms can also update their assessment of the innovation's profitability by conducting their own research and marketing studies. In such cases, and to the extent that there is a first-mover advantage of adopting earlier, firms have to balance the costs of updating their information with potential lost profits due to delayed adoption of a profitable innovation. Finally, an increase in the number of

---

External Influence

Exogenous factors (e.g. changes in regulations, demand-related factors, advances in technology) make an innovation desirable for a certain group of banks with the timing of adoption being a function of firm-specific characteristics.

⇓

A proportion of these banks adopt the innovation based on their individual assessment of that innovation's efficiency or returns

⇓

Internal Influence

Bandwagon Effects Hypothesis		**Rational-Efficiency Hypothesis**
The sheer number of banks adopting an innovation causes a bandwagon pressure prompting other banks to adopt		Banks adopt (reject) innovations based on their updated individual assessment of the innovation's efficiency and returns due to endogenous factors.

Institutional bandwagon	**Competitive bandwagon**	**Updated information**
• Bandwagon pressures on non-adopting banks arising from the threat of lost legitimacy and lost stockholders support.	• Bandwagon pressures on non-adopting banks arising from the threat of lost competitive advantage.	• Information flow from adopting banks to nonadopting banks prompting the latter to update their assessment of the innovation's efficiency and returns. • Returns to innovation increase (decrease) with increases in the number of adopters due to positive (negative) externalities. • Adoption costs decline (increase) with increases in the number of adopters due to the fixed cost nature of new market development (increase in the level of promotional activities).

Figure 6.2 Theoretical background of diffusion models

adopters may induce other firms to view the innovation less favourably because of the lost competitive advantage in the new market. To the extent that early adopters manage to achieve reputational and distributional advantages, other firms have to increase their spending if they are to compete effectively, which increases the expected cost of adoption and thus may discourage subsequent adoption of the innovation.

6.6.2 Bandwagon-Pressure Theories of Innovation Diffusion

The informational-transfer aspect of the rational-efficiency hypothesis assumes that nonadopters' decisions are influenced by new information which flows through channels from early adopters to nonadopters. This, however, requires that there must be (i) information, (ii) channels, (iii) a propensity by adopters to disseminate this information, and (iv) a propensity of nonadopters to be influenced by it (Abrahamson and Rosenkopf, 1993). There are many situations where these conditions are not met. In many competitive markets adopters may not wish to disseminate information about the innovation to nonadopters. Even if some information is disseminated, its impact on nonadopters' decisions can be limited by differences between firms (e.g. differences in current business and customer bases, long-term strategic planning, or cost functions). Finally, firms may not risk waiting for information (from either adopter's experiences or their own research) because they fear that early adopters will have sizeable first-mover advantages in the new market.

Bandwagon theories attempt to explain the diffusion patterns of innovations where one or more of the assumptions underlying the rational-efficiency hypothesis are not met. Bandwagons are diffusion processes whereby organisations adopt (or reject) an innovation, *not because of their individual assessments of the innovation's efficiency or returns*, but because of bandwagon pressure caused by the sheer number of firms that have already adopted this innovation. Two types of bandwagon pressures can be identified; institutional bandwagon and competitive bandwagon. The former refers to pressures on organisations arising from the threat of lost legitimacy and lost stockholder support. The increase in the number of firms adopting the innovation make firms that do not use the innovation appear abnormal or illegitimate to their stockholders. These firms adopt the innovation, not based on their individual assessment of its efficiency or returns, but because of the fear of reputational and shareholder pressures. Competitive bandwagon refers to pressures on organisations to adopt the innovation arising from the threat of lost competitive advantage. In this case, firms do not have sufficient information to assess the innovation's profitability but fear that delay in adoption may cause irrecoverable loss in their current and future market shares. Firms adopt an innovation due to competitive bandwagon pressure in order to avoid a worst-case scenario of being at a great competitive disadvantage in terms of their comparative performance in the industry. In other words, these firms' perceived threat of a competitive disadvantage if they do not adopt and the innovation succeeds, far outweighs the perceived value of the competitive advantage they would gain if they do not adopt and the innovation fails. Innovation adoption due to competitive bandwagon pressure is more likely for innovations that are associated with significant first-mover advantages and relatively small adoption costs.

6.7 CATEGORIES OF ADOPTERS

6.7.1 Internal versus External Adopters

Based on the framework outlined above, we can distinguish between two categories of first-time adopters; external and internal. External adopters are banks which are influenced in their adoption of the financial innovation by initial exogenous factors, such as changes in the regulatory environment or demand factors. Internal adopters refer to banks which adopt the innovation because of bandwagon pressures (institutional and/or competitive) or because of their updated assessment due to endogenous factors (e.g. information transfer and positive/negative externalities). Mathematical diffusion models can be used to provide insight into the structure of diffusion processes of financial innovations. As reviewed in Chapter 5, most of these models are extensions of the Mansfield (1961) logistic curve model:

$$\frac{N(t+1) - N(t)}{\bar{N} - N(t)} = \beta \frac{N(t)}{\bar{N}}, \tag{6.2}$$

where:

$N(t)$ = cumulative number of adopters at time t
$\bar{N}$ = potential number of adopters
β = coefficient of internal influence.

The Mansfield (1961) model postulates that the number of adopters in each period is determined by the cumulative number of adopters in the previous period in a constant way. The non-uniform influence (NUI) model of Easingwood et al. (1983) is an extension of the Mansfield (1961) model which allows for this relationship to vary throughout the diffusion process. This model also has the advantage of allowing for exogenous factors (i.e. that are independent of the number of adopters in previous periods) to influence the number of adopters in each period. The NUI model can be derived by replacing β in the Mansfield (1961) model by $w(t)$ where:[8]

$$w(t) = b\left(\frac{N(t)}{\bar{N}}\right)^{\alpha}. \tag{6.3}$$

The NUI model is then:

$$\frac{dN(t)}{dt} = a(\bar{N} - N(t)) + b\left(\frac{N(t)}{\bar{N}}\right)^{\delta}(\bar{N} - N(t)). \tag{6.4}$$

The left hand side of equation (6.4) represents the increase in the cumulative number of adopters over time, which is equal to the number of first-time adopters in each period. The first term on the right-hand side of equation (6.4) represents the number of adopters due to external influence (i.e. due to exogenous factors). The second term on the right-hand side of equation (6.4) represents the number of first-time adopters due to internal influence at time t.[9] A non-constant internal influence in the diffusion process will be indicated by $\delta \neq 1$. The specification of $w(t)$ in equation (6.3) allows internal influence to be an increasing function (for $\delta > 1$), a decreasing function (for $\delta < 1$) or a constant function (for $\delta = 1$) of the number of previous adopters.[10]

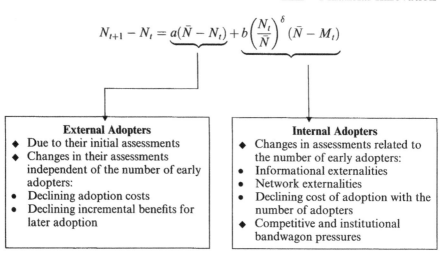

Figure 6.3   External versus internal influence

Figure 6.3 relates the factors identified in Figures 6.1 and 6.2 to the relevant mathematical diffusion models. The finance literature offers support for the structure of the model as well as for some of the individual components. The general structure of the model, for example, is supported by the conclusion that financial innovations grow even after the initial stimulus that led to their emergence is no more in effect (Smith, 1992; Miller, 1986). The implicit assumption of differential assessments of innovation's profitability is supported by the literature on banks' involvement in OBSAs activities which suggest that bank specific factors such as bank risk and assets and loan opportunities affects the probability of entering these markets. On the external side of Figure 6.3, Tufano (1989) offers evidence of declining incremental benefits for later adoption. Declining adoption costs can be justified on basis of advances in information technology. On the internal side, models by Anderson and Harris (1986) and Kapadia and Puri (1995) demonstrate the importance of informational and network externalities in financial markets. The presence of bandwagon pressures is also evident in a number of studies about banks' engagement in derivatives markets and in OBSAs (e.g. Bullock, 1987). Finally, there is no empirical evidence of adoption costs behaviour as a function of the number of adopters.

Testing the above models against data on the number of banks that have adopted an innovation enables us to evaluate whether innovation adoption by one bank makes it more or less desirable for other banks to adopt the innovation (if b is significantly larger/smaller than zero), and how this relationship varies with the number of adopters (if δ is significantly larger/smaller than

1). The effects of exogenous factors can be gauged by evaluating the number of banks that have adopted as a result of the initial stimulus:

$$\text{Number of external adopters at time } t \equiv a(\bar{N} - N_t). \qquad (6.5)$$

It should be noted that even though the number of external adopters is assumed to be distributed uniformly over the diffusion span (since a is constant), the model is flexible enough to accommodate a large number of possible distributions of the number of external adopters over time. This is so because the number of external adopters during any period, and also the total number of external adopters, not only depend on a but also on $[\bar{N} - N_t]$ which, in turn, depends on the value of b and δ. Thus the different combinations of values of a, b, δ allows for more flexibility in depicting the number of external adopters than may be initially conveyed by the constant a examined in isolation.

The number of banks which, though they were not influenced by the initial influence, have engaged in the new market due to competitive, strategic, or informational factors can be given by:[11]

$$\text{Number of internal adopters at time } t \equiv b\left(\frac{N_t}{\bar{N}}\right)^{\delta-1} (\bar{N} - N_t). \qquad (6.6)$$

6.7.2 Repeat Adopters

A limitation of the above models is that they only account for the single-adoption of an innovation, that is, the models only account for the innovation being adopted once by a firm. The NUI model however can be extended to allow for multiple-adoption of an innovation by incorporating a repeat adoption coefficient c, and modelling the total number of adopters, $n(t)$. The resulting repeat model (NUIR) can be written as:

$$n(t+1) = a(\bar{N} - N(t)) + b\left(\frac{N(t)}{\bar{N}}\right)^{\delta} (\bar{N} - N(t)) + cN(t).^{[12]} \qquad (6.7)$$

Note that the interpretation of the parameters in the repeat model is different to that of their counterparts in the single-adoption model. In equation (6.7), the different parameters measure the impact of market entry by new banks at time t on the *number of banks* participating in the market at time $t + 1$, $n(t)$. This number comprises both repeat adopters and first-time adopters. In early stages of the diffusion process, most banks in $n(t)$ will be first time adopters and their number will be determined by the relative values of a and b. In later stages $n(t)$ will be dominated by repeat banks and their number will be determined by c.

6.8 CONCLUSION

A comparison of the literature on financial innovation (Chapters 2 and 3) and technical innovation (Chapters 4 and 5) reveals that the latter has been examined in a more formal and thorough fashion. In particular, the industrial economics literature has examined three main areas:

1. The incentives to innovate at the firm level and the optimal timing and investment rate in the inventive activity
2. The relationship between market structure and the innovative activity by firms (in comparison to the socially optimal levels)
3. The firm- and industry-specific factors affecting the adoption and diffusion of technical innovations.

The literature on financial innovation, on the other hand, has tended to be more descriptive in nature and has focused on exogenous factors that have affected the emergence of a number of specific innovations in the financial industry. These models are more concerned with *why* specific innovations occurred rather than *how* innovation occurs in terms of timing of innovation and investment in new products and the incentives of firms to engage in innovation.

Recently, a more formal literature has developed modelling the incentives of financial innovation (e.g. for a recent survey, see Allen and Gale, 1994, and Duffie and Rahi, 1995) which suggests that new securities play a role in 'spanning', or risk sharing. Although this idea is not new in itself, it is only recently that the process of financial innovation has been formally examined in this context. There is still, however, a big gap in the literature on adoption and diffusion of financial innovations. Although a substantial literature exists on why banks adopt off-balance sheet activities (OBSAs) and the exogenous factors affecting the growth of these instruments (e.g. Benveniste and Berger, 1986, 1987; Pavel and Phillis, 1987; Pennacchi, 1988; Avery and Berger, 1991a; Thomas and Woolridge, 1991; and Boot and Thakor, 1991—see Chapter 2) most of this literature is static, and ignores the informational and strategic aspects of innovation adoption and diffusion. Chapters 4 and 5 showed that strategic competition could have a major impact on competition between firms in innovation. The models by Anderson and Harris (1986) and Kapadia and Puri (1995) show how questions of information-transfer, positive externalities, strategic competition, and free-rider problems can have major impacts on financial firms' decisions to engage innovation. The analysis of the effects of such phenomena on financial innovation have been very limited. Moreover, there has been no detailed treatment of the question of how financial innovation adoption by one firm makes it more or less desirable for other firms to adopt.

The second part of this chapter outlined a framework which analysed innovation adoption by banks and the spread of innovations in the financial industry. This framework distinguishes between two categories of adopters. External adopters are banks which adopt the innovation based on their individual assessments of the innovation's profitability, which is determined by exogenous factors that lead to the initial emergence of the innovation. These banks do not necessarily adopt the innovation simultaneously; optimal timing of adoption is defined by key firm-specific factors which are described by a distribution of values across firms and not a single value. We do not specify these factors, nor do we determine *a priori* the time-pattern of external innovation adoption.

External adoptions of the innovation influence non-adopting banks by either changing these banks' assessments of the innovation's profitability or by exerting competitive and institutional bandwagon pressures on these banks to adopt the innovation. Internal adopters are those banks whose adoption decision is influenced by the number of banks that have adopted the innovation. These banks may base their decision on individual assessments of the innovation's profitability, in which case the change in their assessments is due to positive informational or network externalities related to the number of banks that have adopted the innovation. These banks may also adopt the innovation due to competitive and institutional bandwagon pressures created by the sheer number of banks that have adopted the innovation. In both cases, internal adopters are influenced in their decision to adopt an innovation and in the timing of that adoption by the number of banks that already have adopted the innovation. This relationship is in the form of either updated assessments due to positive network and informational externalities, or in the form of competitive and institutional bandwagon pressures. The framework analysed in this chapter motivates the empirical analysis conducted in the remainder of this book.

ENDNOTES

1. A rare example of patent protection in the financial industry is Merrill Lynch's patent on its Cash Management Account process. The crucial factor in the success of this patent application was the fact that the product made use of a computer for its implementation. The Economist (1996b) reports that there has been a significant increase in banks' efforts to commercialise on their inventions (mainly computer software) by obtaining patents.
2. The assumption of constant R rules out the situation where imitation, competition, or symmetric duopoly are more profitable than monopoly. That is, π_1 is always larger than $\max\{\pi_2, \pi_3, \pi_4\}$.
3. Most of the study, however, is discussed in a two-firm industry framework.
4. This follows Blackman (1972) who used the proportion of output produced by a new technology as a measure of diffusion of that technology.
5. The central difference between equilibrium and disequilibrium models of diffusion concerns the way in which agents acquire the information relevant to their adoption

decisions (Metcalfe, 1988, p. 13). In the equilibrium approach this is given *a priori*. In the disequilibrium approach this is only true for external adopters, and the internal side captures the information transfer aspects of the diffusion process.

6. This change in banks' initial assessments reflects either a positive or negative internal influence.

7. Chapters 4 and 5 covered many studies which model these 'carrot' and 'stick' effects.

8. $w(t)$ measures the time-varying internal influence.

9. Allowing for external adoption in the model allows us to control for exogenous factors that affects the desirability of the innovation to all firms. In the absence of any strategic, competitive, or information transfer aspect of the adoption process (i.e. $b = 0$), all banks would adopt the innovation due to external influence with the optimal timing of adoption (and re-adoption) being determined by firm-specific characteristics. The external influence describes the *normal* diffusion pattern over time by defining the number of adopters at each period of time. This however will be different from the actual number of adopters because of internal influence. Positive internal influence results in a larger number of adopters than is predicted by the external influence alone (i.e. larger than $a(\bar{N} - N(t))$). Negative internal influence indicates that a certain proportion of the firms that would have adopted due to external influence (proportion of $a(\bar{N} - N(t))$) would not adopt due to internal factors. That is, the model not only explains situations in which firms adopt because of internal influence, but also those in which the innovation does not diffuse among all firms because of negative internal influence (negative b), even though the innovation is desirable for each individual bank (positive a).

10. Note that while b determines the sign of the impact of the number of adopters on the rate of diffusion, δ determines the rate of change in this impact as a function of the number of adopters. A positive b and a smaller-than-one δ, for example, indicates that diffusion rate *increases* with the number of adopters at a *decreasing* rate.

11. Most financial innovations survive and continue to grow even after the effects of the initial stimulus are no longer present (Miller, 1986, Allen and Gale, 1994, Smith, 1992, and Harrington, 1992). The distinction between external and internal adopters enables us to separate the effects of initial exogenous factors that led to the introduction of the innovation and those responsible for its diffusion among banks. Initially, certain exogenous factors make an innovation desirable for only a specific number of banks (i.e. external adopters) who base their adoption decision on independent assessments of the innovation's characteristics with the timing of adoption being a function of certain firm-specific characteristics. The critical characteristics of the group of external adopters depend on the innovation (e.g. nationality of banks for NIFs, portfolio of existing business for junk bonds). The existing literature analyses such exogenous factors and characterise firms which are likely to be influenced by them for a number of OBSAs. They do so, however, by implicitly assuming that all banks are external adopters which can introduce a bias in the results of these studies.

12. In the long run, as $t \to \infty$, $N_t \to N$, and the first two terms of the equations drop out. The model reduces to $n(t + 1) = c\bar{N} + u_{t+1}$, where u_{t+1} is a random error term. This suggests that, in the long run, adoption will occur randomly around some fixed mean value of $c\bar{N}$.

Modelling the Diffusion of Financial Innovations: Methodological Approaches

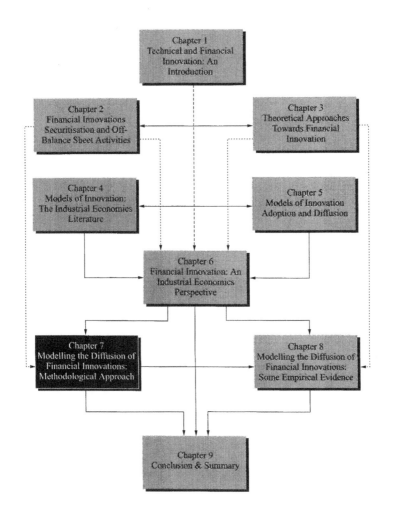

7
Modelling the Diffusion of Financial Innovations: Methodological Approaches

7.1 INTRODUCTION

The framework outlined in the previous chapter motivates the empirical study of this book. This chapter explains the methodology employed in the empirical study. The main goal of this empirical study is to investigate the structure of the diffusion patterns of two financial innovations, junk bonds and note issuance facilities (NIFs). Using mathematical diffusion models we can gauge the importance of internal adoption versus external adoption in the diffusion structure of these financial innovations. Internal adoption reflects the effects that early adopters have on subsequent adopters. External adoption refers to the use of the innovation by adopters whose adoption decisions have not been influenced by the number of earlier adopters. The first part of this chapter defines adoption and adopters in the context of financial innovation. We then outline the single-adoption and repeat-adoption models that can be used to model the diffusion of financial innovations. The final part of the chapter discusses the data sets used in our empirical analysis.

7.2 INNOVATION ADOPTION AND ADOPTERS IN FINANCIAL MARKETS

The diffusion of financial innovations can be measured in a number of ways such as volume, number of issues, number of banks participating in the markets for the innovations, number of issuers of these instruments, or number of investors in these markets. Given that there has been limited application of the innovation diffusion literature to financial innovation (e.g. Jagtiani *et al.* 1995), there is no obvious answer to the question of how one should measure the diffusion of financial innovations. In this book, we measure diffusion using the number of banks in the market because it fits clearly into the theoretical framework outlined above. Also, the population of banks that can enter a new financial market is easier to identify than that of issuers or investors. This will make it possible to compare the results for a number of financial innovations and enable us to shed more light on the competitive and strategic aspects of banks' adoption of financial innovations. We examine the diffusion structure of two innovations, junk bonds and NIFs. For junk bonds, adopters are defined as US investment banks which underwrote (lead managed) a junk bond issue. For NIFs, adopters are international banks which underwrote (and lead or co-lead managed) a NIFs issue.[1]

Based on the framework outlined in the previous chapter, we can distinguish between two categories of adopters; external and internal. External adopters are banks which are influenced in their adoption by initial exogenous factors, such as changes in the regulatory environment or demand factors. Internal adopters refer to banks which adopt the innovation because of bandwagon pressures (institutional and/or competitive) or because of their updated assessment due to endogenous factors (e.g. information transfer and positive/negative externalities). Empirically, we differentiate between the two categories of adopters using mathematical diffusion models. The models we test are either single-adoption or repeat-adoption models.

7.3 SINGLE-ADOPTION DIFFUSION MODELS

7.3.1 The Logistic-Curve Model

The starting point of our empirical analysis is to test whether or not the diffusion structure of financial innovations correspond to the S-shaped curve often encountered in innovation diffusion studies in the industrial economics literature. We aim to test the logistic curve (i.e. a reduced form of the Mansfield (1961) model which excludes profitability and investment size as explanatory variables) against data on the number of first-time adopting banks of junk bonds and NIFs:

$$\text{Log}\left(\frac{N_t}{\bar{N} - N_t}\right) = \alpha + \beta t, \tag{7.1}$$

where
N_t = cumulative number of adopters at time t,
$\bar{N}$ = potential number of adopters,
β = coefficient of internal influence,

α = constant of integration, and

t = time since the introduction of the innovation.

We estimate equation (7.1) using ordinary least squares (OLS) for data on both junk bonds and NIFs. The results are shown in the next chapter.

7.3.2 The Non-Uniform Influence Model (NUI).

The next step in the empirical analysis is to relax two assumptions underlying the logistic model; constant internal influence and the absence of external influence. We do so by testing the NUI model of Easingwood *et al.* (1983). This model is an extension of the Mansfield (1961) model which allows for the internal influence to vary throughout the diffusion process. This model also has the advantage of allowing for exogenous factors (i.e. that are independent of the number of adopters in previous periods) to influence the number of adopters in each period:

$$\frac{\partial N(t)}{\partial t} = a(\bar{N} - N(t)) + b\left(\frac{N(t)}{\bar{N}}\right)^{\delta}(\bar{N} - N(t)). \qquad (7.2)$$

Allowing for external adoption in the model allows us to control for exogenous factors that affects the desirability of the innovation to all firms. In the absence of any strategic, competitive, or information transfer aspect of the adoption process (i.e., $b = 0$), all banks would adopt the innovation due to external influence with the optimal timing of adoption being determined by firm-specific characteristics. The external influence describes the *normal* diffusion pattern over time by defining the number of adopters at each period of time. This however will be different from the actual number of adopters because of internal influence. Positive internal influence results in a larger number of adopters than is predicted by the external influence alone (i.e. larger than $a(\bar{N} - N(t))$). Negative internal influence indicates that a certain proportion of the firms that would have adopted due to external influence (proportion of $a(\bar{N} - N(t))$) would not adopt due to internal factors. That is; the model not only explains situations in which banks adopt because of internal influence, but also those in which the innovation does not diffuse among all firms because of negative internal influence (negative b), even though the innovation is desirable for each individual bank (positive a).

A non-constant internal influence in the diffusion process will be indicated by $\delta \neq 1$. The specification of equation (7.2) allows internal influence to be an increasing function (for $\delta > 1$), a decreasing function (for $\delta < 1$) or a constant function (for $\delta = 1$) of the number of previous adopters. Note that while b determines the sign of the impact of the number of adopters on the rate of diffusion, δ determines the rate of change in this impact as a function of the number of adopters. A positive b and a smaller-than-one δ, for example, indicates that the diffusion rate *increases* with the number of adopters at a *decreasing* rate.

We test the NUI model against data on the number of banks that have adopted junk bonds and NIFs using non-linear ordinary least squares. This enables us to test if innovation adoption by one bank makes it more or less desirable for other banks to adopt the innovation (if b is significantly larger/ smaller than zero), and how this relationship varies with the number of adopters (if δ is significantly larger/smaller than one). The former test helps us to identify whether strategic, competitive, and informational factors affected the diffusion structure of junk bonds and NIFs (i.e. the presence of internal influence in the diffusion patterns of these innovations). The latter test (i.e. the direction of change in the internal influence) helps us to identify whether rational-efficiency factors (e.g. information transfer) or bandwagon pressures factors account for the observed internal influence, if any.

As stressed in Chapters 2 and 3, most financial innovations survive and continue to grow after the effects of the initial stimulus are no longer present. The distinction between external and internal adopters enables us to separate the effects of initial exogenous factors that led to the introduction of the innovation and those responsible for its diffusion among banks. Initially, certain exogenous factors make an innovation desirable for only a specific number of banks (i.e. external adopters) who base their adoption decision on independent assessments of the innovation's characteristics with the timing of adoption being a function of certain firm-specific characteristics. The critical characteristics of the group of external adopters depend on the innovation (e.g. nationality of banks for NIFs, portfolio of existing business for junk bonds). The existing literature analyses such exogenous factors and characterises firms which are likely to be influenced by them for a number of OBSAs. They do so, however, by implicitly assuming that all banks are external adopters which ignores the importance of internal factors in the diffusion process. As our discussion in Chapters 4 and 5 suggests, such internal factors can have significant impacts on the diffusion structure of an innovation.

7.4 REPEAT-ADOPTION MODELS

7.4.1 The Non-Uniform Influence Repeat Adoption Model (NUIR)

We next extend our analysis to allow for multiple-adoption of an innovation by a bank. The NUI model can be extended to account for repeat adoption by incorporating a repeat adoption coefficient c, and modelling the total number of adopters, $n(t)$:

$$n(t+1) = a(\bar{N} - n(t)) + b\left(\frac{n(t)}{\bar{N}}\right)^{\delta} (\bar{N} - n(t)) + cn(t). \qquad (7.3)$$

The NUIR model is estimated using non-linear ordinary least squares to solve for the parameter estimates for both junk bonds and NIFs. The total number of banks that will eventually adopt the innovation, $\bar{N}$ is assumed to be a constant, the value of which is given by the estimate of $\bar{N}$ provided by the NUI model. Note that the NUIR model uses n_t as the unit of analysis on both sides of the model. The independent variable of the model, which is a measure of diffusion, is the number of adopters at each point of time. On the right hand side of equation (7.3), a measures the number of banks which did not adopt the innovation at time t but did so at time $t+1$ due to external factors. The coefficient b measures the number of banks which did not adopt at time t but did so at time $t+1$ due to internal factors. The last term in the NUIR model measures the number of banks that adopted the innovation at time t and continue to do so at time $t+1$. The model thus decomposes the number of adopters at time $t+1$ into two groups, triers (a and b) and repeat adopters (c).

Examination of equation (7.3) shows that first-time adopters and repeat adopters are defined with reference to their behaviour in the previous period of time. That is, if a member adopts the innovation at time $t-2$ and does not adopt the innovation at time $t-1$, then if this member adopts the innovation at time t the model will identify this member as a 'trier'. This member will be part of the number of triers due to internal influence (the second-term) or due to external factors (the first-term). In the former case, this is theoretically inaccurate because it assumes that a member re-adopts the innovation not based on his own experience with the innovation, but rather due to his/her contact with adopters during the last period. In reality, interaction with adopters in the previous period would exert minimal, if any, effects on members who previously adopted the innovation. The unique characteristics of every member of the social system makes his/her own experience with the innovation the most significant factor in their decision of subsequent adoptions. The only case where the structure of the model might be acceptable is where the innovation under examination tends to change significantly over time to the extent that not adopting the innovation for one period would render any previous experience insufficient to evaluate the decision of re-adoption. In such cases it may be assumed that an adopter might rely on his/her contact with adopters during the last period more than he/she does on their previous experience. This can only happen with advanced new technologies which change quickly over time as they are being developed. As noted from previous discussion, modelling the diffusion of such technologies usually requires the application of single-adoption diffusion models. Moreover, if an innovation changes dramatically during its diffusion span, one might argue it should be possibly considered as a new innovation.

When comparing the diffusion patterns of certain innovations, it is interesting to examine how first-time adopters and repeat adopters contribute to the total number of adopters at every point of time, and how the ratio of, say, repeat adopters to total adopters varies over time. This, however, demands that repeat adopters at time t are defined as those who have ever adopted the innovation before time t and re-adopted it during time t. It would be more difficult to extract useful information from the model when first-time and repeat adopters are defined as by Mahajan *et al.* (1983). The number of adopters at time t who have or have not adopted the innovation at time $t - 1$ is difficult to interpret. Its usefulness depends on the characteristics of the innovation. For some innovations for a member to stop adopting the innovation for a single period does not necessarily mean that that member disadopts the innovation. It may very well be that that member possesses cyclical needs. If, for example, the needs of a certain member are such that he/she needs to adopt the innovation every two periods in a regular manner, the NUIR model will classify that member 100% of the time as a first-time adopter. This will overestimate the importance of first-time adopters and underestimate the importance of repeat adopters. Given these considerations, we propose two alternative formulations of the NUIR model below.

7.4.2 The NUIR 1 Model

Because of the disadvantages highlighted above, we suggest that in the case of modelling the diffusion of financial innovations the use of a modified form of the Mahajan (1983) NUIR model where the cumulative number of adopters $(N(t))$, instead of the number of adopters in the previous time period $(n(t))$, are employed in the terms appearing on the right-hand side of the model. The modified model which we will refer to as the NUIR 1 model can be written as:

$$n(t+1) = a(\bar{N} - N(t)) + b\left(\frac{N(t)}{\bar{N}}\right)^{\delta}(\bar{N} - N(t)) + cN(t) \qquad (7.4)$$

The major theoretical difference between the two models is in the way they represent the internal influence. There are two aspects to be compared; the variables employed to represent the internal influence and the behaviour of this effect over time. In the Mahajan (1983) NUIR model, it is assumed that those who did not adopt in the last period, $(\bar{N} - n(t))$, interact with only those who adopted last period, $n(t)$, and that the effectiveness of this interaction is a function of penetration as measured by $n(t)/\bar{N}$. In the NUIR 1 model, it is assumed that those who *never* adopted, $\bar{N} - N(t)$, interact with those who have adopted at least once before, $N(t)$, and the effectiveness of this interaction is a function of penetration as measured by $N(t)/\bar{N}$. This presentation of the internal influence suggests that, since $N(t)$ is an ever increasing number, for a given value of δ, the effect will either increase, decrease or remain constant over the diffusion span. Unlike for the Mahajan (1983) NUIR model, the effect cannot show more than one trend during the diffusion span (i.e. increase at certain periods and decrease at some others). The latter presentation of the internal influence is more appropriate for the following reasons:

1. The standard NUIR model assumes that all adopters due to internal influence adopt as a result of their interaction with adopters during the last period only. It is fair to assume that at least some members of those adopters might adopt as a result of their interaction with adopters from previous periods. The Mahajan (1983) NUIR model does not allow for such a possibility. The form of the NUIR 1 allows the interaction to be made with adopters from any previous adopters, which is probably a more realistic assumption especially when time periods are relatively short.
2. At every point of time, Mahajan *et al.* (1983) assumes that all members of the social system who did not adopt in the last period will adopt due to either internal influence or to external effects. As discussed above, a significant number of those members might adopt based on their own previous experience with the innovation.

Both models, though with different results, introduce time-varying internal influence by expressing the effectiveness of interaction between adopters and nonadopters as a function of the ratio of either total or cumulative number of adopters to the number of potential adopters. The Mahajan (1983) NUIR model has the advantage of allowing the effect to vary in any direction over the diffusion span. Both specifications, however, offer little justification for their particular structure. Whether penetration is measured by the number of adopters or adopting members, it is not very clear how the variability in the effectiveness of the internal influence can be attributed to the level of penetration over time. Most probably this will be a function of several factors outside the model. The factors themselves may be innovation-specific and there may be little use in trying to generalise them to all innovations. Unfortunately, the literature offers little guidance, whether theoretical or empirical, on this subject. We'll come back to this point later in this chapter.

Finally, we examine the long run properties of the model, that is; as $t \rightarrow \infty$. As $t \rightarrow \infty$, $N_t \rightarrow \bar{N}$, so the first two terms on the right hand side of equation (7.4) drop out. This happens when all potential adopters have adopted the innovation at least once. At this stage, equation (7.4) reduces to $n(t+1) = c\bar{N} + u_{t+1}$ where u_{t+1} is a random error term. This formulation of the long run properties of $n(t+1)$ suggests that adoptions occur randomly around some fixed mean value of $c\bar{N}$. This may be a little restrictive. A more flexible long run model might be: $n(t + 1) = c_1 + c_2 n(t) + u_{t+1}$, which allows $n(t + 1)$ to be partly dependent on $n(t)$. Below we discuss a model with such long run properties.

7.4.3 The NUIR 2 Model

Mathematical models of diffusion processes are based on a theoretical background which attempts to explain the dynamics of the diffusion process in general terms. The study of the 'bandwagon effects' (i.e. competitive pressure placed on nonadopters by adopters) of the diffusion process has enhanced our understanding of this process, and it has enabled the development of mathematical models which can depict the process of innovation diffusion (e.g. Mansfield, 1961; Bass, 1969; Mahajan *et al.*, 1983; Skiadas, 1987; Sharma *et al.*, 1993). It is this theoretical background which distinguishes diffusion models from standard regression or time-series analyses. Most of the theoretical contributions however have concentrated on the diffusion of innovations among first time adopters. There has been little effort made to extend the theoretical background to repeat-purchase innovations.

The theoretical aspects of first-time adopter models are reflected in the formulation of the internal influence, that is the assertion that the number of adopters at time t is influenced by the number of previous adopters. The presentation of diffusion models as such is justified by several contributions on the theoretical aspects of diffusion processes. If one wishes to investigate the diffusion of repeat-purchase innovations, the relevance of the findings of single-adoption diffusion models has to be examined. In particular one has to consider two questions; the presentation of the number of first-time adopters and that of repeaters. Regarding the former, we are mainly interested in knowing whether or not the findings of the literature on single-adoption innovations is relevant when examining the behaviour of first-time adopters in a repeat-adoption environment. That is, do we have to differentiate between the influence of repeat-adopters and first-time adopters on nonadopters. For example, we might argue that repeat-adopters have a stronger impact on non-adopters than first-time adopters because their decision to re-adopt is based on more information. If that is the case, we may want to separate these different influences by assigning them to separate terms, the same way we separate the effects of internal and external influences. Therefore, in the first part of our empirical examination, we test the internal-influence model of Mansfield (1961) against data on first-time adopting banks. If the model is found to represent the data well, then we'll be happy with the presentation of first-time adopters in the NUIR 1 model. If the model does not provide a good fit to the data, then we may conclude that single-adoption internal-influence models do not best explain the behaviour of first-time adopters in a repeat-adoption environment. We now turn our attention to the representation of repeat adopters.

In most cases of successful repeat-purchase innovations, the number of repeaters become the most significant proportion of the total number of adopters after a certain period of time. A model which attempts to model the total number of adopters should therefore be able to depict the number of repeaters accurately. Given, however, that theoretical contributions only aid us in depicting the successive increase in the number of first-time adopters, these become of minor importance when we are dealing with repeat-purchase innovations. The theoretical aspects of both the Mahajan (1983) NUIR model and the NUIR 1 model discussed above are presented in the first two terms which sums up the number of first-time adopters (regardless of which definitions of first-time adopters and repeaters are applied). Moreover, the use of the $n(t)$ in the second term of the Mahajan (1983) NUIR model is not consistent with the existing literature. A large part of the success of both models will depend on the formulation of the third term representing the number of repeaters. For both models, there is no theoretical aspect of the formulation of that third term. The success of both models depend on whether or not the behaviour of the number of repeat adopters lend itself to a simple empirical presentation of $cn(t)$ or $cm(t)$ for the Mahajan (1983) NUIR model and the NUIR 1 model, respectively. Both models fail to justify theoretically why a constant proportion of repeat adopters c will continue to re-adopt the innovation at each point of time. On the one hand there are no empirical findings to support such a hypothesis, and on the other hand the existing theoretical literature cannot *directly* provide guidelines as to the formulation of this term.

In the second part of our empirical investigation of the diffusion patterns of financial innovations we will investigate repeat-purchase models. We do so by testing the NUIR 2 model which incorporates a theory-related formulation of the retention coefficient c, and compare this model's results with both the Mahajan (1983) NUIR model and the NUIR 1 model. In the absence of any empirical or theoretical guidelines as how to represent c, one intuitive approach would be to represent c as function of the ratio of repeaters to the cumulative number of adopters $(p(t)/N(t))$. The retention coefficient c thus can be written as:

$$c_t = c\left(\frac{p_t}{N_t}\right)^{\lambda} \tag{7.5}$$

Equation (7.5) postulates that the proportion of the cumulative number of adopters (i.e. the number of members which have ever adopted the innovation before) at time t who will re-adopt during time $t + 1$ is a function of the ratio of repeaters to cumulative number of adopters at time t. This ratio indicates the time-varying significance of repeaters over the diffusion span. Note that c_t is independent of the total number of adopters at each point of time, $n(t)$. c_t

possesses the same properties as $w(t)$ in the Mahajan (1983) NUIR model. Specifically, c_t can either increase, decrease or remain constant over the diffusion span and between each period and the following one. The exact behaviour of c_t will, for a given value of λ, depend on Δc_t in exactly the same way as $w(t)$ discussed above. Whether or not a time-varying coefficient of repeat adoption is necessary is an empirical question, and can be resolved by comparing the performance of the model when λ is estimated by the model and when it is constrained to one.

Replacing c by c_t in equation 7.4 yields:

$$n(t+1) = a(\bar{N} - N(t)) + b\left(\frac{N(t)}{\bar{N}}\right)^{\delta}(\bar{N} - N(t)) + c\left(\frac{p_t}{N_t}\right)^{\lambda}N(t) + \alpha, \quad (7.6)$$

where α is a constant. Note that the constant term α is necessary here in order to get a non-zero long run mean value for the series $n(t)$. As $t \to \infty$, $N_t \to \bar{N}$ and $p(t) \to n(t)$. With $\lambda = 1$, the long run model reduces to $n(t+1) = \alpha + cn(t) + u_{t+1}$. Equation (7.5) provides a mechanism by which the model can estimate a time varying coefficient of retention. In the Mahajan (1983) NUIR model, the number of repeaters estimated by the third term is flexible enough to vary over time because it is represented as a proportion of $n(t)$ which varies freely over the diffusion span. This, however, is achieved by using a rather inconvenient definition of repeaters. The NUIR 1 model defines repeaters properly by representing them as a proportion of $N(t)$ but as a result offers limited flexibility for the estimated number of repeaters to vary (because $N(t)$ increases gradually over time). The NUIR 2 model provides the flexibility of the Mahajan (1983) NUIR model while retaining the definitions and the theoretical aspects of the NUIR 1 model. This has been achieved by adding additional parameters, which has the disadvantage of making the interpretation and comparison of the model's results for various innovations more difficult. In the empirical analysis, the NUIR 2 model is estimated twice; with λ unconstrained and with λ constrained to 1, and the impact on the results is evaluated.

7.5 DATA

As mentioned above, we measure diffusion using the number of banks participating in the market. We examine the diffusion structure of two innovations, NIFs and junk bonds. For NIFs, adopters are international banks which underwrote (and lead or co-lead managed) a NIFs issue.[1] For junk bonds, adopters are defined as US investment banks which managed or underwrote a junk bond issue.

7.6 THE MARKET FOR NOTE ISSUANCE FACILITIES (NIFs)

7.6.1 The Development of the Market

The NIFs market is part of the euronote market which refers to instruments or facilities designed to allow borrowers to issue a series of short term capital instruments and includes NIFs, revolving underwritten facilities (RUFs), euro-commercial paper (ECP), and euro-medium-term notes (EMTNs), each of which dominated the euronote market in different periods; NIFs between 1981 and 1985; ECP between 1985 and 1990; and MTNs between 1991 and 1994. During 1974–80, short term lending activities in the euromarkets were largely confined to direct bank lending. The large volumes of eurodollars resulted in continuing liquidity in the banking system which intensified competition among commercial banks for short-term lending, and caused lending margins to decline. Loans syndicated by a lead manager amongst a group of banks became a common financing structure, with intense competition to win the mandate from a borrower to lead manage such a facility (Bullock, 1987, p. 10).

The euronote market developed as an alternative to the syndicated credit market in the early 1980s. Euronote arrangements became known as note issuance facilities (NIFs), which is an arrangement by which a bank or group of banks agree to act as managers underwriting a borrower's issue of short-term paper as and when required and to back the facility with medium-term credit should the note not find a market. Originally called 'note purchase facilities', NIFs took on a variety of names such as CD-issuance facilities, euronote issuance facilities, or revolving underwriting facilities. The different names were generally used to refer to different distribution methods (e.g. sole placing agency versus tender panel) that commercial banks (i.e. underwriters) used to place the notes with investors.

Between 1982 and 1985, the euronote market was confined to NIFs in its various forms. Since early 1984 NIFs have largely replaced syndicated credit as a means of access to international credit markets for borrowers in developed countries. At least three factors explain the growth of NIFs (Euromoney, 1985, p. 239). First, NIFs provided opportunities to raise funds more cheaply and with more flexibility than the syndicated loan market. A second factor is the decline in the relative popularity with investors of bank deposits and CDs compared with alternative instruments, of which euronotes are one. Thirdly, there was a desire by banks themselves to slow the growth of their balance sheets, improve capital/asset ratios, and boost income from fees derived from OBSAs.

7.6.2 Underwriting Banks in the NIFs Market

Banks joined the NIFs market to compensate for the loss of their traditional lending business. The shift from eurocredit to NIFs has not meant a corresponding removal of large international commercial banks from lending, but has changed their role to one that primarily involves underwriting loans, and only rarely direct lending (Euromoney, 1985, p. 239). Nearly all NIFs have been underwritten by commercial banks. Table 7.1 below shows the top 20 NIFs underwriters in 1985 and 1986 (amount and number of issues).

7.6.3 Arrangers of NIFs

Investment banks benefited from the NIFs market by arranging and managing NIFs issues on behalf of the issuer. Table 7.2 below shows the top 20 NIFs arrangers in 1985 and 1986. An important driving force became the banks' league-table positions for arranging such facilities and their reputation as a placer of paper (Bullock, 1987, p. 48). By 1985, banks recognised that decoupling of the underwriting process from note placement, the main feature of

Table 7.1 Top 20 underwriting banks in the NIFs market (January to November 1986 compared to 1985—Signed facilities only)

Rank			1986		1985	
85	86	Arranger	($m)	No.	($m)	No.
1	1	Banque Nationale de Paris	576.66	53	909.23	65
7	2	Credit Lyonnais	546.62	35	669.16	55
12	3	Algemene Bank Nederland	484.61	31	579.97	41
31	4	Dai-Ichi Kangyo Bank	481.67	40	373.67	34
27	5	Sanwa Bank	467.90	40	413.07	44
37	6	Mitsubishi Bank	459.24	36	323.15	31
25	7	Fuji Bank	453.43	38	423.68	37
4	8	Industrial Bank of Japan	452.50	34	723.23	55
3	9	Credit Suisse	439.17	33	757.04	52
18	10	Barclays Bank Group	438.38	41	503.19	40
6	11	Sumitomo Bank	409.04	31	679.53	52
2	12	Royal Bank of Canada/Orion Royal Bank	400.78	27	823.61	53
17	13	Bank of Tokyo	396.65	34	515.24	35
15	14	Bankers Trust International	389.89	31	531.26	53
9	15	Canadian Imperial Bank Group	381.43	27	606.01	48
41	16	Mitsui Bank	373.34	26	296.28	23
19	17	Societe Generale	358.82	30	479.96	37
23	18	Banque Indosuez	355.42	30	445.09	45
13	19	National Westminster Bank Group	353.81	30	562.01	34
48	20	Tokai Bank	349.35	26	229.04	19

Source: Euromoney, 1987, special survey, p. 12

Table 7.2 Top 20 NIFs Arrangers (January to November 1986 compared to 1985—Signed facilities only)

Rank			1986		1985	
85	86	Arranger	($m)	No.	($m)	No.
2	1	Citicorp Investment Bank	6141.81	18	4980.1	21
4	2	Chase Investment Bank	4368.29	8	3610.0	9
5	3	Morgan Guaranty	3500.00	7	3529.5	14
9	4	Bank of Tokyo	3260.00	6	2635.0	5
50	5	Svenska Handelsbanken Group	2000.00	1	225.0	3
7	6	Merrill Lynch Capital Markets	1565.00	13	3275.0	24
42	7	Barclays Bank Group	1419.75	10	445.0	4
8	8	Bankers Trust International	1387.74	12	3101.0	18
45	9	Shearson Lehman Brothers Int	1360.00	3	300.0	1
14	10	Chemical Bank International Group	1235.00	4	1157.6	3
6	11	Salomon Brothers International	1100.00	5	3320.0	10
1	12	Bank of America International	1085.00	7	7010.0	17
15	13	Goldman Sachs	1020.00	4	1125.0	5
13	14	Lloyds Merchant Bank	1004.29	7	1205.0	8
10	15	Societe Generale	975.00	4	2051.9	4
11	16	SG Warburg	896.77	7	1950.0	12
64	17	NM Rothschild & Sons	859.97	4	78.31	1
12	18	Credit Lyonnais	810.00	2	1435.0	2
65	19	Mitsubishi Bank	800.00	2	75.0	1
34	20	Morgan Stanley International	620.00	2	650.0	3

Source: Euromoney, 1987, special survey, p. 12

commercial paper, ensured distribution advantage over NIFs. Due to these advantages, the ECP market re-emerged in 1985 and continued to grow at the expense of the NIFs market. The dataset for NIFs was constructed from IFR publications and covers all NIFs arranged between January 1983 and until June 1986. Although most of these NIFs issues were arranged in London, issuers and underwriting banks were not confined to one country but came mainly from Europe, America, and Japan.

Figure 7.1 below shows the cumulative number of banks that joined the NIFs market between January 1983 and May 1986, the period of the empirical study. This corresponds to N_t in diffusion models. Within this period more than 505 banks underwrote or managed at least one NIFs issue. After a slow start between 1983 and July 1984, the market started attracting a large number of banks at high rates between July 1984 and until January 1986. Since then the market for NIFs began to decline with limited new entry by banks as a result of the re-emergence of the ECP market.

Note that the cumulative number of banks allows one entry by a single bank and does not take into consideration subsequent entries in future periods. Figure 7.2 shows the number of banks in the market during each month

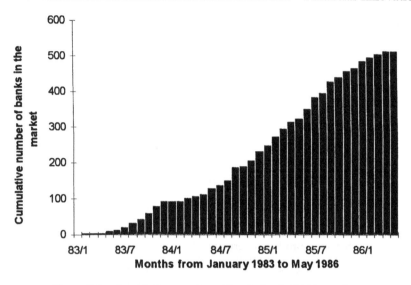

Figure 7.1 Cumulative number of banks in the NIFs market

regardless of whether or not these banks featured in earlier periods. This corresponds to n_t in diffusion models. Figure 7.2 shows more clearly the decrease in popularity of NIFs with banks in early 1986. From more than 140 banks in March 1986, the number of banks engaged in the market dropped to only 33 in April and 3 banks in May.

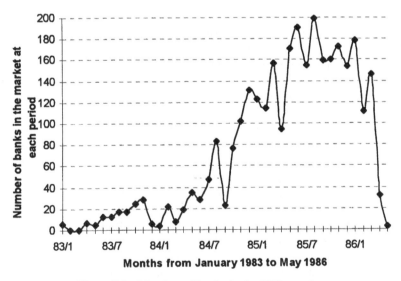

Figure 7.2 Number of banks in the NIFs market

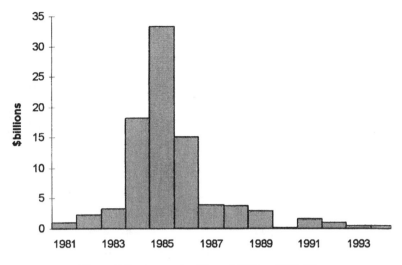

Figure 7.3 Amounts of issued NIFs—1981–94

It should be noted however that n_t filters out re-occurrences of one given bank within the same period of time. That is, a given bank is only counted once *within* a single period (months for NIFs) even though that bank may have under-written more than one issue during that period. This and the fact that usually a large group of banks is involved in each NIF issue means that the number of banks, or n_t, does not necessarily correspond to the number of issues. Figure 7.3 shows the volume of NIFs between 1981 and 1994.

7.7 THE JUNK BOND MARKET

7.7.1 Development of the Market

The junk bond or high-yield debt market consists of bonds rated Ba1 or lower by Moody's, BB+ or lower by Standard & Poor's, or unrated (Howe, 1988). Prior to 1977, the junk bond market consisted primarily of 'fallen angels', companies that were once investment grade issues but whose ratings had fallen below investment grade. The corporate bond market was closed to mid-sized high-growth companies which lacked the size and history that rating agencies required for investment grade bonds. Instead, these companies had to rely on bank debt and private placement to meet their financing needs. The modern junk bond market, which was pioneered by Drexel Burnham Lambert, showed impressive growth rates between 1977 (with 26 new issues totalling just over $US1 bn) and 1986 (with more than 230 new issues totalling more than $34 bn in volume). In addition to total bonds outstanding, the number, size, and type of

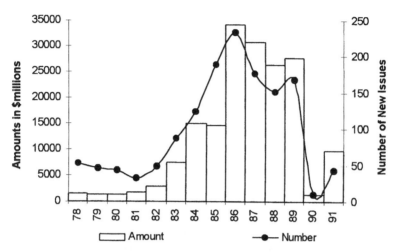

Figure 7.4   Junk bonds market, 1978–1991

issues increased dramatically (Figure 7.4). For over a decade, the junk bond market represented the fastest-growing segment of the US corporate bond market, and in 1988, it accounted for more than 23% of all new public straight debt issues. With the collapse of Drexel Burnham Lambert in 1990, the market suffered considerable shocks and its very survival was questioned. By the end of 1991, however, new issues volume totalled $9.9 bn and total junk bonds outstanding reached a record $209 bn. The market continued to grow, albeit not at the heady rate of the mid 1980s, and in 1995, 177 new junk bond issues were arranged totalling more than $30 bn (The Economist, 1996a).

Our analysis of the diffusion pattern in the junk bond market uses data obtained from Howe (1988) which covers all non-convertible junk bond issues for the period 1977–86. Figure 7.5 shows the cumulative number of banks that managed at least one junk bond issue, or N_t. Unlike NIFs, the junk bonds market attracted a relatively large number of banks during the very early stages (37 banks between January 1978 and September 1980). New entry was then limited to a total of nine new banks during the next three years (46 by June 1983). With the growth in the use of junk bonds in leveraged buy outs (LBOs) more banks started joining the market in the next two years. By 1986 the market for junk bond issues matured in terms of the number of new banks joining the market with only four *new* banks joining the market in 1986, bringing the total to 84 banks.

7.7.2 Participating Banks

Figure 7.6 below shows the number of banks active in the market during each period of time (quarterly data). Table 7.3 lists the major investment banking

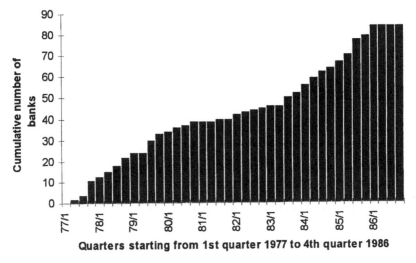

Figure 7.5 Cumulative number of banks in the junk bonds market

firms that acted as underwriters for junk bonds for the four years from 1985 to 1988. Reily (1992, p. 91) points out two important points demonstrated by Table 7.3: (i) the dominant position of Drexel Burnham Lambert (DBL) following its initial efforts to develop the market, and (ii) the gradual deterioration of DBL's position as other firms recognised the opportunities to develop research and underwriting capabilities for high yield debt.

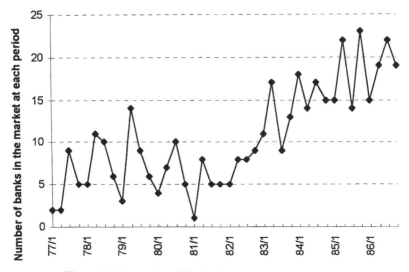

Figure 7.6 Number of banks in the junk bonds market

Table 7.3 Top 10 junk bonds underwriting banks—percentage of totals issued[a]

		1985	1986	1987	1988
1	Drexel Burnham Lambert	49.7	45.6	38.8	40.8
2	Morgan Stanley	7.2	7.8	17.2	14.2
3	First Boston	4.4	4.6	13.8	13.4
4	Merrill Lynch	4.5	10.1	11.7	7.7
5	Salomon Brothers	10.0	7.3	2.3	5.5
6	Prudential-Bache Securities	3.0	1.5	0.2	4.6
7	Donaldson, Lufkin & Jenrette	0.4	1.0	2.2	3.0
8	Goldman Sachs	4.2	3.8	8.4	2.7
9	Kidder, Peabody	0.7	2.6	1.0	2.4
10	Shearson Lehman Brothers	5.3	6.4	0.8	1.2

[a] Percentages do not add to 100 because only the top 10 are listed.
Source: Adapted from Reily (1992, p. 92)

By the time that DBL declared bankruptcy in 1990, several other banks had established expertise and a clientele for these securities, and thus the survival of the market was no longer conditioned by DBL's participation.

7.7.3 Investors in the Junk Bonds Market

It is a positive factor for the liquidity of the market to have more banks involved in underwriting and trading junk bonds. The liquidity of the market is also enhanced by wider distribution of both ownership and issuing firms. As shown in Table 7.4 below, major owners of junk bonds have been mutual funds, insurance companies, and pension funds.

Table 7.4 Percentage ownership of junk bonds: Dec 31 1988

Mutual funds, money managers	30
Insurance companies	30
Pension funds	15
Foreign investors	9
Savings and loans	7
Individuals	5
Corporations	3
Securities dealers	1

Source: Reily (1992, p. 91)

Table 7.5 Distribution of ratings for junk bonds: Dec 31 1988

BB+	13.09%	
BB	3.42	24.88%
BB−	8.37	
B+	12.23%	
B	13.03	49.73%
B−	24.47	
CCC+	15.64%	
CCC	4.09	20.49%
CCC−	0.62	
CC	0.65%	
C	0.19	5.04%
D	4.20	

Source: Reily (1992, p. 91)

7.7.4 Issuers of Junk Bonds

Table 7.5 shows the distribution of S&P ratings for all outstanding high yield issues as of December 31, 1988. The table shows a heavy concentration in the B class which contains almost half of all issues. Generally, wider distribution of issuers' rating class, ownership, and underwriters is a major contributor to the liquidity of this market. Wider distribution of members of these three groups of market participants (i.e. borrowers, investors, and underwriters) gives members of the other groups more choices which meet their portfolio requirements and thus contributes significantly to the development of the market.

7.8 CONCLUSION

This chapter explained the methodological approach to the empirical analysis which will be undertaken in the following chapter. The models to be tested fall into two main groups; single-adoption and repeat-adoption models. Table 7.6 summarises these models. The remainder of the chapter outlined the data set on two financial products, NIFs and junk bonds, which will be used to conduct the following empirical analysis on the diffusion of financial innovations reported in Chapter 8.

Table 7.6 Estimated models

Model	Model Specification	Parameters	Method of Estimation
Mansfield (1961)	$\ln\left(\dfrac{N_t}{\bar{N} - N_t}\right) = \alpha + \beta t$	α, β	Least squares
The Easingwood *et al.* (1983) NUI model	$\dfrac{dN(t)}{dt} = a(\bar{N} - N_t)$ $+ b\,(N_t/\bar{N})^{\delta}(\bar{N} - N_t)$	$a, b, \delta, \bar{N}$	Non-linear least squares (sequential quadratic programming)
The Mahajan *et al.* (1983) NUIR model	$n(t+1) = a(\bar{N} - n(t))$ $+ b\left(\dfrac{n(t)}{\bar{N}}\right)^{\delta}(\bar{N} - n(t))$ $+ cn(t)$	a, b, c, δ	Non-linear least squares (sequential quadratic programming)
The NUIR 1 model	$n(t+1) = a(\bar{N} - N(t))$ $+ b\left(\dfrac{N(t)}{N}\right)^{\delta}(\bar{N} - N(t))$ $+ cN(t)$	a, b, c, δ	Non-linear least squares (sequential quadratic programming)
The NUIR 2 model	$n(t+1) = a(\bar{N} - N(t))$ $+ b\left(\dfrac{N(t)}{\bar{N}}\right)^{\delta}(\bar{N} - N(t))$ $+ c\left(\dfrac{p(t)}{N(t)}\right)^{\lambda}N(t) + \alpha$	$a, b, c,$ δ, λ, α	Non-linear least squares (sequential quadratic programming)

ENDNOTES

1. A few US investment banks, Citicorp Investment Bank, Chase Investment Bank, Morgan Guaranty, Merrill Lynch Capital Markets, Bankers Trust, and Goldman Sachs, participated in the NIFs markets as arrangers. Most underwriters, however, were European and Japanese commercial banks.

8
Modelling the Diffusion of Financial Innovations: Some Empirical Evidence

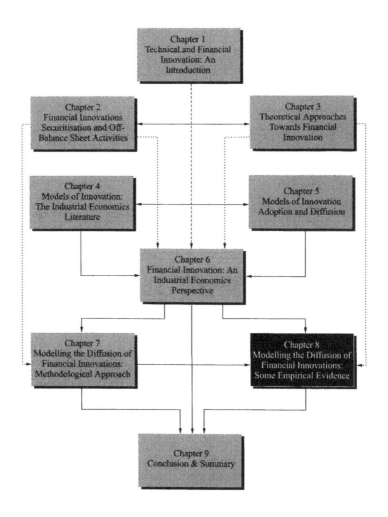

8

Modelling the Diffusion of Financial Innovations: Some Empirical Evidence

8.1 INTRODUCTION

This chapter presents the results of the empirical study in this book. The results obtained from single adoption (the logistic and the NUI models) and repeat adoption (the NUIR, the NUIR 1, and the NUIR 2) models are discussed in the first half of the chapter. Overall the results indicate empirical evidence of internal influence in adoption patterns of both NIFs and junk bonds. This suggests that the innovation adoption by one bank either exerts pressures on its rivals to adopt the innovation (bandwagon pressures) or makes it more desirable to do so (rational-efficiency factors such as enhanced liquidity or decreases in adoption costs).

For both innovations, the results indicate that the time-varying internal influence increases with time. This is more consistent with theories of competitive and bandwagon pressures than with rational-efficiency theories. Although the internal influence is significant for both innovations, its magnitude is much larger for NIFs than for junk bonds. For NIFs, only a few banks adopted the innovation due to the initial stimulus (i.e. external influence) and subsequent entry to the market seems to have been mainly due to competitive and institutional pressures. For junk bonds, entry of few banks into the market in the early stages seems to have made it difficult for competitors to join in. The early stages were dominated by few repeat-adopting banks with limited new entry. Internal influence played a significant role only in the latter stages with the growth in the use of junk bonds in leveraged buyouts and acquisitions.

8.2 SINGLE-ADOPTION MODELS

8.2.1 The Logistic Curve

NIFs

In the first part of our empirical investigations we tested the logistic curve of Mansfield (1961) against data on the cumulative number of first-time adopters for junk bonds and note issuance facilities (NIFs). The results are presented in Figure 8.1 and Table 8.1 below. The speed of adoption as measured by the time coefficient β is positive and highly significant for both innovations. This is consistent with the theoretical background of the logistic model; that is, the proportion of nonadopters (banks not using the innovation) at time t which introduce the innovation by time $t + 1$ is positively influenced by the proportion of their competitors who have already adopted. For both innovations, the general shape of the curve produced by the Mansfield (1961) model does not seem to represent the data accurately. This is particularly the case for junk bonds. The logistic curve always produces a symmetric S-shaped curve with point of inflection occurring when 50% of the banks have adopted the innovation. This is a general limitation of the logistic curve because it indicates the lack of flexibility of the model to adjust to specific data patterns.

Junk Bonds

For junk bonds the number of banks engaged in this new market starts to rise sharply in the early stages of the diffusion span, but then stabilises in the middle

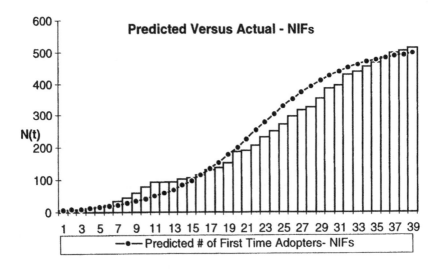

Figure 8.1 The Mansfield (1961) model for NIFs

Table 8.1 The logistic model—NIFs
$$\ln (N_t/(\bar{N}_t - N_t)) = -4.4681 + 0.202t$$

Predictor	Coefficient	Std dev	t-Ratio	P
Constant	−4.4681	0.2030	−22.01	0.000
Time	0.201573	0.008845	22.79	0.000
R^2	93.3%			
R^2-adjusted	93.2%			

stages (early 1980) for almost three years. The diffusion process regains momentum again in the last quarter of 1983 and begins to rise sharply until 1986. The fast growth in the early stages and the slowdown in the middle stages of the diffusion process cause the logistic curve to underestimate the data in the early stages and overestimate it in middle periods. This suggests that the early growth cannot be wholly attributed to internal influence as represented by the model. More important is the fact that the Mansfield (1961) model overestimates the pressures those early adopters, given their relatively large number, have had on nonadopters at that stage (Figure 8.2). This indicates that at some time around late 1980, the significance of the number of adopters in previous periods as an explanatory variable of the number of adopters in subsequent periods (between early 1980 and late 1983) was undermined by certain factors

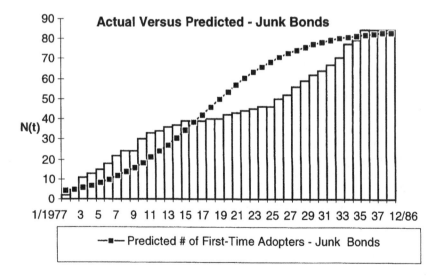

Figure 8.2 The Mansfield (1961) model for junk bonds

Table 8.2   The logistic model—junk bonds
$$\ln(N_t/(\bar{N} - N_t)) = -3.1093 + 0.18t$$

Predictor	Coefficient	Std dev	t-Ratio	P
Constant	−3.1093	0.4227	−7.36	0.000
Time	0.18328	0.01842	9.95	0.000
R^2	72.8%			
R^2-adjusted	72.1%			

or events outside the model. This resulted in an overestimated measure of the effectiveness of the interaction between adopters and nonadopters (β) as defined by the logistic curve (Table 8.2).

One limitation of the logistic curve is that it assumes a constant internal influence. Allowing for time-varying internal influence can help determine the sources of internal influence (rational efficiency versus bandwagon factors). Secondly, the logistic model assumes that all banks introduce the innovation due to internal factors (i.e. all banks are internal adopters). The NUI model of Easingwood *et al.* (1983) avoids both these limitations. Below we estimate this model against data for junk bonds and NIFs and use the results to test the presence and sources of internal influence in the diffusion patterns of junk bonds and NIFs.

8.2.2 The NUI model

Actual versus Expected Number of Adopters

The NUI model was estimated using a non-linear least-squares regression technique with a sequential programming method. The results of the empirical testing of the NUI model are presented in Figures 8.3 to 8.8 and in Tables 8.3 and 8.4 below. Figures 8.3 and 8.4 depict the actual cumulative number of adopters versus the expected number of adopters for junk bonds and NIFs, respectively.

The parameters of the model were all significantly different from zero (a, b, N) for both innovations. This suggests that both internal adoption and external adoption were significant in the diffusion pattern of these financial innovations. The NUI model provides plausible estimates of total number of potential adopters ($\bar{N} = 83.96$ for junk bonds and 544.9 for NIFs). These are slightly larger than the total number of banks in the sample which suggests that diffusion processes of junk bonds and NIFs were near completion. We thus use these estimates $\bar{N}$ in estimating the repeat-adoption models.[1] For both innovations, b was positive indicating that adoption of these innovations by one bank made it more desirable for other banks to adopt, or to hasten their

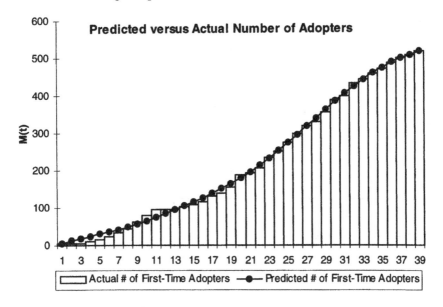

Figure 8.3 The NUI model for NIFs

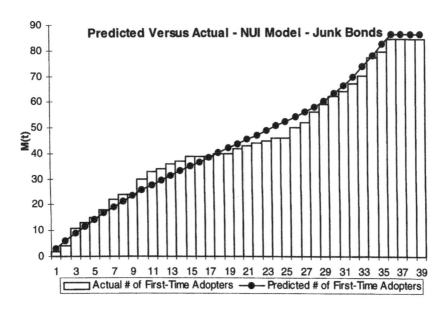

Figure 8.4 The NUI model for junk bonds

Table 8.3 The NUI Model—NIFs

$$N_{t+1} - N_t = 0.109(544.9 - N_t) + 0.209\left(\frac{N_t}{544.9}\right)^{1.63}(544.9 - N_t)$$

Parameter	Asymptotic		Asymptotic 95% confidence interval	
	Estimate	Std. error	Lower	Upper
a	0.1092479	0.0053554	0.0000411	0.0218084
b	0.2098710	0.0721732	0.0631973	0.3565446
δ	1.6338194	0.4578116	0.7034343	2.5642046
$\bar{N}$	544.94401	34.664789	474.49668	615.39131

Table 8.4 The NUI model—junk bonds

$$N_{t+1} - N_t = a(83.9 - N_t) + b\left(\frac{N_t}{83.9}\right)(83.9 - N_t)$$

Parameter	Asymptotic		Asymptotic 95% confidence interval	
	Estimate	Std. error	Lower	Upper
a	0.0363946	0.0058276	0.0245263	0.0482126
b	1.1837817	0.4346332	0.3005006	2.0670629
δ	8.0016731	1.7861245	4.3718312	11.631514
$\bar{N}$	83.968745	0.7369049	82.471174	85.466316

adoption. The rational-efficiency and bandwagon hypotheses offer three factors that can explain this *positive* internal influence:

1. Rational-efficiency hypotheses:
   (i) Information-transfer from adopters to nonadopters reducing uncertainty
   (ii) Reduction in fixed costs associated with developing new markets
   (iii) Increase in expected returns to adoption due to positive externalities (e.g. enhanced liquidity), or
2. Bandwagon pressure hypotheses:
   (iv) Competitive and institutional bandwagon pressures.

Time-Varying Internal Influence

Unfortunately the model does not allow us to separate the effects of these factors. We can however obtain more insight on the factors responsible for internal influence by observing how internal influence varied with the number of adopters. For the first three factors (rational-efficiency hypotheses) we would expect the internal influence to decline with the number of adopters. With only a small number of banks adopting the innovation, adoption by one more bank is more likely to have a greater impact on fixed-cost reduction, information-transfer, and increased liquidity of the market than if there was a large number of banks.[2] That is, although the internal influence increases with the number of adopting banks, it does so at a decreasing rate. The relationship between the bandwagon-pressure internal influence and the number of adopting banks is more ambiguous. In the early stages, we would expect the internal influence to be an increasing function of the number of adopters. This however may stabilise or even reverse in later stages.

The results show that for both innovations δ, the non-uniform internal influence coefficient, was larger than 1; 1.63 for NIFs and 8.0 for junk bonds indicating a time-increasing internal influence. Values of δ greater than 1 indicates a delayed internal influence causing a later and lower peak in the level of adoption. Interestingly, this is in contrast to the studies of the diffusion patterns of consumer durables which generally found a decreasing internal influence (e.g. Easingwood *et al.* 1983, for consumer durables, and Coleman *et al.* 1966 and Mahajan *et al.* 1983 for new drugs). This is mainly due to the fact that the so-called 'word-of-mouth' effect, which underlies the internal influence for consumer durables, loses importance in later stages of the diffusion process. In the financial sector, the behaviour of internal influence depends on how rational-efficiency and bandwagon effects factors vary over time. Figures 8.5 and 8.6 below show how internal influence varied with the number of adopters. The solid lines in Figures 8.5 and 8.6 depict the time-varying internal influence as estimated by the NUI model ($w(t)$ in the NUI model) and the dotted lines depict the constant internal influence as estimated by the logistic curve (β in the Mansfield model). The horizontal axis measures the percentage of firms that have adopted the innovation. An increasing internal influence is inconsistent with the rational-efficiency hypotheses's explanation of internal influence and consistent with the competitive and institutional bandwagon hypotheses. For NIFs internal influence increased at a more or less constant rate during the diffusion period (Figure 8.5). The pressure on nonadopting banks probably stemmed from competitive bandwagon pressures due to the gradual decline in the syndicated market associated with the growth in the NIFs market. Banks actively engaged in the syndicated market faced a threat of losing business in the syndicated market and thus had incentives to compensate by entering the NIFs market.

The results for junk bonds show a different story. Internal influence remained marginally low throughout most of the diffusion period and then increased sharply in the very late stages (Figure 8.7). The controversy associated with the emergence and growth of the junk bond market and the riskiness of this market

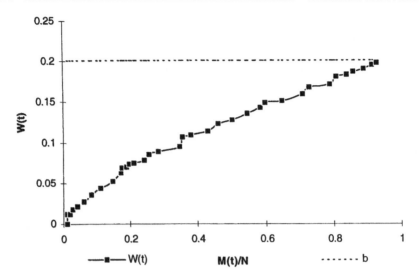

Figure 8.5   Internal influence—NIFs

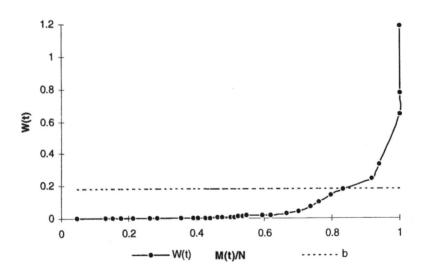

Figure 8.6   Internal influence—junk bonds

could have moderated the effects of institutional bandwagon pressures on non-adopting banks. The sharp increase in the bandwagon pressures in the late stages can perhaps be attributed to the increase in the use of junk bonds in leveraged buyouts and acquisitions. Junk bonds issued to finance leveraged buyouts and acquisitions offered investment banks the opportunity to arrange financing for acquisitions, a business in which they already had experience.

Internal versus External Adopters

The parameter estimates of a, b, δ can be used to decompose the number of adopters into two categories: internal adopters and external adopters.[3] Figures 8.7 and 8.8 show the number of internal adopters and external adopters for NIFs and junk bonds, respectively. For NIFs, the number of external adopters exceeded the number of internal adopters only in the early stages of the market development and thereafter the number of internal adopters dominated. In total, among all the 505 banks which have adopted NIFs, 361 (71%) were internal adopters and only 144 (28%) were external adopters. The 'imitative' nature and institutional bandwagon pressures observed in the diffusion pattern of NIFs among banks, and captured by the NUI model, are explained by Bullock's (1987, p. 50) comments on banks' behaviour during that period '... There were occasions when banks joined the tender panel even when they had no intention of developing placement capabilities, simply because every other bank was invited to join and exclusion was less easy to accept than inclusion ... It became a matter of corporate pride to be included as a tender panel member with exclusion considered a slight.'

Thus the initial factors that led to the emergence of the NIFs were significant only to the extent that they provided the market with initial critical size in terms of banks' expertise, relationships, and reputation and diversity of issuers and investors. The junk bond market, on the other hand, has been dominated by external adoptions for most of the diffusion period (Figure 8.8). The number of internal adopting banks became significant only in the last few periods. Of 84 banks that underwrote junk bond issues, 66 (78%) were external adopters and only 18 (22%) were internal adopters. Most players in the junk bond market in the early stages were influenced in their adoption decisions by the initial factors that led to the emergence of this market. Their entry into the market, however, did not exert enough pressure on their rivals to imitate them. This may be mainly due to the uncertainty and controversy surrounding the junk bond market in the early and intermediate stages of its market development. This is an interesting result as it indicates possible conditions which may undermine the effectiveness of internal influence. In later stages, with the increased use of junk bonds in leveraged buyouts and acquisition, the business domain of a larger set of banks was affected with the developments and growth in the junk bond

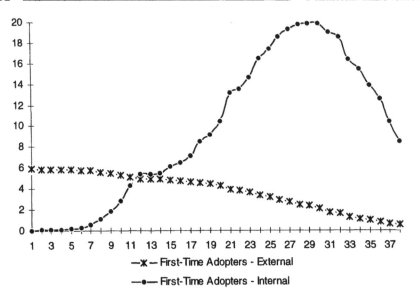

Figure 8.7 Internal versus External Adopters—NIFs

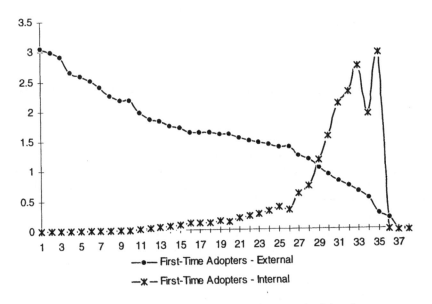

Figure 8.8 Internal versus external adopters—junk bonds

market. The survival of the market and the increased acceptance of its legitimacy revealed its profit potential for banks and far more banks entered the market due to internal influence.

8.3 REPEAT-ADOPTION MODELS: THE NUIR, THE NUIR 1, AND THE NUIR 2 MODELS

In this section the analysis is extended to incorporate repeat adopters into the model. This was achieved by estimating three repeat-adoption models for the data on junk bonds and NIFs.

8.3.1 The Mahajan (1983) NUIR Model

For NIFs, the Mahajan (1983) NUIR model produced insignificant estimates of a, b, and c (see Figure 8.9 and Table 8.5). This suggests that the total number of banks that were engaged in the market for the innovation at time t (and the number of those who were not) has no consistent relationship with the number of banks engaged in the market at time $t + 1$. This is reflected in the insignificance of both b and c. For junk bonds the Mahajan (1983) NUIR model produced significant negative estimate of c and significant positive estimates of a, b, and δ (see Figure 8.10 and Table 8.6). The negative c coefficient suggests a market evolution in which a few early adopting banks monopolised the market and captured increasingly larger market shares making it difficult for rivals to operate in the market. This is consistent with the evolution of the junk bond market (see section 8.3.4 later in this chapter).

8.3.2 The NUIR 1 Model

The Mahajan (1983) NUIR model makes no prediction about the impact of new entry to the market on the total number of banks engaged in the market. The logistic curve and the NUI model established that entry by new banks to the market makes it more desirable for other banks to *introduce* the innovation. The NUIR 1 model assesses the impact of new entry to the market at time t on the number of banks which either *introduce* the innovation for the first time (first-time adopters) or *continue to introduce* the innovation at time $t + 1$ (repeat adopters). Note that $n(t)$, the dependent variable of the model is the sum of these two numbers.

The results of the NUIR 1 model are shown in Figures 8.11, 8.12 and Tables 8.7 and 8.8. The model produced significant positive estimate values for c for both financial innovations. In the case of NIFs, the model produced a

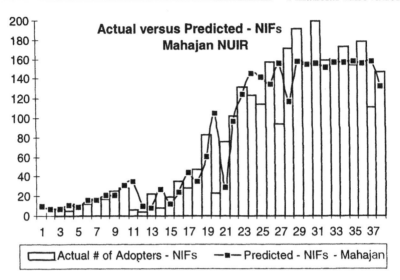

Figure 8.9 The Mahajan (1983) NUIR model—NIFs

Table 8.5 The NUIR model—NIFs

$$n_{t+1} = 0.013(544.9 - n_t) + 4.64\left(\frac{n_t}{544.9}\right)^{1.169}(544.9 - n_t) - 1.66n_t$$

Parameter	Asymptotic		Asymptotic 95% confidence interval	
	Estimate	Std. error	Lower	Upper
a	0.0139866	0.0257569	−0.0383578	0.0663310
b	4.4644142	3.2836703	−2.0290786	11.317363
c	−1.663626	1.5440298	−4.8014727	1.4742194
δ	1.1692098	0.1281377	0.90880258	1.4296171

$R^2 = 1-$ Residual SS/Corrected SS $= 0.84678$

significant positive value for b and an insignificant value for a. The significant estimates of b and δ (i.e. δ is significantly different from 1) indicates significant internal-influence aspects of the diffusion process of NIFs, which is consistent with our earlier results. That is, an increase in the cumulative number of banks that have introduced the innovation makes it more desirable for banks to introduce or continue to introduce the innovation (i.e. either as first-time or repeat adopters). This result suggests that the increase in the desirability of the market for a new financial product associated with new entry into the market by

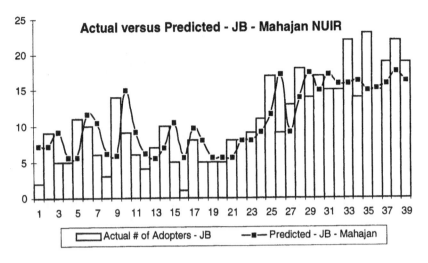

Figure 8.10 The Mahajan (1983) NUIR model—junk bonds

Table 8.6 The NUIR model—junk bonds

$$n_{t+1} = 0.179(83.96 - n_t) + 24.3\left(\frac{n_t}{83.96}\right)^{1.27}(83.96 - n_t) - 12.1n_t$$

Parameter	Asymptotic		Asymptotic 95% confidence interval	
	Estimate	Std. error	Lower	Upper
a	0.17935441	0.0581636	0.0612759	0.2974329
b	24.3768988	8.9287718	6.2505283	42.503269
c	−12.145699	4.7065426	−21.70048	−2.590909
δ	1.27896224	0.0265392	1.2250846	1.3328398

$R^2 = 1 -$ Residual SS/Corrected SS = 0.54905

more banks (due to enhanced liquidity, and other bandwagon pressures) more than offsets the decrease in the desirability of the market due to a larger number of competitors. For NIFs, the NUIR 1 model produced an estimate of $\delta > 1$, suggesting that this relationship is an increasing function of the number of banks that have introduced the innovation at least once before. In the early stages with only a few banks in the market, the entry of new banks in the market at time t had a smaller impact on the number of banks active in the market at time $t + 1$ than in later stages with a larger number of banks operating in the market. This again is consistent with our earlier results and suggests that

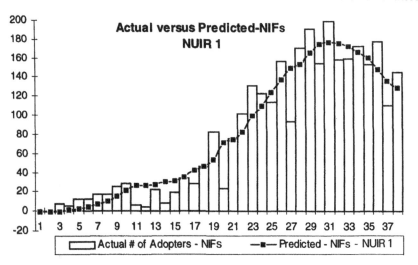

Figure 8.11 The NUIR 1 Model—NIFs

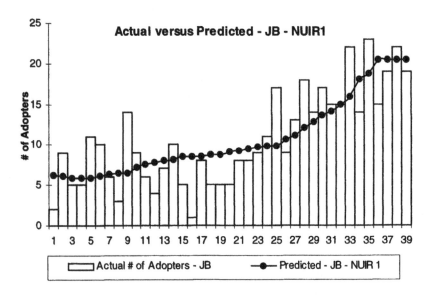

Figure 8.12 The NUIR 1 model—junk bonds

Table 8.7 The NUIR 1 model—NIFs

$$n_{t+1} = -0.00401(544.9 - N_t) + 1.407\left(\frac{N_t}{544.9}\right)^{2.899}(544.9 - N_t) + 0.255N_t$$

Parameter	Asymptotic		Asymptotic 95% confidence interval	
	Estimate	Std. error	Lower	Upper
a	−0.0040195	0.0128880	−0.0302111	0.0221720
b	1.40738286	0.3541593	0.68764449	2.1271212
c	0.25522328	0.0254400	0.20352240	0.3069241
δ	2.89915188	0.4324472	2.02031337	3.7779903

$R^2 = 1 - \text{Residual SS/Corrected SS} = 0.91428$

Table 8.8 The NUIR 1 model—junk bonds

$$n_{t+1} = 0.079(83.9 - N_t) + 0.188\left(\frac{N_t}{83.9}\right)^{0.801}(83.9 - N_t) + 0.243N_t$$

Parameter	Asymptotic		Asymptotic 95% confidence interval	
	Estimate	Std. error	Lower	Upper
a	0.07995758	0.06373779	−0.0494370	0.20935218
b	−0.1882407	0.09416396	−0.3794037	0.00292227
c	0.24358158	0.01927697	0.20444725	0.28271591
δ	0.80181591	0.96099601	−1.1491097	2.75274155

$R^2 = 1 - \text{Residual SS/Corrected SS} = 0.62786$

internal influence is more in the form of bandwagon pressure than rational efficiency factors such as increased liquidity or less uncertainty.

For junk bonds the model produced insignificant estimates of a, b, and δ. This suggests that the cumulative number of banks had no significant impact on banks' decision to participate in the market.

8.3.3 The NUIR 2 Model

The NUIR 2 model produced similar results to those of the NUIR 1 model (see Figures 8.13, 8.14 and Tables 8.9 and 8.10). The results were also similar whether or not λ was constrained to 1. For junk bonds, a, b, and δ were insignificant. The same results were obtained when λ was unconstrained with insignificant estimate of λ.

For NIFs both b and δ were positive and significant reinforcing our earlier

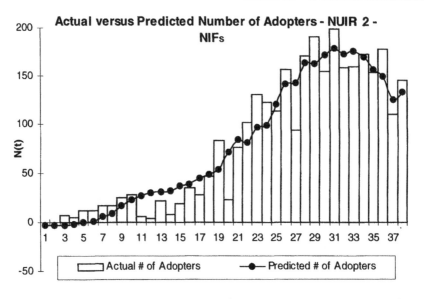

Figure 8.13   The NUIR 2 Model—NIFs

Table 8.9   The NUIR 2 Model—NIFs

$$n_{t+1} = a(\bar{N} - N_t) + b\left(\frac{N_t}{\bar{N}}\right)^{\delta}(\bar{N} - N_t) + c\left(\frac{p_t}{\bar{N}}\right)^{\lambda}N_t + \alpha$$

Parameter	Asymptotic		Asymptotic 95% confidence interval	
	Estimate	Std. error	Lower	Upper
a	−0.3397734	0.06973523	−0.4816508	−0.197896
b	1.81313189	0.50247175	0.79084542	2.8354183
c	−0.3055805	0.23942248	−0.7926892	0.1815281
δ	3.07100484	0.39078385	2.27594911	3.8660605
α	166.533839	31.9260864	101.579728	231.48795

λ Constrained to one
$R^2 = 1 -$ Residual SS/Corrected SS $= 0.91839$

a	−0.2802250	0.05683184	−0.3959877	−0.164462
b	1.88395496	0.52316501	0.81830269	2.9496072
c	−2.6413510	8.74306382	−20.450389	15.167687
δ	3.04483163	0.40889353	2.21194277	3.8777205
λ	137.595222	25.6081030	85.4332229	189.75722
α	3.72816883	4.32228849	−5.0760447	12.532382

$R^2 = 1 -$ Residual SS/Corrected SS $= 0.92302$

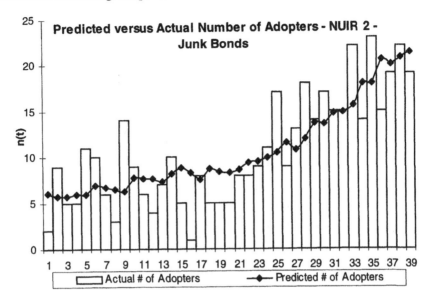

Figure 8.14 The NUIR 2 Model—junk bonds

Table 8.10 The NUIR 2 Model—junk bonds

$$n_{t+1} = a(\bar{N} - N_t) + b\left(\frac{N_t}{\bar{N}}\right)^\delta (\bar{N} - N_t) + c\left(\frac{p_t}{\bar{N}}\right)^\lambda N_t + \alpha$$

| Parameter | Asymptotic | | Asymptotic 95% confidence interval | |
	Estimate	Std. error	Lower	Upper
a	−0.1253531	0.10014188	−0.3288659	0.0781596
b	−0.1652218	0.09531818	−0.3589317	0.0284879
c	0.18265002	0.25141558	−0.3282879	0.6935879
δ	0.74166012	1.09495110	−1.4835482	2.9668684
α	17.2187969	4.81975140	7.42388365	27.013710
λ	Constrained to 1			
$R^2 = 1 -$ Residual SS/Corrected SS $= 0.63371$				
a	−0.1161056	0.21378375	−0.5510519	0.3188406
b	−0.1652145	0.09704804	−0.3626602	0.0322311
c	0.15623716	0.38884667	−0.6348773	0.9473516
δ	0.74348945	1.11289976	−1.5207221	3.0077010
α	16.4578594	16.3405751	−16.787290	49.703009
λ	0.76358233	3.78194238	−6.9308373	8.4580019
$R^2 = 1 -$ Residual SS/Corrected SS $= 0.63373$				

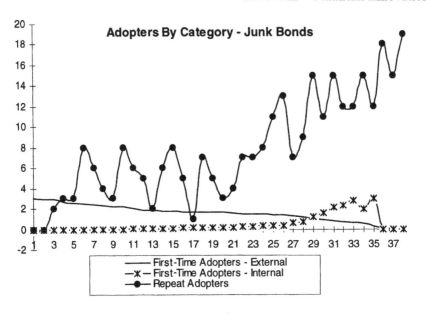

Figure 8.15 Adopters by category—junk bonds

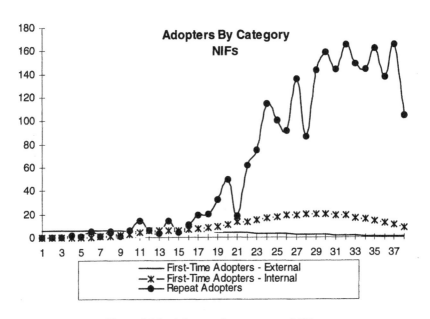

Figure 8.16 Adopters by category—NIFs

conclusion of the relevance of diffusion theory in explaining the diffusion pattern of NIFs. The same results were obtained when λ was unconstrained with insignificant estimate of λ. The NUIR 2 model produced insignificant estimates of c for both innovations suggesting that the long run properties of this model did not provide improvements over those of the NUIR 1 model.

Overall, the results are consistent with the previous results with the internal influence being significant in the structure of the diffusion of NIFs but not for junk bonds.

8.3.4 First-Time versus Repeat Adopters

An important aspect of the diffusion structure of financial innovations is the extent to which the growth of the innovation is concentrated among a small number of repeat adopters. Figures 8.15 and 8.16 show a breakdown of the total number of adopters by category of adoption; first-time adopters due to internal influence, first-time adopters due to external influence, and repeat adopters (actual). Figure 8.15 reveals the relatively high number of repeat adopting banks in the early stages of the junk bond's diffusion process. After the first three periods, most banks active in the junk bond market were repeat adopters, with relatively few new entrants. This might suggest that early adopting banks achieved a competitive advantage in this new market which made it difficult for new banks to join in. Such competitive advantage may have been in the form of a strong reputation for arranging junk bond issues and the ability to market them effectively. By the end of 1986, there had been 84 banks which had managed at least one junk bond issue.

For NIFs, the majority of banks adopting the innovation during the first phase of the diffusion process were first-time adopters with 20 or more banks joining the market every month for the larger part of the diffusion period. The increase in the number of first-time adopters due to internal influence was paralleled with a sharp increase in the number of repeat adopters midway through the diffusion process. The number of repeat adopters began to stabilise in the latter stages of the diffusion period. The inability of a few banks to dominate the NIFs markets may have been due to the wide distribution of issuers' nationalities, where local banks enjoyed the advantages of established customer relationships.

8.4 CONCLUSION

This chapter reports the empirical results of the analysis of diffusion patterns of two financial innovations, junk bonds and NIFs. The models tested focus on the competitive, strategic, and informational aspects of the process of financial innovation diffusion, and it separates these effects from the effects of exogenous factors that led to the initial emergence of the innovation. We find that the initial exogenous factors played a significant role in the diffusion pattern of junk bonds but not NIFs. In the junk bond market, our results suggests that early adopting banks exerted little influence on non-adopting banks, the majority of which have entered the junk bond market because of their assessments of the market's profitability due to the initial exogenous factors. For NIFs only a small number of banks can be attributed to the initial exogenous factors and the majority of banks have entered the market under competitive and institutional bandwagon pressures. This may suggest that banks are more likely to respond to competitive and institutional bandwagon pressures by adopting an innovation when it represents a threat to existing business rather than when it represents new business opportunities. For both innovations, however, we found that innovation adoption by one bank makes it more desirable for other banks to adopt the innovation and that the impact of innovation adoption by one bank on non-adopters increases with the number of adopters.

The above results indicate empirical evidence of internal influence. The literature identified two forms of internal influence (see the first part of Chapter 5); innovation adoption by one bank makes it *more desirable* for other banks to enter the market due to network externalities and/or declining adoption costs (rational-efficiency theories), or innovation adoption by one bank exerts competitive and institutional pressures on its rivals to adopt the innovation (bandwagon pressures theories). Empirically, we can distinguish between the two categories by observing how the internal influence varies over time. Using the NUI model's results, the analysis shows that internal influence is in fact an increasing function of the cumulative number of banks that adopted the innovation. One would expect, however, the internal influence to be a decreasing function of the number of banks that introduced the innovation if enhanced liquidity or reduced uncertainty were responsible for the internal influence. This is so because new entry to the market is likely to have a greater impact in terms of enhanced liquidity and reduced uncertainty in the early stages, when there are few banks in the market, than in the later stages of the diffusion process. Thus it is suggested that an increasing internal influence is mainly in the form of institutional and competitive bandwagon pressure.

The results also show that the magnitude of the internal influence varies between innovations. The NUI model classifies 361 banks out of 505 (71%) that introduced NIFs as internal adopters compared to only 18 out of 84 (22%) for junk bonds. Although it is difficult to arrive at conclusions based on the analysis of the adoption patterns of only two innovations, a few facts emerge from the results. Firstly, the results indicate empirical evidence of the presence of internal influence in financial markets; namely that the number of rival banks that have introduced an innovation affects a bank's decision to adopt the innovation and the timing of adoption.

Secondly, the theoretical literature on innovation adoption and diffusion identifies two sources of internal influence; rational-efficiency factors, such as increased expected returns or declining adoption costs, and bandwagon pressures imposed by early adopters on nonadopters. The time-increasing nature of the internal influence for both innovations suggests that it is the latter that is mainly responsible for internal influence in financial markets. Under bandwagon pressure, a bank does not adopt an innovation based on its assessment of the innovation's profitability, but does so to maintain existing customer relationships and market share in related markets. The results suggest that most banks' entry into the NIFs market was mainly motivated by bandwagon pressures. Most banks that have entered the NIFs market were also active in other euromarkets such as eurobonds and euro-syndicated credit, and thus were eager to maintain their relationships with existing customers and to develop a reputation as being capable of offering innovative packages that met the requirements of their customers.

The results for junk bonds reveal that in the early stages, the market was dominated by the entry of a few banks seeking profitable opportunities (i.e. external adopters). The entry of these new banks had little impact on other banks (in terms of creating bandwagon pressures or making the entry to the market more desirable) during the early and mid stages of the junk bonds market development. This may be due to the uncertainty regarding the continuity of the market at that stage and to the controversy surrounding banks' underwriting of junk bonds. It was only in the latter stages of the evolution of the junk bond market that internal influence had a significant impact. One possible explanation for this might be the increased use of junk bonds in leveraged buyouts and acquisitions. This may have brought the business of underwriting junk bonds closer to the more traditional activities of US investment banks. Also, the survival and growth of the junk bond market, plus academic studies which showed that risk-adjusted returns in the junk bond market exceeded those in investment grade bonds, increased pressures on non-adopting banks. The final chapter outlines the main conclusions and limitations of this book, and discusses possible future research in this area.

ENDNOTES

1. The results of diffusion models are generally insensitive to the assumed values of $\bar{N}$ (Jagtiani *et al.* 1995).
2. Fixed-cost reductions are likely to contribute marginally to internal influence in financial markets because cost of developing a new product is relatively low. Tufano (1989) estimated this cost to range between $50 000 and $5 000 000.
3. See equations (6.5) and (6.6) in Chapter 6.

9

Conclusion and Summary

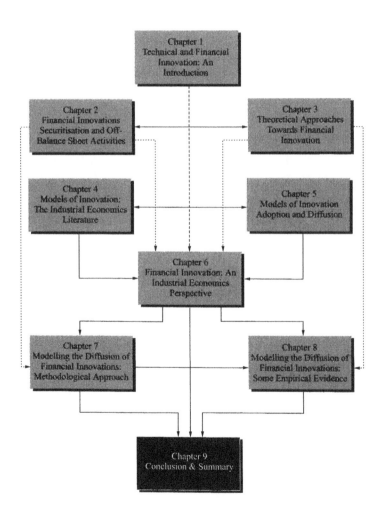

9

Conclusion and Summary

9.1 CONCLUSION AND SUMMARY

The increasing importance of the process of financial innovation has attracted considerable interest in recent years. Financial innovation has been one of the most influential trends prevailing in international financial markets in the 1980s and 1990s. Increased innovation, reflected in the growth of securitisation, for example, has resulted in the emergence and growth of a large number of off-balance-sheet activities (including euromarkets business, contingent banking, bank assets securitisation, and derivative instruments). There are a large number of studies which document the emergence and growth of new financial products and analyse their demand/supply factors. More recently, various theoretical approaches have been advanced that attempt to explain financial innovation as a process. At the same time, a number of hypotheses that explain securitisation and the growth of OBSAs have emerged in the literature. These latter studies are mainly concerned with the question of which banks are more likely to adopt OBSAs.

These studies, however, assume a static framework which ignores the strategic and competitive interactions between firms. The presence of network and informational externalities, two important aspects of innovation competition in financial markets, can have a significant impact on an individual bank's decision to adopt an innovation and on the innovation's diffusion among banks. The industrial economics literature provides an extensive analysis of the competitive and strategic interactions between firms in the context of innovation adoption and diffusion. There has, however, been little effort made to relate the findings of this literature to the banking industry. This book aims to fill this gap.

Chapter 2 examined recent trends in international capital markets and the factors affecting the growth of new financial products. The emergence of many new financial products seems to have been related to certain regulatory constraints. The empirical evidence, however, indicates that the market for these new instruments continues to grow even after the relevant regulations have been removed or reversed. This suggests that once new products are innovated, market participants find new uses for these instruments independent of the factors that led to their introduction initially. Regulatory changes are significant in the extent to which they create sufficient demand for the initial introduction of these instruments. Although some of these factors proved temporary, the initial stimulus was enough to provide the new markets with sufficient critical size (in terms of diversity of intermediaries, issuers and investors and liquidity of the market) to survive their abolition. Other important factors that have led to the emergence of a number of financial innovations include: volatile interest and exchange rates, technological advances, globalisation of financial markets, and increased competition between financial institutions.

Chapter 3 reviews the theoretical literature on financial innovation. These approaches attempt to explain financial innovation as a process. The most influential theories of financial innovation are the constraint-induced hypothesis and the regulatory dialectic model. The former views innovations as attempts by banks to lessen the costs of adhering to certain balance sheet constraints. The latter portrays a picture of continuous struggle between regulators and the regulatees (banks) who innovate to circumvent regulatory taxes. A prominent trend in the literature is to view financial innovation as a *bundling* and *unbundling* process whereby new financial products just simply represent changes in the combinations of certain general attributes of financial instruments (e.g. liquidity, maturity). More recent literature attempts to formalise the view of financial innovation as a bundling and unbundling process by modelling the process of financial innovation in the context of general equilibrium theory. Although more attention is paid now to the study of financial innovation, there is still no generally accepted and unified theory of this process.

Chapter 4 examines the industrial economics literature on market structure and innovative activity. Most of the literature in this area can be characterised as models of R&D competition focusing on the timing and intensity of investing in R&D to perfect a given single innovation. In these models the firms must select the optimal amount to spend on R&D where either the timing or value of the innovation is random. The decision theoretic formulations solve for the optimal rate of R&D spending for a single firm and evaluate the effects of parameter changes on that rate. The game theoretic formulation compares the socially optimal number of research projects with the amount of research performed by firms in a noncooperative game. The important implication of these studies is that the strategic interactions between firms (i.e. each firm takes into consideration the actions of its rivals in making its own decisions) can have significant effects on the eventual equilibrium. This can be seen clearly from the conflicting conclusions obtained by researchers assuming a decision-theoretic versus game-theoretic framework.

Chapter 5 examines models of innovation adoption and diffusion. Motivated by the empirical observation that innovations often *diffuse* over time rather than being adopted by all firms simultaneously, adoption models attempt to explain this observation by analysing the individual firm's decision to adopt an innovation, and the timing of adoption. Adoption models explain diffusion by assuming a heterogeneous population of potential adopters. *Ex ante* heterogeneity stems from differences in firms' characteristics that are critical to the adoption decision (e.g. firm size). *Ex post* heterogeneity stems from either exogenous factors including declining incremental benefits for later adoption and declining adoption costs, or endogenous factors such as bandwagon effects where the sheer number of firms that adopt the product creates a pressure on nonadopting firms.

Empirical diffusion models are general mathematical functions which focus on the aggregate industry diffusion rate by depicting the successive increase in the number of adopters or adopting units of an innovation over time. The most basic of these is a mixed-influence diffusion model which distinguishes between two categories of adopters; internal and external adopters. Internal adopters are firms which are influenced in the timing of their initial adoption by the number of firms that have already adopted the innovation. External adopters, on the other hand, are influenced in the timing of their initial adoption by exogenous factors other than the number of early adopters. In relation to models of adoption, external influence can be viewed to represent the influence of exogenous factors which leads to the initial introduction of the innovation. The differences in the timing of external adopters are due to the *ex ante heterogeneity* in firms' characteristics which affect the optimal timing of adoption. Internal influence, on the other hand, captures the effects of bandwagon pressures, and changes in the return/cost characteristics of the innovation that are related to the number of firms that have already adopted the innovation. That is, it captures the *ex post heterogeneity* generated by, or related to, the number of firms that have already adopted the innovation.

Chapter 6 summarises the implications of the industrial economics literature to the study of innovation adoption and diffusion in financial markets. Firstly, innovations are often developed, adopted, and diffused in a dynamic environment where strategic interactions between rivals can impact strongly on the behaviour of these firms, and on the features of the eventual equilibrium that prevails at the aggregate industry level. Static theoretical and empirical studies of OBSAs which ignore these interactions are inadequate to explain factors determining these instruments' adoption by banks. Secondly, informational and network externalities are two important features of which there is no systematic analysis in the financial context, even though these factors are particularly important in financial markets. These, and the fact that financial innovation often continues to grow even after the initial stimulus is no longer present, form the basis of our proposed framework of innovation adoption and diffusion in the financial industry.

This framework distinguishes between two categories of adopters. External adopters are banks which adopt the innovation based on their individual assessments of the innovation's profitability, which is determined by exogenous factors that lead to the initial emergence of the innovation. These banks do not necessarily adopt the innovation simultaneously; optimal timing of adoption is defined by key firm-specific factors which are described by a distribution of values across firms and not a single value. We do not specify these factors, nor do we determine *a priori* the time-pattern of external innovation adoption.

Internal adopters are banks whose adoption decision is influenced by the number of banks that have adopted the innovation. These banks may base their decision on individual assessments of the innovation's profitability, in which case the change in their assessments is due to positive informational or network externalities related to the number of banks that have adopted the innovation. These banks may also adopt the innovation due to competitive and institutional bandwagon pressures created by the sheer number of banks that have adopted the innovation. In both cases, internal adopters are influenced in their decision to adopt an innovation and in the timing of adoption by the number of banks that have already adopted the innovation. This relationship is in the form of either updated assessments due to positive network and informational externalities, or in the form of competitive and institutional bandwagon pressures. This framework motivates the empirical analysis of the book in which mathematical diffusion models are estimated using data on two financial innovations; junk bonds and NIFs. The datasets used and the models estimated are described in Chapter 7.

Chapter 8 summarises the results of the empirical study. The empirical evidence obtained from the first part of our analysis supports the hypothesis that innovation adoption by one bank makes it more likely that other banks will introduce the innovation. Mansfield (1961) explained this *imitative* nature of diffusion processes, often encountered in the real sector, on the grounds that as more firms adopt the innovation, more information accumulates regarding the innovation's profitability (reduced uncertainty through information transfer from early adopters to other members of the population of potential adopters) and increases bandwagon pressure on nonadopters. Others argued that the profitability of adopting increases (due to positive network externalities), or adoption cost decreases (due to the elimination or reduction of the fixed-cost component of adoption cost) as the number of firms adopting the innovation increases.

Using the non-uniform influence (NUI) model's results, our analysis of the junk bond and NIFs markets show that the positive internal influence increases at an increasing rate with the cumulative number of banks that adopted the innovation. One would expect the internal influence, though positive, to be a decreasing function of the number of banks that introduced the innovation if enhanced liquidity or reduced uncertainty were responsible for the internal influence. This is so because new entry to the market is likely to have a greater impact in terms of enhanced liquidity and reduced uncertainty in early stages when there are few banks in the market, compared with the later stages of the diffusion process. An increasing internal influence, thus, suggests that the rate of innovation diffusion is mainly determined by institutional and competitive bandwagon pressures, and is not based on banks' differential assessments of the innovation's profitability.

The results also show that the importance of the internal influence varies between innovations. The NUI model classifies 361 banks out of 505 (71%) that introduced NIFs as internal adopters compared to only 18 out of 84 (22%) for junk bonds. The diffusion of NIFs was primarily a result of institutional and competitive bandwagon pressures exerted by early adopters on nonadopters. In the case of junk bonds, the market was characterised by substantial repeat adoption by a small number of banks whose adoption decisions were based on their individual assessments of the market's profitability and limited internal influence. That is, the adoption of junk bonds by these banks exerted little influence on their rivals in terms of either attracting them or exerting pressures on them to enter the market. In the latter stages, the growth of the junk bond market and its increased use in leveraged buyouts and acquisitions brought the market closer to more traditional investment banking activities and more banks joined the market due to internal influence. Overall, however, internal adoption has been much less dominant in the diffusion pattern of junk bonds compared with NIFs.

9.2 LIMITATIONS OF MODELLING THE FINANCIAL INNOVATION PROCESS

The framework adopted in this book presents a general approach to analysing the determinants of banks' adoption of financial innovations. In its general form, this framework is applicable to most financial innovations. This however requires that no innovation-specific factors are directly incorporated into the models. On an innovation by innovation basis it may be useful to incorporate specific factors into the analysis to evaluate their effects on the spread of the innovation among banks. Changes in the regulatory environment is a good example of external factors that can be incorporated into the analysis.

Even though the formulation of the non-uniform internal influence shows more flexibility than constant internal influence, the number of different patterns it can depict is still limited. For example the internal influence might not be continuous but rather a step-like function of the number of adopters. That is the number of adopters may only exert an influence after it exceeds a certain minimum limit, after which each successive adoption exerts equal effect. There is no limit to different patterns of internal influence which can be envisioned. Our choice among the alternative specification has to be guided by theoretical and empirical studies of the market for new financial products. There is a lack of both theoretical and empirical studies of innovations in financial markets which limits our choice to general specifications like the ones estimated in this book. We know very little of *how* the entry of some banks into new markets affects the decision-making of their rivals. This book provides general evidence of the presence of internal influence and some of its characteristics. But much theoretical and observational work remains to be done in this area if we are to achieve a good understanding of the relationship between market structure and financial innovation to the extent to which it has been achieved in the industrial economics literature. Having said that, it should be acknowledged that many of the aforementioned limitations have resulted from the fact that the theoretical adoption models and the empirical diffusion models have developed in separate literatures. This book aims to unify the two bodies of literature in a workable framework but has been constrained in its choices by existing diffusion models.

On a more specific note, the main limitations of the framework adopted can be summarised as follows:

1. The analysis does not define the certain characteristics that define external adopters (that is, which banks are external adopters?). We would expect these characteristics to differ from one innovation to another and thus identifying these characteristics should be done at the innovation level. For example, for one type of financial innovation external adopters might be defined by banks' size, whereas for another it may relate to the regulatory taxes these banks incur, and so on. Alternatively, one may investigate the identities of banks that adopt the innovation during each period and compare these to the breakdown of external and internal adopters as predicted by the model (e.g. in a period when several banks adopt the innovation, and the model identifies some as internal adopters and others as external adopters, one may check to see whether these share common distinguishing characteristics. This exercise can be repeated for each period to see if any pattern emerges, especially in periods where all banks were identified as external or internal adopters).

2. The mathematical diffusion models tested assumes *a priori* the distribution of the number of external adopters at each period over the diffusion span independent of the key characteristics that define external adopters, but more importantly independent of the key characteristics that determine their optimal time of adoption. Theoretical models exist that use more sophisticated (and probably more realistic) methods that define the number of banks that will adopt the innovation at any period of time, using the distribution of the critical bank-specific characteristics that determine whether a bank would adopt the innovation or not. Thus if the criterion

is that a bank would adopt an innovation if its size exceeds a certain critical size, then by making appropriate assumptions regarding the distribution of banks' size, and the rate at which the critical size varies from one period to another (say as a function of time) then it is possible to determine the number of banks that would adopt the innovation during each period. Such theoretical models are however difficult to estimate empirically and requires that the critical characteristics affecting individual banks' adoption decisions, and their distribution across firm and over time, are known precisely. The framework adopted in this book is not aimed at representing accurately the *real-world mechanism* generating the observed data, but is rather intended to provide a model that is plausible and informative.

3. The method of identifying the factors responsible for internal influence (rational efficiency versus bandwagon effects) is not precise. Existing diffusion models assume that the mathematical formulation of the internal influence is the same regardless of which factors underlie the internal influence. It may also be argued that although banks do influence each other by the timing of their adoption, this may happen in a way that cannot be mathematically detected by modelling the time series of the number of adopters. This limitation is partly due to the fact there has been little integration of theoretical adoption models with empirical diffusion models. This literature seems to have been developed independently. Future research should aim to further unify these two areas.

4. The mathematical diffusion models implicitly assume that the population of internal adopters is homogenous. This assumption runs both ways; the adoption of the innovation by one bank is *likely* to have an *equal impact on all other banks* in the population of potential adopters, and the influence of an adoption by one bank is the same regardless of the identity of *this bank*. That is, the diffusion models deal with the *number* of banks rather than their identities. One may imagine situations where the internal influence is not only a function of the number of banks, but also of their identities. Banks are more likely to be under competitive and bandwagon pressures caused by the adoption of one bank if this bank is in the same peer group. The significance of information transfer is also likely to be larger if this transfer takes place between similar banks. The identities of the adopting banks can also play a part in determining the internal influence regardless of which banks still do not adopt the innovation. One would expect, for example, that the adoption of the innovation by a large bank would contribute more significantly to the liquidity of the market. Non-uniform diffusion models could allow for such patterns only if the identities of the adopting banks can be correlated with time. That is, since the non-uniform influence parameter allows for the internal influence to increase (decrease) with time, then certain groups of banks can be allowed to exert stronger (weaker) internal influence if these banks tend to adopt later or earlier than other banks.

Another approach is to investigate the effects of innovation adoption by a specific bank or financial firm, say Merrill Lynch, given the adopted framework. In this case, one could analyse the deviations of actual values from predicted values for the period next to the one during which that bank adopted the innovation (this is similar to the use of event studies to investigate stock market reactions to a given event). The diffusion model provides the *normal* or expected value, and deviations from this can be attributed to the fact that it is a particular bank which has adopted the innovation. In event studies, however, it is unlikely that other events are responsible for the deviation (or abnormal returns) because the data are measured in short periods of time (usually daily or hourly). In diffusion models the deviations can be attributed to a larger number of causes since the data periods are longer (monthly and quarterly in our case) and even ignoring any external factors, the fact that more than one bank adopted the innovation during a given period means that adoption by any one of these banks could have been the cause for the deviation. Such an approach can only be useful if it is known *a priori* that a specific pattern exists (e.g. US banks adopt the innovation during these specific periods). Even in this case any further analysis of the results of the diffusion model have to be motivated by the predictions of well defined hypotheses (e.g. the entry of US banks into the market are likely to exert larger internal influence). Currently, the literature offers no such hypotheses as to the possible variations in internal influence created by the adoption of financial innovations by different banks.

9.3 FUTURE RESEARCH

The contribution of this book is not limited to the empirical findings. These findings are presented in the spirit of a beginning rather than an end. The theoretical framework motivating the empirical analysis was based on a review of two distinct literatures (theoretical models of innovation adoption and empirical models of innovation diffusion) which seem to have developed separately. The bringing together of this literature and identifying interrelations and links should provide many interesting and important ideas for future research. Our review of the industrial economics literature, for example, shows that innovations are developed, adopted, and diffused in a much more dynamic environment than is often assumed by banking researchers. Our empirical findings suggests that strategic, competitive, and informational factors play an important role in shaping the diffusion pattern of financial innovations. These findings should stimulate further work on modelling the process of financial innovation.

Economists have benefited from a substantial empirical and observational literature on innovation and market structure in formulating their theoretical models of technical innovation. The lack of empirical studies of financial innovation limits our ability to develop theoretical and mathematical models of competition in the innovative activity and timing of innovation in financial markets. This is so because the choice of the many alternative formulations have to be guided by empirical observations. Studies such as Drew (1995) provide a good start. In particular we need to know more about *how* one bank's decision to enter a new market is influenced by, and influences the decisions of, its rivals (if it does at all). This book proposed some ways in which the internal influence is created. These findings, however, need to be verified by a better understanding of the decision-making processes of banks. Future research in this area could attempt to answer questions such as: under which conditions are we likely to observe bandwagon effects and what factors govern the extent of these effects? Which banks are more likely to create bandwagon pressures and which banks are likely to be influenced by these pressures? Which type of financial innovations are likely to be dominated by external adoption or internal adoption? Finally, the analysis could be extended to relax the assumption of *constant initial* external influence by incorporating exogenous variables into the model so as to assess their impact on the diffusion of financial innovations in a more dynamic environment.

Bibliography

Abrahamson, E. and Rosenkopf, L. (1990) When do bandwagon diffusions roll? How far do they go? and when do they roll backwards? A Computer Simulation. Proceedings of the Academy of Management Best Paper, pp. 155–9.

Abrahamson, E. and Rosenkopf, L. (1993) Institutional and competitive bandwagons: using mathematical modelling as a tool to explore innovation diffusion. *Academy of Management Review* **18**, 487–517.

Abramovitz, M. (1956) Resource and output trends in the United States since 1870. *The American Economic Review* **46**, 5–23.

Akhtar, M.A. (1983) Financial innovations and their implications for monetary policy: an international perspective. Bank for International Settlements, Monetary and Economic Department, Basle: BIS Economic Papers, no. 9.

Alderson, M.J. and Fraser, D.R. (1993) Financial innovations and excesses revisited: the case of auction rate preferred stock. *Financial Management*, Summer, 61–75.

Ali, A. (1994) Pioneering versus incremental innovations: review and research propositions. *Journal of Product Innovation Management* **11**, 46–61.

Allen, F. and Gale, D. (1988) Optimal security design. *Review of Financial Studies* **1**, 229–63.

Allen. F. and Gale, D. (1989) Optimal security design. *Review of Financial Studies*, **1**, 229–363.

Allen, F. and Gale, D. (1990) Incomplete markets and the incentives to set up an option exchange. *General Papers*, Risk Insurance, 15, pp. 17–46.

Allen, F. and Gale, D. (1991) Arbitrage, short sales and financial innovation. *Econometrica* **59**, 1041–68.

Allen, F. and Gale, D. (1994) *Financial Innovation and Risk Sharing*. MIT Press.

Alpar, P. (1992) Automation of banking functions and its managerial implications. *IEEE Transactions On Engineering Management* **39**, 378–85.

Altman, E.I. (1988) Measuring corporate bond mortality and performance. NYU Working paper, also *Journal of Finance*, September 1989, pp. 909–22.

Altman, E.I. (1992) Revisiting the high-yield bond market. *Financial Management*, Summer, 78–92.

Amemiya, T. (1985) *Advanced Econometrics*. Basil Blackwell, Oxford.

Anderson, R.W. and Harris, C.J. (1986) A model of innovation with application to new financial products. *Oxford Economic Papers* **38**, 203–18.

Anderson, R.W. and Sundaresan, S. (1993) Design and valuation of debt contracts. Working paper, School of Business, Columbia University.

Arnold, B. (1986) Securitisation and loans. Speech presented at the Securitisation of Loans Seminar, Federal Reserve Bank of New York, October 23rd.

Arrow, K.J. (1962) Economic welfare and the allocation of resources for invention. In R. Nelson (ed.), *The Rate and Direction of Inventive Activity: Economic and Social Factors*, NBER Princeton University Press.

Arrow, K.J. (1964) The role of securities in the optimal allocation of risk-bearing. *Review of Economic Studies* **30**, 91–6.

Arrow, K.J. and Debreu, G. (1954) Existence of equilibrium for a competitive economy. *Econometrica* **22**, 265–90.

Artus, P. and Boissieu, C.D. (1988) The process of financial innovation. Chapter 5 in A. Heertje (ed.), *Innovation, Technology, and Finance*. Basil Blackwell, Oxford, pp. 101–26.

Asquith, P., Mullins, D.W. and Wolff, E.D. (1989) Original issue high yield bonds: ageing analyses of defaults, exchanges, and calls. *The Journal of Finance* **44**, 923–52.

Avery, R.B. and Berger, A.N. (1988) Risk-based capital and off-balance sheet activities. Proceedings of the Conference on Bank Structure and Competition, Federal Reserve Bank of Chicago, Chicago, pp. 261–87.

Avery, R.B. and Berger, A.N. (1991a) Loan commitments and bank risk exposure. *Journal of Banking and Finance* **15**, 173–92.

Avery, R.B. and Berger, A.N. (1991b) Risk-based capital and deposit insurance reform. *Journal of Banking and Finance* **15**, 847–74.

Baer, H.L. and Pavel, C.A. (1988) Does regulation drive innovation?. Federal Reserve Bank of Chicago Economic Perspectives, March/April, pp. 3–16.

Bank of England (1983a) The nature and implications of financial innovation. *Bank of England Quarterly Bulletin*, September, pp. 357–62.

Bank of England (1983b) Competition, innovation and regulation in British banking. *Bank of England Quarterly Bulletin*, September, pp. 363–72.

Bank of England (1988) International capital and banking markets. *Bank of England Quarterly Bulletin*, May, pp. 209–19.

Bank of England (1991) The international bond market. *Bank of England Quarterly Bulletin*, November, pp. 521–28.

Bank of England (1994) Structured floating rate notes. *Bank of England Quarterly Bulletin*, February, p. 26.

Banker, The (1995) Fast track on forex, November 145 (837), pp. 37–42.

Banking World (1994) Syndicated loans 12(7), p. 32.

Barzel, Y. (1968) Optimal timing of innovations. *Review of Economics and Statistics* **50**, 348–55.

Bass, F.M. (1981) [1969] A new-product growth model for consumer durables, pp. 457–75. In Wind *et al.*, *New Product Forecasting*. D.C. Heath, Lexington, MA. (Also in *Management Science* **15**, 215–27, 1969).

Beath. J., Katsoulacos, Y. and Ulph, D. (1987) Sequential product innovation and industry evolution. *Economic Journal* **97**, 32–43.

Ben-Horim, M. and Silber, W.L. (1977) Financial innovation—a linear programming approach. *Journal of Banking and Finance* **1**, 277–96.

Benveniste, L.M. and Berger, A.N. (1986) An empirical analysis of standby letters of credit. Proceedings of the Conference on Bank Structure and Competition, Federal Reserve Bank of Chicago, Chicago.

Benveniste, L.M. and Berger, A.N. (1987) Securitization with recourse—an instrument that offers uninsured bank depositors sequential claims. *Journal of Banking and Finance* **11**, 403–24.

Berger, A.N. (1991) Market discipline in banking. Proceedings of the Conference on Bank Structure and Competition, Federal Reserve Bank of Chicago, Chicago, pp. 419–27.

Berger, A.N. and Udell, G. (1990) Collateral, loan quality, and bank risk. *Journal of Monetary Economics* **25**, 21–42.

Berger, A.N. and Udell, G. (1993) Securitisation, risk, and the liquidity problem in banking. In M. Klausner and L.J. White (eds), *Structural Changes in Banking*. Irwin Publishing, Homewood, IL, pp. 227–91.

Bhattacharya, U., Reny, P. and Spiegel, M. (1995) Destructive interference in an imperfectly competitive multi-security market. *Journal of Economic Theory* **65**, 136–70.

BIS (Bank for International Settlements) (1986) *Recent Innovations in International Banking*, BIS, Basle.

BIS (Bank for International Settlements) (1994) Public disclosure of market and credit risks by financial intermediaries. *The Fisher Report*, Basle Committee on Banking Supervision, BIS, Basle.

BIS (Bank for International Settlements) (1996) The international securities market. *International Banking and Financial Markets Development*, BIS, Basle.

Blackman, A.W. (1972) A mathematical model for trend forecasts. *Technological Forecasting and Social Change* **3**, 441–52.

Blackman, A.W. (1974) The market dynamics of technological substitutions. *Technological Forecasting and Social Change* **6**, 41–63.

Blaug, M. (1963) A survey of the theory of process-innovations. *Economica* **30**, 13–32.

Bonus, H. (1973) Quasi-Engel curves, diffusion and the ownership of major consumer durables. *Journal of Political Economy* **81**, 655–77.

Boot, A.W. and Thakor, A.V. (1991) Off-balance-sheet liabilities, deposit insurance, and capital regulation. *Journal of Banking and Finance* **15**, 825–46.

Boreham, G.F. (1984) Financial innovation in Canada. Series Number 46A, SUERF.

Bretschneider, S.I. and Mahajan, V. (1980) Adaptive technological substitution models. *Technological Forecasting and Social Change* **18**, 129–39.

Bretschneider, S.I., Carbone, R. and Longini, R.L. (1977) An adaptive approach to time-series forecasting. *Journal of Technology* **10**, 241–48.

Bright, J. (1968) *Technological Forecasting for Industry and Government: Methods and Applications*, Prentice-Hall, Englewood Cliffs, NJ.

Brown, M. (1996) Derivative instruments. In E. Gardener and P. Molyneux (eds), *Investment Banking*, 2nd Edition, Euromoney Books, London.

Budd, C., Harris, C. and Vickers, J. (1993) A model of the evolution of a duopoly: does the asymmetry between firms tend to increase or decrease? *Review of Economic Studies* **60**, 543–73.

Bullock, G. (1987) *Euronotes and Euro-Commercial Paper*. Butterworths, London.

Caranza, C. and Cottarelli, C. (1987) Financial innovation in Italy: a loop sided process. In M. de Cecco (ed.), *Changing Money: Financial Innovation in Developed Countries*. Basil Blackwell, Oxford, pp. 172–211.

Carbone, R. and Gore, W.L. (1978) An adaptive diagnostic model for air quality management. *Atmospheric Environment* **12**, 1785–91.

Carbone, R. and Longini, R.L. (1977) A feedback model for automated real estate assessment. *Management Science* **24**, 241–48.

Carlston, C.T. and Samolyk, K.A. (1995) Loan sales as a response to market-based capital constraints. *Journal of Banking and Finance* **19**, 627–46.

Carter, M. (1991) Uncertainty, liquidity and speculation: a Keynesian perspective on financial innovation in the debt markets. *Journal of Post Keynesian Economics* **14**, 169–82.

Chatterjee R. and Eliashberg, J. (1989) The innovation diffusion process in a heterogeneous population: a micromodeling approach. Working paper, Marketing Department, Krannert Graduate School of Management, Purdue University.

Chen, Z. (1995) Financial innovation and arbitrage pricing in frictional economies. *Journal of Economic Theory* **65**, 117–35.

Clarke, R. (1985) *Industrial Economics*. Basil Blackwell, Oxford.

Clemenz, G. (1992) Market structure and R&D competition. *European Economic Review* **36**, 847–64.

Coleman, J.S. (1964) *Introduction to Mathematical Sociology*. Free Press, New York, p. 490.

Coleman, J.S., Katz, E. and Menzel, H. (1966) *Medical Innovation: A Diffusion Study*. Bobbs-Merrill, Indianapolis.

Cooley, T.F. and Prescott, E.C. (1973) Systematic (non-random) variation models varying parameters regression: a theory and some applications. *Annals of Economic and Social Measurement* **2/4**, 463–73.

Copeland, T.E. and Weston, J.F. (1988) *Financial Theory and Corporate Policy*. 3rd edition, Addison-Wesley, Reading, MA.

Cornwall, R.R. (1984) Introduction to the use of general equilibrium analysis. North-Holland: Amsterdam, New York.

Cuny, C.J. (1993) The role of liquidity in futures market innovations. *Review of Financial Studies* **6**, 57–78.

Dasgupta, P. and Stiglitz, J. (1980) Industrial structure and the nature of innovative activity. *Economic Journal* **90**, 266–93.

David, P.A. (1969) A contribution to the theory of distribution. Research Memorandum No. 71, Research Center in Economics Growth, Stanford University.

Davies, S. (1979) *Diffusion of Process Innovations*. Cambridge University Press, Cambridge.

Davies, S. (1989) *Surveys in Economics: Economics of Industrial Organisation*. Longman, New York.

Davis, E.P. (1995) The Eurobond market. Chapter 5 in D. Cobham (ed.), *Markets, Dealers, and the Economics of the London Financial Markets*. Longman, New York, pp. 111–37.

Debreu, G. (1959) *Theory of Value: An Axiomatic Analysis of Economic Equilibrium*. Yale University Press, New Haven, CT.

Delbono, F.R. (1989) Market leadership with a sequence of history dependent patent races. *Journal of Industrial Economics* **38**, 95–101.

Demange, G. and Laroque, G. (1995a) Optimality of incomplete markets. *Journal of Economic Theory* **65**, 218–32.

Demange, G. and Laroque, G. (1995b) Private information and the design of securities. *Journal of Economic Theory* **65**, 233–57.

Demsetz, H. (1969) Information and efficiency: another viewpoint. *Journal of Law and Economics* **12**, 1–22.

Denison, E.F. (1974) *Accounting for United States Economic Growth; 1929–1969*. Brookings Institution.

Desai, M. and Low, M. (1987) Measuring the opportunity for product innovation. In M. de Cecco (ed.), *Changing Money: Financial Innovation in Developed Countries*. Basil Blackwell, Oxford, pp. 112–40.

Dodson, J.A. Jr and Muller, E. (1978) Models of new product diffusion through advertising and word-of-mouth. *Management Science* **24**, 1568–78.

Dosi, G. and Orsenigo, L. (1988) Industrial structure and technical change. Chapter 2 in A. Heertje (ed.), *Innovation, Technology, and Finance*. Basil Blackwell, Oxford, pp. 14–37.

Drew, A.W. (1995) Accelerating innovation in financial services. *Long Range Planning* **28**, 11–21.

Dufey, G. and Giddy, I. (1981) The evolution of instruments and techniques in international financial markets. Series No. 35A, SUERF.

Duffie, D. and Jackson, O. (1989) Optimal innovation of futures contracts. *Review of Financial Studies* **2**, 275–96.

Duffie, D. and Rahi, R. (1995) Financial market innovation and security design: an introduction. *Journal of Economic Theory* **65**, 1–42.

Easingwood, C.J., Mahajan, V. and Muller, E. (1981) A nonsymmetric responding logistic model for forecasting technological substitution. *Technological Forecasting and Social Change* **20**, 199–213.

Easingwood, C.J., Mahajan, V. and Muller, E. (1983) A nonuniform influence innovation diffusion model of new product acceptance. *Marketing Science* **2**, 273–96.

The Economist (1966a) The reincarnation of junk bonds. *Finance and Economics, The Economist*, January 6th, pp. 69–70.

The Economist (1996b) A dose of patent medicine. *Finance and Economics, The Economist*, February 10th, pp. 93–94.

Elul, R. (1995) Welfare effects of financial innovation in incomplete markets economies with several consumption goods. *Journal of Economic Theory* **65**, 43–78.

Eskin, G.J. (1973) Dynamic forecasts of new product demand using a depth of repeat model. *Journal of Marketing Research* **10**, 115–29.

Euromoney (1985) The NIFTY way to beat euroloans. *Euromoney*, October, pp. 239–43.

Euromoney (1987) *Annual Financing Report on Underwriting Business*, Special Survey, March.

Euromoney (1991a) Common sense creeps in. *Euromoney*, January, pp. 59–63.

Euromoney (1991b) Financial innovation fine tunes EMTNs. *Euromoney*, January, p. 62.

Euromoney (1993) The six men who rule world derivatives. *Euromoney*, August, pp. 45–51.

Euromoney (1994) The polymaths of the dealing room. *Euromoney*, January, pp. 65–68.

Fabozzi, F.J. (1986) *Floating Rate Instruments: Characteristics, Valuation, and Portfolio Strategies*. Probus Publishing, Chicago, IL.

Fabozzi, F.J. and Modigliani, F. (1992) *Capital Markets: Institutions and Instruments*. Prentice Hall, Englewood Cliffs, NJ.

Farrel, J. and Saloner, G. (1985) Standardization, compatibility and innovation. *Rand Journal of Economics* **16**, 70–83.

Ferguson, P.R. (1988) *Industrial Economics: Issues and Perspectives*. Macmillan Education, Basingstoke.

Finnerty, J.D. (1988) Financial engineering in corporate finance: an overview. *Financial Management* **17**, 14–16

Finnerty, J.D. (1993) An overview of corporate securities innovation. *Journal of Applied Corporate Finance* **4**, 23–39.

Flath, D. and Leonard, E.W. (1979) A comparison of two logit models in the analysis of qualitative marketing data. *Journal of Marketing Research* **16**, 533–38.

Floyd, A. (1968) A methodology for trend forecasting of figures of merit. In J. Bright (ed.), *Technological Forecasting for Industry and Government: Methods and Applications*. Prentice-Hall, Englewood Cliffs, NJ, pp. 95–109.

Forsyth, J.H. (1987) Financial innovation in Britain. In M. De Cecco (ed.), *Changing Money: Financial Innovation in Developed Countries*. Basil Blackwell, Oxford, p. 141.

Fourt, L.A. and Woodlock, J.W. (1960) Early prediction of market success for new grocery products. *Journal of Marketing* **25**, 31–38.

Freeman, C. (1982) *The Economics of Industrial Innovation*. 2nd edition. Frances Pinter Publishers, London.

Freeman, C. (1988) Diffusion: the spread of new technology to firms, sectors and nations. Chapter 3 in A. Heertje (ed.), *Innovation, Technology, and Finance*. Basil Blackwell, Oxford, pp. 38–70.

Freeman, C. and Tabellini, G. (1991) The optimal of nominal contracts. Working paper, Institute for Economic Research, University di Brescia and Innocenzo Gasparini.

Fudenberg, D. and Tirole, J. (1985) Preemption and rent equalization in the adoption of new technology. *Review of Economic Studies* **52**, 383–401.

Fudenberg, D., Gilbert, R.J., Stiglitz, J. and Tirole, J. (1983) Preemption, leapfrogging and competition in patent races. *European Economic Review* **22**, 3–31.

Galbraith, J.K. (1952) *American Capitalism*, Houghton Mifflin, Boston, MA.

Gardener, E.P.M. (1991) International bank regulation and capital adequacy: perspectives, developments, and issues. Chapter 6 in Norton (ed.), *Bank Regulation and Supervision in the 1990s*, LLP, Lloyds of London Press, London.

General Accounting Office (1994) Financial derivatives: actions needed to protect the financial system. *United States General Accounting Office Report to Congressional Requesters*, May.

Gilbert, R.J. and Newbery, M.G. (1982) Preemptive patenting and the persistence of monopoly. *American Economic Review* **72**, 514–26.

Globerman, S. (1975) Technological diffusion in the Canadian tool and die industry. *Review of Economics and Statistics* **57**, 428–34.

Goldfeld, S.M. (1975) Comment: speculation on future innovation. In W. Silber (ed.), *Financial Innovation*, D.C. Heath, Lexington, MA, pp. 173–76.

Grabowski, H.G. (1968) The determinants of industrial research and development: a study of the chemical, drug, and petroleum industries. *Journal of Political Economy* **76**, 292–306.

Greenbaum, S. and Heywood, C. (1973) Secular change in the financial services industry. *Journal of Money, Credit, and Banking* **5**, 571–603.

Griliches, Z. (1957) Hybrid corn: an exploration in the economics of technological change. *Econometrica* **25**, 501–22.

Grossman, G.M. and Shapiro, C. (1987) Dynamic R&D competition. *Economic Journal* **97**, 372–87.

Hamilton, A. (1956) *The Financial Revolution*. Penguin Books, London.

Hara, C. (1992) A characterisation and generic inefficiency of transaction-volume-maximising contracts. Working paper, Department of Economics, University College London.

Hara, C. (1995) On the commission revenue maximization in a general-equilibrium model of asset creation. *Journal of Economic Theory* **65**, 258–98.

Harrington, R. (1992) Financial innovation and international banking. Chapter 3 in H. Cavanna (ed.), *Financial Innovation*, Routledge, London, pp. 52–68.

Harris, C. and Vickers, J. (1985) Perfect equilibrium in a model of a race. *Review of Economic Studies* **52**, 193–209.

Hart, O. (1979) On shareholder unanimity in large stock market economies. *Econometrica* **47**, 1057–84.

Harvey, A.C. (1990) *The Econometric Analysis of Time Series*. 2nd edition, Philip Allan, Oxford.

Hassan, M., Karels, G. and Peterson, M. (1994) Deposit insurance, market discipline, and off-balance sheet bank risk of large United States commercial banks. *Journal of Banking and Finance* **18**, 575–93.

Heertje, A. (1988) Technical and financial innovation: Chapter 1 in A. Heertje (ed.), *Innovation, Technology, and Finance*, Basil Blackwell, Oxford, pp. 1–13.

Holland, R.C. (1975) Speculation on future innovation: implications for monetary control. In W. Silber (ed.), *Financial Innovation*, D.C. Heath, Lexington, MA, pp. 159–71.

Horsky, D. and Simon, L.S. (1983) Advertising and the diffusion of new products. *Marketing Science* **2**, 1–18.

Howe, J.T. (1988) *Junk Bonds, Analysis and Portfolio Strategies*, Probus Publishing, Chicago, IL.

IMF (1993) The growing involvement of banks in derivative finance. *International Capital Markets, part II*, August, International Monetary Fund World Economic and Financial Surveys.

IMF (1994) Derivatives and supervisory issues. *International Capital Markets*, September.

Isaac, R.M. and Reynolds, S.S. (1988) Appropriately and market structure in a stochastic invention model. *Quarterly Journal of Economics* **103**, 647–71.

Jagtiani, J., Saunders, A. and Udell, G. (1993) Bank off-balance sheet financial innovations. Working Paper Series, S-93-50, Stern School Of Business, Salomon Center, New York University.

Jagtiani, J., Saunders, A. and Udell, G. (1995) The effects of bank capital requirements on bank off-balance sheet financial innovations. *Journal of Banking and Finance* **19**, 647–58.

Jensen, R. (1982) Adoption and diffusion of an innovation of uncertain profitability. *Journal of Economic Theory* **27**, 182–93.

Jensen, R. (1984a) Adoption of an innovation of uncertain profitability with costly information. Working paper no. 84-8, Ohio State University.

Jensen, R. (1984b) Innovation adoption with both costly and costless information. Working paper no. 84-22, Ohio State University.

Jensen, R. (1984c) Information capacity and innovation adoption. Working paper no. 84-33, Ohio State University.

Jeuland, A. (1981) Parsimonious models for diffusion of innovation: derivation and comparisons. Working paper, Marketing Department, Graduate School of Business, University of Chicago.

Johnson, L.T. (1987) Theoretical approaches to financial innovation. *Discussion Paper no. 51*, School of Accounting, Banking and Economics, Research Papers in Banking and Finance, University of Wales, Bangor.

Johnson, S. and Murphy, A. (1987) Going off the balance sheet. *Economic Review*, September–October, Federal Reserve Bank of Atlanta, pp. 23–35.

Judd, J.P. (1979) Competition between the commercial paper market and commercial banks. Federal Reserve Bank of San Francisco, Bulletin, Winter, pp. 39–53.

Judd, K. (1985) Closed-loop equilibrium in a multi-stage innovation race. Discussion Paper no. 647, Management Economics and Decision Science, Kellogg Graduate School of Management, Northwestern University.

Kalwani, M.U. and Silk, A.J. (1980) Structure of repeat buying for new packaged goods. *Journal of Marketing Research* **17**, 316–22.

Kamien, M.I. and Schwartz, N.L. (1970) Market structure, elasticity of demand and incentive to invent. *The Journal of Law and Economics* **13**, 241–52.

Kamien, M.I. and Schwartz, N.L. (1972) Timing of innovations under rivalry. *Econometrica* **40**, 43–60.

Kamien, M.I. and Schwartz, N.L. (1974a) Risky R&D with rivalry. *Annals of Economic and Social Measurement* **3**, 276–77.

Kamien, M.I. and Schwartz, N.L. (1974b) Patent life and R&D rivalry. *American Economic Review* **64**, 183–87.

Kamien, M.I. and Schwartz, N.L. (1976) On the degree of rivalry for maximum innovative activity. *Quarterly Journal of Economics* **90**, 245–60.

Kamien, M.I. and Schwartz. N.L. (1978a) Self-financing of an R&D project. *American Economic Review* **68**, 252–61.

Kamien, M.I. and Schwartz, N.L. (1978b) Potential rivalry, monopoly profits and the pace of inventive activity. *Review of Economic Studies* **45**, 547–57.

Kamien, M.I. and Schwartz, N.L. (1980) A generalised hazard rate. *Economics Letters* **5**, 245–49.

Kamien, M.I. and Schwartz, N.L. (1982) *Market Structure and Innovation*. Cambridge University Press, Cambridge.

Kane, E.J. (1977) Good intentions and unintended evil. *Journal of Money, Credit and Banking*, February, 55–69.

Kane, E.J. (1978) Getting along without regulation Q: testing the standard view of deposit-rate competition during the 'Wilde-card experience'. *The Journal of Finance* **33**, 921–32.

Kane, E.J. (1980) Accelerating inflation, regulation and banking innovation. *Issues in Bank Regulation*, Summer, 7–14.

Kane, E.J. (1981) Accelerating inflation, technological innovation, and the decreasing effectiveness of banking regulation. *Journal of Finance* **36**, 355–67.

Kane, E.J. (1983) Metamorphosis in financial-services delivery and production. In *Strategic Planning for Economic and Technological Change in the FSI*. San Francisco: 49–64.

Kane, E.J. (1984a) Technological and Regulatory Forces in the Developing Fusion of Financial-Services Competition. WPS 84-4, Ohio State University, Columbus, OH.

Kane, E.J. (1984b) Microeconomic and macroeconomic origins of financial innovation. Chapter 1 in *Financial Innovations: Their Impact on Monetary Policy and Financial Markets*, The Federal Bank of St. Louis. Kluwer-Nijhoff, Boston, pp. 3–20.

Kapadia, N. and Puri, M. (1995) Financial innovation under uncertainty. Paper presented at the *Conference on Derivatives and Intermediation* sponsored by *The Federal Reserve Bank of Cleveland* and *Journal of Money, Credit and Banking*, November 1–3, Cleveland, OH.

Katz, M.L. and Shapiro, C. (1985) Network externalities, competition and compatibility. *American Economic Review* **75**, 424–40.

Katz, M.L. and Shapiro, C. (1987) R&D rivalry with licensing or imitation. *American Economic Review* **77**, 402–20.

Kennedy, P. (1994) *A Guide to Econometrics*. Blackwell, Oxford.

Kim, T. (1993) *International Money and Banking*. Routledge, London.

Klepper, S. (1992) Entry, exit and innovation over the product life cycle: the dynamics of first mover advantages, declining product innovation and market failure. Paper presented at the 1992 International Schumpeter Society Meeting, Kyoto, Japan.

Koppenhaver, G.D. (1986) The effects of regulation on bank participation in the guarantee market. Federal Reserve Bank of Chicago, September, Chicago, IL.

Koppenhaver, G.D. and Stover, R.D. (1991) Standby letters of credit and large bank capital. *Journal of Banking and Finance* **15**, 315–27.

Koppenhaver, G.D. and Stover, R.D. (1994) Standby letters of credit and bank capital: evidence of market discipline. *Journal of Banking and Finance* **18**, 553–73.

Kumar, U. and Kumar, V. (1992) Technological innovation diffusion: the proliferation of substitution models and easing the user's dilemma. *IEEE Transactions on Engineering Management* **39**, May, 158–68.

Lavaraj, U.A. and Gore, A.P. (1992) Modelling innovation diffusion—some methodological issues. *Journal of Scientific and Industrial Research* **51**, March, 291–95.

Lawrence, K.D. and Lawton, W.H. (1981) Applications of diffusion models: some empirical results. In Wind *et al.* (eds), *New Product Forecasting*. D.C. Heath, Lexington, MA, pp. 529–41.

Lee, T. and Wilde, L.L. (1980) Market strucure and innovation: a reformulation. *Quarterly Journal of Economics* **94**, 429–36.

Levin, R.C. (1978) Technical change, barriers to entry, and market structure. *Economica* **45**, 347–61.

Lewis, M.K. and Davis, K.T. (1987) *Domestic and International Banking*. Philip Allan, Exeter.

Lilien, G.L. and Rao, A.G. (1978) A marketing promotion model with word of mouth effect. Working paper 976-78, Sloan School of Management, Massachusetts Institute of Technology, Cambridge, MA.

Lilien, G.L. Rao, A.G. and Kalish, S. (1981) Bayesian estimation and control of detailing effort in a repeat purchase diffusion environment. *Management Science* **27**, May, 493–506.

Lippman, S.A. and McCardle, K.F. (1988) Preemption in R&D Races. *European Economic Review* **32**, 1661–69.

Llewellyn, D. (1992) Financial innovation: a basic analysis. Chapter 2 in H. Cavanna (ed.), *Financial Innovation*, Routledge, London, pp. 14–51.

Loury, G.C. (1979) Market structure and innovation. *Quarterly Journal of Economics* **93**, 395–410.

McCardle, K.F. (1985) Information acquisition and the adoption of new technology. *Management Science* **31**, 1372–89.

McClean I.W. and Round, D.K. (1978) Research and product innovation in Australian manufacturing industries. *The Journal of Industrial Economics* **27**, 1–12.

Mahajan V. and Muller, E. (1979) Innovation-diffusion and new product growth models in marketing. *Journal of Marketing* **43**, 55–68.

Mahajan, V. and Peterson, R.A. (1978) Innovation diffusion in a dynamic potential adopter population. *Management Science* **24**, 1589–97.

Mahajan, V. and Peterson, R.A. (1985) Models for innovation diffusion. In Sage University Paper Series on Quantitative Applications in the Social Sciences. **48**, Sage Publications, Beverly Hills and London.

Mahajan, V. and Schoeman, M.E.F. (1977) Generalized model for the time pattern of the diffusion process, *IEEE Transactions on Engineering Management* EM-24, pp. 12–18.

Mahajan, V., Bretschneider, S.I. and Bradford, J.W. (1980) Feedback approaches to modeling structural shifts in market response. *Journal of Marketing* **44**, Winter, 71–80.

Mahajan, V., Wind, L. and Sharma, S. (1983) An approach to repeat-purchase diffusion analysis. *Proceedings of the American Marketing Educator's Conference*, American Marketing Association, Chicago, pp. 442–6.

Makridakis, S. and Wheelwright, S.C. (1977) Adaptive filtering: an integrated auto-regressive/moving average filter for time series forecasting. *Operations Research Quarterly* **28**, 2, 425–37.

Malerba, F. and Orsenigo, L. (1990) Technological regimes and patterns of innovation: a theoretical and empirical investigation of the Italian case. In A. Heertje and M. Perlman (eds), *Evolving Technology and Market Structure*. Michigan University Press, Ann Arbor, MI.

Malerba, F. and Orsenigo, L. (1993) Technological regimes and firm behavior. *Industrial and Corporate Change* **2**, 26–43.

Malerba, F. and Orsenigo, L. (1995) Schumpeterian patterns of innovation. *Cambridge Journal of Economics* **19**, 47–65.

Mamer, J.W. and McCardle, K.F. (1985) Uncertainty, competition, and the adoption of new technology. Mimeo.

Mansfield, E. (1961) Technical change and the rate of imitation. *Econometrica* **29**, 741–66.

Mansfield, E. (1968) Industrial research and technological innovation. Norton, London.

Marshall, A. (1898) *Principles of Economics*. Macmillan, London.

Marx, K. (1900) *Capital: A Critical Analysis of Capitalist Production*, translated from the 3rd German edition by S. Moore and E. Aveliny and edited by F. Engels. London, S. Sonnenschein.

Matthews, J. (1994) *Struggle and Survival on Wall Street: The Economics of Competition Among Securities Firms*. Oxford University Press, New York.

Mayer, H. and Kneeshaw, J. (1988) Financial market structure and regulatory change. Chapter 6 in A. Heertje (ed.), *Innovation, Technology, and Finance*. Basil Blackwell, Oxford, pp. 127–57.

Merton, R.C. (1995) Financial innovation and the management and regulation of financial institutions. *Journal of Banking and Finance* **19**, 461–81.

Metcalfe, J.S. (1970) Diffusion of innovation in the Lancashire textile industry. *The Manchester School* **38**, 145–59.

Metcalfe, J.S. (1988) The diffusion of innovation: an interpretive survey. Discussion Papers in Economics **60**, Department of Economics, University of Manchester.

Midgley, D.V. (1976) A simple mathematical theory of innovative behavior. *Journal of Consumer Research* **3**, 31–41.

Miller, M.H. (1986) Financial innovation: the last twenty years and the next. *Journal of Financial and Quantitative Analysis* **21**, 459–71.

Modigliani, F. and Miller, M.H. (1958) The cost of capital, corporation finance and the theory of investment. *The American Economic Review* **48**, 261–97.

Modigliani, F. and Miller, M.H. (1963) Corporate income taxes and the cost of capital: a correction. *The American Economic Review* **53**, 433–43

Needham, D. (1975) Market structure and firms' R & D behavior. *The Journal of Industrial Economics* **23**, 241–55.

Nelson, R.R. (1959) The simple economics of basic scientific research. *Journal of Political Economy* **67**, 297–306.

Ng, Y.K. (1971) Competition, monopoly and the incentive to invent. *Australian Economic Papers* **10**, 45–49.

Niehans, J. (1983) Financial innovation, multinational banking, and monetary policy. *Journal of Banking and Finance* **7**, 537–51.

Ohashi, K. (1995) Endogenous determination of the degree of market incompleteness in futures innovation. *Journal of Economic Theory* **65**, 198–217.

Oliver, F.R. (1964) Methods for estimating the logistic growth function. *Applied Statistics* **13**, 57–66.

Oren, S. and Schwartz, R.G. (1988) Diffusion of new products in risk-sensitive markets. *Journal of Forecasting* **7**, 273–87.

Pavel, C. (1987) Securitization. *Economic Perspectives*, Federal Reserve Bank of Chicago, Chicago, IL, pp. 16–31.

Pavel, C.A. and Phillis, D. (1987) Why commercial banks sell loans: an empirical analysis. *Economic Perspectives*, Federal Reserve Bank of Chicago, May/June, pp. 3–14.

Pawley, M., Winstone, D. and Bentley, P. (1991). *UK Financial Institutions and Markets*. Macmillan, London.

Pennacchi, G.G. (1988) Loan sales and the cost of capital. *Journal of Finance* **43**, 375–96.

Pennings, J.M. and Harianto, F. (1992) The diffusion of technological innovation in the commercial banking industry. *Strategic Management Journal* **13**, 29–46.

Pesendorfer. W. (1995) Financial innovation in a general equilibrium model. *Journal of Economic Theory* **65**, 79–116.

Petruzzi, C., Del Valle M. and Judlowe, S. (1988) Patent and copyright protection for innovations in finance. *Financial Management* **17**, 66–71.

Phillips, A. (1966) Patents, potential competition, and technical progress. *American Economic Review* **56**, 301–10.

Podolski, T.M. (1986) *Financial Innovation and the Money Supply*. Basil Blackwell, Oxford, New York.

Porter, R. and Simpson T. (1980) Some issues involving the definition and interpretation of the monetary aggregates. In *Controlling Monetary Aggregates* **3**, 161–234, Conference Series, Federal Reserve Bank of Boston.

Quirmbach, H.C. (1986) The diffusion of new technology and the market for an innovation. *Rand Journal of Economics* **17**, 33–47.

Radner, R. (1968) Competitive equilibrium under uncertainty. *Econometrica* **36**, 31–58.

Rahi, R. (1993) Adverse selection and security design. Working paper, Department of Economics, Birkbeck College, University of London.

Rahi, R. (1995) Optimal incomplete markets with asymmetric information. *Journal of Economic Theory* **65**, 171–97.

Reily, F.V. (1992) *Investments*, 3rd edn. New York, Dryden Press.

Reinganum J.F. (1979) Dynamic games with R & D rivalry. Ph.D. thesis, Northwestern University.

Reinganum, J.F. (1981a) Dynamic games of innovation. *Journal of Economic Theory* **25**, 21–41.

Reinganum, J.F. (1981b) On the diffusion of new technology: a game theoretic approach. *Review of Economic Studies* **48**, 395–405.

Reinganum, J.F. (1981c) Market structure and the diffusion of new technology. *Bell Journal of Economics* **12**, 618–24.

Reinganum, J.F. (1982) A dynamic game of R and D: patent protection and competitive behavior. *Econometrica* **50**, 671–88.

Reinganum, J.F. (1983) Uncertain innovation and the persistence of monopoly. *American Economic Review* **73**, 741–48.

Reinganum, J.F. (1984) Practical implications of game theoretic models of R&S. *American Economic Review* **74**, 61–66.

Reinganum, J.F. (1985) Innovation and industry evolution. *Quarterly Journal of Economics* **100**, 81–99.

Reinganum, J.F. (1989) The Timing of Innovation: Research, Development and Diffusion. Chapter 14 in R. Schmalensee and R. Willig (eds), *Handbook of Industrial Economics*, North-Holland, Amsterdam, pp. 849–908.

Riordan, M.H. and Salant, D.J. (1994) Preemptive adoptions of an emerging technology. *The Journal of Industrial Economics* **42**, 247–61.

RISK (1994) Books of revelations? 7(9), pp. 91–102.

Roa, V.R. (1981) New-product sales forecasting using the Hendry system. In Wind *et al.* (eds), *New Product Forecasting*. D.C. Heath, Lexington, MA, pp. 499–510.

Robenson T.S. and Lakhani, C. (1975) Dynamic price models for new product planning. *Management Science* **21**, June, 1113–22.

Roberts, B. and Schulze, D.L. (1973) *Modern Mathematics and Economic Analysis.* Norton, New York.

Rogers, E.M. (1962) *Diffusion of Innovations.* Free Press, New York. [1965] Collier-Macmillan, London.

Romeo, A.A. (1977) The rate of imitation of a capital-embodied process innovation. *Econometrica* **44**, 63–69.

Rosenberg, N. (1976) *Perspectives on Technology.* Cambridge University Press, Cambridge.

Ross, S.A. (1989) Institutional markets, financial marketing, and financial innovation. *Journal of Finance* **44**, 541–56.

Salter, W. (1960) *Productivity and Technical Change.* Cambridge University Press, Cambridge.

Scherer, F.M. (1967) Research and development allocation under rivalry. *Quarterly Journal of Economics* **71**, 359–94.

Scherer, F.M. (1980) *Market Structure and Economic Performance.* Rand McNally, Chicago, IL.

Schmittlein, D.C. and Mahajan, V., (1982) Maximum likelihood estimation for an innovation diffusion model of new product acceptance. *Marketing Science* **1**, 57–78.

Schmookler, J. (1966) *Invention and Economic Growth.* Harvard University Press, Cambridge, MA.

Schumpeter, J.A. (1934) *The Theory of Economic Development.* Harvard University Press, Cambridge, MA.

Schumpeter, J.A. (1939 [1964]) *Business Cycles*, McGraw-Hill, New York.

Schumpeter, J.A. (1942 [1994]) *Capitalism, Socialism, and Democracy.* Unwin, London.

Sharif, M.N. and Kabir C. (1976) A generalised model for forecasting technological substitution. *Technological Forecasting and Social Change* **8**, 353–64.

Sharif, M.N. and Ramanathan, K. (1981) Binomial innovation diffusion models with dynamic potential adopter population. *Technological Forecasting and Social Change* **20**, 63–87.

Sharma, L., Basu, A. and Bhargava, S.C. (1993) A new model of innovation diffusion. *Journal of Scientific & Industrial Research*, **52**, 151–58.

Silber, W. (1975) Towards a theory of financial innovation. In W. Silber (ed.), *Financial Innovation*, D.C. Heath, Lexington, MA, pp. 53–85.

Silber, W. (1983) The process of financial innovation. *The American Economic Review,* May, pp. 89–95.

Sinkey, J.F. Jr, (1992) *Commercial Bank Financial Management in the Financial Services Industry*, 4th edition, Maxwell Macmillan International Editions.

Skiadas, C.H. (1987) Two simple models for the early and middle stage prediction of innovation diffusion. *IEEE Transactions on Engineering Management*, EM-**34**, 2.

Smith, A. (1776 [1922]) *Wealth of Nations.* London, Methuen.

Smith, A.D. (1992) *Performance in International Financial Markets.* NIESR, Cambridge University Press.

Solow, R.M. (1957) Technical change and the aggregate production function. *Review of Economic and Statistics* **39**, 312–20.

Speece, M.W. and MacLachlan, D.L. (1992) Forecasting fluid milk package type with a multigeneration new product diffusion model. *IEEE Transactions on Engineering Management* **39**, 169–75.

Stapleton, E. (1976) The normal distribution as a model of technological substitution. *Technological Forecasting and Social Change* **8**, 325–34.

Stewart, M.B. (1983) Noncooperative oligopoly and preemptive innovation without winner-take-all. *Quarterly Journal of Economics* **98**, 681–94.

Stoneman, P. and Ireland, N. (1983) The role of supply factors in the diffusion of new process technology. *Economic Journal* (Supplement), **93**, 66–78.

Suzuki, Y. (1987) Financial innovation in Japan: its origins, diffusion, and impacts. In M. de Cecco (ed.), *Changing Money: Financial Innovation in Developed Countries*. Basil Blackwell, Oxford, pp. 229–59.

Swamy, P.A.V., Conway, R.K. and Leblanc, M.R. (1989) The stochastic coefficients approach to econometric modelling, Part III: Estimation, stability testing and prediction. *Journal of Agricultural Economics Research* **41**, 4–20.

Thomas, M. and Woolridge, J.R. (1991) The wealth effects of asset-backed security issues. Working paper, Pennsylvania State University.

Tufano, P. (1989) Financial innovation and first-mover advantages. *Journal of Financial Economics* **25**, 213–40.

Van Horne, J.C. (1985) Of financial innovations and excesses. *The Journal of Finance* **15**, 621–31.

Varma, R. and Chambers, D.R. (1990) The role of financial innovation in raising capital—evidence from deep discount debt offers. *Journal of Financial Economics* **26**, 289–98.

Vickers J. (1986) Notes on the evolution of market structure when there is a sequence of innovations. *Journal of Industrial Economics* **35**, 1–12.

Vittas, D. (1985) How far is the US ahead in financial innovation? *The Banker*, May, pp. 47–53.

Von Bertelanffy, L. (1957) Quantitative laws in metabolism and growth. *Quarterly Review of Biology*, 217–71.

Von Neumann, J. and Morgenstern, O. (1947) *Theory of Games and Economic Behavior*, 2nd Edition. Princeton University Press, Princeton, NJ.

Walmsley, J. (1988) *The New Financial Instruments*. John Wiley and Sons, Chichester.

Walras, L. (1874) *Elements d'Economie Politique Pure*. L. Corbaz, Lausanne: In 1954 translated by William Jaffé as: Elements of Pure Economics. Irwin, Homewood, IL.

Waterson, M. (1990) The economics of product patents. *American Economic Review* **80**, 860–69.

Wind, Y., Mahajan, V. and Cardozo, R.C. (1981) *New product forecasting: models and applications*. D.C. Heath, Lexington, MA.

Young, P. (1993) Technological growth curves—a competition of forecasting models. *Technological Forecasting and Social Change* **44**, 375–89.

Zecher, J.R. (1984) Financial innovations in the 1980s. Chapter 6 in *Financial Innovations: Their Impact on Monetary Policy and Financial Markets*. The Federal Bank of St. Louis, Boston. Kluwer-Nijhoff, Lancaster, pp. 151–67.

Index

Index compiled by Indexing Specialists

Printed and bound by CPI Group (UK) Ltd, Croydon, CR0 4YY

23/04/2025

14660956-0009